FISHING FOR TUNA AND MARLIN

CAPTAIN PETE BARRETT

FISHING FOR TUNA AND MARLIN

CAPTAIN PETE BARRETT

THE FISHERMAN LIBRARY
1620 Beaver Dam Road
Point Pleasant, New Jersey 08742

© 1992, FISHING FOR TUNA AND MARLIN
THE FISHERMAN LIBRARY CORP.

ALL RIGHTS RESERVED. No part of this book may be used or reproduced in any form or means without the written permission of the publisher, except in the case of brief quotations embodied in writer's reviews.

PRINTED IN THE UNITED STATES OF AMERICA
Library of Congress Cataloging-in-Publication data
ISBN 0-923155-16-3

THE FISHERMAN LIBRARY CORP.
1620 Beaver Dam Road
Point Pleasant, New Jersey 08742

Publisher . . . . Richard S. Reina
Associate Publisher . . . . Pete Barrett
Editor . . . . Linda Barrett
Design . . . . Allison Eagle-Rudnick
Cover design . . . . Steve and Terri Goione
Paste-up . . . . JoAnne Clemens and Janet Glassman

INTRODUCTION

If my grandfather could only see me now. My grandparents gave me a pole and reel that started a life-long fishing journey that evolved from boyhood fun in creeks and ponds to a full-time adult vocation along the edge of the ocean. Fortunately, the daily business of fishing is no less enjoyable or challenging than the fresh dreams of youth.

Fishing For Tuna and Marlin had its beginnings back in the early 70s when Ted Glicksman of the Manasquan River Marlin & Tuna Club offered me a ride on his Whales Tales to the canyons off the New Jersey Coast. Previously, I had fished for big game such as white marlin, sailfish and wahoo in Florida and the Bahamas, but the 75-mile run to the Continental Shelf opened new fishing opportunities. Nothing on the inshore grounds would ever again hold my interest like fishing offshore.

I owned a Mako center console at that time and began plotting ways to make the long run to the blue water on my own. What held me back was lack of specific information, not enthusiasm. There were no books or videos to offer guidance, so I talked to other fishermen and captains who ventured offshore. They shared experiences, frustrations and a few victories. The many stumbles along the way only made the successes that much sweeter.

With a big dose of humility, I offer this book to those fishermen just starting their offshore quest, or who are searching for new tips, tricks or techniques that will fool a few more fish. I make no claim to being an expert, I just like to fish and I enjoy meeting others who love this sport. Much of the information presented here came from the many ideas learned from other captains and offshore anglers. The learning experience never ends, and even veterans with many years of blue water fishing accomplishments will tell you they discover new ideas with each passing season.

No one can ever hope to learn it all and perhaps that is one of the most fascinating aspects of offshore fishing; there is always a new way to rig a bait, a new lure to put in the trolling pattern, and new horizons to point the bow towards. Offshore fishing is never boring!

Most of my fishing experiences are along the northeast coast in the summer, North Carolina in the spring and fall, with winter trips to Florida and the Bahamas. That I like to catch yellowfin and bigeye tuna will be evident as you read the following pages, because these fish are so readily available where I fish most of the time. The more glamorous marlin often get the lion's share of the spotlight in many sport fishing books and magazines, but on a daily basis, the tuna are the mainstay of charter and private boats from Massachusetts to the Carolinas. Tuna are the "meat and potatoes" of the offshore fishery, billfish are the sweet dessert.

My wish would be to run a full-time charter boat off the rich waters beyond the Virginia or North Carolina Coasts, but the realities of family, business and financial common sense prevails. My hat is off to those hard-working captains and mates who are blessed with the chance to live most every day of the year on the water.

It has been my good fortune to meet many top-notch, innovative fishermen along the east coast who cheerfully passed along their knowledge to help me, and many others, gain more pleasure from the sea. Among those I owe a special "Thank you" are Captain John Bayliss of the Tarheel, Captain Eric Burnley, Steve Goione and his superb art, Bill Goodman of Sevenstrand Lures, Bob Hawie of So-Lo Marine, Frank Johnson of Mold Craft Lures, my fishing buddy Jeff Merrill, Ed Mesunas and the crew at Penn Reels, Captain Matt Muzslay, Bill Munro and the crew at Ande and Mako Marine, Ed and Frank Murray of Murray Brothers, Captain Al Ristori, Captain Robbie Robinson of Huntington Drone Lures, Bill Shedd and his crew at AFTCO, Mark Sosin for his kind words, Captain Spider of the Marker 32, Captain Sal Sorace of Sir-Ace Lures, Captain Lou Truppi an offshore pioneer, Captain Greg Venturo, Bob Walker of Bimini Marine and Captain Dick Weber of South Jersey Marina.

I have also had the tremendous good luck to work with, and be partners with, Rich Reina and Richard S. Reina, the father and son publishing team of *The Fisherman* who have given me and my family some remarkable opportunities and support in the past 20 years. I've written over 500 stories for the magazine and some of those original ideas are expanded in this book.

My wife, Linda, is my right arm in this wonderful life of fishing. She manages the office, and has been a good sport when "The Fever" strikes and I leave to hunt for tuna or billfish. She has also proven her own fishing abilities on the offshore fishing grounds. My son, Rich, keeps me thinking young and for this I am grateful. It is with great pride that I now watch him venture offshore on his own fishing adventures.

They say you earn only what you spend. *Fishing For Tuna and Marlin* is a culmination of ideas from many fishermen and captains who so willingly helped me get so much more from offshore fishing. I hope this book returns the favor and gives many other fishermen some enjoyable reading, some fishing tips and the chance to shout "Fish On!" a few extra times.

Captain Pete Barrett

DEDICATION

To Rich, my son and fishing buddy, who shares my love of the sea, beautiful sportfishing boats and the challenge of the offshore blue waters.

TABLE OF CONTENTS

1. MEET THE SPECIES 11
2. TACKLE AND EQUIPMENT 37
3. RIGGING FOR ACTION 69
4. THE OFFSHORE BOAT 91
5. OFFSHORE TROLLING LURES 109
6. OFFSHORE TROLLING BAITS 155
7. LIVE BAITS AND CHUNK BAITS 177
8. LOCATING FISH 203
9. THE TROLLING STRATEGY 217
10. ATLANTIC BLUEFIN TUNA 241
11. FISH ON! 255
12. CARING FOR THE CATCH 279
13. TAGGING FOR THE FUTURE 287

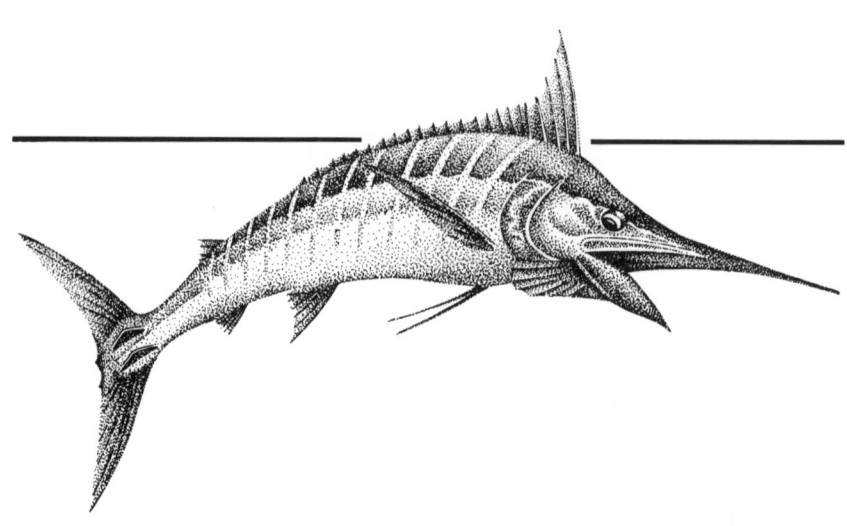

Chapter One

MEET THE SPECIES

Billfish and tuna are at the top of the fishing world. For sheer beauty, speed and challenge, no other group of fish come close to matching their fighting qualities or strength. Once the sport of the rich, today's big game fishermen are a delightful mix of everyday people, just like you and me. Whether you fish two miles offshore of Palm Beach, Florida; 40 miles offshore at The Point off Oregon Inlet, North Carolina; or head 70 miles to the edge of the Continental Shelf off Brielle, New Jersey, the chance to catch these great fish is there waiting for you.

The excitement, the lore, the challenge, and the chance for success are within the grasp of everyone. The rumble of powerful engines, brilliant blue water, lures dancing merrily in the snowy wake and the sudden surprise as a huge fish crashes a lure or bait are images and sounds that are simply unforgettable. Once you've seen the wild aerial shows of a blue marlin or slugged it out on stand-up tackle with a powerful bigeye tuna, the appeal of smaller, lesser game fish, pale by comparison.

Fortunes have been won, and lost, in search of marlin and tuna. Reputations of charter skippers and well-known anglers often hinged on their ability to consistently seduce these magnificent game fish into taking a well-rigged bait or finely-tuned lure. Many fishermen devote their entire lives to the quest for billfish and tuna. No matter how many of these awesome fish they catch, they never learn enough, never quite satisfy the need to catch and see the next one, never sleep easy once bitten with "The Fever."

Big game fishing is addictive. The only cure, and a delightful one at that, is to fish, and you must do that frequently. An occasional trip is just not enough to satisfy the need to hunt, find and fight these unique fish. It is a delightful sport that will provide years of challenge, enjoyment, and great rewards for your efforts.

The Billfish Clan

Billfish are considered the ultimate catch for the big game angler. Their size can be awesome and their apparent intelligence exasperating. Perhaps no other group of fish inspires so much angling attention and emotion. The billfish we'll be looking at are the blue marlin, white marlin, sailfish and longbill spearfish. They are all three members of the sub-order *Scombroidei,* in the *Istiophoridae* family.

Up until a few years ago, marlin were all placed in the genus *Makaira*, a magical name that embodied the spirit and mystique of the fish. Biologists occasionally change the classification of fish as more knowledge about the species becomes available. The white marlin is now classed in the genus *tetrapturus,* a very awkward sounding name for such agile fish! The sailfish remains in the *Istiophorus* genus. Today only the blue marlin is still in the genus *Makaira.* The spearfish is in the genus *tetrapturus* and is not a commonly caught billfish.

Marlin are cold-blooded fish, their body temperature rising and falling with the surrounding water environment. They cannot withstand waters much cooler than 50 degrees for blue and white marlin, and 60 degrees for sailfish, so they are for the most part creatures of the warm tropical, subtropical or temperate zones of the earth's oceans.

Powerful of muscle for fast swimming, they also have the ability to pump water through their gills to add to their overall speed; a sort of rocket booster for extra bursts of speed to help catch bait or escape enemies. Fortunately for fishermen they have a high rate of metabolism and require lots of food to maintain their physical well-being. They must eat frequently, and regularly.

The ocean waters support, or float, the body weight of the billfish and they are much like astronaut space voyagers, or in this case, aquanauts, utilizing the effects of near weightlessness to move through their environment. According to marine biologists, a 300-pound blue marlin will only weigh about 15 pounds in the water! This nearly weightless condition allows billfish to literally fly through the water with little effort and accounts for their great speed.

Their swim bladder also aids this buoyancy effect but is more important as a hydrostatic adjuster as the fish makes plunges to deep water and then rises again to feed or bask near the surface. They can withstand dramatic changes in water depth with no apparent ill effects.

A highly developed lateral line with a chain-like pattern of nervous system receptors, serves as the primary sensory organ that records changes in the fish's environment such as water temperature, water depth (pressure) and the vibrations caused by nearby moving fish

While frustrated fishermen may swear that billfish are "smarter than we are", they actually have a small brain which emphasizes the development of the senses of sight and smell. They are well equipped to react to any stimulus with highly developed instincts but it is unlikely they are really "smart" with the ability to reason. There are many documented reports of the same marlin being hooked several times within a short period of time so they apparently don't always learn that fish hooks are bad medicine. However, there are just as many reports from skippers who feel that marlin fishing can be way off the mark for a few days after a tournament. Did the fish get spooked by lures and hooked baits, or did they get the jitters because of added boat traffic, noise and disturbances on the billfish grounds?

Description

Sleek and muscular, each of the billfish bears a spear-like extension of their upper jaw - hence the name billfish. The bill may serve several purposes such as an aid to cut through the water for super fast bursts of speed, or it can be used to gather food either by spearing large fish or stunning smaller fish. It may also help as a defensive weapon and there are numerous verifications of sharks, and other billfish, that have been caught with spear holes in their bodies, probably administered by an attacking marlin.

Their powerful bodies are propelled by a large lunate tail that pushes the fish to speeds of over 40 miles per hour. The dorsal fins are pronounced and vary from each species, serving as easy identification markings from the huge sail of the aptly named sailfish to the pointed dorsal of the blue marlin and the rounded dorsal of the white marlin.

Billfish have a unique ability to expel their stomach to help get rid of unwanted weeds or undigested food - and baits or lures with hooks in them! They seem to suffer no ill effects from this gastronomic feat and there are numerous records of tagged marlin that were later recaptured after the angler witnessed the stomach reversal trick. One blue marlin I caught off Walker's Cay in the Bahamas looked in bad shape with its belly hanging out of its mouth. It lay on its side slowly swimming away when suddenly the stomach disappeared as the fish apparently swallowed it back where it belonged.

Marlin and sailfish spawn in tropical to subtropical waters and will do so year-round when conditions are right. Although marlin usually do not school, some concentrations of fish are observed in the Caribbean and Gulf of Mexico when spawning is believed to occur.

The eggs drift at the mercy of the currents and the wind. Out of a million spawned eggs, 10 will survive to attain the status of an adult

FISHING FOR TUNA AND MARLIN

BLUE MARLIN

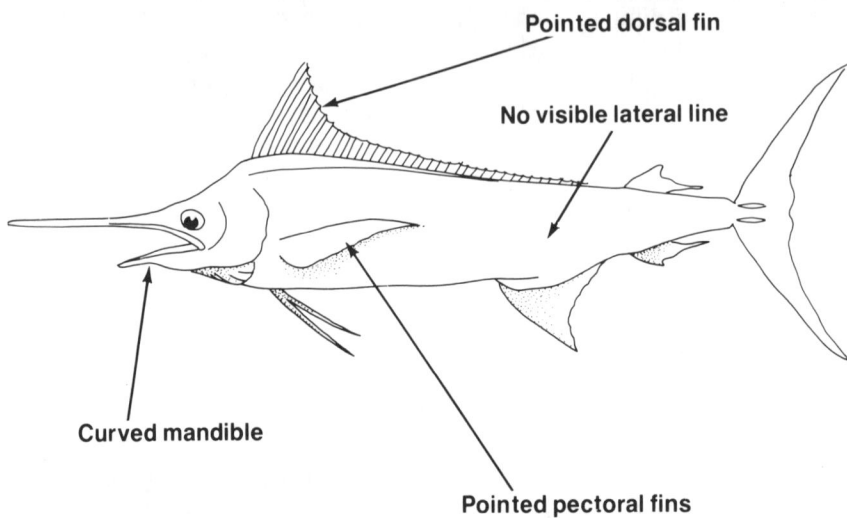

WHITE MARLIN

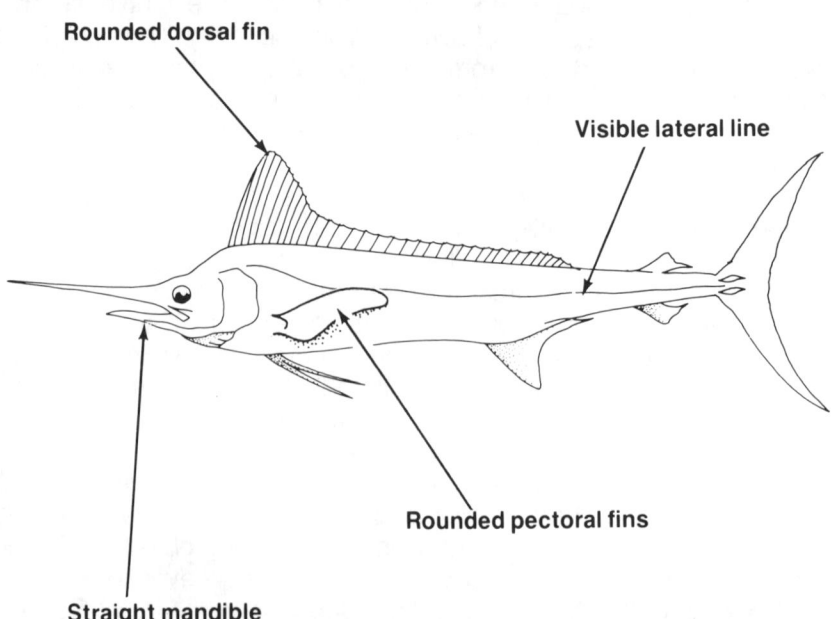

MEET THE SPECIES

SPEARFISH

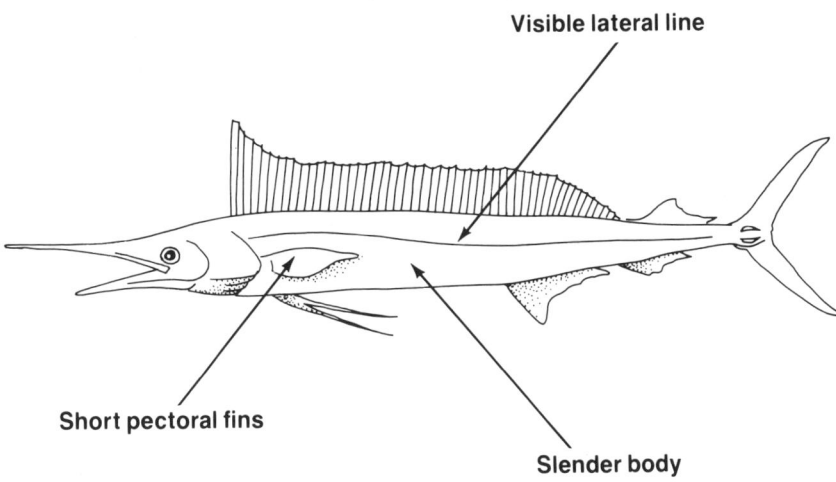

SAILFISH

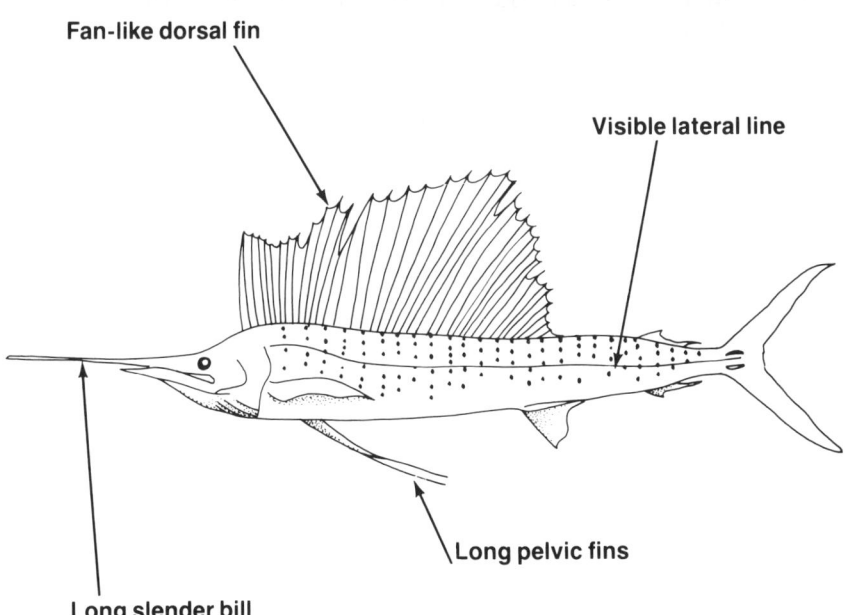

fish. Fortunately, marlin spawn eggs in great quantities to overcome this high morality, but it is easy to see how unrestricted fishing pressure can exceed the carrying capacity of the species to recruit new fish to the overall population.

Sailfish were once thought to be relatively short-lived fish, although recent tag returns show that their life expectancy is much longer than previously believed. At 10 years of age, a sail is probably an old fish, with most tagged returns from fish of about 3 to 6 years of age. The marlin seem to live longer and specimens examined by biologists have been recorded at over 20 years of age.

Billfish hear differently than humans do. They have no external ear, but rely instead on the lateral line to help pick up vibrations of sound. The inner ear is well developed and since the fish is suspended in its watery environment, the inner ear is able to pick up vibrations immediately and from great distances. The inner ear also serves as a sensory apparatus to balance the fish in its near weightless environment so it knows which way is up.

Would you believe that billfish talk? Not like we do, of course, but they are known to make noises at mating times and to warn of approaching danger. They can rub jaws and gill plates and vibrate their air bladder to produce sounds that, while not understood by humans, are communicated to other billfish. If they can "talk", then perhaps they are intelligent. Again, not in the sense of human intelligence, but with such highly developed instincts and sensory organs like the lateral line and good hearing, they are able to react swiftly to danger and to catch food.

Billfish are frequently seen lazing on the surface of the water. Some biologists believe this is a form of sleeping or at least a resting period for the fish when their senses are tuned to watch for danger, but their bodies are relaxed.

While billfish do have a well-developed sense of smell, they probably don't rely to any great extent on their sense of taste. When attacking a bait, they zone in on the motion, shape and smell of the bait, rather than how well the bait may taste. A meal is a meal, is a meal, is a meal. Marlin aren't interested in the sizzle, they just want food to survive.

Their vision is excellent and they can easily determine differences in contrast and color. Since their eyes are positioned on the side of their head, they have monocular vision and therefore lack good depth perception to judge distances. This is probably why marlin and other billfish sometimes seem to have difficulty in striking bait. Monocular vision forces the billfish to favor attacking a lure or bait from one side or the other, rather than straight on from behind. At the instant the bait is directly in front of the fish, it probably cannot see the bait.

Feeding Habits

Billfish feed on a wide range of food and will eat anything from fast surface fish like members of the tuna tribe to slower but easier to catch bottom dwellers like whiting, cod, tilefish, grouper and shellfish. Their primary food is squid, small fish like ballyhoo and flying fish, mackerel, small tuna and dolphin.

Each of the billfish are very fast - fast enough to catch the speediest of tunas. There are recorded blue marlin that have had yellowfin tuna in their bellies that weighed in excess of 100 pounds. Other marlin have shown up at dockside examinations with mackerel, bluefish, squid, and dolphin in their stomachs. A small marlin I saw hooked while fishing off Treasure Cay in the Bahamas, spit up large chunks of barracuda when only a few feet from the boat.

Food Value

Since billfish hold a special place in the hearts of many anglers, most American billfishermen today prefer to release their catch rather than destroy such a magnificent game fish. Unless a trophy is to be mounted, most serious billfishermen promote the concept of tag and release of all marlin. Current East Coast regulations place the following restrictions on the size of billfish, measured from the tip of the lower jaw to the fork of the tail:

```
Blue marlin  . . . . . . . . . . . . . . . . . . . . . . . . . . . . . . . . . . . . .86 inches
White marlin  . . . . . . . . . . . . . . . . . . . . . . . . . . . . . . . . . . . .62 inches
Sailfish  . . . . . . . . . . . . . . . . . . . . . . . . . . . . . . . . . . . . . . . . .57 inches
```

It cannot be over-emphasized that hanging fish at the dock for the sake of a picture and then wasting the fish by towing it back out to sea to be dumped is a sin. Release any billfish you do not have to keep.

Atlantic Blue Marlin

The elite of the Atlantic big game fisherman, the blue marlin, *Makaira nigricans,* is the largest and toughest fighting of the billfish. They can attain sizes beyond 1,500 pounds, but the most common are fish in the 200 to 500-pound range.

They usually inhabit the warmer waters off Cuba, Florida and in the Caribbean, but blue marlin can be caught from Brazil to Cape Cod.

Scientists disagree if the Atlantic blue marlin and the Pacific blue marlin are the same fish. Although the Atlantic blue is usually smaller than its Pacific counterpart, the International Game Fish Association world record Atlantic blue is less than 75 pounds apart from the Pacific blue. They are no less a sporting and dazzling performer when caught on rod and reel!

Blue marlin have brilliant colors when alive and they are famous for "lighting up" in iridescent colors as they strike a bait or lure. A bright cobalt blue back is accented by glistening silver sides that reflect a bronze tint when the fish jumps. Bright blue or lavender vertical stripes are beautiful on a fresh fish still in the water, yet quickly fade in death. Not all blue marlin "light up" when hooked, but it is an amazing sight to witness when one of these awesome fish turns on its neon lights.

The blue marlin is generally much larger than his close cousin the white marlin, yet small blues may be confused as whites by novice anglers. The positive giveaway identification distinction is the dorsal fin and pectorals which are pointed on the blue marlin, rounded on the white.

Little is known of the marlin's life history in comparison to many other species more easily studied by biologists. It spawns year-round in tropical water and ripe females have been most frequently caught in the waters near Cuba and the Virgin Islands. It is generally believed

One of the world's greatest game fish, blue marlin are considered trophy fish and are usually tagged and released by sports anglers.

the eggs drift with the currents and perhaps marlin prefer spawning in the major currents, such as the Gulf Stream.

Blue marlin usually travel as single fish preferring their solitude. Occasionally they travel in pairs but rarely in small groups, although on a trip to Chub Cay I saw a group of four blue marlin free jumping as we trolled baits in the Tongue of the Ocean leading into the Northwest Passage.

The most productive fishing areas seem to lie from Montauk to Cape Hatteras, then south to the Caribbean and along the South American Coast to Brazil, and in the waters of the Gulf of Mexico. They prefer deep waters of 50 to 500 fathoms and fishermen often see them along severe drop-offs at the edge of the Continental Shelf where the bottom contours fall to dizzying depths.

Blue marlin feed on a wide variety of fish including squid, bonito, dolphin, mackerel, small members of the tuna tribe and other billfish. There are numerous reports of blue marlin with tuna of 100 or more pounds in their bellies when cut open at the dock after weigh in! They feed on the surface as well as at great depths taking bottom species such as tilefish, cod and whiting.

White Marlin

The white marlin, *Tetrapturus albidus,* is more abundant and more easily caught (some say) than the blue marlin. Average size will range from 30 to 70 pounds with occasional fish going over 100 pounds. There are reports of commercially-caught whites approaching the 200-pound mark but this size fish has eluded rod and reel anglers. The current world record of 181 pounds, 14 ounces was caught off Brazil in 1979.

They range from South America to Cape Cod, and are most abundant in tropical waters. Summer fishing from Block Island south to Cape Hatteras can be good to excellent depending on the water temperature. It is common for warm water eddies to break off from the main part of the Gulf Stream and make their way closer inshore thus providing fast action along much of the Atlantic Coast.

As the year progresses, white marlin tend to migrate northward along the Atlantic up to Cape Cod then swing offshore and return south to the Caribbean or on to South America. Another group of white marlin migrate along the west coast of Florida. These two groups of fish do intermingle.

Spawning females are taken off Cuba, the Bahamas and Florida so spawning appears to take place in these waters in the summer months but may also take place year-round. Just as with the blue marlin, eggs of the white marlin drift with the currents.

The bill of the white marlin is shorter in proportion to its body length than other billfish. The dorsal fin is capped by a rounded shape clearly identifying this fish and telling it apart from the blue marlin with its pointed dorsal. As previously mentioned the pectorals are also rounded in shape, unlike the pointed pectorals on the blue marlin. The dorsal is often tinted with a lavender or light blue hue and has deep purple or dark blue spots sprinkled through it.

The back of the fish is deep blue to almost black, with vertical stripes readily apparent in live fish, especially vivid as they attack a bait or lure. The vertical striped will shine a neon lavender, purple or brilliant blue. The sides of the fish are bright silver, the belly a whitish to silver color. Like the blue, there may at times be a sheen of copper or gold to the sides when battling a fish.

Since the white marlin is the most numerous of the billfish of the Atlantic Coast, the white is more readily available to sport anglers who fish the offshore waters from Maryland to New Jersey. In fact Ocean City, Maryland calls itself the "White Marlin Capital of the World"! Many anglers believe the white marlin is the best performing of the billfish, making more leaps than either the sail or the blue. While this can be argued, there's no doubt that it is a fine game fish!

Atlantic Sailfish

There's no mistaking what species you caught when you land a sailfish! The huge dorsal, fan-like in appearance and covering the entire back of the fish, is a sure giveaway in identifying this famous fish. Scientists call the sailfish by its fancy name of *Istiophorus platypterus*. The sail is perhaps the most sought after billfish as tens of thousands of anglers descend on Florida each winter seeking a trophy fish and aerial displays unmatched by many other fish.

Florida's sailfish average 25 to 60 pounds and are most common, from Stuart to the upper Keys. Larger specimens can be found in the Gulf of Mexico where sails of 70 to 90 pounds are common, many going over 100 pounds. Further north along the coast, their numbers dwindle until sailfish are rarely seen above Rudee Inlet, Virginia.

Sailfish can frequently be found in loose groups or "schools" and they have been known to cooperatively work together to herd bait, selectively picking off their meals. This "balling" of bait is a common sight along parts of Florida and some outstanding catches have been recorded during these times when these graceful fish feed with abandon and with little regard for the dangers from sports anglers looking to hook a sailfish.

The shimmering colors of the sailfish are beautiful to behold. The dorsal is usually a dark blue in color with darker spots sprinkled through it. The back is dark blue to purple, with a bar of bronze running down the lateral line on fresh caught fish. Vertical stripes, just as with the marlin, are a light blue to lavender and quickly fade after being boated.

Sailfish are not prized as food fish, yet many of them are taken each year as trophy fish to serve as a reminder of fishing skills or a memorable day on the water while decorating a den or office wall. They do make an impressive mount. Since they can be relatively abundant in the right season, it is not unusual to take several fish in one day thereby allowing the angler to have his mount and also to release the excess catch. A better bet is to take advantage of an offer now made by most taxidermists who will mount a sailfish for you without even requiring the killing of the fish. Most taxidermists have a wide range of molds available for any size sailfish. My son, Rich, wife, Linda and I had a great day off Islamorada tagging and releasing 14 sails in one day while fishing with Captain Ted D'Esposito on the Sump N Special. Back at the marina, I asked the dockmaster to order us a fish to commerate the day. Not only do we have a beautiful mount but we didn't have to kill a single fish to get it.

The major spawning areas of the sailfish are Florida, the Bahamas and the Caribbean during April to September. Tagging studies show that there is no long range migration of sailfish, although some fish do move from Florida water into areas along Mexico off Cozumel and Cancun, and to the south off Venezuela.

Sailfish tend to inhabit only the upper layers of water and are found in much shallower water than the marlins. Sailfish are caught in the Keys along the edges of reefs in water of only 50 to 150 feet deep. Further up the Florida Coast most fish are caught along the edge of the blue water where the depth drops off just past the reefs or where the depth exceeds 120 to 240 feet.

Spring and summer migrations are northward, the fish moving with the predominant currents. In late fall they begin to reverse the migration and return to the south. Often they will run with the sea for great distance on the edge of a cold front, moving south of Palm Beach into the Keys. When the weather changes they again move north until the next weather pattern moves through the area moving the fish south again.

Longbill Spearfish

A close cousin of the white marlin, the spearfish is a rare catch and when one is boated, many anglers think it's just a strange looking white marlin. The longbill spearfish, *Tetrapturus pfluegeri,* can be distinguished from its cousin by the sleek, slender body and the slightly higher dorsal that ends in a pointed tip rather than the rounded tip of the white. They are generally much thinner than a white and a biologist once described it to me as a sailfish with a blue marlin dorsal fin.

Most spearfish are on the small side weighing 30 to 50 pounds and measuring up to 60 inches. They do get larger and the only spearfish taken on the Linda B was a 74-inch fish caught while my friend, Captain Matt Muzslay, was at the helm on a Hudson Canyon trip.

The Tuna Tribe

While marlin often get top billing in the press, many fishermen consider the tuna tribe, especially the Atlantic bluefin and the bigeye to be the supreme game fish. For New England and mid Atlantic fishermen, tuna are the day to day star performers in the world of 50 to 80-mile runs to the edge of the Continental Shelf, or to the closer 20 and 30-fathom inshore banks.

In other parts of the world where billfish are more common, the tuna are still a prime game fish, even if caught more by accident than by design. Tuna are the street fighters of the big game world and each one gives the ultimate fight against a tight line. For my money, tuna are THE best big game fish. I've heard it said that there are no easy tuna, some just fight harder than others.

Tuna, large or small, belong to the large family of fish known as *Scombridae* which includes the mackerels and close cousins like the wahoo and bonito. In this book, we'll take a close look at the bluefin, bigeye, yellowfin and longfin albacore, plus a few close relatives like the wahoo, skipjack and blackfin tuna; but we'll leave out the many small members of the tuna and mackerel tribe because their small size hardly classifies them as big game fish.

Unlike most fish, tuna are warm-blooded and can register body temperatures of up to 93 to 95 degrees as verified by studies of longfin albacore, even while living in 60 degree water. Bigeye have been recorded with body temperatures of 14 degrees or more above the surrounding water. Warmed muscles can produce more power than cold muscles, so the warm-blooded tunas are better able to use their powerful muscles to extreme advantage.

Tuna swim constantly to accelerate the flow of oxygen over their gills which then helps produce more body heat. This need for constant, rapid motion requires even more oxygen so the process never ends; it must swim, or die. They can't "stand still" and they breathe by forcing water over their gills while they swim, moving at least the distance of one body length every second. As a comparison, an Olympic swimmer may not be able to swim that fast at full speed!

MEET THE SPECIES

It has adapted to its speedy life with some remarkable evolutionary changes. The forward dorsal fin and the pectoral fins fold into recesses in the body to help streamline the fish superbly to minimize energy-wasting water friction. The tiny finlets along the top and bottom of the tuna aft of the dorsal and anal fins further reduce water friction and turbulence.

Excessive loss of body heat into the cooler surrounding water is amazingly solved with a vascular system that works like a heat exchanger. Cold blood coming from the gills is warmed as it passes through a mesh of blood vessels carrying hot blood from the body muscles on its way to the gills. This interwoven, net-like system warms the cool blood coming from the gills as it travels to the body core to maintain and stabilize the tuna's body temperature. When a tuna exerts itself when chasing bait, or fighting an angler, the heat exchanging vascular system helps dissipate heat away from muscle tissues so the fish doesn't overheat.

Tuna are fast, very fast. Bluefin can hit speeds of 50 miles per hour! Yellowfin cruise in search of food at 10 miles per hour, 24 hours a day. Many fishermen can tell stories of reels that literally have had drag washers fried as a huge bluefin or bigeye made its dash for freedom after eating a hooked bait. Screeching drags sound like a cliche', but for tuna fishermen, the drags do screech.

A triple header of yellowfins! Tuna offer terrific fishing opportunities and are the mainstay of offshore anglers from Cape Hatteras to Cape Cod.

Growth is rapid in the big game tunas. Take for example the bluefin that in 10 years time can grow from an inch-long larva to a 7-foot, 400-pound adult. While no other tuna reaches the immense size of the bluefin, the growth rates of yellowfin, bigeye and longfin albacore are also quite rapid.

Tuna roam the worlds oceans avoiding only the coldest of polar waters, preferring the more comfortable tropical and subtropical waters. Biologists have recently discovered magnetite crystals in a cavity of the skull of bluefin tuna. These magnetite crystals are also found in homing pigeons, salmon and whales and may help explain how tuna can migrate such long distances to ancient spawning grounds year after year, without ever losing their way.

Description

All members of the tuna tribe, *Thunnini,* are distinguished by having two separated dorsal fins, dorsal and anal finlets, and a generally streamlined barrel shape. Their sickle-like lunate tails and muscular, streamlined bodies are built for great speed. The pectoral fins and dorsal fins even fold into grooves to reduce water friction to an absolute minimum when the tuna travel at top speed.

If you have never done so, it's enlightening to carefully view a tuna you have boated to see the streamlined shape, the retracting fins and the shape of the tail. Even the eyes of the tuna are molded so they don't cause any excess water friction. These are fish that have adapted amazingly to their underwater environment.

Tuna are pelagic, meaning they wander the open seas, usually near, or just below, the surface of the water, but they can dive to extreme depths in search of food or to avoid danger. Unless absolutely necessary to go deeper, they will remain above the thermocline, a layer of water usually found 30 to 150 feet below the surface and fed by a churned mixture of cold deep water and the milder upper temperature layer. The thermocline offers comfort and a ready food supply since many species of smaller fish and squid live just above the thermocline.

At spawning, the tuna egg is only about one millimeter in diameter and it would take 25 eggs laid side by side to equal one inch. Spawning females release approximately 100,000 eggs for every 2.2 pounds of body weight. A 220-pound yellowfin could therefore release approximately 10 million eggs!

The eggs drift at the whim of the ocean's currents. During their early development, tuna are food for other, larger fish, birds, and even their parents and most do not survive. Those who do get beyond larval stage, experience explosive growth. For instance, a yellowfin tuna at the end of its first year would weigh about 6 pounds, 33 pounds at two years, 95 pounds at three years and 175 pounds at five years of age.

Juveniles and adults blend in well with their environment being light on the belly and darker on top. Depending on the species, additional colors such as bright yellow finlets serve an unsure purpose, other than beauty. Vivid slashes of gold or neon blue and dark vertical bars can be seen when the fish are excited, feeding or in danger.

Feeding Habits

The tuna's constant need to move uses up enormous quantities of energy that must be fueled by food. Tuna may eat up to 25% of their body weight each day; a fortunate situation for big game trollers since tuna may therefore feed several times a day. The more they feed, the more likely they will be fooled by a trolled bait or lure.

Their diet consists of a wide variety of food, including squid, sand eels, shrimp, ling, whiting, butterfish, bunker and juveniles of many other species. Their meals do not have to be small fish. Witness the famous photos from Murray Brothers tackle shop in Riviera Beach, Florida, taken by Paul Murray, of the Cookie Too. The series of six photos shows a giant bluefin tuna chasing, then finally missing a 12-pound bluefish off Cape Cod. The bluefin is caught by the shutter leaping clear of the water in its quest for a meal.

Food Value

Unfortunately for the tuna, its flesh is delicious. The Japanese consider tuna to be a delicacy, depending on the species and how it is served. The United States, Japan, France, Spain, Italy and Germany consume nearly 90% of the entire world's commercial catch of tuna. This demand has placed extreme commercial pressure on several of the tuna species.

For recreational anglers, the chance to head home after a day at sea with a good supply of tuna steaks is a reward that we all look forward to. There are few fish that taste so good as a properly prepared tuna. The flesh is firm and mild flavored. Steaked out, the tuna can be served grilled, baked, steamed, barbecued, poached and even raw. Most every seafood recipe book has delicious advice on how to prepare tuna.

FISHING FOR TUNA AND MARLIN

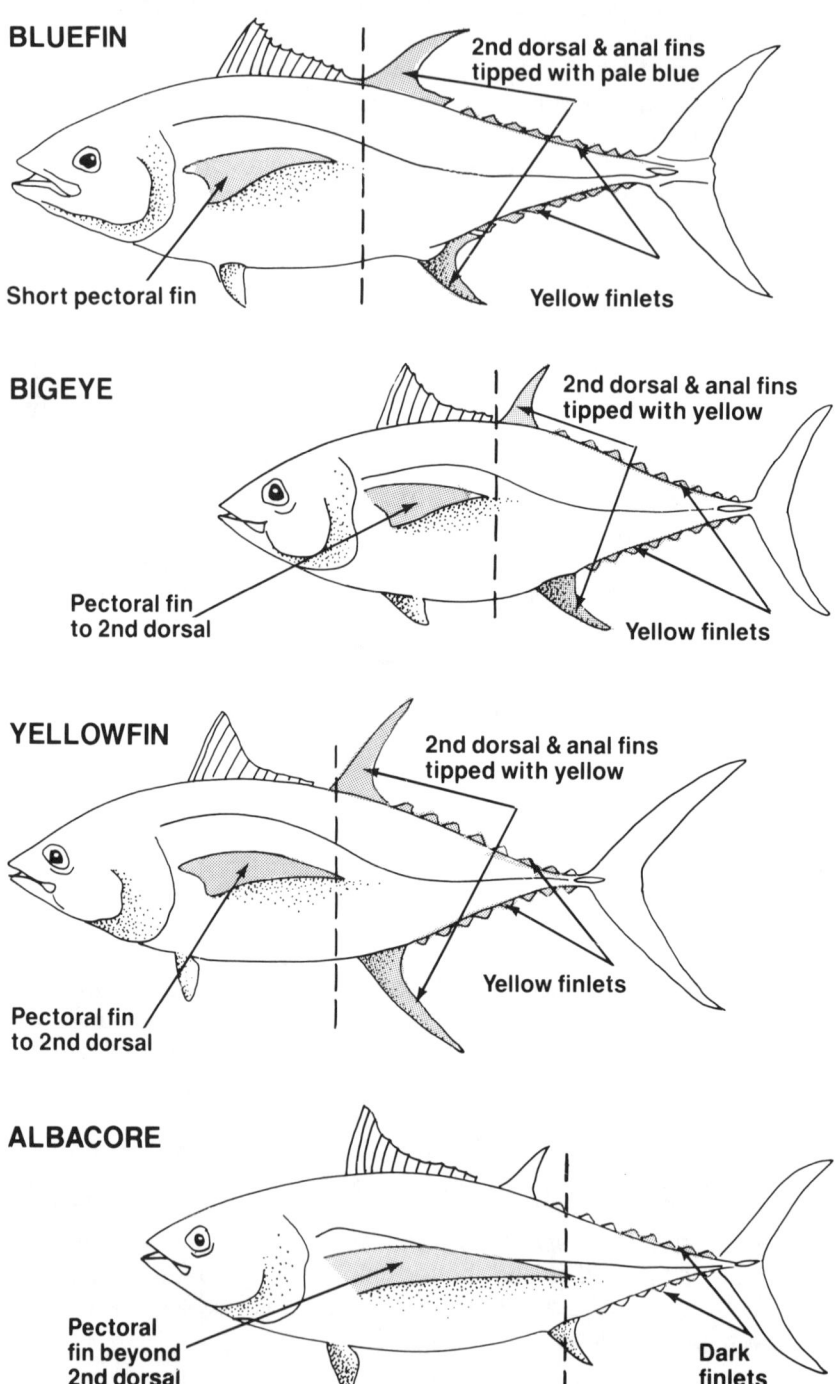

MEET THE SPECIES

BLACKFIN
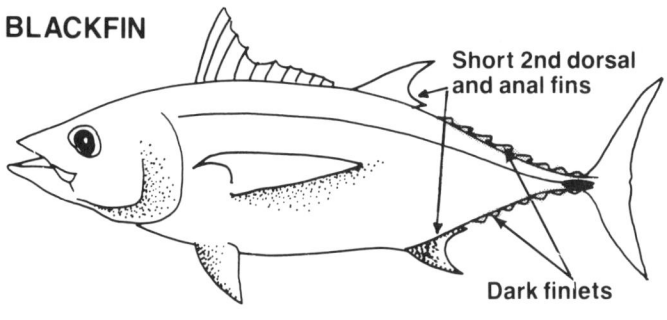

SKIPJACK
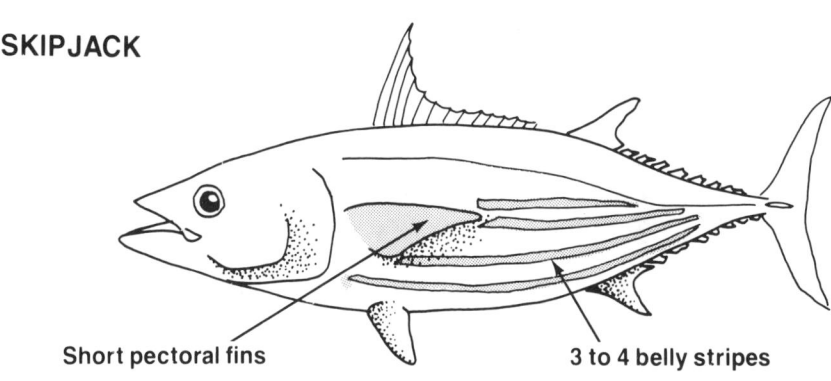

LITTLE TUNNY
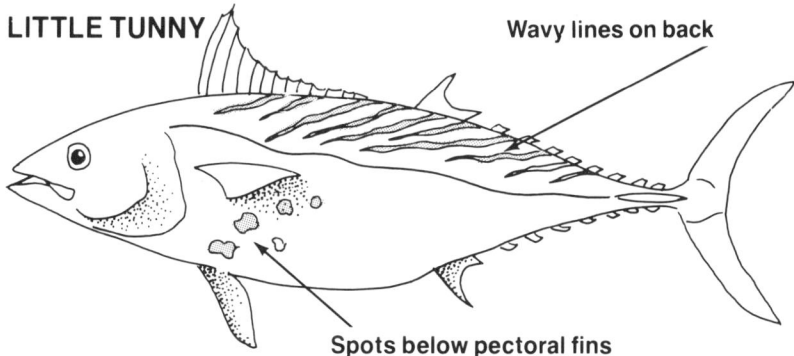

WAHOO
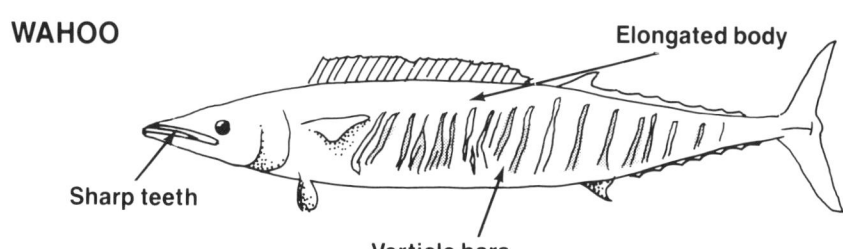

Atlantic Bluefin Tuna

The "big bad boy" of the tuna world, Atlantic bluefin tuna, *Thunnus thynnus,* may reach weight of 2000 pounds, yet none have yet been caught that large on rod and reel. As big as bluefin may get, they are the most devastated of the tuna species due entirely to the greed of commercial fishermen, including those so-called sportsmen who sell their catch to the eager Japanese buyers. When the Atlantic bluefin tuna was worth barely a nickel a pound, the fish was caught for sheer pleasure and the angling challenge these immense fish could give. Today, with prices of a single fish often exceeding the $30,000 mark for an individual fish, sport fishing has virtually ceased and only a handful of big game fishermen still pursue the giant tuna for sporting purposes rather than the lure of the almighty dollar.

The Atlantic bluefin tuna is found from Argentina to Labrador, Canada. Depending on the size of the fish they move along the East Coast from south to north each spring. The smallest fish may move quite close to the coast while the larger fish may stay in the slope waters of the Continental shelf. The major wintering areas are the Caribbean, Gulf of Mexico and South America.

Bluefin tuna are dark blue on the back with silver sides and white belly. Unique smokey gray lines and spots mark the sides of the fish when alive. Juveniles may have vivid dark vertical bars along the sides when fresh caught, but these lines disappear in adult fish. The short pectoral fins and the pale blue tint to the second dorsal and anal fin are distinguishing marks that help identify the bluefin from other tuna.

Atlantic bluefin tuna grow quickly but don't mature until the sixth year of life, measuring nearly 6 feet in length and weighing in excess of 300 pounds. Protection of the spawning class of fish is essential to the future of the species, yet the intense commercial pressure is aimed directly at these huge fish so vital to their continuation. Spawning takes place in April through June in the Caribbean and Gulf of Mexico, along the edge of the Shelf in June and July for smaller bluefin from North Carolina to New York.

Bluefin feed on a wide variety of ling, whiting, small pollock, butterfish, sand eels, smelt and other predatory fish like other small tuna, bonito and bluefish.

Bigeye Tuna

The bigeye tuna is a tough, beautiful fish much sought after by offshore fishermen. Next to the Atlantic bluefin, it is the largest tuna found on the East Coast and may reach sizes in excess of 300 pounds. The largest we've taken on our boat is a 314 pounder caught in the fall at the Hudson Canyon, but bigeye of better than 350 pounds have been taken off Maryland and North Carolina.

Thunnus obesus is dark metallic blue on the back with silver sides and a white belly set off with bright yellow finlets along the tail and tinges of yellow in the dorsal and anal fins. Although similar in appearance to the yellowfin tuna, the bigeye does have a larger eye, a chunkier body shape and a prominent lateral keel on the caudal peduncle. A look at the gill arches will reveal 23 to 31 gill rakers. A sure-fire way to tell a bigeye is to check the liver when cleaning the fish. A tuna with striations (lines) on the underside of the liver is definitely a bigeye.

We tag many of the bigeye and yellowfin tuna we catch on the Linda B and liver examinations are therefore not practical. Our only solution is to make realistic guesstimates using length and weight to determine the species we are about to tag. Examining the liver kills the fish so we eyeball the catch and call tuna over 100 pounds bigeye, those under 100 pounds yellowfin.

We do, however, check livers on fish that are iced down and brought home for dinner. Several times we have found some small tuna of 40 to 80 pounds that we guessed as yellowfin that were actually bigeye. One summer when hefty bigeye were abundant off the Jersey Coast, a 246 pounder we caught was not an unusual catch until we cleaned the fish back at the dock and discovered it was actually the biggest yellowfin we'd ever caught and was not far off the state record!

Bigeye are sexually mature at three years of age and measure about 3 feet in length. Spawning may occur year-round but most

Bigeye may reach 300 pounds and are great sport on stand-up or trolling tackle.

activity occurs from April to February. Females may spawn twice a year, distributing up to 6 million eggs. Bigeye seem to prefer deeper water and are rarely caught on the inshore grounds, as yellowfin and bluefin. They also have a preference for night feeding and are especially active at dawn and dusk.

Yellowfin Tuna

While the Atlantic bluefin tuna has been on the decline in the last decade, sport fishing catches of yellowfin have generally been better than ever. *Thunnus albacares,* has been the primary targeted tuna species when anglers say they are heading for the northeast and mid Atlantic canyons. They may hope to land a blue marlin or a white, but they count on catching yellowfin.

As bluefin have disappeared from much of the inshore waters, yellowfin tuna have frequently moved inshore to waters where they were previously unknown. With varying degrees of abundance, the last ten years have seen some impressive catches of yellowfins not far from sight of land. The fish move into these inshore waters to gorge themselves on the large quantities of bait available. From Virginia to New England, the last several years have seen fair to excellent inshore catches of yellowfin in 20 to 30 fathoms of water. The fishing changes each year, seeming to depend on the relative abundance of the number of small bluefin available at these inshore areas. When the bluefin are abundant, the yellowfin are scarce.

As previously mentioned, yellowfin may be confused with the bigeye tuna because they are similar in coloration with metallic blue backs blending to silvery sides. The yellowfin tuna, however, is less robust, has a smaller diameter eye, and has slashes of yellow along its sides when fresh caught. When brought to the boat and the mate yells, "I see color!", the golden yellow slash down the side can be quite bright and easy to see, quickly giving away the identity of the fish. I've seen this bright glow of color when yellowfin attack a flat line lure pulled a few feet off the transom. What a sight!

Some specimens have graceful, elongated second dorsal and anal fins, and biologists used to classify these yellowfin as allison tuna, a name no longer used, as if they were a seperate species. Detailed examination shows there is no difference between the longer finned yellowfin and the shorter finned brothers and sisters. One explanation given for the shorter fins was the wearing down of these fins in close, tightly packed schools of smaller fish. Yellowfin may have variegated dark marks along the sides and belly when first caught or excited, especially younger fish.

Yellowfin spawn in spring and summer when water temperatures reach 78 degrees. Fortunately they mature quickly, unlike the unfortunate bluefin, and usually spawn by their second year. A 60-inch female is capable of laying over 6 million eggs, and some females may spawn more than once in a season.

Yellowfin do not live long but their growth is rapid. In the first two weeks of life they grow from an egg to a 2-inch fish. At the end of the first year of growth they measure 20 inches and will reach 68 inches in seven years and weigh in the 200-pound range.

Albacore Tuna

The albacore, *Thunnus alalunga,* has several local names depending on where you fish. Some anglers use the name longfin albacore, or just longfin. Northeast anglers may call this fish a "true" albacore to lessen any confusion between the albacore and the inshore "false" albacore, more correctly called a little tunny. No matter what you call him, the albacore is a great game fish and can be very abundant. If you catch one albacore, chances are there are many more waiting to jump on a lure or bait because they often travel in large schools.

Dark metallic blue on the back, they blend to a silvery white on the sides and belly. They lack the pretty yellow finlets of many other tunas, but may exhibit a beautiful neon blue splash of color down the side when excited or fresh caught. The best way to identify an albacore is by the extremely long pectoral fin. Some fishermen nickname the albacore "airplanes" or "turkeys" because the fins look like wings of a plane or bird as the fish moves through the water.

Albacore roam the Atlantic Coast from Brazil to New England and can be found in the Caribbean, but unlike other tuna, they are absent from the Gulf of Mexico. They like waters of 54 to 75 degrees and frequently mix with schools of yellowfin and blackfin tuna.

They become sexually mature at five years when they are about 30 to 36 inches in length. Like other tuna, they disperse millions of eggs into the warm waters of the Gulf Stream and the eggs drift with the current until they reach several inches in length and can fend for themselves. At the end of the first year of life, an albacore will measure 18 inches, 24 inches at three years and nearly 4 feet at 10 years.

Wahoo

The wahoo is famous for its super-fast runs and its razor-sharp set of dentures. Unlike most other tuna, this sleek fish is long and slender rather than short and chunky. Scientists know this fish as *Acanthocy-*

YELLOWFIN MIGRATIONS

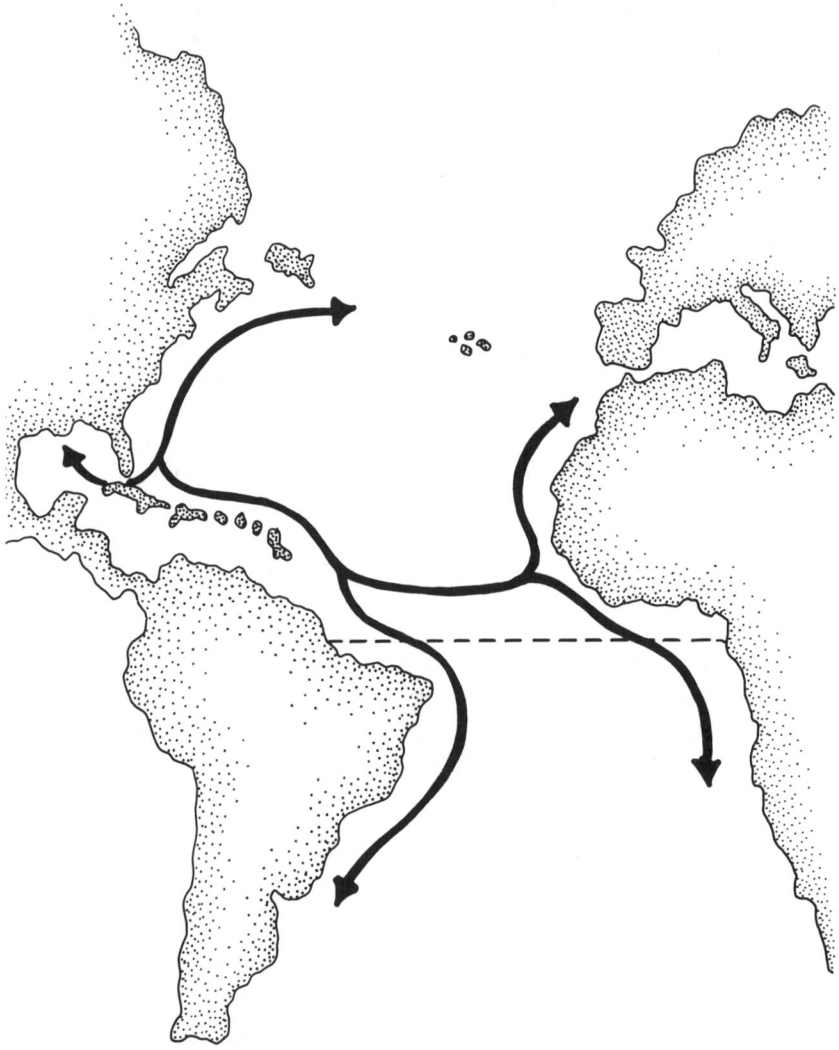

Yellowfin travel along known routes, dependant upon bait and water temperature. The intermixing of yellowfin from the East Coast of the United States to the West Coast of Africa has been documented by tag returns. Yellowfin probably move from north to south at the approach of winter in the northern hemisphere, yet year-round fishing for yellowfin and bigeye occurs off North Carolina's Outer Banks.

MEET THE SPECIES

BLUEFIN MIGRATIONS

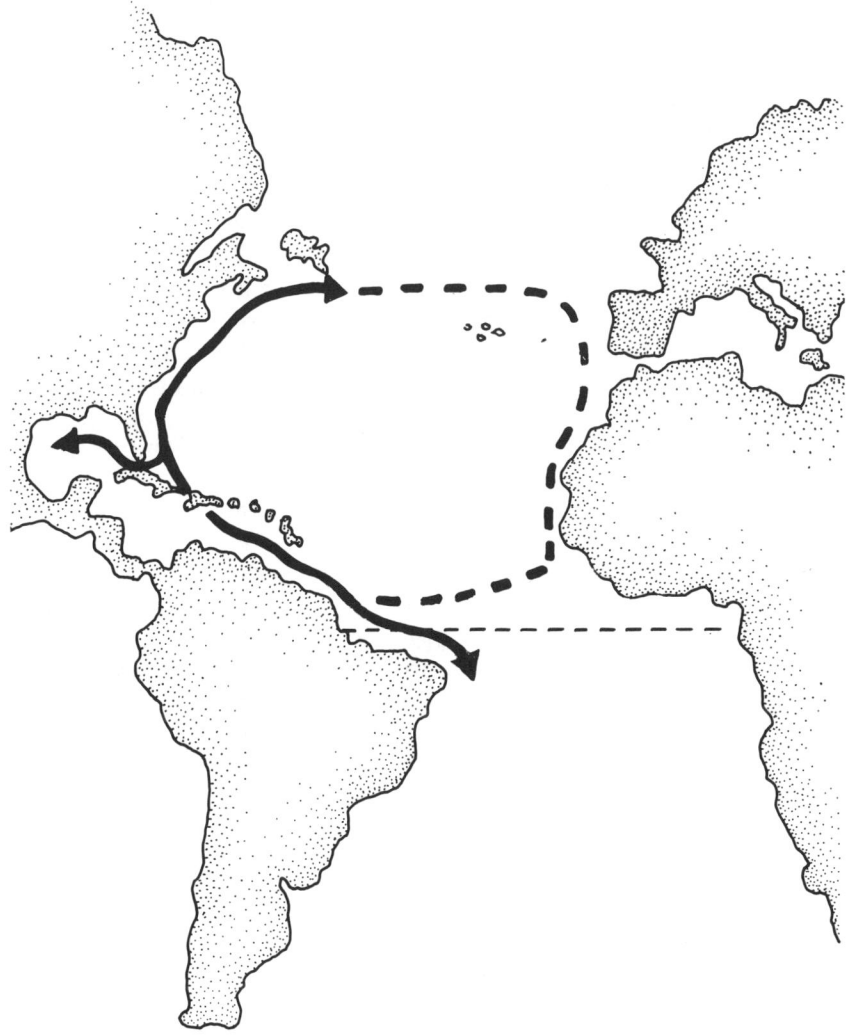

The Atlantic bluefin tuna spawns in the Gulf of Mexico. As the spawners leave the Gulf, they head south and north, with the primary migration heading north to the Canadian Maritimes. Before the extreme decimation of bluefins by commercial interests, there was limited documentation by tag returns of bluefin migrating across the Atlantic.

bium sloanderi, fishermen know the wahoo for its strong fighting ability and appreciate it for its excellent table fare.

It is found in tropical and subtropical waters of the Atlantic Coast, rarely being caught above Montauk, although Massachusetts offshore fishermen occasionally do see wahoo. It is much more common from Virginia southward to Florida. Wahoo eat other fish almost exclusively and examination of stomach contents after boating a wahoo will usually reveal butterfish, sand eels, squid, small tunas and mackerel, small dolphin, flying fish, jacks and ballyhoo.

A beautiful steel blue when alive, the body is accented with 25 to 30 blackish-blue vertical bars. There's no mistaking the wahoo and it makes a superb fish mount for a den or office.

Wahoo do not live long, yet they grow rapidly. At one year of age a wahoo will measure about 40 inches and weigh about 15 pounds. At four years it will stretch the ruler to 60 inches and weigh about 45 pounds. They can reach weights of 100 pounds although fish over 80 pounds are not too common. Both males and females reach sexual maturity during the first year of life with spawning taking place in June, July and August from approximately North Carolina to Florida and the Caribbean.

The flesh of wahoo is a delight. It is slightly more oily than most other tuna but not strong in flavor. It is ideal when cooked on a charcoal grill. The meat seems to freeze better than other tuna, perhaps because of the slight extra oil. Small, pear-shaped parasites, called trematodes, are found in the stomachs of wahoo, but not the flesh. They are harmless to man and are usually discarded with the carcass of a filleted fish.

Blackfin, Skipjack & Little Tunny

"Pound for pound," many an angling story starts out, and then finishes with that anglers opinion of the best, fastest, jump'nest, hardest fight'nest, biggest or toughest fish in the ocean. I've always believed the fish on the end of your line at any given moment is really the best fish, but I do confess to having a lot of fun with the several species of small tunas found along the coast from Massachusetts to Florida.

The blackfin tuna is one of the smaller members of the tuna family but a popular one, especially with southern anglers. *Thunnus atlanticus* prefers waters above 68 degrees and swims the coast from the Caribbean to Virginia, occasionally straying to New Jersey waters. It can be confused with school bluefin tuna but lacks the yellow finlets. Most blackfin are 18 to 30 inches when caught but they may exceed 36 inches and weigh up to 35 pounds. I caught a 28-pound blackfin on 12-pound tackle while fishing at Walker's Cay in the Bahamas and would have qualified for a world record if we hadn't eaten the fish that night. I realized my mistake several weeks later when another captain suggested I take a look at the IGFA record book.

The skipjack, *Katsuwanus pelamis,* and little tunny, *Euthynnus alletteratus,* are found all along the coast from the Caribbean to New England. While frequently caught at the canyons, they can also be caught on the 20 to 30 fathom banks all along the coast. Pound for pound they are great game fish testing the skill of the angler and the limits of the tackle.

Known as the bonito to southern fishermen, false albacore to anglers north of Delaware, the little tunny really isn't a bonito at all nor is he an albacore. With wavy lines across his back and spots just below the pectoral fins he's easy to identify. Skipjack have bold strips along their bellies, winning them the nickname of watermelons.

Blackfins are very good tasting as is the skipjack, although many fishermen rarely eat skippies. The little tunny is a stronger flavored tuna that many fishermen prefer to use as strip baits yet I've met fishermen who marinate the little tunny fillets in milk before cooking and they say the tunny makes a good meal.

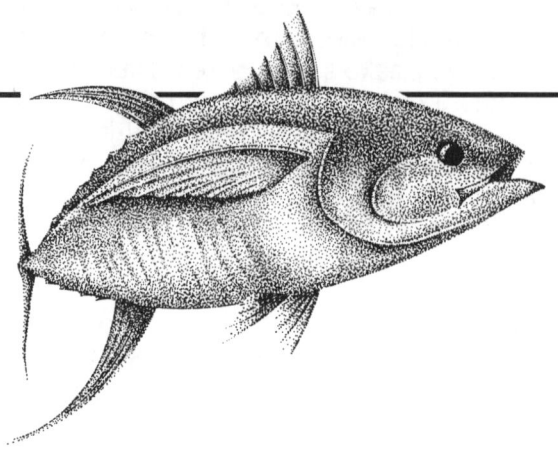

Chapter Two

TACKLE AND EQUIPMENT

Tomi Vadset of the Billfish Foundation worked the rod beautifully. She was hooked solidly into a good-sized yellowfin tuna pulling hard against 20 pounds of drag pressure. Tomi's knees were bent slightly and her legs flexed with the motion of the waves against the hull. The aluminum rod butt rocked in the gimbal belt as she pumped the fish towards the boat. The rod tip gently pulsated with each sweep of the tuna's powerful tail, transmitting the struggle through the rod blank to her hands and arms. She had complete control of tackle and fish.

Soon, we saw the first splash of color as rod pressure lifted the fish from the depths. The tuna splashed wildly at boat side in a last ditch attempt to break the line, or the angler. Both held, and my son, Rich, reached over the cover boards to pop the tag into the back of the fish.

"Looks about 36 inches", he yelled so I could make the entry on the tag card. A quick twist of the lure hook with a leather-gloved hand and the yellowfin zipped away in a blur of gold, silver and blue. We all shouted, cheered and laughed, then got back to the business of trolling another fish. Lures were dropped back into the pattern, drags checked and anxious eyes watched the foamy wake. The search for offshore action continued.

Using the right tackle, balanced not only to the size of the fish being caught, but also to the size and strength of the angler, and the size and style of boat, is vital to consistent success on the offshore grounds. The wrong tackle can lose a fish, possibly a trophy-sized marlin or tuna - maybe the fish of a lifetime. The right tackle will make the fighting of every fish a pleasure, and the angler, like Tomi Vadset, will enjoy the fun of battling the fish and be in complete control of fish and tackle at all times.

Tackle Selection

Like many offshore fishermen I have some strong opinions of what makes a good, balanced rod and reel combination. I've formed these opinions on the proving grounds of the northeast canyons, the edge of the Stream off Oregon Inlet, along the Florida Keys and in the Bahamas in boats I've owned and operated that ran in size from a 25-foot center console to my present boat, a 38-footer. The size of the boat, not just the species of fish, will also dictate the class of tackle being used. A heavy duty 130 International is not handy to use on a smaller center console boat and will literally shake the flush mount rod holders loose from their mountings. Likewise, a 30-pound outfit to troll big baits for giant bluefin tuna or grander blue marlin is no match to the task. In most trolling situations, tackle that is somewhere between these two extremes is a more reasonable choice.

The terms heavy tackle and light tackle are vague and open to wide interpretation. A 50-pound class rod and reel used to subdue a 25-pound yellowfin would hardly be called light tackle, yet the same rod and reel, if used to land a 500-pound blue marlin, a 10 to 1 ratio of fish weight to line strength, could be considered light tackle fishing. Most fishermen prefer to use tackle that will allow them to get a fish to the boat in a comfortable length of time, with no undue strain on the angler and with some fun to the fight. A two-to-one, or three-to-one ratio of fish weight to tackle pound test rating is more in line with what most fishermen use on the day to day fishing grounds.

Heavy and light mean different things to different fishermen, but for the sake of comparison, let's classify offshore trolling tackle into these categories:

Heavy	130 pound	Giant tuna and blue marlin of 500 or more pounds.
Medium	80 and 50 pound	Blue marlin, bluefin tuna, bigeye tuna, yellowfin tuna of 100 to 400 pounds.
Light	20 and 30 pound	White marlin, sailfish, yellowfin, bluefin and albacore of 25 to 100 pounds.
Ultralight	12 and 16 pound	White marlin, sailfish, school-sized tuna of 5 to 50 pounds.

TACKLE AND EQUIPMENT

These tackle classifications are meant as a general guideline and there is plenty of room for overlap. Sometimes the overlap occurs as a surprise. A blue marlin I caught off Islamorada, Florida hit a 20-pound pound class outfit meant for dolphin and school tuna, but two hours later my wife, Linda, grabbed the leader and we released a blue one that we estimated at 250 pounds. At The Point off Oregon Inlet, North Carolina, fishing on Captain John Bayliss' Tarheel, I had a 240-pound bigeye hit a 50-pound outfit meant for the 30 to 50-pound yellowfin we had been catching all morning.

Good tackle can land big fish if used properly. Many fishermen, however, are surprised that super-heavy tackle just isn't needed for most of the fish we catch. There's no point to using 80W reels, filled with 100-pound monofilament line, to catch fish that average less than 100 pounds. It's overkill and the level of challenge and enjoyment decreases considerably when excessively heavy tackle is used.

The strength of the angler must be considered, too. Heavy tackle is not only bulky but it also weighs a lot. If the drag is set at one third the breaking strength of the line, 100-pound line on an 80W with a drag set at 33 pounds of pull is too much for any but the most experienced angler to use. The pressure will exhaust the fisherman before the fisherman tires the fish. On the other hand, a 50W with 60-pound line and a drag setting of 20 pounds is not too much for most adults to handle. If the angler is comfortable with the tackle, maximum pressure can be applied during every minute of the fight. Since the angler isn't tired out, sensibly balanced tackle can actually subdue big fish in less time than heavy tackle can.

I remember a bigeye we hooked at the Toms Canyon that nearly broke the back of a hefty guy who thought he was in shape to handle anything. Our charter that day swore they had "lots of canyon experience" and wanted the heavy tackle brought out for bigeye tuna. I had seen the strike and it looked like someone threw a Volkswagen into the water the splash was so terrific. I thought the fish might break the 200-pound mark and the angler struggled mightily with the fish. After fifteen minutes or so, however, I watched the angler more carefully and could see he wasn't working the rod properly, nor was he applying maximum pressure. Most times the rod was pointed towards the fish with no hard bend in the rod. He struggled to wind in line desperately, though he gained barely a few inches for his great attempts at lifting the rod.

The tackle wore him down until finally he had to get out of the chair and hand off the tackle to his buddy. The second angler obviously had more experience with tuna and used short lifts of the rod tip to gain line a foot at a time until ten minutes later the gaff finished the fight as the tuna, a 186-pounder the dock scales said later, was lifted from the water across the cover boards. The second angler was a gentleman and gave credit to his pal who had "worn out the fish so my job was easier" but he and I both knew the toll the tackle had taken on the first angler.

In my opinion, the best all round rod and reel combination is the 50W size reel filled with 50 or 60-pound line, 80 pound at the most. I've used this tackle from Block Canyon to Chub Cay, for blue marlin and bigeye, yellowfin and albacore and have never felt handicapped because the tackle was too light for big fish, nor did it overpower smaller fish. The line capacity is generous, the reels are rugged and durable, and the tackle light enough in weight that fishermen (men or women) of average stature can handle it without getting exhausted.

The 50Ws work well in small skiffs and on a larger sportfisherman. This tackle is on the light side for fish over 200 pounds, but we've taken blue marlin over 450 pounds on this gear and bigeye to just over 300 pounds. The 50Ws are not so heavy that a 50-pound yellowfin won't still put up a good fight.

Ultimately, it's your boat and you should use what pleases you, not what everyone else thinks you should use. I know plenty of anglers who use tackle that is heavier, or lighter, than what I consider to be ideal, but if it works fine for them, that's the right tackle to use.

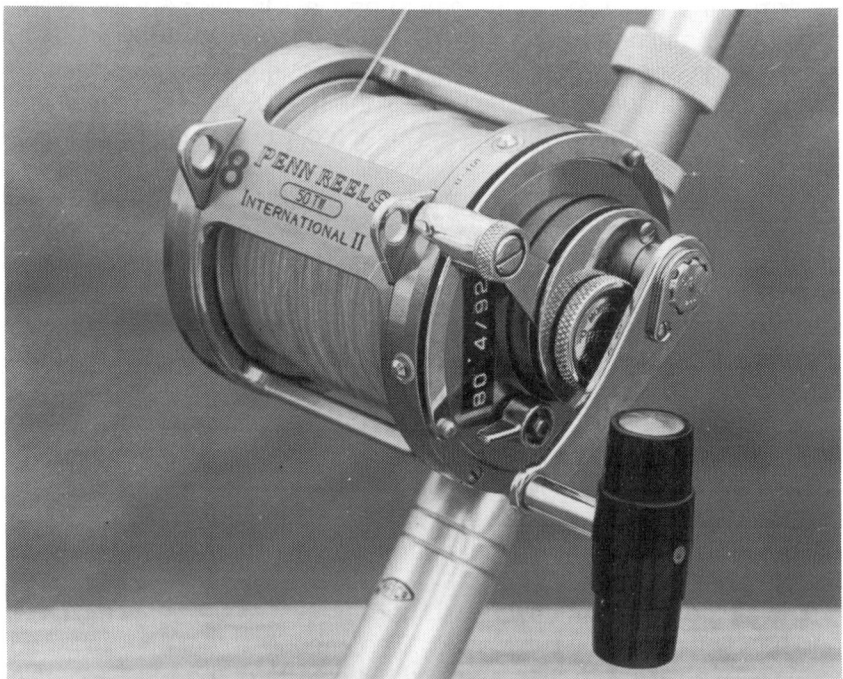

The wide-spool 50TW lever drag reel is favored by many offshore fishermen because of its relatively small size and light weight, in comparison to larger reels. It is a good choice for stand-up and traditional trolling tackle.

The Reel Choice

When we look at the reels available today, it's obvious that fishing tackle technology offers an extensive array of high quality equipment to choose from. The old standards from Penn and Fin-Nor are now challenged by Shimano, Daiwa and Abu-Garcia. Star drag reels are still popular with fishermen on a budget, and work especially well for inshore species. Over the years many records have been set with star drag reels attesting to their quality.

The major drawback of the star drag reel is its limited range of drag settings, along with the lack of ability to quickly and accurately change the drag setting while fighting a fish. Further, the total surface area of the drag washers in a star drag reel is far smaller than the drag surfaces of a corresponding lever drag reel, which may have at least ten times more drag surface area.

Lever drag reels are the primary choice for offshore fishing. From a utility viewpoint, they are much more rugged than a star drag reel and will withstand repeated years of hard fishing. From a functional viewpoint, they are better fish fighting tools. The larger drag surfaces do not heat up and expand as readily and the drag setting can be varied while fighting a fish to increase or decrease drag as needed.

They are expensive at first purchase but since they last so long, they are actually less costly in the long run. My original Penn 50s were purchased 14 years ago and are still going strong after hundreds of fish. By comparison, several star drag reels I used during the same time period lasted only several seasons before gears, drags, spool shafts and other parts wore out. If you fish offshore only occasionally, then a star drag reel may be fine for your tackle choice. However if you plan to fish hard and often, then lever drags are the way to go.

Aluminum is still the material of choice for heavy duty tackle and most lever reels are now produced in a tubular frame design that is strong yet light weight. They are usually classed based on the length and pound test rating of the line they will hold. A 130 reel is meant to hold approximately 800 yards of 130-pound test line; an 80 will hold 800 yards of 80-pound; a 50 will hold 800 yards of 50-pound line and so on down the size classes through 30, 20 and 12-pound test.

Some reels are sold in wide-spool versions such as 80W, 50W and 30W, which have the same reel frame diameter as a standard 80, 50 or 30 pound reel. The wider spools will hold 25 to 40% more line than the standard reels, or they can be filled with one pound test heavier line. For instance, a 50W would hold 1200 yards of 50-pound line or about 800 yards of 80-pound line. The advantage of the wider spool reels, especially for small boat fishermen is their lower center of gravity, lower position of the handle in relation to the rod blank and the fact that they maintain their spool line diameter when fish take large amounts of line. A narrower spool will lose more of its line diameter at a faster rate and the effective drag setting is increased as the spool diameter gets smaller.

On the down side, wide-spool reels, when used with a heavier pound test line do not retrieve line as quickly as a standard spool reel. For instance, a 50W filled with 80-pound line will not take in the same length of line as a larger diameter 80 size reel for each turn of the reel handle. The spool diameter of the 50W is about 20 to 25% smaller than the spool on the standard 80 reel.

Graphite composites are now receiving wide acceptance for their light weight, ruggedness and resistance to corrosion in the saltwater environment. Manufacturers like Shimano and Penn have taken advantage of graphite's attributes and introduced lever drag reels that will suit the budget minded offshore angler. At present, these graphite reels are meant to be fished with 12 to 50-pound line and range in size from the ultralight to medium weight reels.

One of the greatest innovations for stand-up fishermen has to be the popularizing of the two-speed reel. They have to be used to be appreciated. The standard high speed retrieve is great while fighting a fish that is out and away from the boat, but once a hefty bluefin or blue marlin starts to nose dive to the depths, a quick shift into a lower gear ratio can keep the situation under the control of the angler. With a single speed reel, the down deep fight of a tuna leaves the angler on the "short end of the stick." The two-speed reel, shifted into its lower gear ratio and with the angler working the rod in short lifting strokes will beat some very big fish on relatively light, 30 or 50-pound tackle.

My son had his first experience with a two-speed reel while struggling with a bigeye of better than 200 pounds. He worked the tackle well but the big fish just didn't want to come up so we could see him. Rich gained line with great effort until he remembered the two-speed feature on the Penn 50SW he was using. Dropping down to the lower gear made all the difference in the world and he gained line quickly to bring the fish to the gaff. Two-speed reels are a definite advantage and well worth the extra price tag if you fish often. The primary advantage of the two-speed reel is its capability of working up a fish from deep water, such as a blue marlin or bigeye that has sounded and must be lifted foot by foot until within gaffing or tagging range.

Using Lever Drag Reels

Setting the drag correctly assures maximum performance. A lever drag reel is always in gear and there is no free spool as in conven-

TACKLE AND EQUIPMENT

From top to bottom; 80TW for giant bluefin and blue marlin; 50TW for bigeye, yellowfin and mid-size blue marlin; International 114H for yellowfin, albacore, bluefin; and the 12T for school tuna, sailfish and white marlin.

tional reels with a push button or free spool lever control to disengage the gears from the spool. On a lever drag reel, the gears are meshed to the spool at all times. The "free spool" setting is actually a position where all tension on the drag is removed so the spool can spin freely, but the gears are still meshed to the spool. By moving the lever forward, the drag is increased and the reel is then "in gear".

Lever drag reels have two (sometimes more) positions within the arc that the drag lever can be moved. The Strike position is designed to be set at 25% of the breaking strength of the line and the fish is usually fought with the lever in this position. The Full position does not mean 100% drag - the line would break on every fish. Ideally the Full setting should produce a drag setting of approximately 33% of the breaking strength of the line on the spool.

Big fish anglers, especially those who seek giant bluefin tuna, using 100 to 130-pound test lines may use even greater drag settings. It can be crucial to the successful outcome of a battle with a 1000-pound fish to stop the initial run quickly to keep the angler in control at all times. In this case, the Strike position drag may be set at 33% of the line strength, the full setting resulting in a 50% drag setting.

To adjust the drag, the lever must first be in the free spool position. The drag tensioning knob is then turned to increase or decrease the drag setting. The new drag setting is checked by moving the lever back to the Strike position and pulling on the line. To do this accurately, a hand scale should be used. Many anglers make the mistake of trying to adjust the drag with the lever still in the Strike position. While some change in the drag setting may occur, the setting will not be accurate unless the lever is placed in free spool before turning the adjustment knob.

The staff at Shimano ran some informal tests and proved that most fishermen cannot properly set drags without a hand scale. They asked hundreds of fishermen they met at sport shows to set drags by hand and then tested the settings with a scale. Most fishermen were off by a wide margin on the low side of the scale which prevents maximum power being applied to the fish to bring the catch to the boat. On my own boat, visiting fishermen often question the seemingly tight drags on our reels. It takes a gloved hand to yank line from a Penn International 50W filled with 80-pound line and with the drag set at 20 pounds of pull. It feels too tight to the hand, but it is just right by the scale.

Too light a drag results in lost fish. Stories of huge tuna or marlin that dumped an entire spool of line have to be entirely the anglers fault with an improperly set drag. A 100-pound tuna can swim forever against a 10-pound drag setting even if the angler is using 80 or 100-pound line. It wasn't the strong fish that emptied the spool, it was the lightly set drag that never applied tiring pressure to the fish.

TACKLE AND EQUIPMENT

Lever drag reels are all designed to be used within a range of line pound tests and the reels, as previously mentioned, are named for the recommended line. For instance, a 50 size reel is made to be fished with 50-pound line. Usually the fisherman can elect to use the next pound test lighter line if he needs more line capacity or the next heavier pound test line if more pressure is needed against the fish and in either case the reel will still perform flawlessly. The 50 reel can be successfully used with 30, 50 or 80-pound test. The drag system as engineered by the manufacturer's design team will adequately provide a range of settings for lines within these limits.

A major problem occurs when the fisherman exceeds the limits of the reel and uses, let's say, 100-pound test line on a 30TW. A properly set drag would give 25-pounds of pull at strike, a setting which on the 30TW is beyond the limits of the drag system. The adjustment knob will not even be able to dial in such a powerful drag setting so there is no advantage to using the heavier line. With too heavy a drag setting, the lever may not be able to be moved forward without damage to the reel. With a drag setting that exceeds the limits of the designed drag range, a small movement of the lever from free spool into gear will have the drag already at its maximum setting. This causes rapid wear on the reel, tackle failure and no advantage in drag setting. The innovative Shimano Tiagra reels offer a wider range of available drag settings and have an adjustable full drag position to match the line being used. While allowing a wider range of lines, they still won't work well beyond reasonable limits.

Drags should be set with a hand scale, rod bent as if fighting a fish, on each and every trip.

The drag setting is modified while trolling. Pulling lures at 6 to 9 knots puts a tremendous amount of pressure on the line at the moment a fish strikes the lure or bait. If the lever was placed in the Strike position, set at 25% of the line strength, there could still be enough shock at the impact of the strike to snap the line. I learned that lesson the hard way on my first canyon trip many years ago in my Mako 25. With drags at the Strike position, four bigeye jumped our lures at the edge of the deep. Two lines snapped immediately, sounding like rifle shots. Fortunately the other two fish were boated after a good fight.

When trolling, the lever should be pulled back from strike to a setting about 15% of the line strength. With 80-pound line that's about 12 pounds of drag; plenty of punch to set the hook but light enough to prevent snapped lines. After the rush of the initial hook-up and once the angler is in the chair or strapped into the gimbal belt, the lever is then shoved to strike to fight the fish. The lever can be pushed to full to gain more power when lifting the fish, backed off to strike when the fish makes a run.

When trolling with baits, opinion varies as to the proper drag setting. Sailfish and white marlin fishermen often fish with the drag lever pulled back so there is only slight drag pressure, just enough to keep the spool from backlashing at the strike of fish and enough so the bait is maintained in its trolling position in the wake. At the strike of a fish, there is little resistance from the drag to spook the fish as it mouths the bait, turns it and swallows the offering. At this moment, the angler shoves the lever to strike and sets the hook.

Bait trollers using swimming baits and running at the same speeds as lure trollers will usually use a drag setting about 15% of the strength of the line. Most tuna will hook themselves at the strike, but a billfish may need to be played with to get the fish to eat the bait. The angler must be attentive so he can work the tackle and free spool the reel to drop the bait back to the fish if the initial strike did not result in a solidly hooked fish.

Using heavier lines puts a strain on the drag washers and drags can wear out from hard use and big fish. They can also collect moisture from wet, sloppy days trolling or too much water from the hose at cleaning time. It pays to service the drags periodically, either to remove the washers and rub them on 400 grit wet or dry paper, hard cardboard or other fine polishing surface, or to replace them with new washers.

Rod Selection

Most offshore fishermen will choose a standard trolling rod for their fishing and simply match the rod to the reel. An International 50 reel would match up with a rod labeled for 50-pound test line. It sounds simple, but there are a few wrinkles to be aware of. Years ago there were two classes of offshore trolling rods; one for the West Coast and another for the East Coast. They were all about 6'8" in length but the West Coast rods had a softer action than the stiffer East Coast versions.

Today the West and East Coast labels have disappeared but the mix of blanks is still there. Compare one manufacturer's 50-pound rod to another's and you are likely to find a significant difference in how the rods feel and how they flex and bend while working a fish. You can tell the difference easily by placing the tip of the rod on the floor (carpeted so you don't scratch the rod) while holding the rod butt in your hands. Put a good bend in the rod and see how it feels. Careful examination of rods from a dealers shelf will disclose 50-pound class rods that feel like another manufacturers 80-pound class rod. As a frame of reference, check out the Fenwick and Penn 50 pound class rods. They are, in my opinion, about ideal in length, action and "feel" for 50-pound test tackle.

My preference is for a rod blank that has a firm butt action and a slightly limber tip. Not a fast taper blank, just a tip action that doesn't feel like a broomstick. A rod of this type will feel good when you play a fish and is not so tiring as a very stiff rod that doesn't bend with the pull of the fish. It's the cushioning bend of the rod that protects the line (along with the drag) and applies constant tiring pressure against the pull of the fish.

Most traditional trolling rods are 6'6" to 6'10" in length for a reason; the rod blank must be long enough so that when the butt is placed in the fight chair gimbal, the tip top roller will clear the transom cover boards so the line won't become chafed by rubbing against the boat. There's no magic to selecting the length, it's based on the reality of the size of the boat's cockpit and the distance from the fight chair to the outside edge of the center of the transom.

Standard trolling rods are often called IGFA rods in reference to the International Game Fish Association that sets the criteria by which world record catches are judged. The IGFA sets reasonable regulations for record fish but they do not, however, set the design guidelines for rod blank tapers. So long as a rod meets IGFA's minimum requirements of a 40-inch tip section and butt section no longer than 27 inches, the rod action can be anything the angler or the manufacturer wants it to be. Manufacturers usually label their rods based on IGFA regulations for line classes that match record categories (12, 16, 20, 30, 50, 80 and 130) and to match the reels that use similar pound tests. A so-called IGFA 30-pound rod would be used with a 30-pound class reel, and 80-pound rod with an 80-pound class reel.

There is a wide range of high-quality rods available from several manufacturers. The best rods have AFTCO aluminum Unibutts and roller guides secured with double-wrapped, epoxy-coated threads for maximum strength to hold the guides in position. Foam style grips are about standard, but harder cork grips are superior. Foam squeezes under the strain of a big fish and causes undue strain and fatigue of the angler's forearm.

Avoid wooden butts if possible, and never use a rod with a foam lower butt. Once the foam is water soaked from spray while trolling, it will be nearly impossible to remove the rod from the rod holder once a fish is hooked and the rod is bent over from the pull of a good fish.

A small point, but AFTCO makes two styles of Unibutts; one with a squared off gimbal and the other with a rounded ball-shaped gimbal. The squared AFTCO butts are almost universally used by most manufacturers of factory-built rods and by most custom rod builders. The ball gimbal is less damaging to teak decks, to the edges of rod holders and slips more easily into gimbal belts. If you can find rods with the ball style end, they are a better rod. Custom rod builders can order the ball end butts at any time.

At one time there was quite a battle between those fishermen who favored graphite rods and those who preferred fiberglass rods. Fiberglass is a heavier material than graphite so a glass rod will always weigh more than a comparable graphite rod. Graphite has a high modulas, which is a $5 way to say it returns to its unbent state more quickly than fiberglass. It is also less forgiving when a fish is at boat side and makes a sudden dive. Graphite is more costly than fiberglass. As you can see, each has its advantages and drawbacks.

New innovations in fiberglass technology have introduced lighter, stronger glass rods that bring them closer to their graphite counterparts at a more reasonable price. The traditional E-glass blanks offer the maximum durability under hard fishing conditions where rods may get knocked around. Most offshore fiberglass rods today are a version of E-glass.

Some early graphite rods literally blew up under strain of a big fish. I had a 50-pound class rod shatter on a yellowfin of about 100 pounds. It was awesome, and frightening, as I imagined graphite slivers flying in every direction. Actually there was only a small puff of dust where the rod broke. The sound of the blank cracking was worse than the break itself.

Offshore graphite rods are no longer 100% graphite. Present designs use a blend of graphite and fiberglass to make rods that are more durable and yet still offer the attributes of graphite. I have another graphite rod that has seen six seasons of hard use (sometimes abuse) and it will no doubt continue to take tuna for many more years to come.

TACKLE AND EQUIPMENT

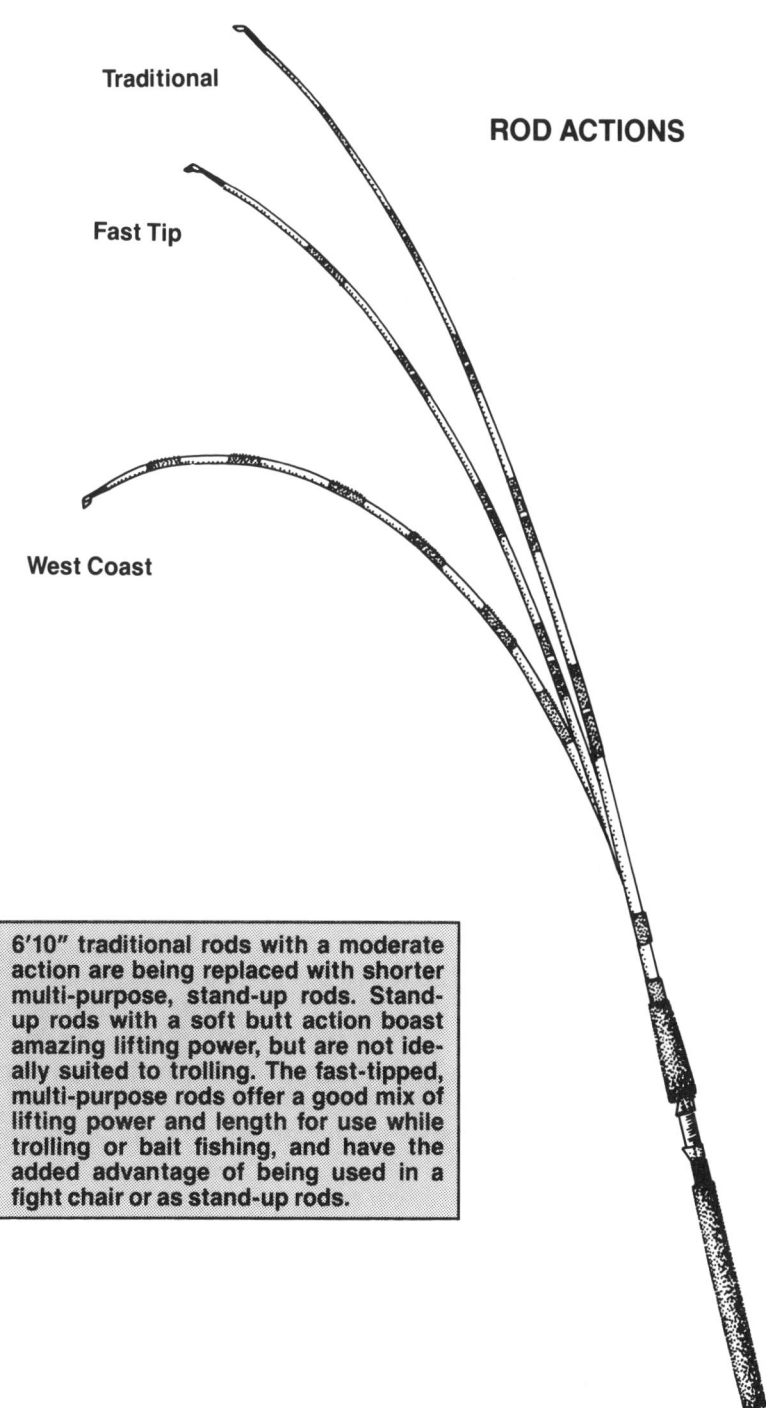

ROD ACTIONS

Traditional

Fast Tip

West Coast

6'10" traditional rods with a moderate action are being replaced with shorter multi-purpose, stand-up rods. Stand-up rods with a soft butt action boast amazing lifting power, but are not ideally suited to trolling. The fast-tipped, multi-purpose rods offer a good mix of lifting power and length for use while trolling or bait fishing, and have the added advantage of being used in a fight chair or as stand-up rods.

Stand-up Trolling Rods

The introduction of the West Coast style stand-up tuna rods hit the East Coast like a tidal wave sweeping anglers, tackle shops and custom rod builders into a new era of big game fishing. Fishermen from Maine to Florida purchased the stand-up rods at record breaking sales for many tackle shops and the rods are now being used for inshore bluefins, canyon yellowfins and bigeye.

There is some confusion about what the stand-up rods can and can't do. When used as they were designed they perform superbly but like any fishing rod they aren't perfect for all types of tuna or big game fishing. The rods were originally built for use on the party boats making long-range trips to the Baja Coast. Since party boats have no fight chairs, the only way the big yellowfins, wahoo and marlin could be fought was standing at the rail, aching muscles and all.

Traditional offshore rods with long, stout tips offered little leverage against these big fish and tired the angler quickly. They were designed to perform in a fight chair, not as stand-up rods. Early experiments with shoulder harnesses and belly gimbal belts didn't help the situation very much. In fact, on a long fight the shoulder harness caused more fatigue of the back muscles because the pull of the rod against the harness actually yanked the angler off balance and made the fish fighting experience a grueling one.

Some inventive angler realized the fishing rod was like a seesaw. If both sides of the seesaw are about even, it takes little effort to keep it working. Grabbing hold of the rod higher up the blank increased the leverage for the fisherman and made the fight easier. Ideally, if the distance from the gimbal to the hand grip could match the distance from the grip to the rod tip, the rod would function like a well balanced seesaw and the fight would be much easier on the fisherman.

This balancing of the pulling forces of the angler and the fish is the basic idea behind the West Coast style rods. They've been designed to let the fisherman grip the rod closer to the balancing center of the "seesaw" action while fighting a fish. They work best with fish that fight down deep directly below the angler, not on fish that make long runs away from the boat.

To take full advantage of these rods, however, some extra gear is needed. The angler should wear a wide, padded gimbal belt as low on his thighs as possible. This increases the angler's side of the "seesaw" and puts more pressure on the angler's legs which are far stronger than his arms. A kidney style fighting harness that crosses and supports the lower back completes the duo of necessary equipment and allows the fisherman to use his body and legs against the fish instead of weaker arms.

TACKLE AND EQUIPMENT

The well-dressed, stand-up fisherman with gimbal at mid thigh. Kidney harness across the back is also attached to top of reel with snaps. Angler fights the fish with leg muscles, leaning back to raise the rod tip and lift the line, gaining line by leaning forward on the down stroke.

Traditional Rods VS Stand-up Rods

The goal is to make fighting the fish as fatigue-free as possible. So which rods work better? Big game tackle gurus Bill Shedd and Greg Stotesbury of AFTCO proved it dramatically a few years ago at the New York Boat Show with a simple experiment. Using a special scale with digital readouts to show pounds of pull, Bill and Greg were able to show how each style rod functioned under conditions similar to real fishing situations.

Strapping me into a gimbal belt they had me pull on a standard trolling rod to maintain a steady pressure of 40 pounds. Within a few seconds my arms started to shake with the effort of maintaining that pressure. Switching to a stand-up type rod, it was dramatically easier to arc the rod and maintain that 40 pounds of pull for several minutes with no arm shake or muscle fatigue.

Both outfits were fitted with 300-pound test mono so we also measured the maximum pull I could register on the scale. With a standard trolling rod I hit the 80-pound mark but could not hold that pressure for any length of time. With the stand-up rod I applied over 90 pounds of pressure and could maintain that amount of pressure with little or no discomfort.

Actually this last test needs some interpretation for the real world of fishing. Typical outfits for tuna fishing would have 50 or 80-pound test line on the reels with drag settings of 12 or 20 pounds. That's all the pressure the angler can apply before the drag slips. The important point here is that the stand-up rods will allow the fisherman to hold that maximum drag setting with far less muscle and back fatigue than with a trolling style rod.

On a battle with a bigeye or yellowfin in excess of 100 pounds, many anglers fold under the pressure within 5 or 10 minutes when using a standard trolling rod. Yet that same fisherman can slug it out toe to toe for over an hour with the stand-up style rods with their greater lifting advantage to the fisherman; especially if the fisherman is using the proper gimbal belt and kidney harness.

For stand-up fishing, West Coast style rods with the longer butts and extended fore grips are clearly superior to the traditional trolling rod. Does this make the "old fashioned" rods ancient history? No way, and the second part of Bill and Greg's testing shows why.

They also had a fight chair installed at the show and while seated in the chair, pulling with the same standard trolling rod that gave me arm shakes while standing up, I was able to maintain 40 pounds of pull with far less arm fatigue. But, that's not exactly how a fight chair was designed to be used.

Once seated in the chair with a fanny bucket under my butt and harnessed to the reel lugs I could use my legs to apply pressure. There was virtually no fatigue at all and it was far less effort to maintain 40 pounds of pull in the fight chair than it was when pulling 40 pounds with the stand-up rod and kidney harness.

Just for comparison's sake I was able to maintain nearly 120 pounds of pressure with no fatigue and could have gone beyond that with a properly adjusted harness. Again, although this does not relate to real fishing conditions, it still proves that a fight chair and standard trolling rod has the capability to apply MORE pressure than a stand-up angler.

So which is better, the stand-up rods or the traditional rods with a fight chair? Actually neither is better. They are both different and should be used for the fishing situations and conditions where they each work the best.

Stand-up rods won't work well in a fight chair because they are so short. The very thing that makes them "super rods" for stand-up battles, works against them when used in a chair. With a full bend in the rod and a tuna holding straight below the boat, the short rods don't have enough length to keep the line clear of the stern of the boat and the rub rail.

Stand-up rods feel the best and apply the greatest pressure when the fish are being fought from below the boat. The lifting power is absolutely amazing with the short rods. That's why they work so well while baitfishing where the fight is nearly vertical. While trolling, however, the shorter rods lose their edge. Not only can the short length cause problems when the fish is brought to the boat, longer trolling rods feel better when working a fish that is high in the water crashing a surface trolling lure. Trolling anglers still seem to prefer the standard trolling rod with a beefier tip action. Fighting a hefty bigeye, a bluefin or a blue marlin of several hundred pounds is more efficient and less tiring when done from a fight chair, with the angler seated in a bucket to allow full use of strong leg muscles.

Small boaters, even while trolling, may find the stand-up rods perfect for their style of canyon fishing where a fight chair is often too large to mount in their boat. The added advantage of being able to fight a big fish for an hour or more is a bigger benefit than the extra care needed to work a fish around outboard engines.

Super Stand-up Trolling Rods

The reality of big game trolling along the East Coast, especially when tuna are present, is that we often get multiple hook-ups. Only one angler gets the chair, the others struggle standing up whether they want to or not. And, many of the fish we catch are far from record breakers, averaging 40 to 125 pounds and easily outgunned if fought from a fight chair.

The trend among many charter captains is toward 6-foot rods with lots of power in the butt section matched to a firm but flexible tip action. These rods are stiffer than many of the original stand-up rods which were meant purely for lifting purposes and which bent in a severe "U" shape under pressure from a fish, the tip arced over so far as to nearly be in line with the rod butt under strain of battle. This does make for less stress on the angler but gives the fish the advantage if it dives under the boat or makes a mad dash around the transom. A wimpy action rod does not have enough length to get the line safely around underwater parts of the boat. Since these rods are made for lifting a fish from the depths they don't work well when pulling on a fish that is 100 yards behind the boat trying to drag your lure to Bermuda!

The firmer actions are better suited to the East Coast. Some factory rods work well, like the Daiwa SP20XH and Penn ARA 2260. Unlike the easily bendable rod, these stiffer action rods handle trolled tuna with more authority. Since the rod action is firmer, there's more line control when gaining line after a tuna strikes a trolled lure or bait 100 feet back in the wake. Using the short stroke technique of rapid, but short, lifts of the rod and quick cranks of the reel handle are a deadly tactic on tuna, especially on smaller boats of 24 to 34 feet.

Over the last few years I've gathered opinions and advice from rod crafters like John Bishop, Kevin Bogan, Ron Fuering, Bob Fox, Fred Klawitter, Roger Green and captains like Dave Preble and Al Anderson in Rhode Island and Frank LoPresti of California. Many other fishermen had already tried rods that were similar to what I had in mind and I gladly took their tips and advice. I wanted a rod that would blend the best attributes of the short stand-up gear with the longer IGFA style trolling rods. I settled on the Calstar 6455 blank to build the rods I thought would be my own version of the Super Stand-Up Rod.

Dave Arbeitman and Grant Toman of the Reel Seat in Point Pleasant, New Jersey did the actual rod construction and talked me through several versions of the blank. I wanted a tip that was light enough to provide enough flex to make a battle with a 40 pound fish as much fun as a 200 pounder. The light tip action allowed the blank to be used as a stand-up rod so the principles of leverage and mechanical advantage were on the angler's side, not the fish's. The hefty butt provided lifting power and hook setting ability. There are three versions of the 6455 blank; the H, XH and XXH. I choose the XXH to make the stand-up 80s we have used on the Linda B for the last several years.

The overall length of 6'2" was significantly longer than typical stand-up rods, but shorter than a standard IGFA trolling rod. This length proved to be ideal when working a trolled fish that already had 100 yards of line off the reel. A very short rod can't gain line when the

TACKLE AND EQUIPMENT

fish are far away from the boat. This length was still short enough to be comfortable when tuna sounded near the boat and had to be lifted from the depths.

The rod was also long enough to be shoved into the water up to the reel seat to gain precious inches to clear an outboard lower unit, or rudders and wheels on an inboard boat. The longer blank allowed fish to be steered to the boat if they made a strong run off to the side. On many occasions these rods literally turned the heads of yellowfin up to 130 pounds by sheer rod pressure, something nearly impossible to do with a short 5-foot rod, unless pulling straight up and down.

These rods are not perfect; no rod is perfect, but they are the best I've ever used for my style of fishing and they are a real pleasure to handle. Everyone who has fished aboard the Linda B and who had a chance to pull against some tuna, remarked how well the rods fished and how comfortable they felt.

Although we usually use them as stand-up rods, preferring to battle our fish standing up at the stern, they are long enough that if a truly big fish is hooked, they can be slipped into the gimbal of the fight chair and worked from the chair. The tips are long enough to clear the cover boards at the transom.

East Coast stand-up rods boast powerful butt actions, a light tip and 6-foot lengths to help work lines around outboard engines and rudders when fish dive beneath the boat.

SUPER STAND-UP RODS

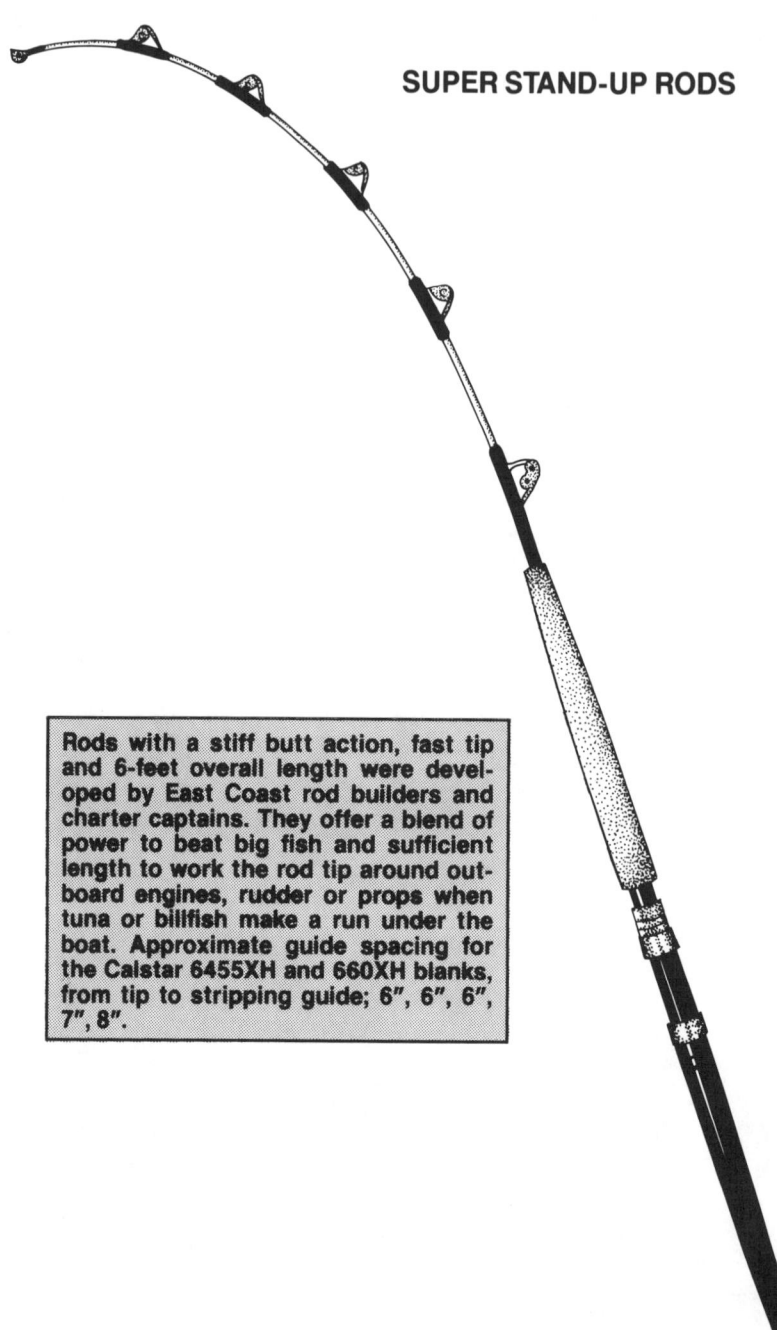

Rods with a stiff butt action, fast tip and 6-feet overall length were developed by East Coast rod builders and charter captains. They offer a blend of power to beat big fish and sufficient length to work the rod tip around outboard engines, rudder or props when tuna or billfish make a run under the boat. Approximate guide spacing for the Calstar 6455XH and 660XH blanks, from tip to stripping guide; 6", 6", 6", 7", 8".

The rods have Aftco UB2 Unibutts with the rounded gimbal and AFTCO roller guides. Starting at the tip, a #16 tip top is followed by four #41 rollers and one #51 roller. The guides are spaced (tip to butt) at 5½, 6, 6, 6 and 7 inches apart. The grip is 12 inches in length. It's 24 inches from the lower guide to the Unibutt ferrule.

Rod building is a matter of inches. I used the full length of the tip, only cutting the butt to achieve the overall 6'2" length. The butt had to be turned down slightly to fit the ferrule of the UB2 Unibutt. Using the XH or H versions of this blank would make 50 and 30 pound class stand-up rods. Fenwick, Lamiglas, Loomis, Fisher and others make blanks that are similar to the Calstar so you may want to do some searching to find your own Super Stand-Up Trolling Rod.

Super Stand-up Chunking Rods

Many East Coast charter captains and individual fishermen who from their own boats have also selected beefier rods for fishing chunk and live baits. The theory here is again gain added butt power and a slightly longer tip length. The butt power helps fight the fish that make a long run away from the boat. The lighter tip still works well when lifting the fish when it dives deep and the added length provides insurance to work a line around an outboard engine, rudders and props.

There are several excellent blanks that make up into Super Stand-Up Chunking Rods, such as the Lamiglas WSU764E which makes a great 50 or 80-pound class rod depending on how much tip is trimmed, and the Calstar 660 series. The 660 is the grand daddy of the stand-up rod, designed by Leon Todd over 20 years ago and it still is a terrific blank. Available as the 660L, 660, 660H and 660XH, rods can be custom made to cover 20-pound to 80-pound class tackle. My chunking rods are all 6-feet long, and sport a full set of roller guides and aluminum butts.

Lighten Up

It only takes a few minutes for a 100-pound fish to have a big, brawny guy sweating bullets as he pulls mightily against 80-pound tackle. With the drag set at 20 to 30 pounds of pull, arm and back muscles get that burning feeling in a few minutes. As arms start to tremble and shake, the angler lowers the rod tip to ease the pressure. Now the tuna laughs. With less pressure on the line the fish heads to the depths. As the angler continues to struggle, muscles cramp. The rod tip soon rests on the cover boards. The tuna laughs again and as the hole in his jaw wears larger, the hook pops free and he escapes.

This scene gets played many times at the inshore and offshore grounds and it's the stuff that "the big one that got away" stories are made of. Tuna and billfish have a reputation for fighting hard so most fishermen believe extra heavy tackle is essential to land these fish. Sure, they fight hard, but lighter tackle is actually a more effective fish fighting tool. I'm not advocating stunt fishing with thread-like lines to tackle 1000-pound giant bluefin or grander blue marlin. Ultralight gear is for special occasions. For huge fish you need a bucket harness and 80 to 130-pound tackle.

But, if a 700-pound bluefin can be caught on 130-pound tackle, a 5 to 1 ratio of fish weight to line pound test, then it stands to reason a 100-pound yellowfin or a 70-pound white marlin should readily be taken on 20-pound tackle. Some offshore anglers might think I'm nuts when we talk about anything lighter than 80-pound gear for offshore fishing but the reality of day to day fishing, not dock-side stories, indicates that for most of us, 50-pound tackle is ideal for trolling. When I first started running to the canyons, I used a set of 4 International 80s, but the tackle was so heavy the flush mount gunnel rod holders were nearly torn out of the fiberglass. In rough seas we could barely hold the rod and reel while struggling to get into the fight chair. The tackle was beating my boat and the anglers, not necessarily the fish.

I sold the 80s and purchased a set of lighter weight 50s. I've never regretted it and even though we now run a larger boat, I still fish the same tackle because it is the better fish fighting equipment for the job. The 50-pound tackle can dish it out and we've taken bigeye to 314 pounds and blue marlin to 400 pounds, so I know it works.

The key issue with lighter gear is tackle handling. If you can't put the hurts to the fish, it will take a long time to get that fish to the boat to be gaffed or tagged and released. If it takes too long to boat the fish, he's putting the hurts to the angler and may win his freedom from tackle failure, line fatigue or angler fatigue.

After the hook-up, 50-pound tackle allows the fisherman to apply maximum pressure at all times. The drag setting is much less than with 80-pound tackle so there is less strain against the angler. He can work the rod and reel to continually gain line. It's easier for the fish to make strong runs on light tackle and this worries some fishermen who are new to tuna fishing or to light tackle fishing, but these runs are what exhaust the tuna and finally allow the fish to be brought to the boat.

On heavy gear when the fish and angler are at a standstill and fish circles 30 fathoms below the boat, the tuna is regaining strength; the angler is losing strength. As the battle continues, the angler is continually worn down, and the tuna is getting refreshed.

The worst cases of angler fatigue I've seen on our boat occurred when a tuna of 100 pounds or more was fought on 80-pound stand-up gear. Between the rocking of the boat and the last minute evasive maneuvers of tuna as they aim at rudders and props to cut the line, the angler strapped into 80-pound gear is past the borderline of control. I've watched a single tuna wear down four fishermen, each taking a 10-minute turn at getting harnessed into the heavy gear as the boat rocked and rolled and the sun went down. Another angler, on the same boat, hooked up at the same time but using 40-pound line decked his fish in less than 15 minutes.

Twenty-pound tackle is about as light as we go but I've watched fishermen land 80 to 120-pound yellowfin on 15-pound test tackle! My son, Rich, has landed yellowfins in excess of 130 pounds using 20-pound test tackle. For several years I kept track of the average fish we caught and found that our tuna averaged 76 pounds in 1988, 102 pounds in 1987, and back in 1986 and 1985 when large bigeye tuna made us all heroes, the average was 163 and 146 pounds. Our fish have ranged from small school yellowfin of 15 pounds to bigeye in the mid 200-pound range. At no time have we felt handicapped by the 50-pound tackle and in fact the lighter tackle has helped us catch more fish with fewer pulled hooks after long battles.

Hand 'Em a Line

Imagine the predicament of big game fishermen back in the pioneer days of the 1920s and 1930s. The linen lines of the day had to be carefully washed, cleaned, then dried so they would not rot and weaken. Special large diameter, wooden spools were designed just for the purpose of easily removing the line from the early reels. After a thorough washing, the line was stored out of the harsh rays of the sun so it could dry in time for the next fishing trip. Perhaps we don't know how easy we have it today!

DuPont first invented nylon in 1935 but it was not until 1939 that it was introduced as a fishing line. The early monofilament lines were a far cry from the soft, supple lines we now use. Many of the original mono lines were brittle, or became brittle with minimal use, and had to be changed, or at least cut back from the fishing end of the line frequently or the line would part with little strain.

Advances came quickly and by the 1950s monofilament line had virtually replaced all other types of line. It offered reasonable price, high quality and wide availability. Best of all, it did not need to be washed and dried in between fishing trips. Monofilament line technology continues to bring new advances in line formulations that offer greater abrasion resistance, impact resistance, controlled stretch and resistance to the deterioration caused by exposure to the sun's ultraviolet rays.

Monofilament is the ideal fishing line for most fishermen and it is used by 95% of the offshore fishing fraternity. Another choice is braided Dacron, another DuPont formulation from the pre-Second World War days. Braided Dacron has one especially outstanding quality that make it the choice for some big fish anglers. It has virtually no stretch at all. When the fisherman pulls back against a giant bluefin tuna, he is assured of gaining at least a foot or two of line. With the controlled stretch factor of monofilament, an angler may lift the rod tip a foot or two but all he's done is stretched the mono to a longer length, not necessarily lifted the fish closer to the boat.

I used Dacron line for several years and we beat some big fish in a relatively short period of time with the Dacron line. I could use the rocking action of the boat as it would rise and fall with the waves to gain line each time the boat would fall down into trough. The next swell would lift the boat, and the fish, so more line could be gained on the next descent into a trough.

The lack of stretch was a disadvantage at boat side if a fish would make a last ditch lunge under the boat. With no cushioning stretch, we did occasionally break off a big fish. One blue marlin we had hooked and battled for quite some time in the Florida Keys did just that. The very rough 4 to 6-foot seas made it difficult to keep the boat down-wind of the fish and on one fast dive under the boat, the angler could not react fast enough and the line parted. For the many times Dacron helped get us a trophy fish, that time it cost us the fish.

As I moved up to a larger boat and became more involved in chartering, I switched to monofilament line. It is less expensive so I can replace it more frequently. Most of all, though, was the need for a line that was a bit less critical to use. The stretch of monofilament was easier to handle on a daily basis and its ability to stretch saved many a fish that made wild attempts to break free just out of reach of the waiting gaff. Today I only use monofilament for tackle up to 80-pound class, Dacron for the 130-pound stuff.

There is no best fishing line. Monofilament and braided Dacron are both high quality fishing tools to be used where their advantages can best be utilized by the fisherman. Dacron is usually favored by fishermen seeking the biggest of offshore fish, with 130-pound tackle, perhaps 80-pound tackle, where the targets are the giant bluefin and the blue marlin. Monofilament is the usual choice for all tackle of 80-pound class and under.

No matter which line you choose, it pays to buy high quality line. In the long run it is the least expensive part of the tackle system and it makes no sense to skimp on line. I'm amazed when I hear someone complain at replacing line when they've already spent a lot of money on rods and reels, fuel, boat, electronics and equipment. The few dollars saved with a cheap line is foolish economy and could cost you the fish of a lifetime.

TACKLE AND EQUIPMENT

Fishing on a buddy's boat several years ago late in the season, we lost a bragging-sized bigeye because of line failure after only several minutes into the battle. Reeling in the slack line it was obvious the mono was brittle from exposure to sunlight and repeated baths in saltwater. It would have cost my friend only $30 to re-fill his reel. He saved the money on the line and instead spent $300 on fuel and lost a tournament winning. Dumb, real dumb.

I put fresh line on all my reels each spring before we begin the season looking for early action with yellowfin tuna off the Outer Banks. The reels are slightly overfilled because the first fish usually stretched the line real tight and the line will lay lower in the spool after even one day of fishing. I cut back the end of the line after each and every trip to remove the worn end that has been exposed to fish, salt, UV sunlight and possible abrasions.

By mid season we'll be off our home waters in New Jersey and I'll change the line on any spools that are low in line capacity from continued cutting off of the line ends. Some rods and reels get more use than others, such as the outrigger outfits, so these reels may need line replacement much sooner than the outfits used for the flat lines. By the fall we are wrapping up in New Jersey and getting ready to head south. Line will again be replaced if needed.

Everyone seems to have their favorite line to use, and with the many high quality lines to choose from there are many good choices. Stick with the known brands and you can't get hurt. Look for lines that stress resistance to abrasion, impact strength and low stretch.

Tackle Storage

Each fall when I prepare the boat for winter and take off the tackle, lures and equipment for cleaning and repair, I'm amazed at how much stuff we carry on the boat. As I look at the mound of gear piled on the dock waiting to be carried to the workshop, it sometimes seems inconceivable all that stuff actually fits on the boat. And, each winter I go through the same ritual of trying to choose what not to put back on the boat in the spring, yet I always have the same amount of equipment, sometimes more, the next fall. I guess it's all necessary - at least I think it is.

Storage of all this gear can be critical on any offshore boat, no matter how large, or small it is. I know fishermen who run 48 footers who wonder where to put everything and others who run a 25 to 30-foot outboard who have plenty of room because they have good storage. It's critical to your fishing success to keep everything organized and ready for instant use. Thoughtful storage also keeps gear out of the way so the deck is clear and ready for action. Good storage also keeps your equipment dry so it won't rust, rot or fall apart.

For several years now I've been using Rubbermaid storage boxes, like the kind sold in department stores to hold sweaters, shirts and other clothes. I've begun to see them in hardware stores now too and they are readily available. They are sold in several sizes and I use a compact 7 X 12 size for small items and a larger 11 X 16 size for bigger items like groups of lures, ballyhoo or bait rigs, rigging tools and equipment, spare parts for electronics, tools, fish flags, folded charts, tagging kits, spare flashlight, loran books, hats, suntan lotion, sunglasses and gloves.

While a lot of my gear is stored in drawers inside the cockpit tackle locker, I use the storage boxes to keep many items organized and stored under bench seats at the helm, in the cabin or in the engine room. Bulk quantities of small items like snap swivels, hooks, rubber bands and crimps are stored in plastic peanut butter jars. Zip lock plastic bags keep small items rust-free. Canyon Products mesh compartmented bags hold lures and daisy chasin rigs.

Rigging Box: Hi-Seas crimping tool and line cutter, Manley fishing pliers, boxes of Hi-Seas and Sevenstrand crimps, leader spools, single strand wire coils, waxed thread, rigging needles in several sizes, dental floss, #32 and #64 rubber bands, copper rigging wire, boxes of hooks, fillet and bait knives, de-boner, sharpening stone, hook file, snap swivels, rolls of red and yellow 3M plastic tape.

Lure Box #1: Primary lures that I use on virtually every trip. These lures are my main selection of about 14 proven fish grabbers.

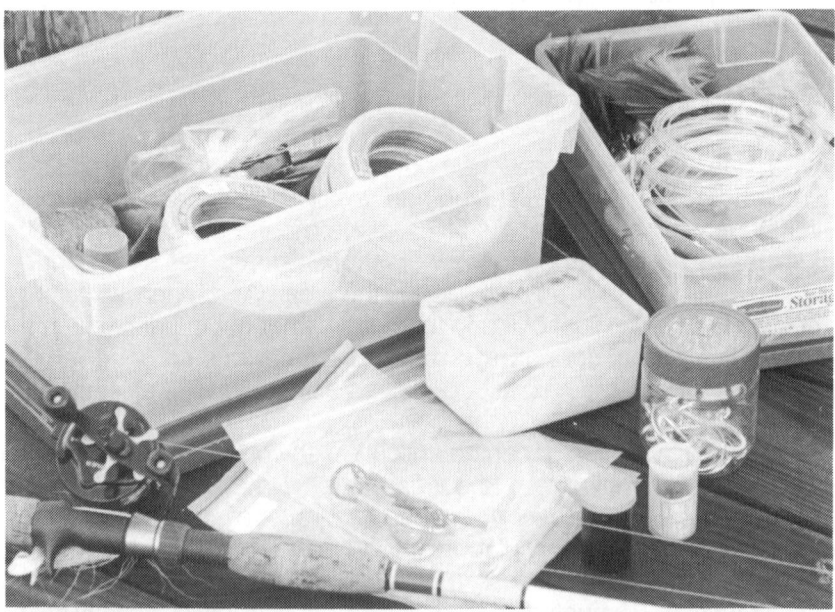

Rubbermaid storage boxes hold lots of lures, rigging tools, ballyhoo rigs, extra leaders, hooks and lots more.

Lure Box #2: Back up lures of various sizes and colors that I need occasionally. Also holds some duplicates of the primary box in case a good lure that is producing well is lost, or if we want to put several of the same lure in the pattern.

Ballyhoo Rig Box #1: 6-dozen ballyhoo rigs, some with skirts, some without, all rigged for tuna and blue marlin on 200-pound test mono.

Ballyhoo Rig Box #2: 2-dozen ballyhoo rigs, some with skirts, some without, rigged for white marlin on 125-pound test mono.

Catch All Box: Holds suntan lotion, fish flags, sunglasses, loran number books, fish tags, Rolaids, spare pliers, small flashlight.

While running to the fishing grounds, the boxes are kept dry and out of the way but ready for quick use when needed.

Belts, Harnesses and Buckets

Balancing out the newest in tackle innovations are some impressive improvements in gimbal and kidney harness designs. As previously mentioned, we elect to fight most of our fish standing up, whenever possible. Fish over 100 pounds demand the use of a gimbal belt and large back supporting kidney harness; unless you want to go home a soprano with a backache. Most of the fish we catch are less than 100 pounds and can be handily fought with a gimbal belt only, no kidney harness needed.

I keep a variety of belts on board to be prepared for any size fish we meet, from hefty belts for Big Beauford, if he ever hits one of our baits, to a selection of lighter stuff for the smaller fish. The Braid Blu-Fin Harness matched to the Yellowfin Belt is ideal for the biggest of tuna. So is the Reliable stainless belt and wide back harness. For the fish in the 60 to 150 pound range we prefer the smaller Braid Marlin harness and the Manta belt. For fish up to 60 pounds I've been using a soft belt from Canyon Products. Since it's soft and comfortably padded, this small belt can be worn all day so it is always ready to help the angler fight a fish.

For truly big fish that can only be fought from a chair, we use either a Murray Brothers bucket harness or large kidney harness across the angler's back. Both systems allow the angler to slide forward and back in the fight chair to work the rod efficiently.

Gaffs and Tag Sticks

A selection of gaffs is needed depending on the size of the fish you are looking for. I have several gaffs ready and waiting for use, each with an 8-foot handle and the following hook sizes; a 4-inch bite straight gaff, a 6-inch bite straight gaff, an 8-inch bite fly gaff and a 12-inch bite fly gaff with the hook reinforced with a support rod welded to the back of the bend. Both fly gaff ropes have 5/8, three-strand nylon line spliced to the gaff heads with the line cut to special length so when the rope is secured to the base of the fight chair there's only enough line to reach out at arm's length to gaff the fish.

Many fly gaffs are factory rigged, or dealer rigged, with up to 25 feet of line. This is usually about 10 feet too much line. The goal is to subdue the fish next to the boat not hook the fish on a heavy line and let him swim 25 feet away from the boat. When rigging your own fly gaffs, lay the gaff line on the deck and have a buddy reach out from the transom corner as far as he can while holding the gaff. While he's holding the gaff, stretch the remaining line to the base of the fight chair or an appropriate cleat if you don't have a chair. This is the longest the line needs to be. Add an eye splice at the end of the gaff line.

When I first started fishing offshore, I lost several fish because of extra long fly gaff ropes. A marlin can get up quite a head of steam within a 25-foot leap and literally rip the gaff hook out of his body. I had a tuna make a run under the boat, after being gaffed, where he wrapped the gaff rope around a wheel. We only got the fish by diving in the water and going under the boat ourselves to untangle the mess. Yes, we did get the fish, too.

Fly gaffs are a must for jumbo blue marlin if you plan to kill one for a trophy mount. Fly gaffs can also be used on giant tuna, but many of the best tuna captains use a straight gaff with a 15 to 25-foot rope attached at the gaff head and along the shaft at the midway and top end points. A wildly twisting marlin would not be a safe animal to stick with a gaff of this type because the mate or the boat could get banged by the gaff handle, but for big tuna, a Reliable TunaKit gaff with an 8-foot shaft and a 5/8" 8-inch bite is an ideal piece of equipment.

I get a big kick out of tagging and have several tag sticks handy. To be ready when we get multiple hook-ups, I keep a pair of tag sticks rigged with the tags mounted in the pin, ready to get poked into a tuna or billfish. Many tackle shops now sell tag sticks and they are readily available. Some rod builders make beautiful sticks complete with fancy diamond wraps to match the customer's trolling rods. There are factory made tag sticks from AFTCO, So-Lo, Reliable and Pompanette.

Gloves

These small tackle items are vitally important to a well organized cockpit. Ed Murray showed me how to use large sized, leather welders gloves with a pair of fingerless cotton gloves over them for big fish use. Smaller fish are readily handled with the Hi-Seas Grand Slam glove with the rubber palm grip.

Several pairs of gloves are kept on hand at all times and they are laid out and ready for use while trolling, not stashed in a drawer where they can't be found.

Safety lines are inexpensive but can save valuable tackle from going overboard.

Safety Lines

So far, I've been lucky on my boat and have never yet lost a rod and reel over the side, but I've seen it happen to someone else. It was heart breaking to see the 80W and the custom rod slip from the angler's hands as he tried to get the rod and reel out of the rod holder while a fish tried to steal all the line it could. The man slipped on the deck, lost his grip and it was bye-bye rod and reel.

A safety line would have prevented the loss. I've been using lines made from 3/8-inch nylon three strand line. A small stainless, spring loaded clip is spliced to one end, an eye splice added at the other end. The lines are ten feet in length so they are long enough to allow the rod and reel to be carried to the fight chair before they are unsnapped after the angler is settled in position.

Many giant tuna fishermen will leave the safety line in place all through the fight until the fish is boated. Others add a second safety line that runs from the fight stanchion up the back of the chair and then clips onto the back of the bucket harness. The line is long enough to not interfere with the angler, allowing full movement to raise up high in the chair to apply full leg power against the fish, but short enough to stop the angler if he loses control and starts to take a rocket ride out of the chair.

Tail Ropes

A selection of tail ropes in 8 and 10-foot lengths can make boating a big fish much easier. After the gaff is solidly in the fish and the catch is ready to be hauled aboard, ropes can be slipped around the fish's tail (and head if needed) so a second or third man can help haul the fish over the cover boards.

My ropes are made of 1/2-inch nylon three strand line with a loop spliced into each end. Loops are formed in the tail rope by passing one end of the tail rope through the eye splice loop at the other end. The nylon line slips easily against itself and the loop can be drawn up tight against the fish. These are better, and simpler tail ropes than the kind sold with snaps and other hardware attached.

It only takes one fish to start thrashing and twisting at the side of the boat, digging the snap into the gel coat or paint finish to make you leave the complicated tail ropes back at the dock.

Coolers and Fish Bags

Since we tag most of our fish we don't need coolers for our catch but instead use the coolers to carry lots of ice. Those fish that we do keep, are held in the Canyon Products fish bags, encased in bags of ice. The fish will be so cold they'll hurt your hands when it's fillet time back at the dock. We'll go into greater detail on fish preparation and how the bags work later in the book.

Rigged baits, like ballyhoo, mullet or mackerel are best stored in a smaller cooler of 24 to 54-quart size, depending on how many baits you will rig and use in a day's fishing. I like a cooler that is large enough to provide plenty of room inside to lay six to eight baits side by side so the leader coils don't get too tangled up. When you need a new ballyhoo, eel or mullet because a sailfish or white marlin is

TACKLE AND EQUIPMENT

playing havoc with your baits and lines, getting a new bait clipped to the line to replace a chopped up bait can be critical to hooking the fish. You don't want to spend time untangling baits while a hungry billfish is saying "feed me, feed me."

SSI, Igloo, Coleman and Gott all make excellent coolers. White reflects the sun's heat and keeps your catch and the ice colder, longer. Depending on the size of your boat bring the largest you can carry if you plan to take tuna home for dinner. It's a shame to run out of ice on a long trip and have your hard-fought tuna spoil before you get it home.

To keep the ice coolers from sliding on the decks, lay a wet towel or a soft rubber place mat like the kind used for picnics under the cooler and it will stay put in the worst of sloppy seas.

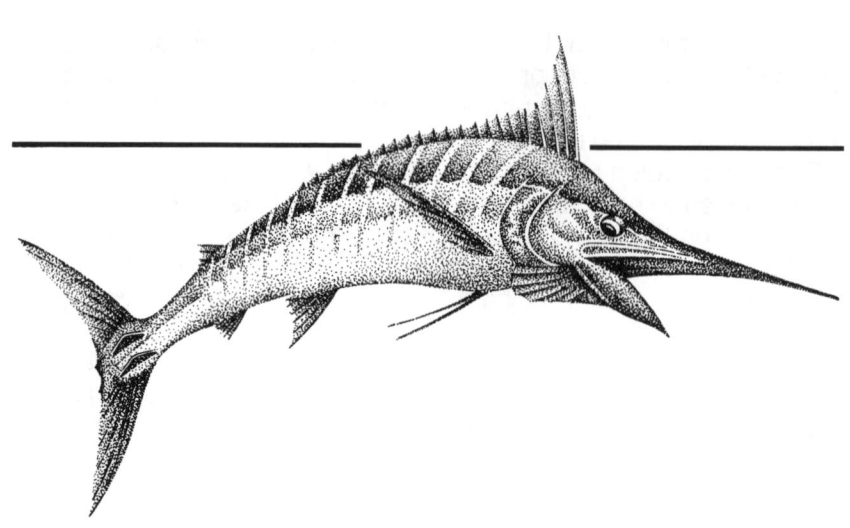

Chapter Three

RIGGING FOR ACTION

The angler, tackle and line can only do their best job if the knots used to join them to the fish do their job effectively. Tying good knots is a frequently overlooked skill yet the right knot, properly tied, is THE vital connection between the fisherman and the fish. The choice of which knot to use is an important decision every fisherman makes when tying on a snap swivel or a lure, or when joining two lines together or when adding a double line at the end of the main fishing line.

Unfortunately, even the best knots usually cause a slight weakening of the line. The wrong knot, or a poorly tied knot, can cause a severe loss of line strength and possibly the loss of a fish. Most knots weaken the line as the twisting coils cut into, or flex against, one another. To minimize, or totally defeat the loss of line strength, the bimini twist is used to build up line strength. The bimini twist and the waxed thread double line are the only knots I am aware of, that when tied properly, test at 100% of the unknotted line. Others may come close at 95 to 98%, but they do not hit the optimum 100% mark.

Some offshore knots may seem intimidating if you've never tied them before but brief practice is all it takes to master any of them. Innovative fishermen are finding new ways to splice monofilament to Dacron and to tie leader systems that can be reeled right to the rod tip with no bulky knots to jam in roller guides or tip tops.

The knots and splices in this chapter have been proven on the offshore grounds of the East Coast by charter captains and tournament winning fishermen so you know you can rely on them.

Double Lines and Strong Leaders

Doubling up the end of the main fishing line effectively increases the strength of the end of the line, a distinct advantage when bringing a fish near the boat. No matter how spectacular the aerial battle of a marlin or how impressive the runs of a tuna, the final few minutes when the fish is only yards away from feeling the gaff or tag stick, is the ultimate moment of truth.

When a double line is tied into the end of the line, the angler can gain added pulling power once a few turns of the doubled line are on the spool. The angler can then use hand pressure on the spool to increase the drag setting, or move the drag lever forward from Strike to Full, to horse a big fish at boat side. The last few feet can be the hardest when battling a big bluefin or marlin. The doubled line and its increased strength give the angler more control so the leader man and gaff man can do their job.

Instead of a double line, other fishermen prefer to splice a length of heavy monofilament into the end of the main fishing line. Although these connections for so-called wind-on leaders are more time consuming to tie, they offer the great advantage of being able to slip through roller guides much more easily than a bulky knot.

The International Game Fish Association, the keeper of the sport fishing rules and regulations, allows the use of a double line of up to 15 feet for lines of 20-pound class and below, or 30 feet for lines of 30-pound and above. Careful reading of the rules will also show that the combined length of the double line and the leader for the lighter tackle must not exceed 20 feet overall, 40 feet overall for the heavier tackle.

The three most common knots used to tie a double line in monofilament are the bimini twist, spider hitch and waxed thread double. Those fishermen who use Dacron line favor a special line splice to create the double line.

Bimini Twist

Also called the 20 times around knot, the bimini twist was first used decades ago when linen line was being replaced by Dacron and monofilament. This is still a good knot today and ties very well with modern monofilament lines.

Some fishermen never learn the bimini twist because they heard the knot was difficult to tie. Anyone who uses the bimini regularly will agree that the knot isn't the easiest to tie but it sure isn't the hardest either. With practice it can be tied in only a few seconds. My son, Rich, has had some fun in the cockpit with newcomers by tying a bimini in less than one minute. All it takes is a bit of practice.

RIGGING FOR ACTION

Properly tied, with neat rolls and twists, it tests at 100% of the breaking strength of the main fishing line making it the best knot to use when a double line is required. It can be used with a wide range of line from 20 to 130-pound test.

Long double lines of 15 to 30 feet as used by big game trollers require a second person to help tie the knot. Have a buddy walk off the required length of doubled line so he is at the end, or bend, of the loop. You should be holding two legs of line; the main line and the leg of the loop. Hold your end tight and have your buddy make 20 twists in the line. It's easy to do this by placing the wrist of one hand through the loop and then twisting the wrist until 20 line twists are built up.

After the twists are in place, hold your end steady by squeezing the main line and the tag end of the line between your fingers while your buddy walks towards you spreading the two legs of the double line between the fingers of one hand (place one leg of the line loop between the thumb and forefinger, the other between the forefinger and middle finger).

As he walks toward you, the separated line is allowed to drop to the floor or deck. When only a few feet away from you, the tension on the twists will build and he can then grab one leg in each hand. Your buddy will pull the legs apart much like the knees separate the legs in the accompanying illustrations. As tension on the twists continues to build, feed the tag end of the line so the knot rolls over itself. Once the twists start rolling over, the knot ties just like in the illustrations.

Don't let the illustrations fool you. The bimini only looks tricky. Tie it four or five times and you'll quickly get the hang of it.

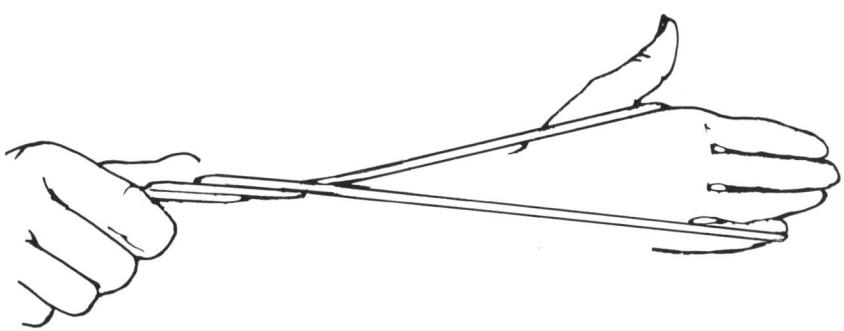

1. **Measure off a little more than twice the length of the double line desired and double it back forming a long loop. Hold the standing line and the tag end and have a mate rotate the end of the loop 20 times, putting twists into it.**

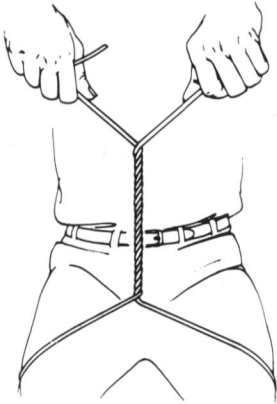

2. Your mate can slip the loop over a stationary post, get inside the loop and "walk" the twists toward you until they are about 18 inches from the tag end. Sit in a chair, put your feet on the two lines and spread your legs slightly to put tension on the twists.

3. The twists will now be verticle in front of you. Hold the standing line in one hand, the tag end in the other hand so it is 90 degrees to the twists. Keep tension on the loop with your knees and gradually relax the tension on the tag end. It will roll over the verticle twists.

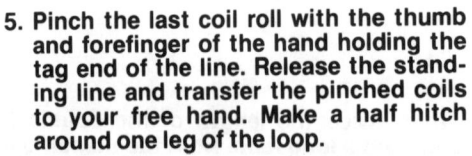

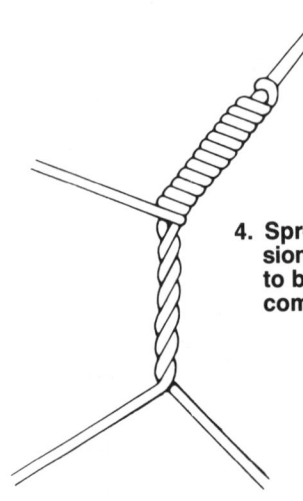

4. Spread your legs slowly to maintain tension on the loop. Roll the tag end from top to bottom in tightly spaced coils until it completely covers the twists.

5. Pinch the last coil roll with the thumb and forefinger of the hand holding the tag end of the line. Release the standing line and transfer the pinched coils to your free hand. Make a half hitch around one leg of the loop.

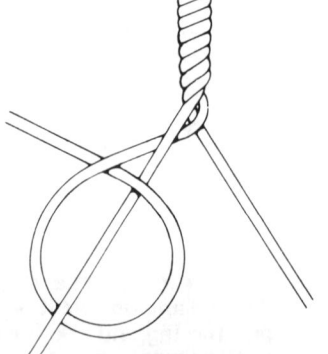

RIGGING FOR ACTION

6. With the half hitch holding the knot, relax some knee pressure, but keep the loop taut. Make a loose loop around both legs of the bimini.

7. Make two more turns with the tag end around both legs, winding inside the bend of the line formed by the loose loop and towards the main knot. Pull the tag end slowly, forcing the three loops to gather in a spiral wrap.

8. When the loops are pulled tight against the knot, clip the tag end, but leave 1/4" sticking out from the knot.

Spider Hitch

The spider hitch is another good knot to make a loop of doubled line. It is easier to tie than the bimini but may not always test at full 100% of the line strength. To assure that the knot draws up tightly, wet the coils with saliva, then draw the coils down slowly and be sure they are even before snugging the coils tight. When first learning the spider hitch there is a tendency for the coils to wrap back over themselves so watch for this. If the coils don't look like the illustration, tie the knot again.

FISHING FOR TUNA AND MARLIN

The spider hitch should be re-tied after each big fish and at least after each day's fishing. The pressure and flexing of the knot under strain of playing a fish will slowly weaken the knot. The older it gets, even by a few hours, the weaker it gets. It's a good idea to get into the habit of re-tying terminal connections and leaders after each fishing trip anyhow so the spider will rarely fail you if you always tie fresh knots.

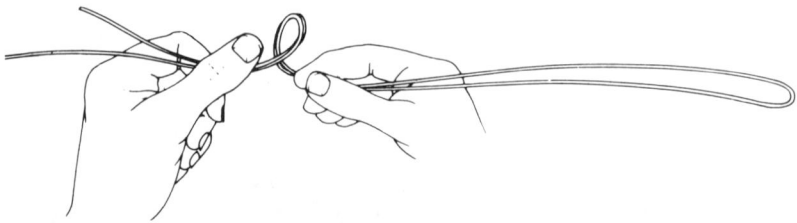

1. Form a double line loop to the desired length. Near the tag end, twist the strands in a reverse loop.

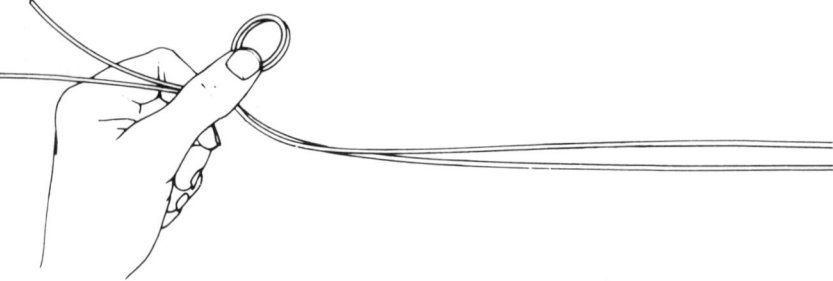

2. Hold the small loop between your left thumb and forefinger, with the thumb well extended above the finger.

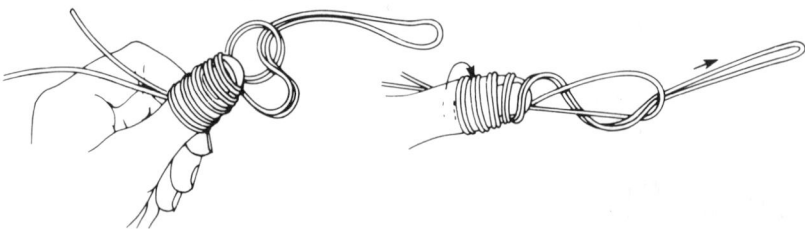

3. Wind the double line around your thumb and the reverse loop strands, taking five parallel turns. Pass the end of the original loop through the small loop, pull the slack out and pull the five turns off your thumb.

4. Pull the tag end standing line strands against the loop strands to tighten the knot. Pull the standing line only against the loop for final tightening and clip off the tag end.

RIGGING FOR ACTION

Waxed Thread Double Line

This knot takes longer to tie than a bimini but it will last far longer since there are no interlocking coils and turns of line to flex and cut into each other. The waxed thread, or dental floss, flows through rod guides with ease and never gets hung up like the bulkier bimini or spider. The waxed thread double line is ideal for heavier monofilament lines of 50 to 130-pound test that don't always pull down neatly when tied in a bimini or spider.

Start by forming a loop the length of double line you want to make and hold both legs of the loop parallel to one another at the forward end of the loop (the part of the loop nearest to the reel). Using a length of dental floss or Gudebrod Waxed Rigging Thread about five to six feet in length, secure the waxed thread with a lark's head knot to lock it in place.

Tie a half hitch around both legs of the loop, pulling the knot tight. Continue with four more half hitches. Separate the legs of the loop and tie a half hitch around one leg, then the other. Tie another five half hitches around both legs, then a single half hitch around each leg. Tie in a total of eight sets of hitches, five around both legs, one around each leg, then five more around both.

Finish with five half hitches around both legs and the knot is ready to fish.

1. Form a loop to the desired length.

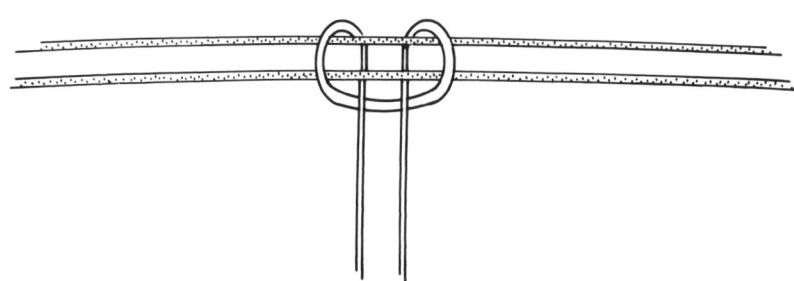

2. Make a clove hitch around the double line with a 24" length of Gudebrod Waxed Riggin' Thread.

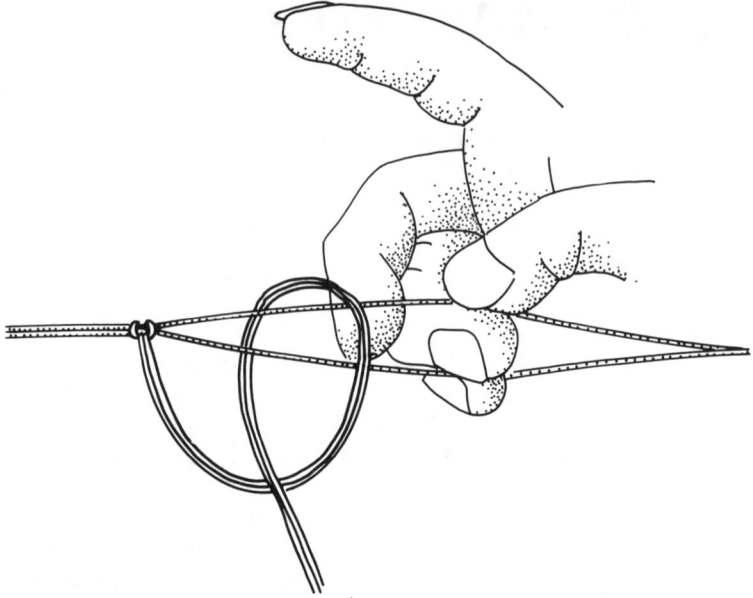

3. Make five half hitches around both strands, wrapping towards the loop of the double line.

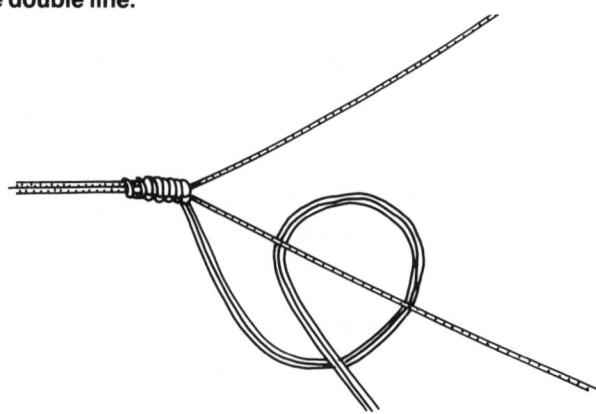

4. Spread the legs of the double line and make a half hitch around one leg, then the other.

5. Repeat the five half hitches around both lines, followed by half hitches around each single leg for six more sets of wraps. A dab of Krazy Glue or Pliobond will secure the final thread wraps.

RIGGING FOR ACTION

Dacron Double Line Splice

Most Dacron lines sold today are of the hollow braided type and a length of double line can be handily spliced into the line with no loss of line strength. The splice works much like a Chinese finger handcuff that we all played with when we were kids. It is strong, reliable and its slim profile flows through rod guides the best of any double line knot. Manufacturers of Dacron lines usually include a splicing needle with each bulk spool of line they sell, plus instructions on how to make the double line splice.

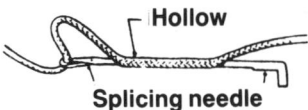
Hollow
Splicing needle

1. With the end of the line towards you, insert the splicing needle about 6" from the end. Run the needle about 3" inside the hollow line, the out, and catch the main line with the hook end of the splicing needle.

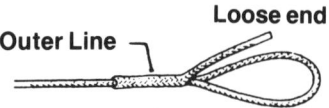
Loose end
Outer Line

2. Bring the needle back through the line, pulling the main line with the needle. Detach the needle and hold the newly formed loop with thumb and forefinger of the left hand, pulling the line with the right hand until the braided line actually turns inside out.

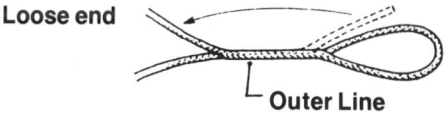
Loose end
Outer Line

3. The tag end will now be facing the standing part of the line. Pull the slack leg until the loop of double line is to the desired length.

Main Line

4. Insert the splicing needle about three inches up the main line from where the tag end has been pulled through. Catch the tag end with the hook and pull back through the line.

5. Cut off any exposed excess tag end and roll the splice between the fingers to neatly smooth it.

FISHING FOR TUNA AND MARLIN

Splicing Dacron to Dacron

Rather than doubling the end of the line, some big game fishermen will splice a length of heavier Dacron to the main fishing line. For instance, when fishing with 50-pound line, a length of 80 or 100-pound Dacron would be spliced into the main line instead of making a double line. Although this spliced in heavier is not twice the original line test, for many fishermen, this is of little consequence, especially for light tackle anglers who always use very heavy leaders.

The more the lines differ in pound test, the harder it is to make a clean, neat splice but with care, even 130-pound line can sometimes be spliced into 50 pound. The advantage of this connection is the ease of motion of the line through rod guides.

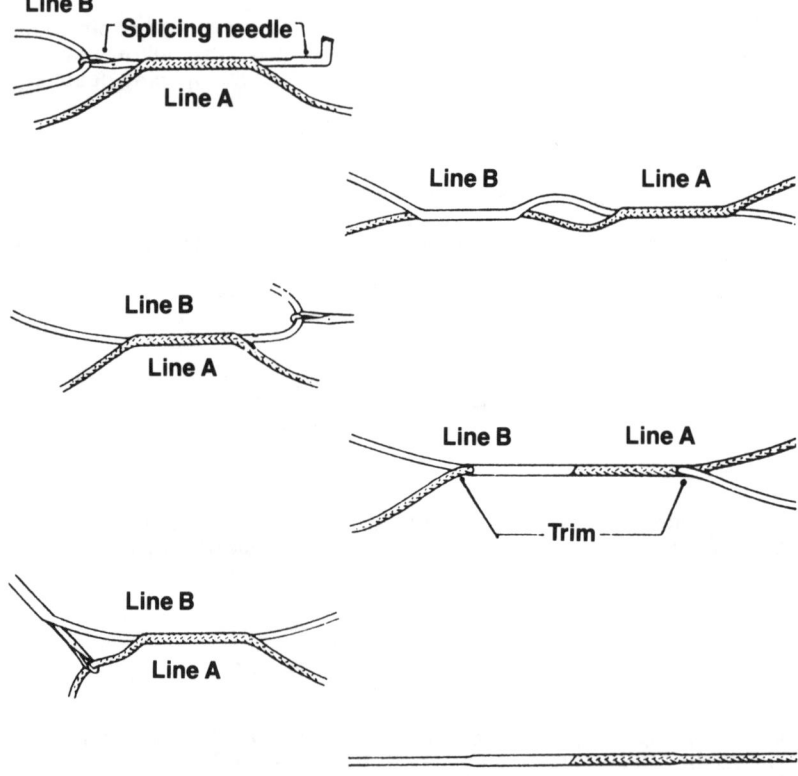

Insert needle in line about 4" from end for a distance of 1". Pick up end of line B, pull back through line A and detach needle. Approximately 1" from splice, insert needle in line B. Pick up loose end of line A in needle. Smooth splice by pulling both loose ends to work splice together. Trim.

RIGGING FOR ACTION

Mono to Dacron Splice

This connection is used by offshore fishermen who want maximum pound test mono leaders when fishing for giant bluefin tuna or blue marlin with Dacron line as their main fishing line. It allows an incredible amount of pressure to be applied to big fish without worrying about a bulky bimini getting hung up in rod guides.

Care must be taken to work the mono up into the hollow Dacron for at least a distance of four feet when using 80-pound Dacron and a 200-pound test leader, up to eight feet when using 130-pound Dacron and a 300-pound leader. I know giant tuna fishermen who painstakingly splice 12 feet of heavy leader into the Dacron line.

Rub the end of the mono with sandpaper to avoid any sharp edge that might poke into the side of the Dacron as the mono is worked up into the braided line.

Waxed thread is applied in half hitches at the bottom end of the leader (the snap swivel or lure end) and at several places along the splice where the mono is held inside the Dacron. The waxed thread helps prevent the mono from slipping out from the grip of the Dacron.

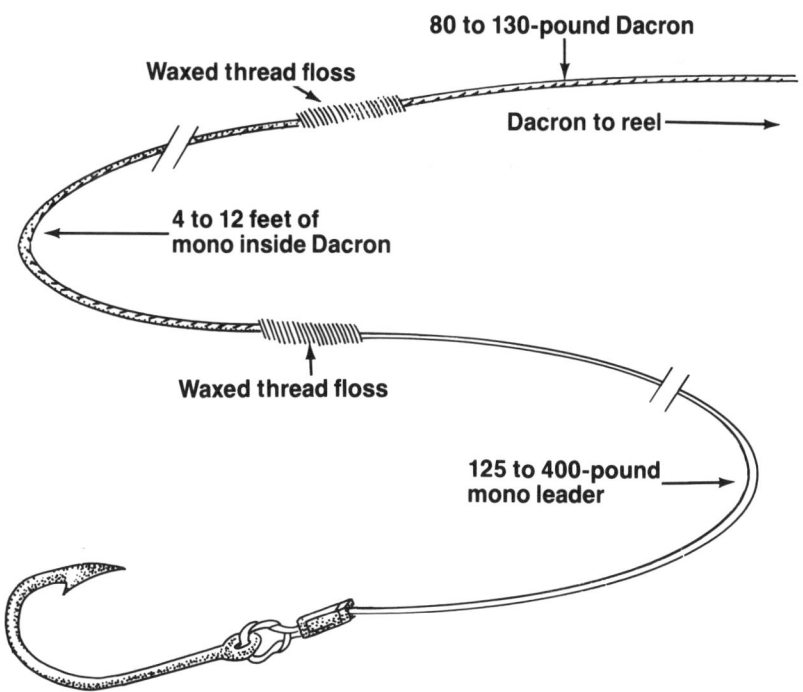

Mono to Dacron to Mono Leader

A variation of the Dacron to mono splice can be used to add a length of heavy leader to the end of monofilament line so the heavy leader can be reeled right to the snap swivel. These wind-on leaders are most popular with marlin fishermen in the Caribbean, but are slowly spreading to big game ports along the East Coast.

A 6-foot length of 130-pound Dacron is spliced to a 200, 300 or 400-pound test leader as described above. A loop is spliced into the end of the Dacron that will be joined to the loop formed by tying a short bimini into the end of the main fishing line.

Pass the bimini loop through the loop formed in the Dacron, then slip the tag end of the leader through the loop of the bimini. Pass the tag end through a second time to form an exceptionally strong interlocking loop that firmly joins the bimini to the Dacron and heavy mono leader.

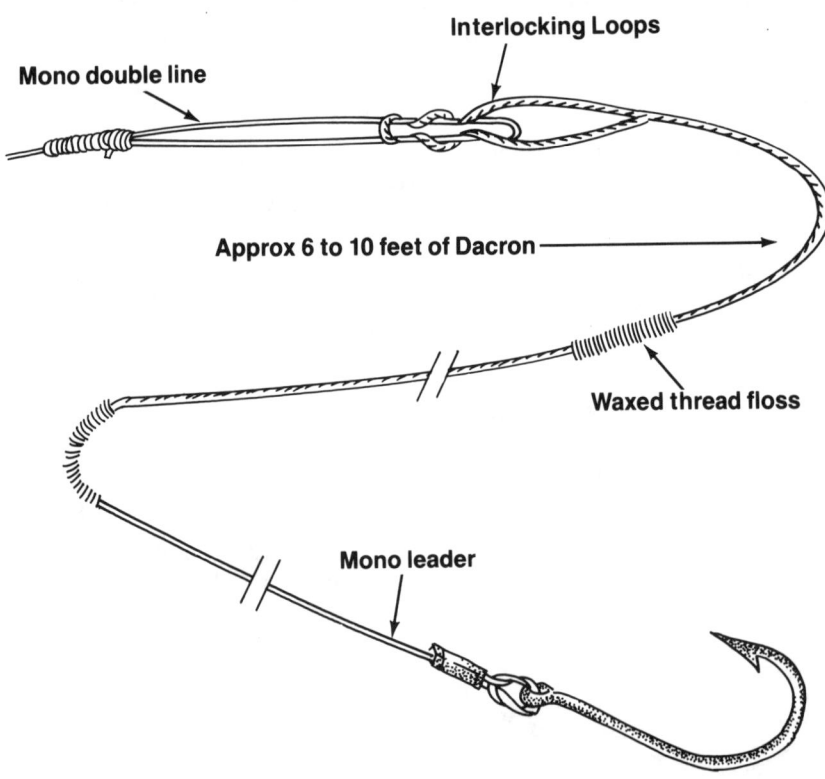

Offshore Swivel Knot

This is the traditional knot for attaching a snap swivel when using a double line. Originally used for Dacron lines, also works well with monofilament lines of 50-pound test or heavier.

Be sure to put the half turn in the knot before folding the loop back over the double line. This locks the knot so that if one leg of the double line breaks, the entire knot will not fail or unravel.

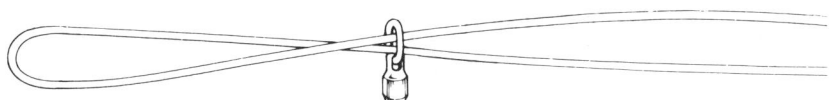

1. Slip loop end of double line through eye of swivel. Rotate loop a half turn to put a single twist between loop and swivel eye.

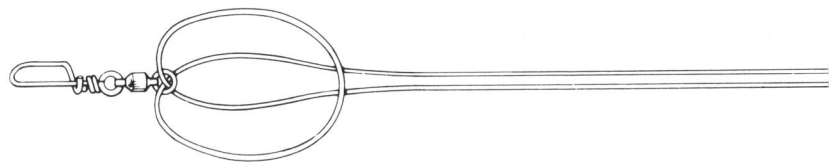

2. Pass the loop over the swivel. Holding end of loop against both double line legs, let swivel slide to junction of the double loops now formed.

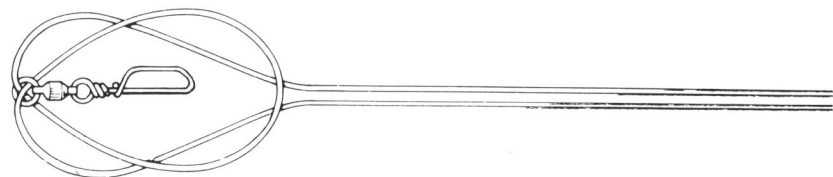

3. Still holding the loop and double line, use other hand to rotate swivel through the center of both loops at least six times.

4. Hold both legs tight, but release the loop and draw the knot tight by pulling on the swivel.

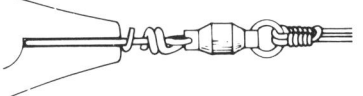

5. Continue to pull the knot tight with pliers on the swivel. You may have to push the coils to prevent the knot from jamming.

Double Improved Clinch Knot

An alternative to the offshore knot when using monofilament lines of 50-pound test or less is the double improved clinch knot. Tests by the crew at DuPont's Stren testing laboratory indicate the double improved clinch is superior to the offshore knot in monofilament lines from 20 to 50-pound test and at least as good when used with 80-pound test line. Heavier 130-pound test mono is too stiff to allow the knot to be tied effectively.

Dupont's tests have shown the Improved Clinch Knot to provide 90 to 98% of the breaking strength of the line depending on how carefully it is tied. Since the double line is already twice the strength of the main fishing line, no real loss of strength is apparent.

Be sure to make at least five twists around the standing part of the line. Fewer turns will make a weak knot but any more than seven twists may also weaken the knot because of the excessive effort then needed to draw the knot tight. Too many coils may also cause the knot to jam so it can't be drawn up tight.

It is important to draw the knot down with no loose or overlapping coils which cause the most dramatic loss of line strength. It also pays to lubricate the knot with saliva when drawing it tight so the coils don't fray against one another or build up excess heat as the coils tighten. Don't yank it tight, just pull firmly with no jerks.

It is also important to add the last tuck of the tag end of the line under the loop formed when the tag end is brought back towards the snap swivel eye. The extra tuck is what adds to word "Improved" to the Clinch Knot. Leave out the extra tuck and the knot loses about 25% of its strength. That extra tuck prevents the line from slipping, the main reason for knot failure.

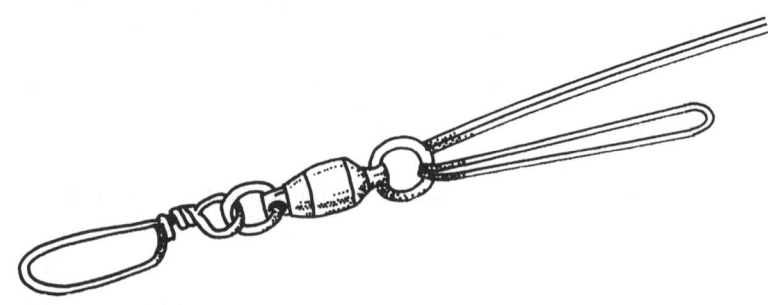

1. **Push the double line loop through the eye of the swivel and back over the standing line for about 18 inches.**

RIGGING FOR ACTION

2. With the thumb and forefinger of the right hand pinching the loop at the eye of the swivel, make five turns of the tag end around the standing line.

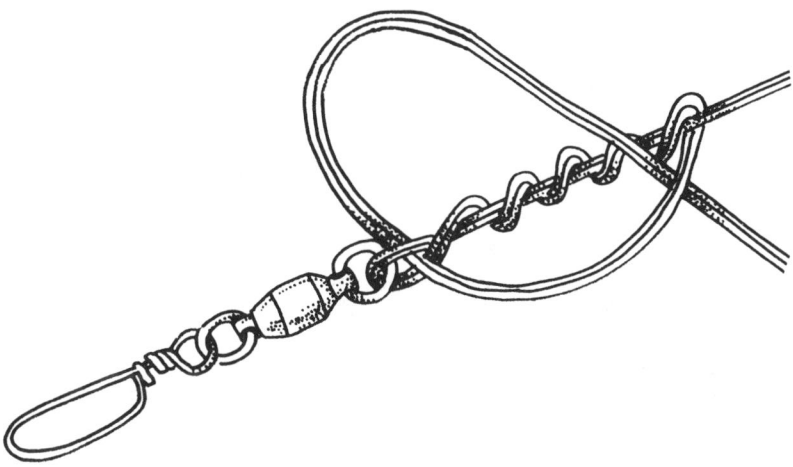

3. Pass the tag end through the small loop between the swivel eye and the wraps and then through the loop formed over the wraps.

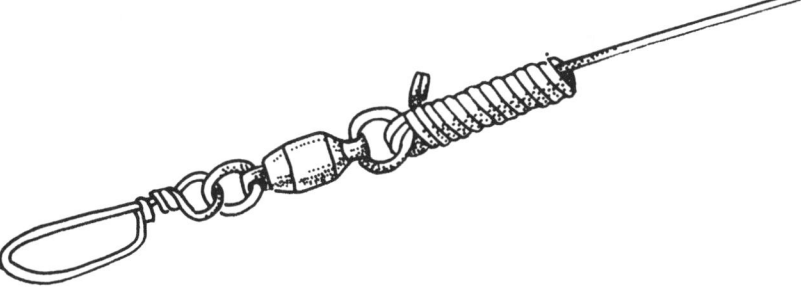

4. Wet the knot and carefully draw down until tight. Clip off the tag end.

Uni-Knot

The Uni-Knot can be used in place of the double improved clinch with lines of 80-pound test or less. In many ways it is the best knot to use although slightly more complicated to tie than the improved clinch. A major advantage is the knot's consistent high strength as it provides 97 to 99% of the breaking strength of the line. A poorly tied Uni-Knot will usually test out higher than a poorly tied improved clinch knot.

The knot gains exceptional strength because it adds an extra layer of the main fishing line beneath the knot coils. This effectively cushions the cutting forces as the knot is flexed and tensioned when casting or fighting a fish. The knot is durable and does not have to be re-tied after each fish or each day's fishing, although better fishermen will always re-tie as a matter of habit, just to be sure.

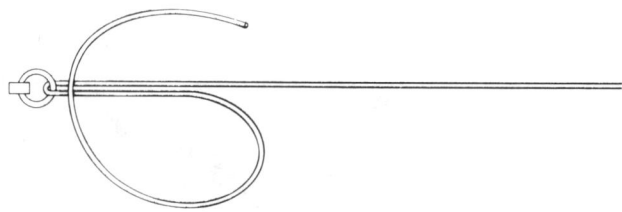

1. Run line through eye of hook or swivel at least 10 inches and fold back to make parallel lines. Bring tag end back in a circle toward hook or swivel.

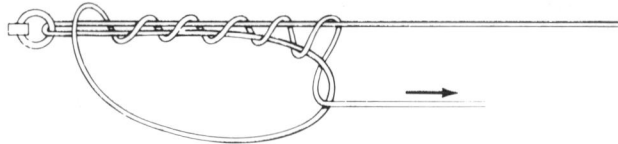

2. Make six turns with tag end around the doubled line and inside the loop. Hold double line at point where it passes through eye and pull tag end to tighten knot.

3. Pull standing line to slide the knot up against the eye of the hook or swivel.

4. Continue pulling until the knot is tight. Trim tag end near to the closest coil.

Crimp Loop

Charter captains of North Carolina like to keep things simple and they rely on the crimped loop connection to add snap swivels to their fishing lines. The crimped loop is redone before each trip to assure maximum line strength.

This connection works best with 50 to 130-pound test line and if high quality crimps are used, it will approach 100% of the line's strength. It is usually used with no double line at the end of the main line. Keep in mind that if blue marlin are the target species, longer leaders on the bait rigs or lures are needed to prevent any chaffing of the line by the fish's tail.

The offshore loop at the end of a single mono leader is also used by a number of giant tuna fishermen to attach the snap swivel when trolling with mackerel spreader bar rigs.

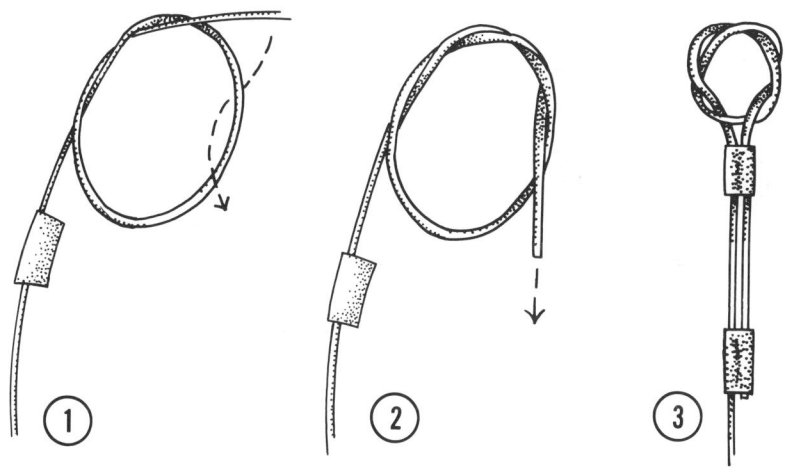

1. Slide a crimp onto the line, then form a loop in the end of the line or leader.

2. Pass the tag end of the line through the loop a second time.

3. While holding the line and tag end in one hand, use fingers of the other hand to slide the knot to form a small loop. Push the crimp in place, snug against the loop and swag with a crimping tool. The diagram shows a second, optional crimp in place as used on 300 to 500-pound test leaders.

Add a Bead

To prevent a knot or crimp from jamming when the leader is reeled right to the rod tip, add a small bead to the line before tying the knot or making the crimp connection. Many tackle shops sell the beads, or you can buy a bag full for pennies at a craft store.

The bead offers another advantage. When a fish is near the boat and angled deep, it can be hard to see the line as it gets lost in the sparkles of the water or glare from the sun. The bead, small as it is, can usually be clearly seen to give the captain a reference to locate the line. As the fish moves, especially if it makes a quick dash, the bead will leave a small wake or splash and again helps the captain follow the line, and therefore the fish. Some of the best tricks cost next to nothing, but reap valuable rewards.

A small bead just ahead of the snap swivel prevents the knot or crimp from jamming in the tip top guide. Rite Angler bead (top) has a groove so bead slips over knot and first ring on the snap swivel.

Surgeon's Knot

A relatively easy knot to tie, the surgeon's knot is a quick knot to add a length of heavier leader when fishing with chunks or live baits. Since it tests out at about 75% of the breaking strength of the line, it must only be used in conjunction with a Bimini twist or spider hitch. The doubled line created by the Bimini and spider also doubles the strength of the line. Even though the surgeon's knot weakens the double line by 25%, the double line is still far stronger than the single strand main fishing line.

1. Lay line and leader parallel, overlapping by 12 inches.

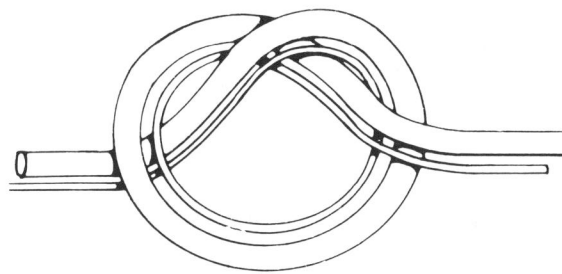

2. Tie an overhand knot, pulling the entire tag end of the leader through the loop.

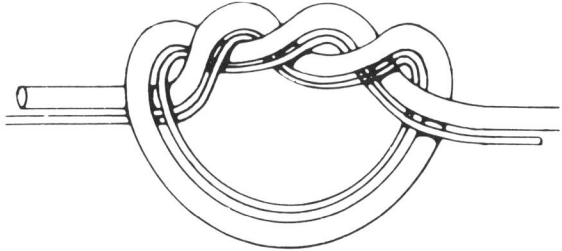

3. Push tag end through the loop a second time.

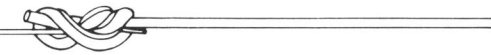

4. Hold both lines and both ends to pull knot tight. Clip ends close to knot to avoid hang-up in rod guides.

Palomar Knot

A quick, yet strong knot used to attach a hook to a leader when chunking with dead bait or when fishing a live bait.

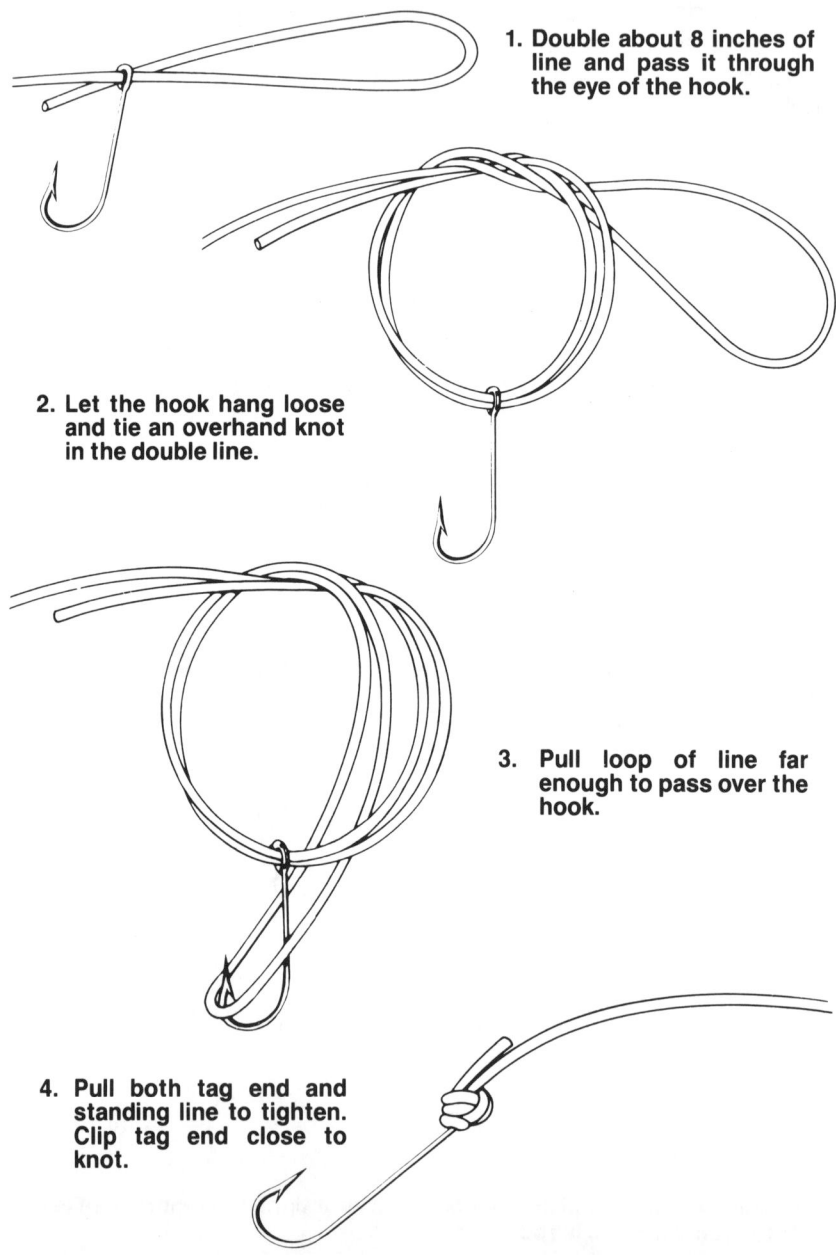

1. Double about 8 inches of line and pass it through the eye of the hook.

2. Let the hook hang loose and tie an overhand knot in the double line.

3. Pull loop of line far enough to pass over the hook.

4. Pull both tag end and standing line to tighten. Clip tag end close to knot.

RIGGING FOR ACTION

Snell Knot

Many chunkers or bait fishermen prefer the snell knot when attaching a hook to a leader. Unlike the Palomar or clinch knot that can slide off to one side of the hook eye ring when a tuna slurps down the bait, the snell always assures that the leader will lie in a straigt line to the hook shank. The accompanying diagram shows a reverse snell that is preferred when attaching a hook to leader that is already tied to the main fishing line.

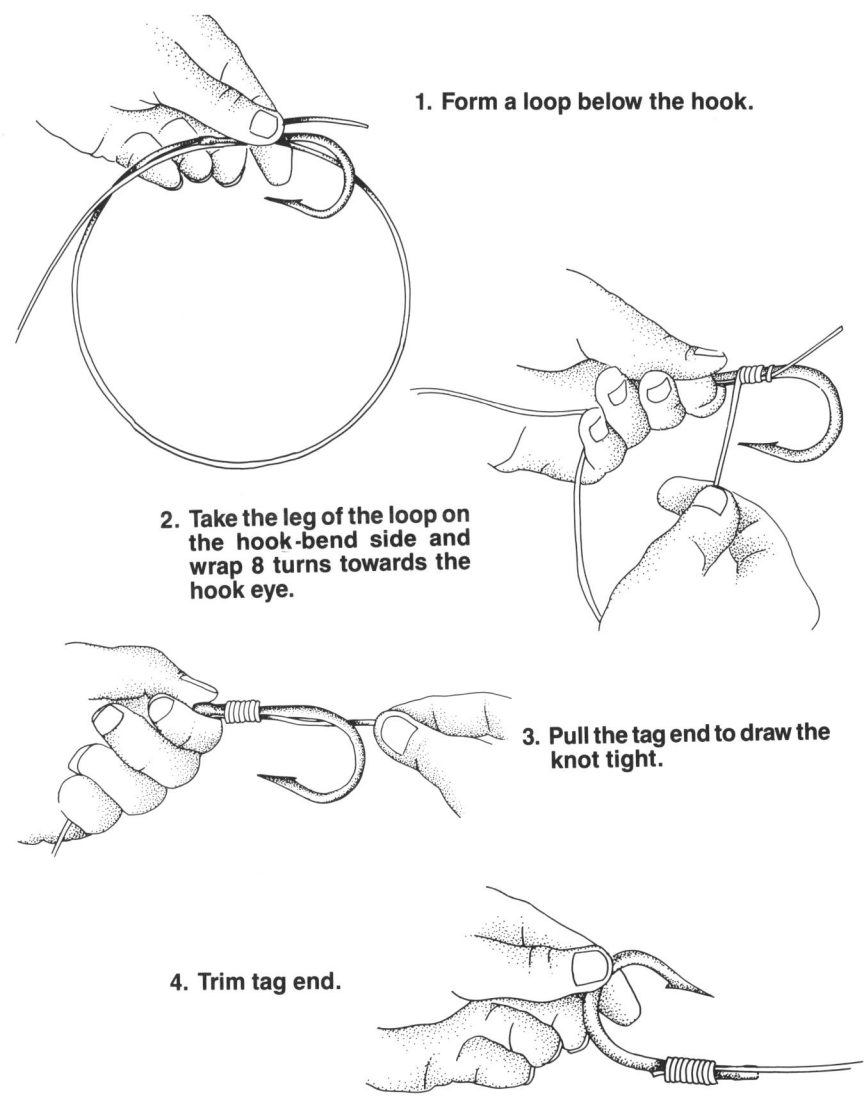

1. Form a loop below the hook.

2. Take the leg of the loop on the hook-bend side and wrap 8 turns towards the hook eye.

3. Pull the tag end to draw the knot tight.

4. Trim tag end.

Chapter Four

THE OFFSHORE BOAT

Walking the docks at Oregon Inlet, Palm Beach, Brielle, Ocean City, Snug Harbor or Montauk to look at the fleet of local sport fishing boats is always a pleasant way to spend idle time. I never tire of looking at the fishing boats and there is always plenty to see; pretty Carolina boats, ageless Ryboviches and Merritts, speed wagons from Monterey and Jim Smith, plus a host of factory boats from Post, Topaz, Hatteras, Viking, Blackfin, Ocean and Bertram. Vest pocket machines from Mako, Grady White, Phoenix and Ocean Master satisfy the budget minded as do the commercial style New England downeasters from JC Boats, Crosby, and Duffy.

Sportfishing boats display a wide range of boat-building thinking and technology. Some are beautiful, others plain Jane; some are all glitz, others simple and effective. They all reflect the owner's, or captain's, personal preferences of what he thinks a boat should be. Checking out the small rigging details of boats is an enjoyable on-going project for many captains; the way a boat's outriggers are rigged, the layout of tackle lockers and bait rigging stations, electronics boxes, cockpit layouts, the overall look of a boat.

I've been fortunate to fish on a wide variety of boats from hard-working charter boats to pampered 65-foot, million dollar tax write offs. And, I've been lucky to own several good boats that treated me well and opened doors to new fishing experiences. Someone said the two happiest days of a boat owner's life are when he buys the boat and then later when he sells it. Perhaps this is true, but each boat I've owned has a special place in my fishing memories. The excitement of moving into a new boat was always tempered by the loss of an old friend.

Boats are like people. They have personalities, quirks and moods but if you take the time to get to know them, to crawl around the bilges, nurse the engines and take care of the boat, a good fishing boat will turn out to be your best fishing buddy. A boat takes you fishing, gives you something to tinker with and provides an extra purpose to your fishing life that is hard to explain to anyone who doesn't own a boat.

My first boat was an aluminum skiff that took me up and down the coast, fishing jetties and inshore striped bass hot spots. Over the years I graduated to a Mako 25, through several inboard boats and now to a Ricky Scarborough. With 500 to 600 hours per year of operating time on these boats, plus the time to service them, repair them, clean them, and keep them looking like new, I've developed some ideas on what makes a good offshore fishing boat. I've also found that there is no perfect boat. Even the best of boats still represent some compromises, but there is plenty of room to adapt, modify, or customize virtually any boat into a fish-raising offshore sportfisherman.

What to Look For

Despite the many changes in technology, new hull designs and the selection of construction materials, the basics of what makes a good fishing boat are similar today to what they were nearly 50 years ago when the Rybovich and Merritt families began turning out their timeless sportfishing boats. These early designs set the stage for what we know as modern sport boats and most of today's boats still reflect the designs of these pioneer builders. It could be argued that today's boats are better in the sense that they take advantage of the latest materials and refined hull designs, but the best of today's boats still imitate the basic layouts of these early boats.

A close comparison will show that the early boats are different in many respects than many of today's breed. They have cockpits that are longer than they are wide. They have built-in bait rigging and tackle storage at the forward end of the cockpit and at the aft bulkhead of the salon. They are easy to clean and maintain. Best of all, they were built from the get-go primarily for fishing.

Compare these boats to some of today's boats that stress family comfort first, fishing second. Some of today's boats have cockpits that are so short there's barely any walk-around space much less space for a crew, coolers and gear. Easy maintenance has often been replaced with the need for mirrored cabin bulkheads, washing machines, thick pile carpeting and wet bars. What happened to tackle storage, rod storage, fishing space and visibility? Not every modern boat has gone the "floating condo" route and the best of the factory boats do offer a good blend of live aboard amenities and fishing qualities.

Rybovich and Merritt still make their classic boats using the latest in boat building materials and techniques, and they cost a pretty penny. However, a custom boat doesn't have to cost an arm and a leg as seen by the Carolina boats that can be constructed for about the same price as a factory boat; probably less if you do away with the lace curtains and suede sofas. A valuable trip for anyone contemplating a new boat would be a visit to the Outer Banks of North Carolina to check out the simple, but absolutely beautiful Carolina-style hulls. The charter boats vary from functional, simple interiors to some more elaborate treatments with sleeping space, microwaves, showers and enormous tackle storage.

A walk along the dock at Oregon Inlet Fishing Center or Pirates Cove is like a visit to the mecca of fishing boats. These are true sportfishing boats - beautiful, clean, roomy, fast, economical and imminently fishable.

The classic Merritt 37 was designed to catch bluefin tuna off Bimini and Cat Cay, sailfish off Florida. It combined beautiful lines, generous cockpit space, nimble maneuverability, seaworthiness and speed that is still imitated.

What Size and Style?

The size of the boat is a big factor in its fishing ability. While many big game anglers run 24 to 30-foot boats great distances in search of marlin and tuna, they probably wish for a larger boat if they had the budget to afford one. However, a point is reached when a boat gets too large and in some cases smaller really is better.

The great Tommy Gifford, father of many of today's tackle and fishing innovations, preferred a 29-foot boat for his fishing along the Florida Keys and in the Bahamas for giant tuna because the boat offered him the best blend of maneuverability, speed and fishing space. A 37-foot boat was once thought to be the ideal length for a day boat, according to Buddy Merritt, and many of his early Merritts were built to this length. Captains liked them because they could spin on a dime while battling a giant tuna or a blue marlin. Crews liked them because they had room to work the cockpit - all the tackle, rigging gear and baits were close at hand. Fishermen liked them because they caught fish like few other boats did. Some are still running today, like Captain Elly Brown's beautifully restored Do Stay, a classic 37 Merritt.

Later, the envelope expanded to 43 feet and a new generation of Merritt's set the pace for many boat builders. Good examples of these fast, roomy boats are the Murray Brothers Cookie Too and Captain Wink Doerzbacher's Sheria. While larger boats have been built, and fished effectively, as proven by the many 50-foot Vikings, Posts, Bertrams, Oceans and others being fished today, fishing ability may suffer as the comfort level increases. Most of today's top captains still prefer boats in the 40-foot range as the ideal length.

Flybridge boats offer the added living space of the salon and enlarged cabin spaces. The captain has optimum visibility from his elevated position above the cockpit, however he is also remote from the actual fishing and cannot easily lend the mate or crew a hand on troublesome fish. Many flybridge boats get around this by installing cockpit throttle and shift controls, sometimes a steering wheel, in the cockpit just to one side of the salon door. The captain can now control the boat and be only an arm's length away from lending a hand.

Open boats with a level deck from cockpit to helm, or with a step up to the helm deck are called express or day boats, yet many fishermen do spend a night, sometimes a weekend, on this style boat while chunking tuna or making long range canyon trips. The slightly elevated helm deck is only a step or two away from the cockpit and can be used for additional tackle storage and crew seating. The captain is fairly close to the action too, but his fishing visibility suffers unless the boat has a tower. Perched in the tower, however, the captain is again remote from the fishing and the crew, just as with a flybridge boat. Boats of this type were made famous by Topaz and Grady White, followed by Luhrs, Pursuit and now Ocean Yachts.

A cross between the open boat and the flybridge is the raised helm style, where the helm deck is about 4 to 5 feet above the cockpit. This layout offers generous seating and tackle storage, good visibility and close access to the cockpit by every crew member, including the captain. Another advantage is the huge engine room under the helm deck that can provide even more storage space and superb access to all sides of the engines for service. Most of these boats are built by custom builders of Stuart and Palm Beach, Florida and in North Carolina.

Many boats in the 24 to 28-foot range are designed as center consoles. They offer 360 degrees of walk around room, a big plus when fighting fish on stand-up tackle, and they have plenty of deck space for anglers, gear and equipment.

Powered by twin outboards, they have a lot of speed to get you to and from the fishing grounds. In the northeast, where the offshore runs can be long and the weather cool, quite a few center console boats have T-tops added and a full enclosure built around the front and sides of the T-top. This keeps the crew dry while cruising on the way to or from the fishing grounds. With the enclosure rolled up or removed once on location and trolling, the full deck space is again available.

Cockpit of the Bimini 29 is deep and wide, offering plenty of room for angler in the fight chair and the rest of the crew on deck.

Some Things to Look For

Cockpit - Longer than wider, crowned deck and large scuppers for fast water drainage, tackle locker and bait rigging stations, non-skid or teak deck surface, hinged and guttered deck hatches to keep water and fish blood out of the bilges, 25 to 28 inches of freeboard, under gunwale gaff storage, at least eight storage rod holders, four to eight flush-mount rod holders on cover boards, adequate walk-around space, plus space for bait tanks and ice coolers, and saltwater and freshwater wash down.

Helm- Seating for captain and mate, visibility to bow and cockpit for captain to see while docking or to see an angler playing a fish from the fight chair, electronics storage with easy visibility, throttle and shift controls at waist height, extra tackle storage.

Cabin - Sleeping space for three-quarters of the crew and anglers, refrigerator, microwave, shower, rod storage, extra tackle and gear storage.

Notice that most of the important considerations for a fishing boat are listed in the cockpit. It's nice to have the beautiful carpets, the teak coffee table and the TV, but without the right cockpit layout and sufficient space, the boat is a poor choice for offshore fishing. There are many center console and small cuddy cabin boats of 24 to 30 feet that have more cockpit space, hence more fishing space, than some 45-foot flybridge boats.

Engine Options

The choices narrow down to outboards verses inboards. Many years ago, Bertram modified one of their 28-foot flybridge boats to accept a pair of twin Evinrude outboards. The test boat highlighted the versatility of outboards and surprised everyone by proving that the outboard engines could equal or surpass the fuel economy of a gas powered inboard. The outboards did consume more fuel per hour but they traveled faster. The net fuel consumption was actually less with the outboards than with a gas-powered inboard. While revolutionary in its time, outboards are now an accepted power option for boats up to 32 feet in length, especially with the trend toward ever larger, higher horsepower rated outboards.

Twenty years ago, a boat rigged with a pair of 135 horse engines was barely able to push a 25 footer, much less a 26 to 30-foot boat to sufficient speeds for long distance running. Now we can choose from engines of 200 to over 300 horsepower. These bigger engines are not just higher in horsepower ratings, they are as different as ponies to farm horses when comparing the new engines to the small engines of yesteryear.

To calculate the required horsepower for an offshore boat powered by outboards, use the following formula:

1. Add the weight of the hull, fuel, engine, passengers, fishing gear and accessories.	2. Divide by 25 for a deep-vee hull. Divide by 30 for a modified-vee hull.

The result will closely match the horsepower required for that boat. As an example, my Mako 25 weighed approximately 8000 pounds fully loaded and ready for an offshore canyon trip. Because of the deep vee hull, I divided by 25 to get 320 horsepower. The twin 150 Mercuries I hung on the transom were close to the formula's suggested engine rating. They proved to be a perfect choice, performing flawlessly for six years with exceptionally good fuel economy and cruise speeds of 24 to 27 knots and a top end in the high 30-knot range.

A rule of thumb to achieve optimum fuel economy is to run outboard engines at approximately 2/3 throttle. My twin Mercury package ran best at 3800 to 4000 rpms for 12.8 gallons of fuel consumed per hour. I burned less fuel while trolling and usually achieved 10.3 gallons per hour over an entire canyon trip of 18 to 20 hours total duration.

While there is no pat answer to the question, "Which is better, inboards or outboards?" For many offshore fishermen, the only way to go is with inboards, either gas or diesel. Inboards supposedly make better sounds while trolling, yet there are days when the outboards will catch better than inboards do. I had great days on the Mako when we seemed to do no wrong while others around us caught fewer fish. Other days we got bit by the snake while others did more catching.

More important than engine noise is boat speed. Outboards do not provide as much "push" in rough water. The engines are meant for high speed operation and the relatively small props in relation to the larger props of inboard boats just don't have the oomph to push through large swells without letting the boat slow down, then speed up as the boat runs off the back side of the swell. Setting the trim on the engine all the way in the down position causes the bow to dig in and push more water. This can help the situation and get a steadier speed in rough water, plus make a better wake behind the boat. Other outboard boats run better with the trim tabs up and the engines tilted to cause the stern to squat low in the water to throw larger wake.

When comparing gas to diesel inboards, the primary consideration is cost. The diesels may cost an additional $20,000 to $40,000 but will offer superior fuel economy and much more safety since there is little danger of fire or explosion with diesel fuel. Diesel engines also offer greater range for the same volume of fuel. Gas engines burn about 25 to 40% more fuel than a diesel engine.

On offshore boats of 40 or more feet in length, diesel is often the only engine option. The choice then becomes one of which brand is preferred by the owner and how much horsepower is needed to push the boat to the desired speed. Unless you are on a very tight budget, there should be no contest between gas and diesel engines for an offshore boat. The added range, the less expensive fuel costs, the added safety and the ultimately higher resale value of the boat with diesels overwhelms the gas engine option.

Hull Designs

The forerunner of the ubiquitous 31 Bertram, the Moppie, set the boating world on its ear when it won many offshore races nearly 30 years ago. Its deep-vee hull design was copied, refined and adapted to a wide range of fishing boats, and many boats today can trace their basic hull design back to the Bertram 31.

As horsepower ratings rose in the 1950s, the traditional hulls of the 1930s and 1940s simply could not handle the added power without an excessively hard ride. Hull designs needed to catch up with the technology of new engines. The deep-vee was the result and it cut through tough water and softened the ride to everyone's satisfaction.

Unfortunately the deep-vee hull required a lot of power to keep it running. The deeper hull also meant there was more hull in the water so water drag had to be overcome with more power. More power often meant excessive, and expensive, fuel consumption. This was eventually overcome in the 80s with innovative use of hull and deck materials, like balsa coring, that made boats lighter. More efficient engines, gas and diesel, gave more power with less weight. Today's deep-vee hulls are not the same fuel hogs of the old days.

The modified-vee uses the same deep-vee entry forward on the hull but tapers it to a more gentle vee at the stern. The result is usually a more efficient, fuel saving hull. There may be some noticeable improvement in stability when trolling in a beam sea, but also a harder ride in very rough seas.

The Carolina style hull uses a nearly flat after section at the stern with an extreme deep-vee forward. Once underway at cruise speed, the sharp entry slices through choppy water while the hull rides economically on the flatter after section. There is very little water drag and the ride is soft, dry and stable.

Fuel Capacity

No matter what size boat you run for offshore fishing, it must have enough fuel to get you there, allow fishing time and then get you back home. A major breakthrough for outboard fishermen came when manufacturers realized we needed fuel, and lots of it, to get offshore. Many early outboard fishing boats had small fuel tanks of less than 100 gallons. Twin outboard canyon boats need at least 200 gallons of fuel to feed a thirsty pair of 150 to 200 horsepower outboards capable of drinking 12 to 18 gallons of Arab gold per hour while cruising; 6 to 12 while trolling for an average of 10 to 14 gallons for the entire trip, perhaps more if you are heavy handed with the throttle.

Larger boats may seem safer because they are bigger but if they lack sufficient fuel they'll be useless. I had the chance to tow a larger boat back to the inlet after it ran out of fuel. I can only imagine how the other guy must have felt as 25 footer pulled the 41 footer through the inlet to the fuel dock. Fuel capacity can be just as important as size.

Most engine manufacturers will supply a fuel consumption curve for their engines if you ask them. Calculate the anticipated fuel burn by multiplying the time it takes to get to the offshore grounds by the gallons per hour indicated at cruise on the manufacturers fuel burn.

Fishermen in the Northeast, Mid Atlantic and Gulf Coast regions need to be more concerned about fuel consumption because of the distances they travel to get to the good fishing areas. It would not be unusual to travel 75 miles offshore in quest of tuna or billfish. At a cruise speed of 25 knots, it takes three hours to get to the fishing grounds, another 3 hours to get back. If your twin diesel boat burns 24 gallons per hour, you've used up 144 gallons of fuel just getting there and back. If the boat only holds 200 gallons, you barely have enough fuel to troll for a few hours before having to head home.

Most canyon capable boats need a fuel supply that is equivalent to twice what the fuel consumption is to run to, and return from, the fishing grounds. This is true for outboard and inboard boats. My current boat holds 300 gallons of diesel juice and the Volvo's burn 22 gallons per hour at 23 to 24 knots. To fish a location 100 miles offshore, I'll run 8 hours round trip, consuming 180 gallons, still leaving a balance of 120 gallons for trolling and reserve fuel.

When fishing about 75 miles offshore, my Mako burned nearly 80 gallons of fuel, out and back, leaving 120 gallons for trolling and reserve. Extra fuel can be safely added on outboard boats with 12 and 18-gallon portable tanks sold by Tempo. They are Coast Guard approved, plastic tanks that stow easily and are 100% safe. They are sold with the proper outboard fuel line fittings in place and stow easily under consoles, or at the stern. Burn these first on the way out then tie them forward so they are out of the way while fishing.

Diesel boats can use 18-gallon chemical storage tanks. Gas inboards are best left as is, no extra tanks on deck that could cause a severe fire or explosion. If your gas boat doesn't have the range, book a charter or hitch a ride with a friend with a diesel boat.

If you aren't sure of your boat's capabilities and fuel consumption, try an inshore spot within 20 to 40 miles of the coast for inshore tuna, like bluefin, before heading off to the distant canyons. Keep track of the fuel burn and speed and after two or three trips to these not so distant areas you will have enough experience to make the right choices for long range fishing sorties.

Electronics

Electronics are essential for navigating, finding fish, locating temperature breaks and to keep in touch with fellow fishermen. The basics include:

MUST HAVE	OPTIONAL
VHF radio	Single side band
VHF radio (backup)	Loran (backup)
Loran	Color scope (cockpit)
Surface temperature gauge	Plotter
Radar	Auto pilot
Color scope	Engine synchronizer
Digital depth finder	EPIRB
FloScan fuel meter	

Accessories

There is a wide range of custom, after market accessories that will enhance the fishability of a sport fishing boat. Some of the most popular include:

Outriggers: Besides adding to the good looks of an offshore boat, outriggers provide several primary fishing advantages. They keep distance between the baits in the pattern, they add to the action of the lures and they allow the boat to manuever when turning sharply to approach fish, structure or surface schools of bait.

Tommy Gifford is generally credited with using some of the earliest outriggers, made of bamboo, to allow a pause, or drop back, when sailfishing with trolled baits. The original idea was to give the sail a few seconds of slack line to mouth the bait before the line came tight. It still works the same today when trolling baits, although when trolling with lures, no drop back is necessary.

Avoid canting the outriggers too far back. It may make the boat look racy but it removes some of the spread from the outriggers and therefore decreases their effectiveness. A number of boat manufacturers insist on raking the riggers way back so the boat looks racey and sleek, yet this defeats the ability of the outriggers to spread the baits correctly in the pattern.

Tuna or Marlin Towers: Add enhanced visibility to see the baits, lures, signs of fish, color changes, rips or other fishing opportunities. The Bimini tuna boats have towers that reach so high you feel you think you'll get a nose bleed climbing to the top. Many captains prefer the safer, and generally just as effective, lower marlin tower. The tower hard top, mounted just over the flybridge, serves as a support for an overhead electronics box, antennas and radome.

Fight Chair: For battles with the biggest of trophy fish, there's nothing to compare to a fight. Despite all the hoopla about stand-up techniques, a bent butt rod fished from a chair gives the angler the maximum power to apply to a fish. An angler in good shape, with a bucket harness and 130-pound class tackle can put up to 70 or 80 pounds of pressure against a 1000-pound bluefin. Giant tuna and blue marlin fishermen can not be without a good fight chair.

A thoughtfully equipped Grady-White with full electronics, hardtop, twin outboards and a generous fuel supply is an ideal offshore fishing boat.

The chair should match the boat. A small chair, like the Murray Brothers Sailfish chair is ideal for small boats, either center consoles or cuddy cabin. Since there isn't much side to side deck space, added pulling power is gained by the angler placing his feet on the gun'ls or on a reinforced hinged splash well just forward of the outboards. The chair can help land some hefty bigeye tuna or blue marlin.

Larger boats can use a larger chair and many anglers like the idea of installing a Large Tuna Chair, partly for comfort, partly for prestige. I use a Murray Brothers Small Tuna Chair on the Linda B and have never felt hampered. The overall size of the chair is just a tad narrower than the Large Chair, and the foot rest and back rest are also a bit smaller. On the plus side, I like the added room I gained. The chair is capable of handling fish over the 1000-pound mark.

Anglers who seek white marlin, sailfish, tuna up to 300 pounds, kingfish and wahoo will do well with a compact size 80-pound class chair.

Tuna Door: Also called a transom door, the swing out door makes easy work of boating extra large fish. With the increased emphasis on releasing marlin, the giant tuna fishermen are more apt to need a transom door. Many offshore trollers use a tuna door to handle bigeye and yellowfin of 100 to 300 pounds and feel it is much easier to slide these fish aboard through a transom door rather than struggle to haul a big fish over the cover boards.

Gin Pole/Tower Pull: Big fish are often hauled aboard with a block and tackle mounted on a special gin pole or from a reinforced eye mounted on a tower leg. It's a second best to a tuna door, but much less expensive.

Fish Boxes: In-deck, or transom fish boxes, are a great way to keep bait and boated fish out of the way. Many are insulated to help preserve the catch until dockside filleting. Some fish boxes can be converted to bait wells, or refrigerated chill boxes.

T-Top/Hard Top: The T-top offers good electronics storage for center consoles and with a vinyl enclosure can keep crew and captain DRY. Not every trip back will be a dry, smooth ride. Cuddy cabin boats use a hard top for similar purpose as the T-top. Both styles of tops also provide mounting platforms for outriggers and antennas so they are out of the way while fighting a fish.

Rocket Launcher/Tackle Seat: Rod storage is always a welcome addition, especially on boats of less than 30 feet in length where space can be at a premium. Although they usually show up on center consoles I've seen many cuddy boats rigged with them in Florida where the emphasis is on sailfishing. My own boat has a rocket launcher that holds ten 50W size rods and reels. They hold rods while traveling to the grounds and while trolling since rod holders are tough to mount at the transom with the outboards in the way.

Bait Well: Depending on where you live and fish, bait wells are more or less important. Florida sailfish experts use live goggle eyes, northeast bigeye fanatics use live snapper blues, but most trolling fishermen use little in the way of live bait. I find it handier to use an above-deck live well that can be removed from the boat when I don't need it. The space that would have been used for the live well can provide under deck storage of extra lines, cleaning supplies, float balls and miscellaneous gear.

A Case for "Mini" Boats

There are still skeptics who don't believe a 25 to 30-foot boat can successfully fish the offshore grounds yet there are many fishermen proving the fishability of these boats every season from Massachusetts to the Bahamas. I recall one tournament we fished in my old 25 Mako nearly 15 years ago when the crew and I had taken quite a ribbing at the captains meeting, but justice was eventually to be ours. We were the smallest boat in a fleet of larger sportfishermen dominated by 35 to 54 footers. Several captains offered help, "Give a shout if you get into trouble." Others chuckled at our little boat and its "coffee grinder engines".

We broke the inlet at midnight running a slow cruise to the mouth of the Hudson Canyon to be in position at dawn. With the spray hood up, we had a cabin of sorts and two men slept on foam backpack pads and sleeping bags while two men stood watch and ran the boat. At dawn we drew first blood with a pair of yellowfins. I called a committee boat to report the catch and within minutes a dozen or more 40 footers were breathing down our necks. The hardest part of trolling now was avoiding the other boats as the trolling patterns got frenzied while captains towed their lures over the spot we had hooked up.

At 8:30 we scored again as three bigeye blasted our lures. A larger boat turned sharply hoping to get a shot at the same school and cut one of our fish off. Give us a break! That boat hooked up immediately with a pair of fish. Other boats came in fast and several more bigeyes were hooked up before the school sounded with a case of lockjaw.

We finally boated our two fish just as the northwest winds began to blow. After wrapping the bigeyes in a large tuna bag with several bags of ice packed around the carcasses, we headed home. The seas were perfect for the Mako once we got the right rpms figured. At about 3500 we made a decent 19 to 20 knots with no pounding and since the seas were dead off the bow there was no uncomfortable spray either. We passed nearly every larger boat in the fleet, waving as we passed them just to rub it in a little. The combination of swells and chop was nearly ideal for the Mako, while the larger boats pounded into the 6-foot seas sending sheets of spray over the tops of fly bridges. We laughed at them all the way home.

Two other tuna beat out our 219 pounder so we missed third place by a few pounds, but gained a lot of respect for the Mako as several captains thanked us for calling them into fish. "That's one heck of a boat. Boy, you sure blew by me on the way in!" After the ribbing the night before, this was sweet music indeed.

During the five years I ran that boat, we made approximately 60 canyon trips, plus ran the boat to the Bahamas, spent winters fishing it in the Florida Keys and made hundreds of inshore tuna trips. Some people thought we were half way gone to run a boat that size to the canyons, others knew we were half way there!

If you keep a weather eye and common sense at hand at all times, a small battle wagon of 25 to 30 feet can easily handle offshore duties. Keep in mind, too, that there were also days when the seas gave us a tough ride back home while the bigger boats were dry and cozy.

Author's 25 Mako made numerous runs of up to 115 miles to the northeast's offshore canyons.

An Ultimate Offshore Boat

If I won the lottery, or a long-lost uncle willed me a million dollars, I'd build a brand new Linda B but it would be virtually identical to the 38 footer I'm running right now. It's an open boat with a raised helm and a center console. Built by Ricky Scarborough in Wanchese, North Carolina of juniper and marine plywood, glassed over with West System epoxy and then sprayed with Interlux 800, the boat is lighter and stronger than a comparable fiberglass boat. Powered with a pair of Volvo diesels she burns 20 gallons an hour at cruise, 11.5 gallons average for an offshore trip. She'll run effortlessly all day at 22 to 24 knots and can be pushed to a top end of 29 knots.

I came upon the boat by chance. For several years I had kept an "Ideal Boat" file, filling it with photos, deck layouts and sketches of various boats I had seen over the years that had caught my eye. I even drew plans for a raised helm boat that I dreamed of building. While looking to move into a larger boat, I saw an ad for a boat located in Palm Beach. Imagine my surprise when I first saw the boat and realized it was nearly identical to the designs I had sketched out on paper so many times. There was no way I could pass her up and a month later she was running up the coast to her new home on the Metedeconk River. Built in 1983 for Bob Herder, an innovative offshore angler from Maryland, she's been refurbished and is still running to the blue water grounds in search of billfish and tuna.

With raised helm and center console, the Linda B has huge cockpit, exceptional visibility, and fuel capacity for long-range offshore trips.

Unlike many boats with hulls that quickly warp from a deep-vee to a wide, full hull up forward to make a huge cabin, this Carolina boat has a deep forefoot that cuts through nasty water like a warm knife through butter. There's no hard ride and virtually no spray to roll up over the bow. Any slight spray thrown by the hull is deflected by the distinctive wide flaring Carolina style hull. It's a rare day that we get water on the eisenglass, unless it rains.

The deep forward entry does take away some deck space in the forward cabin, but only at foot level. The wide flaring bow adds space up higher in the cabin, so storage space in cabinets for the head, dinnette and hanging lockers is generous.

Before purchasing the boat, I spent time with Sunny Briggs, of Briggs Boat Works in Wanchese. His craftsmanship and experience as a charter captain helped me develop many ideas to make the boat even more fishable. We added a tackle locker, bait rigging station, improved electronics boxes, and gave her a new coat of polyurethane paint so she looks brand new. Bill Laing at Ocean Towers in Point Pleasant, New Jersey added a rocket launcher and tower rod holders for critical rod storage. Murray Brothers crafted the twin helm chairs and cockpit fight chair. With new electronics and the refurbishing, she's sharp-looking.

The cockpit is longer than it is wide so there is plenty of space for

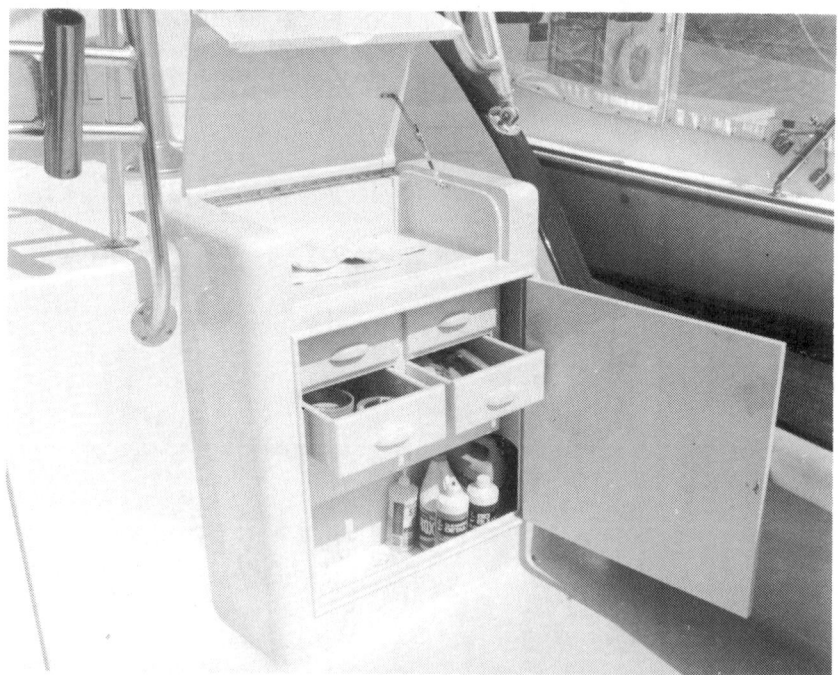

Tackle locker adds storage and makes cockpit more fishable with bait rigging gear close at hand.

THE OFFSHORE BOAT

the fight chair and there's still walk around room behind the chair for coolers, fish bags, tackle and for the crew to move as a fish is battled. The raised helm is four feet above the cockpit and is high enough to offer excellent visibility of the baits and lines while working a trolling pattern. It is only a few short steps from the helm to the cockpit so I can assist with boating a fish, checking the baits or moving a lure in the wake.

The helm layout assures all the crew members of comfort, clear visibility and easy communication, something especially important when working on a billfish or a blast of several tuna. I don't miss the full salon cabin at all, and in fact, prefer the way the raised helm keeps the captain and crew within close touch and not separated by an "apartment" in between the helm and the cockpit. While I admire the more traditional cabin boat with salon and cabin amenities, I can't imagine being so far from my crew, or from the fishing action.

She's a quiet boat with hardly more than a very dull roar from the engines even at cruising speeds. The resonance through the hull from the diesel engines seems to draw fish into the boat very well.

Before You Purchase

Before purchasing your dream sportfisherman, it's a good idea to visualize the use of the deck space while actually fishing. If the dealer will let you, bring a cooler and a rod or two to see how things fit. Imagine the cockpit with four of your buddies standing in it, working rods, baits, fighting fish, gaffing fish and bringing a fish aboard. Ask yourself, "Is there enough space?"

Check out the ride of the boat in reasonable seas. Does the wake break away from the hull chine amidships indicating a dry running boat, or does it break far forward indicating a wet ride in moderate seas. Get the feel of the boat to see if it leans excessively, or rides bow high. Do the engines smoke badly, does the hull get up on plane quickly? Try backing down as if battling a fish. How does it handle when maneuvering to dock the boat? Does it roll in a beam sea?

It's your boat and your money. All anyone can do is recommend and give opinions. I've given some of mine in the preceding pages but the ultimate decision of what boat to run depends on you. It's your money, your pride, your satisfaction and your boat. Ultimately, it's all a lot of fun.

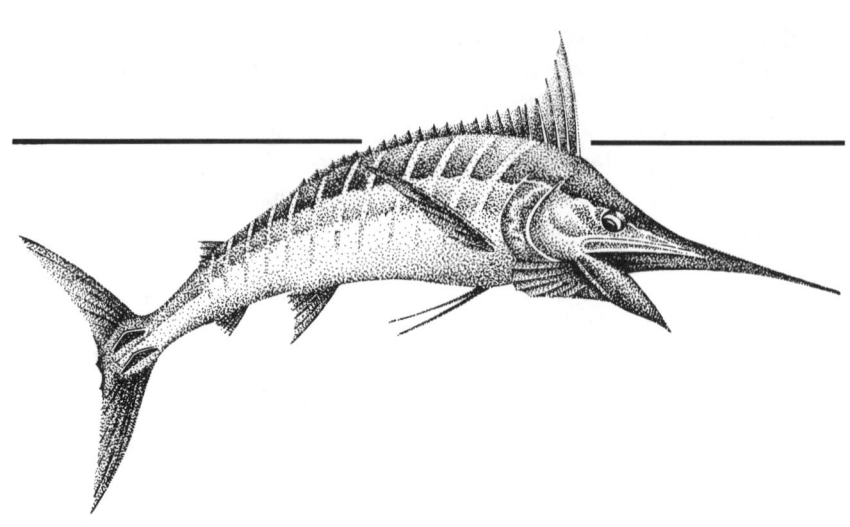

Chapter Five

OFFSHORE TROLLING LURES

Snap, snap! Szizzz, szizzz! Two rods went off at once, yanked from their rigger clips by the smashing strike of a pair of yellowfin tuna. Now the fun began. Using stand-up tackle, the anglers danced the "tuna ballet" as each fish went in a different direction. The captain could only maintain bare headway, trying to keep the stern to the wind and to the fish, to prevent an end run around the bow of the boat.

"Watch out, my fish is going to the left. Lift your rod, I'm going under you! Pull ahead just a little, my fish is running towards the bow! Here's the double line, there's the fish. Look at the size of that fish! I'm ready for the gaff. Someone grab the damn leader! Gaff him, gaff him, quick! Okay, there's one; now let's get the second one on the boat."

The controlled confusion, shouts, and the electricity in the air is pure heaven for a fisherman. Few of life's experiences can match big game fishing for sheer excitement and wild enjoyment. The mayhem, the powerful fish, the blue ocean, the tackle strained to the limit all add up to a unique experience.

For many offshore fishermen, trolling with lures is the favorite way to go. The lures themselves have a magical quality about them, some with special mother of pearl shells embedded in the epoxy molded heads, others with huge eyes, special woods and shapes, or reputations built on the tournament circuits of the world. Just watch a big game fisherman visit an offshore tackle shop; it's a well disciplined man who can walk out the door without buying another lure - the next secret weapon that will call fish into the pattern and assure trolling success.

We live in a plastic world and while many of us bemoan that fact in our daily lives, plastic has brought many innovations to the big game fisherman. The dramatic increase in tuna and marlin catches over the last decade are probably due in some part to the plastic offshore high speed trolling lures. Rigging trolling baits required skill; but pulling plastic lures put offshore trolling into everyone's realm. The trick in fishing plastic lures lies in matching the action, weight, size and color of the lures for the most appealing lure pattern.

Head Shapes

The most popular head shapes are the pointed, bullet, Yap, flat-face, Kona, cupped, jet and rule. Manufacturers have come up with an infinite number of variations on these basic head shapes to match any possible fishing situation.

The action of the lure may vary due to the overall weight and size of the head shape, balanced by the skirt. The length of the skirt, its weight and whether it's a single or double skirt may also effect the action of the lure. My own preference is for light weight lures, simple head shapes and light weight skirts.

The pointed and bullet-shaped heads usually run on the surface, splattering water and skipping along much like a natural ballyhoo bait. They fish very well from outriggers. Heavier heads may dip below the surface and pull air to stream a short length of bubbles.

The Yap lure was made famous in Hawaii, then made its way to the Gulf of Mexico where Texas and Louisiana fishermen used it with telling success. It runs straight and pushes a lot of water. As it dips below the surface it will pull a pocket of air with it and stream a long plumb of bubbles.

Flat-face lures are a shortened version of the Yap and are generally favored by tuna fishermen, although I've taken marlin in the Bahamas and in the Keys on these same lures. They gulp huge volumes of air and spew lots of jet stream bubbles. Angle-face versions of these lures may splash a bit more water when they surface before gulping the air diving a few inches below the surface again.

Kona heads were once the most popular lure but their swimming, darting motion has proven to be not as effective as a straight running lure. The scooped out face of the Kona head does act as an enticing teaser lure and may draw fish into the pattern where they will hit another lure.

Cupped-face lures may also swim erratically but the side to side motion is more like a vibration rather than a distinct darting motion like the Kona, cupped-face lures will push a lot of water, spray it wildly on the surface and then dart below the surface to smoke bubbles. They

OFFSHORE TROLLING LURES

LURE HEAD SHAPES

Bullet

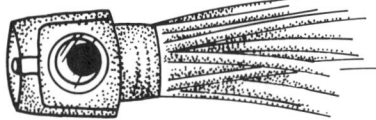
Flat

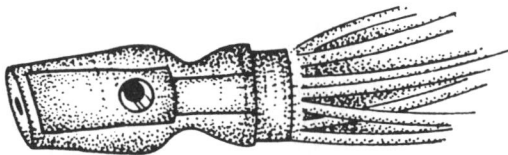
Area Rule

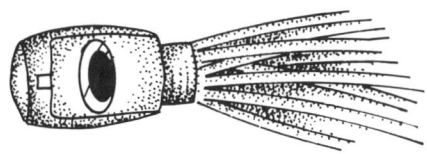
Cupped

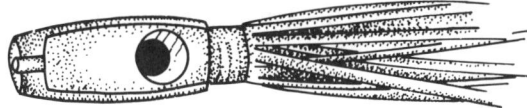
Yap

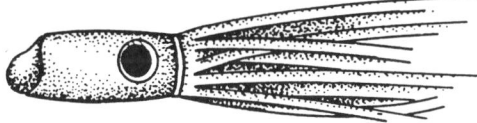
Kona

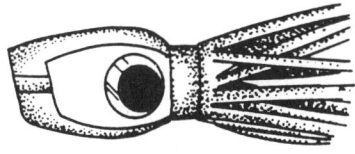
Angled

often work very well at slower trolling speeds and can be trolled with a mix of natural bait and lures.

Area Rule lures use an aeronautical idea to allow the lures to track well at high speeds. The narrowed waist keeps the lure running straight and true even at speeds up to 10 knots or more. The flat, angled face smokes well and splashes on the surface before diving.

Jet head lures are usually heavy metal with a chromed finish but they may also be constructed of lighter weight plastic or machined aluminum. Many fishermen swear by them and they do attract fish. They run deeper than many other lures and will run jet streams of bubbles when they momentarily get to the surface to slurp a pocket of air before diving.

Which head shape is best? There's no answer to that, or rather the answer keeps changing from year to year. I've found some winners that pulled fish like a magnet one year and the next year they were duds. My basic favorites are a mix of pointed, bullet, flat-face and Yap style lures. My two all-time best producers are the Mold Craft Soft Head wide range, a small Yap style head; and the Sevenstrand Psyclone bullet head. Also top-notch producers are the Murray Brothers, Sir Ace, the C & H Stubby and Hacksaw, Boone Sea Minnow, Tournament Tackle Ilander and others. I usually fish pointed, bullet and Yap lures from the outriggers; flat-face, jets and cupped lures from flat lines or directly from the rod tip. Larger flat-face or Yap lures are run straight down the center of the pattern.

The lure's action is probably more important than its color. Flat-face lures that trail long, jet streams of air bubbles may not need any color at all. It's the smoke that draws the fish. In fact, I used a lure with a clear head for several seasons with a semi-transparent skirt that caught very well. Nearly colorless, it reminded me of squid I had seen while snorkeling once over a shallow reef in the Keys. It was a nearly perfect imitation of the natural thing.

Marlin fishermen believe that an odd-sized lure will be the best catcher. This is probably true with tuna also. The odd lure may consistently get single strikes and be a steady taker of fish on all days, especially when the fishing is a slow pick. Multiple hook-ups usually occur with lures of the same or similar size.

Colors

The bright green Sevenstrand Psychobead turned many a frustrated bait troller into a fishing hero back about 20 years ago when fishing the canyons along the East and Gulf Coasts first became popular. Up until then, most everyone fished with rigged ballyhoo. Lures were something used in Hawaii not here at home.

The Sevenstrand Psychobead in bright green, is still popular today, often imitated and frequently one of the favorite lures in most every captain's trolling pattern. Nicknamed the Green Machine, it made lure fishing popular and quickly gained a reputation for fooling a lot of fish. Its light weight and pointed head shape gives it good trolling action in almost any kind of sea. Rough water or calm, the Machine could be counted on to splatter along the surface much like a natural bait. It sputtered and fussed with an action that drew tuna and billfish, with uncanny ability.

There's no doubt green is a remarkably good color. It may imitate a dolphin but a better reason why it's so good is based on science. Light is made up of many different wave lengths, each penetrating the water to varying depths. The color green is highly reflective, unlike red which loses its color only a few feet below the surface. Since green is more visible, fish may see a green lure more readily than lures of other colors.

As good a color as green is, there are other colors that work well; sometimes better. Frank Johnson of Mold Craft lures schooled me on the importance of presenting a variety of colors in the trolling pattern. He kids fishermen to "Buy one of each color, it's good for my business," but his thoughts are based on the facts learned from some of Frank's best customers; the charter captains around the world who use his lures. "Dark lures are very good because they stand out against the bright sky. Fish are looking upward at your lures. The surface of the water is very light in color because of the bright sky. A dark lure really shows up well and gives the fish a clear target to strike at."

It made sense to me and trolling several dark lures in my pattern helped add more fish to the day's catch. My log book entries verified how well color combinations like black and red, purple and red, and blue and red really worked. Over the last several seasons, many of the tuna caught on my boat were fooled by dark lures. I believe the dark lures are more enticing to bigeye and larger yellowfin. I've seen several instances when bigeye ignored larger lures that must have looked like a bigger meal to strike at a smaller, darker lure.

A lure I often run straight down the middle in the shotgun position is a mix of the bright and dark, scoring frequently in the last few seasons. It's a bright green and dark blue Sir Ace lure with a flat, angled face. It's pulled in bigeye and grabbed the attention of a 300-pound blue marlin as we trolled along the edge of a rip just inside of the shelf at the Baltimore Canyon.

At the other end of the color scale is another favorite color, pink. It is especially good for longfin and I use this color not only in single lures but in a daisy chain made from several 6-inch Tuna Clones, bullet-head lures with a larger lure trailing at the end. Pink has also taken a number of big dolphin for us and one of our largest bigeye, a

289 pounder, ate a pink and white Murray Brothers lure.

Presenting a good mix of colors is a valuable strategy. Frank Johnson's theory is that the attacking tuna or billfish focuses on the weakest link in the lure pattern and that's the lure the fish strikes. If the pattern has several bright lures and only one dark lure, the dark one is likely to be the piece of plastic that gets the attention. I troll a single dark lure right down the center so the lures sits on the sixth wake. We call it the dive bomber and it often gets smashed by the biggest fish of the day.

Changing light conditions can make some colors better producers than others. I like to start off the day at sunrise with mostly darker colors in the pattern and then switch to brighter colors as the day wears on. I troll seven lures most of the time and at dawn four or five of them will be dark. By nine or ten in the morning we start to switch over so there are four or five brighter colors in the pattern.

The best colors may change during the day depending on the available light. Many trollers prefer dark colors like black, purple and red at the early morning hours and again at the end of the day, switching to brighter colors like green, yellow, orange and blue in midday. My log shows some good early morning catches on bright colors when the bright color was the only bright lure in the pattern. Perhaps this is the fish showing a preference for the odd color rather than an overall preference for dark or bright colors.

Multiple hook-ups on tuna will usually all be on the same color lure. If I have seven lures in the pattern, five green ones and a pair of odd colored lures, and we get four strikes at once, it is almost a guarantee that they'll all have hit the green lures. On the other hand, when we get single strikes, it is almost a sure thing that the odd lure may have done the catching. Not always, but frequently. The odd colored lures become very important to our fishing success on those slow days when it's a pick one here, pick one there kind of a day. By the end of a slow day like that, if we picked three or four singles, we've had a good trip, while another boat, trolling one color in its pattern may go fishless.

Size and Weight

Light weight lures usually have a more predictable action and they work well in all kinds of seas. Heavy lures tend to dig into the sea, then fly out causing the lure to tumble. Choose lures that stream long jets of bubbles as they work just below the surface. They should occasionally come to the top, gulp a pocket of air and then dive with a long trail of "smoke". The actions should be straight, not violently side to side.

It's a good idea to mix the size of the lures, using smaller lures in close and larger lures dropped back in the pattern. The largest lure is usually run down the center and dropped back onto the fifth to seventh wake; sometimes even further back.

I usually prefer to fish lures of similar weights in the pattern, rather than mixing lures of heavy and light weights at the same time. Put one heavy lure in the pattern, in the wrong place, and you will cause either the heavy lure to work poorly or if you tune your speed to make the heavy lure work correctly, the rest of the light lures may then work poorly. All the lures in the pattern must work well together. On calm days, lighter lures are generally better, while heavy lures are preferred by some captains in rough water. Lighter lures tend to work best from the outriggers, while heavier lures tend to work best off the flat lines.

The old fishing adage that "bigger is better" does not always work with tuna. Sometimes smaller is better. Checking the log books of tournament winners, charter captains and lure manufacturers like Don Combs of C & H Lures and Frank Johnson of Mold Craft seems to prove that the mid-sized lures are the best producers of fish.

Most successful tuna trollers will work one jumbo-sized lure, usually a Kona style head that throws a lot of water somewhere in the center of the lure pattern. The majority of the remaining lures will emphasize mid-size lures in the 8 to 10-inch range and perhaps a pair of lures of only 5 to 7 inches will be run off flat lines.

One season, Sevenstrand Tuna Clones worked so well it was like feeding jelly doughnuts to Boy Scouts. There were massive schools

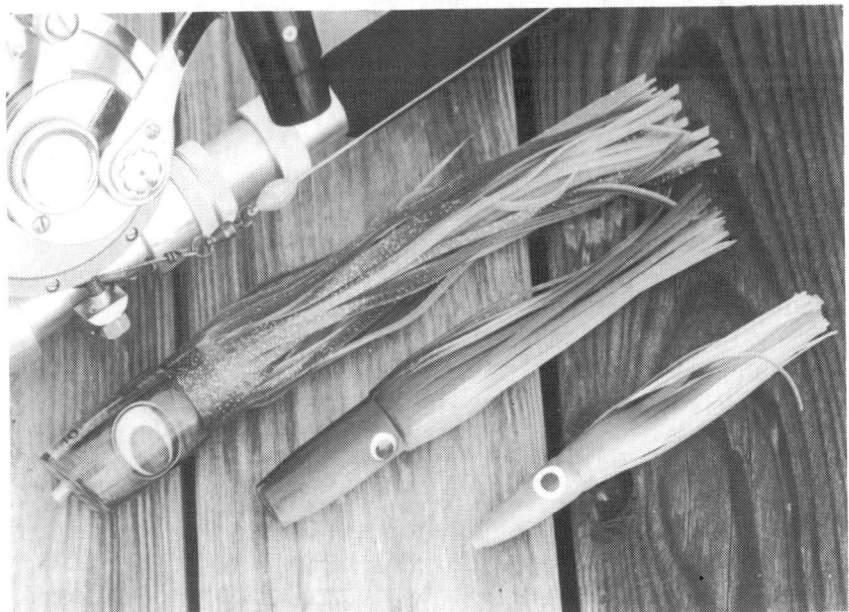

A good mix of offshore lure sizes (l to r) includes Sir Ace #10, Mold Craft Wide Range and Sevenstrand Tuna Clone.

of squid of only 4 to 8 inches in size and since this was the prevalent bait on many days, the larger lures went untouched, while the Clones fooled fish after fish. And it wasn't only small fish that hit the smaller lures. Several bigeye in the 150-pound class blasted the small Clones, too, disproving the bigger is better adage.

I keep records on every fish we catch on the Linda B and over a nine-year period over 70% of our fish have hit on lures of less than 12 inches. Approximately 20% have hit on lures of less than 8 inches and only 10% have hit large lures. Our largest fish, whether tuna or marlin have all been taken on 10-inch lures.

Rigging Lures

An offshore lure incorporates several parts; the head, the skirt, the hooks and the leader. Most lures are sold ready to fish right out of the package from the manufacturer. Some lures must be "built" before they are ready for the water. Many offshore fishermen customize factory lures by adding new skirts, or they just replace skirts that have been torn up in fist fights with tuna or billfish. Customizing your lures allows you to try new head shapes, new colors and new ideas that may catch more fish.

Rigging is an easy skill to learn but it does take some practice, and there are numerous variations on ways to make up leaders, tie or crimp hooks to the leader, forming loops and how to tie on skirts. The methods shown here are "proven in combat" but can be modified to suit your own special big game trolling techniques or needs.

Wrap-around Skirts

Ed Murray of the famous Murray Brothers Tackle Shop in Riviera Beach, Florida showed my son, Rich, how to rig big lures meant for marlin. The following photos show the technique Ed uses on all sizes of lures. He likes the wrap-around skirts because he can make an infinite variety of color combinations, including solids and metallic, to imitate any species of baitfish.

To rig the wrap-around skirts you'll need: lure head, several Mold Craft or Trawlite skirts, Gudebrod Waxed Rigging Floss or dental floss, reflective prism tape or colored plastic tape, scissors and a single edged razor blade.

Wraps of dental floss will hold the skirts in position while the various colors are added to the head. You'll get a better looking lure if the skirt is rolled into position with no excessive stretching. When the tension is released, the skirt will get smaller and gaps may appear in the finished lure.

OFFSHORE TROLLING LURES

1. Pull off 12 feet of Gudebrod Bait Riggin' Floss, double it over. Form a loop at the end and make a lark's head knot around the back of the lure head.

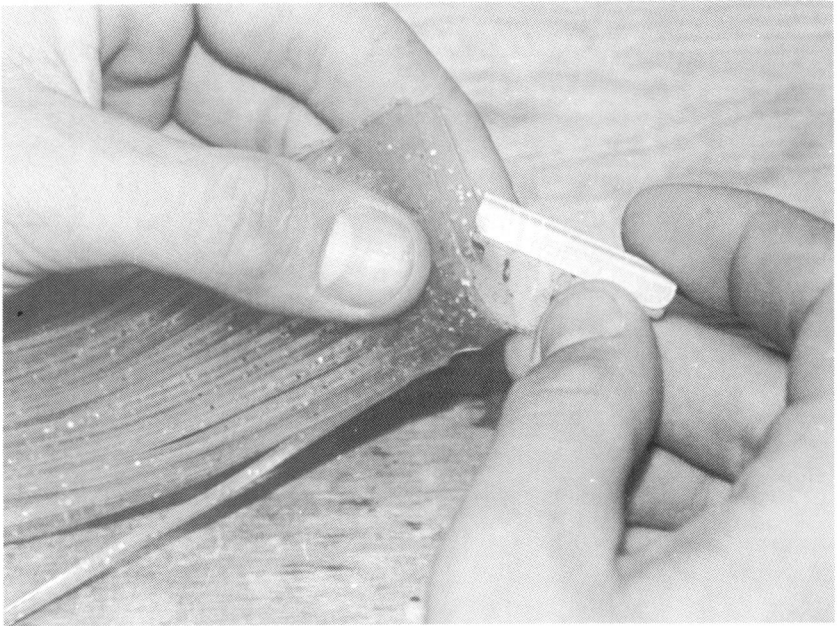

2. Select a light color skirt for the under skirt. Fold it in half and make a tiny slit with the razor blade to mark the center of the skirt.

FISHING FOR TUNA AND MARLIN

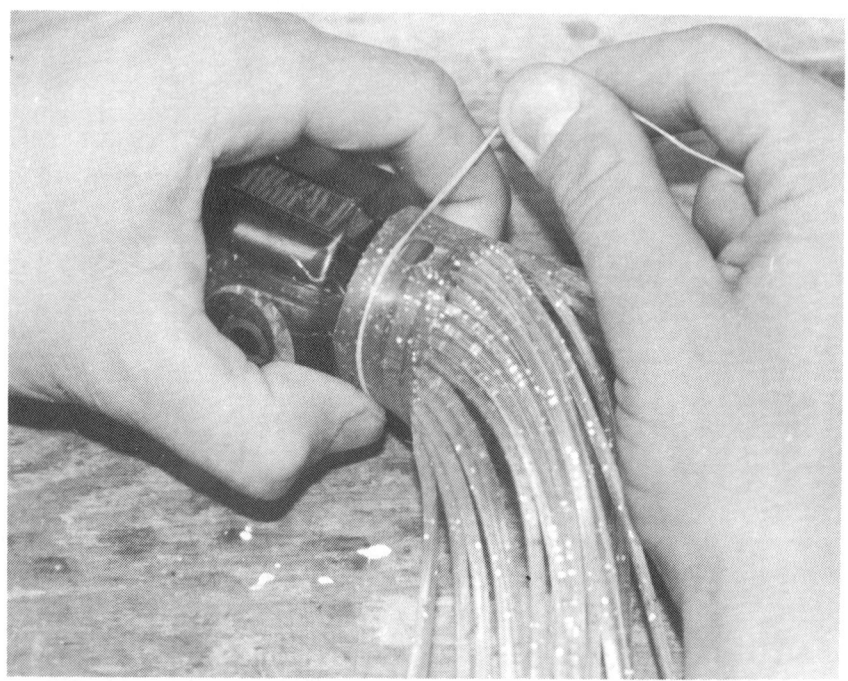

3. Place the skirt in position so the center mark is at the top center of the lure head. Wrap with several turns of floss.

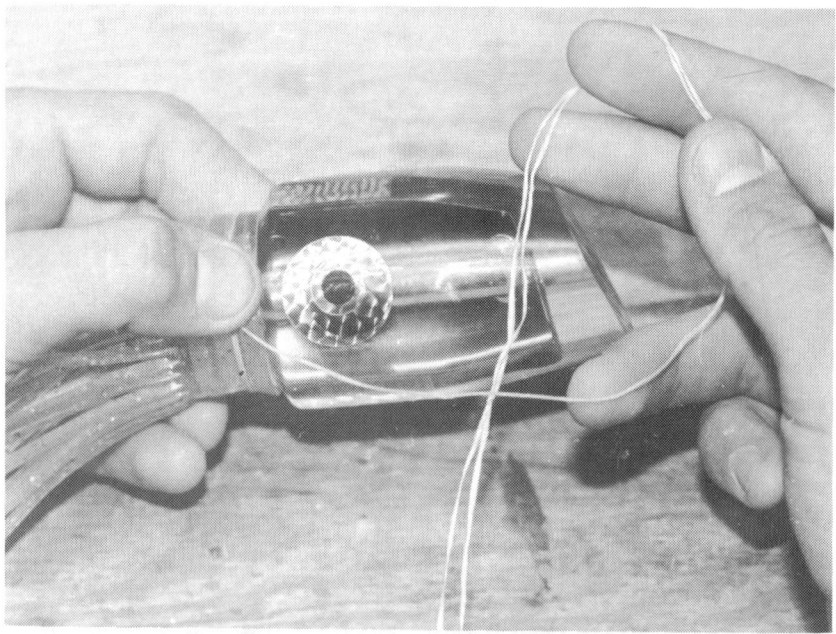

4. To hold the floss in place while readying the next skirt, make a half hitch, drop it over the lure head and pull tight to lock the floss.

OFFSHORE TROLLING LURES

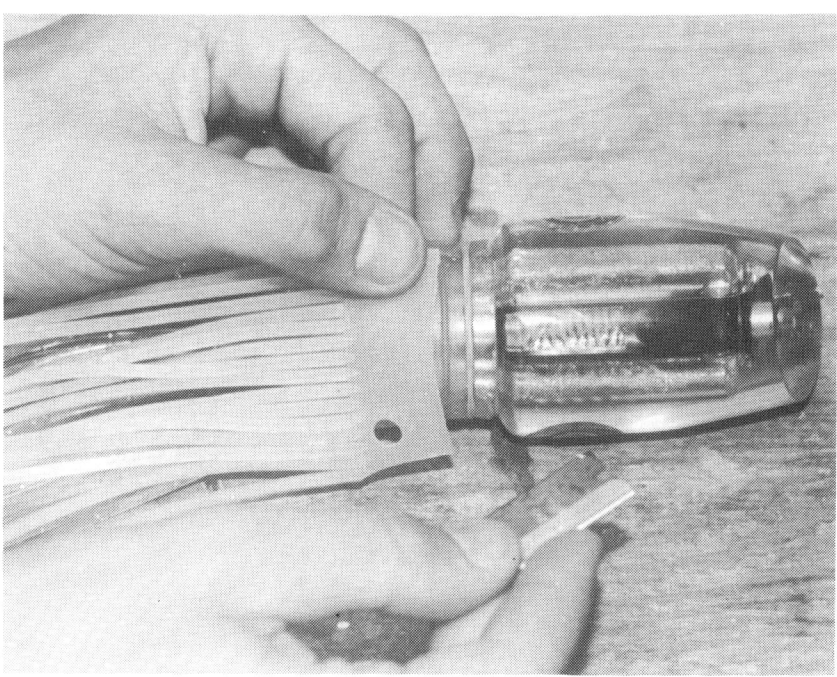

5. On a large lure head, there may be a gap at the belly of the lure. Cut a small piece of skirt to fit and wrap in place.

6. Add a second layer of skirts, usually a darker contrasting color, in the same manner as the under skirt.

FISHING FOR TUNA AND MARLIN

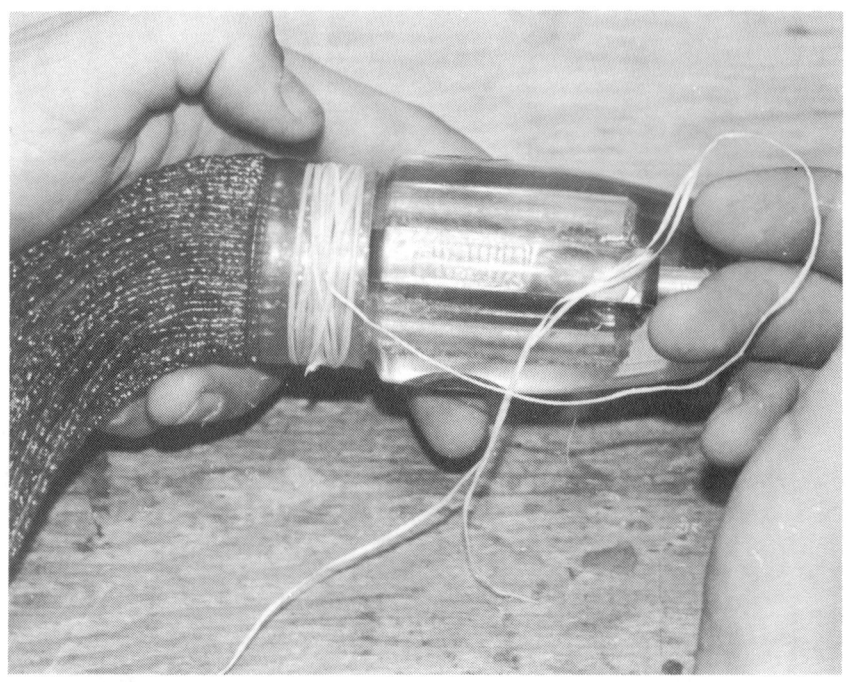

7. Make several more tight wraps with the floss to secure the skirts and lock in place with half hitches.

8. Wrap prism tape or colored plastic tape around the skirts and floss to add color, attraction and to protect the floss from becoming unraveled.

OFFSHORE TROLLING LURES

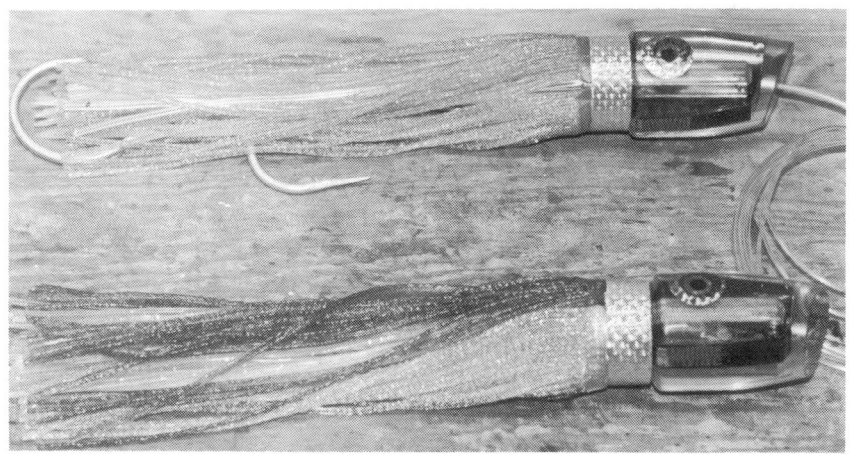

9. A pair of finished lures; the top one tied and rigged by Ed Murray.

Slip-on Skirts

Most every offshore tackle shop worth its salt has a wide variety of slip-on skirts available. They can be used to re-rig old damaged lures or to make new creative lures with special head designs, colors or skirt lengths.

To build a lure with slip-on skirts, you'll need: two skirts (usually a light under skirt and a dark over skirt, dental floss or Gudebrod Waxed Rigging Floss, silicone spray or liquid soap and scissors.

1. What you need: lure head, floss, two skirts, silicone spray, scissors.

FISHING FOR TUNA AND MARLIN

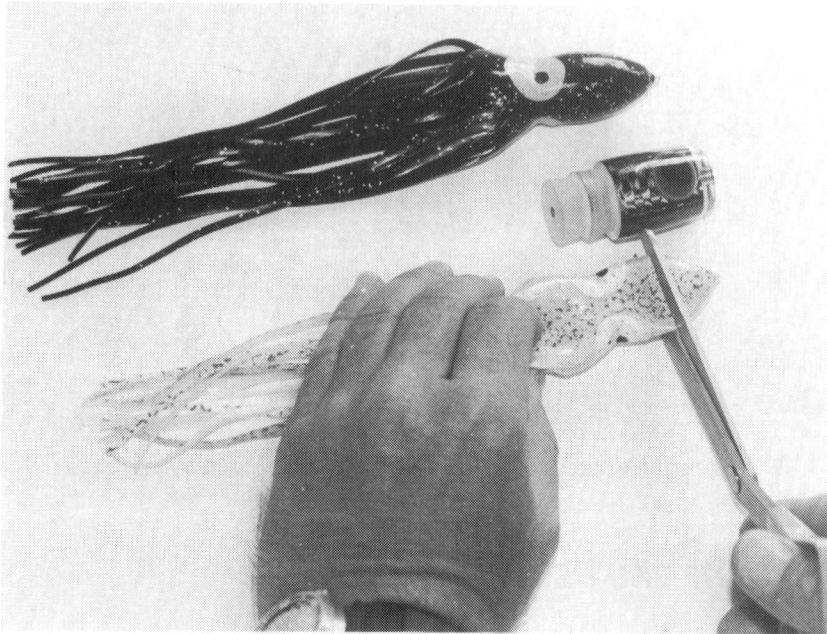

2. Lay skirts next to lure head, trim off excess forward part of the skirt. Opening of the skirt should be slightly smaller than the diameter of the back of the head shape.

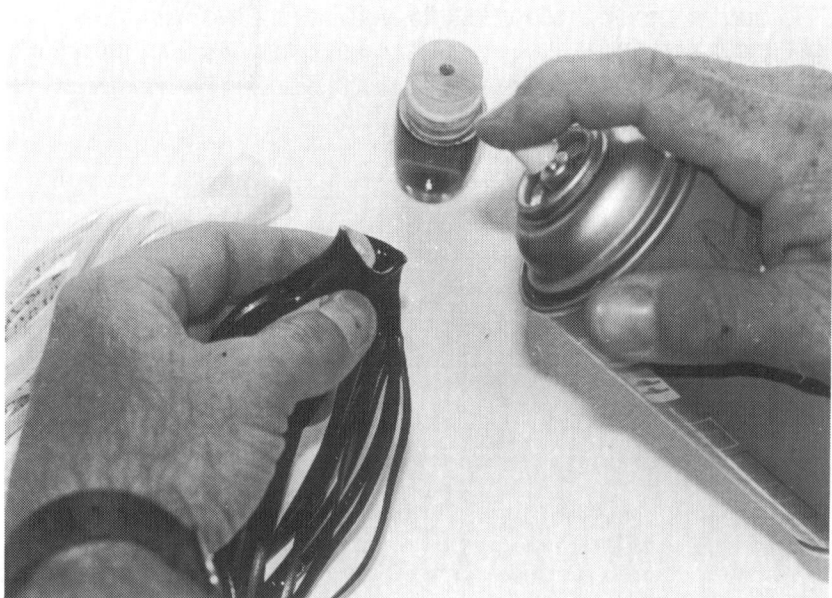

3. Turn both skirts inside out. Spray the under skirt with silicone, then spray the lure head.

OFFSHORE TROLLING LURES

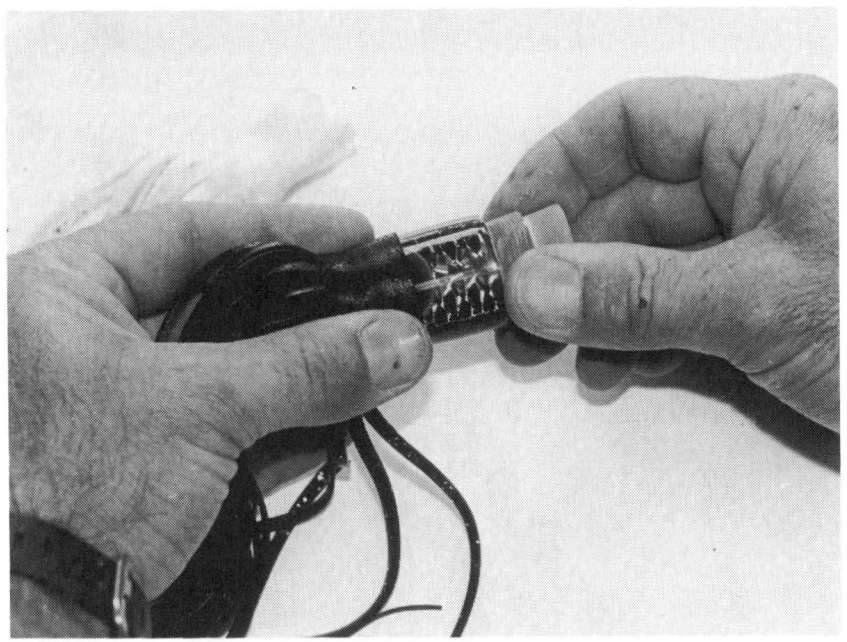

4. Slide the under skirt over the front of the lure head until the skirt stops at the rear of the lure head.

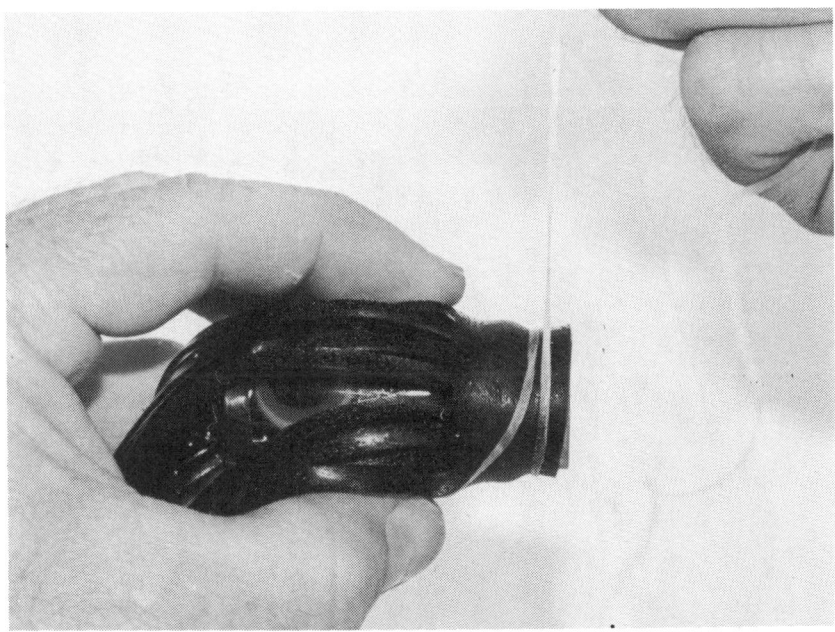

5. Use about 2 feet of doubled over floss, make several wraps, then secure with several half hitches.

FISHING FOR TUNA AND MARLIN

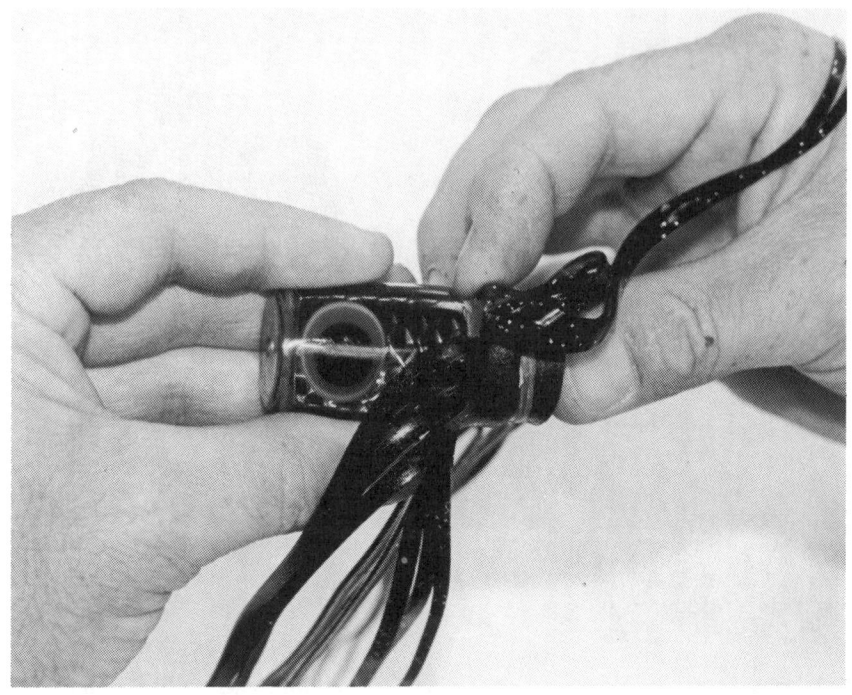

6. Roll the skirt back so it is right side out and positioned correctly.

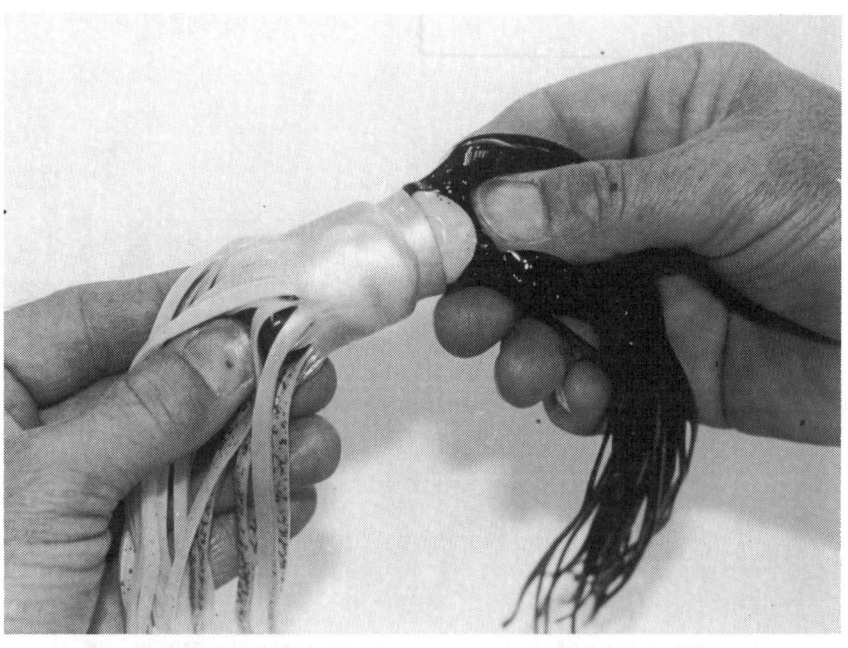

7. Install the outer skirt in the same manner as the under skirt.

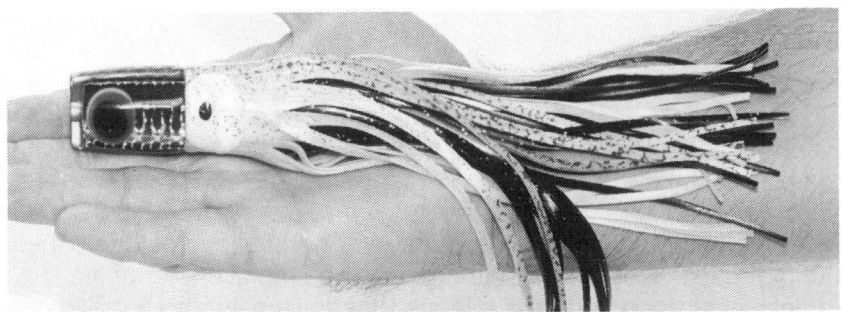

8. The finished lure ready for rigging with hooks.

Leaders

Lures are fished with mono leaders; wire is rarely used. I use 125-pound test mono for white marlin and inshore tuna, 200-pound test for yellowfin and longfin, 300-pound test when blue marlin and bigeye are expected. My lure boxes are organized so lures of the same pound-test leader are all stored together. Most of my lures are rigged on 200-pound mono. A handy way to keep track of the size of the leader is to use different colored leaders for different pound tests. For instance, I use smoke gray for 125-pound test, green tint for the 200-pound leaders and clear for the heaviest leaders. I can always tell at a glance what strength leader a lure is rigged with. Most manufacturers offer several color tints of mono, or you may have to use more than one brand name to get enough different leader colors.

Manufacturers like Ande, Maxima, Hi-Seas, Jinkai and Triple Fish package leader mono on handy spools of 50 to 100 yards of line. These relatively small spools store easily in tackle lockers, cabinets or tackle boxes and are ready for instant use. Some fishermen prefer to purchase their mono leaders on large bulk coils and this does save a bit of money. However, my experience with bulk coils has too frequently resulted in tangled coils that cause more problems than the small amount of money they save.

Tradition says leaders should be 15 to 25-feet long, but practicality says that long leaders must be handlined to the boat before the fish can be gaffed. Shorter leaders of 8 to 12 feet, especially for small boat trollers and tuna fishermen, lose no fish attracting ability and allow the fish to be reeled by the angler much closer to the boat. When playing a fish, the angler lifts the rod tip as the snap swivel reaches the tip. The tuna will be within gaffing reach, usually without need for a leader man, a great asset when you have three or four fish on at once and no one free to handle the gaff.

Crimps

Leaders must have a fast, reliable, strong method to have hooks attached and attachment loops formed. This is usually done with crimps like the Hi-Seas, Sevenstrand, Nico-Press or Jinkai sleeves. Most manufacturers make a wide section of sizes and list the size of the crimp in the box they are sold in. As a general rule of thumb, use a crimp that is .1 or .2 millimeters larger than the diameter of the line. For instance, Ande 200-pound leader has a diameter of 1.3 millimeter so I use a Hi-Seas or Jinkai 1.4mm crimp.

There are two styles of crimps, the oval shaped aluminum and the formed copper. Both can be used for crimping two sections of line, as when forming an offshore loop or a simple loop to add a hook. There are also round crimps that are used as stoppers when making daisy chains or to position a hook under the skirt where the leader enters the back of the lure head. I've been using the Hi-Seas and Jinkai double crimps for years and swear by them. The Sevenstrand crimps are another good choice, especially the single style crimp.

The crimping tool is critical to a strong connection. The best of tools will swage a nice neat crimp with equal pressure being applied to the entire crimp. The inexpensive crimping tools that look like a jagged edged pair of cutting pliers actually crush the mono, deform it and may cause the leader to be weakened at the point where the crimp

Crimps come in several sizes and styles. Good swaging tools are worth the extra cost, so is a top quality mono cutter. Thimbles add protection to loops formed with crimps.

is installed. Be sure to match the crimping tool to the style of crimp being used. Both Hi-Seas and Jinkai market two distinctly different crimps, the formed copper and the oval aluminum, and each uses a different crimping tool for maximum preservation of the strength of the leader.

Hooks

There are several good offshore hooks to use when rigging lures. My favorite hooks are the VMC 9229PS Southern Tuna hooks in 6/0 to 10/0 for most yellowfin, albacore and bluefin lures. The same hook is 12/0 to 14/0 is excellent for giant bluefin and blue marlin. Other good hooks include the Mustad 7734 and 7731. Both hooks come in brazed eye for mono leaders, or needle eye for wire leaders. Eagle Claw makes the Titan Ocean style in similar sizes and the 254 for rigging small lures with single hooks, like feathers and short nylons.

I listened to a marlin captain from Louisiana giving a talk at a sport show in Virginia Beach who said, "I use the biggest damn hook I can find. Marlin don't care, if they want the lure they'll eat it. You better have a strong hook to hold him." He had caught more blue marlin than I may catch in my entire lifetime so he may be right, yet I've met other captains like Sal Sorace of Sir-Ace Lures who says, "Hide the hook so the fish can't see it. Lay that hook right under the skirt so he doesn't know anything is wrong until it's too late and he's got the hook stuck in his jaw."

I rig all my lures with hooks that just about match the width of the lure's skirt. If the bend of the hook is wider than the skirt, I drop down one size hook.

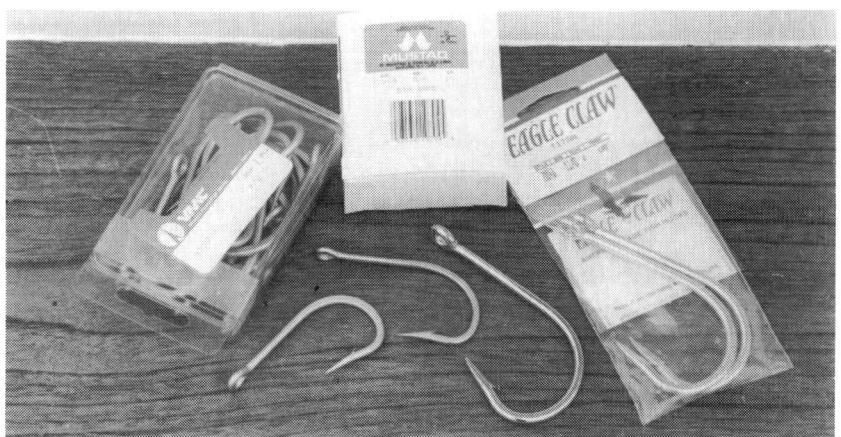

VMC, Mustad and Eagle Claw offer many styles of offshore hooks for rigging lures.

Double Snell Rig

For many years offshore lure manufacturers sold their lures rigged with a single hook at the tail end of the skirt. Careful observation from tuna towers, however, by many captains indicates that most times tuna hit a lure from the side, perhaps coming up alongside the lure to scan it then turning suddenly to blast it at the head end of the lure. A lot of fish can be missed at the strike if a second hook is not positioned up near the head of the lure.

Frank Johnson of Mold Craft showed me the double snell rig, nicknamed the "pro rig" by Gulf Coast trollers off Florida, Mississippi and Louisiana. The rig is simple and can be tied without need of crimps and hardware.

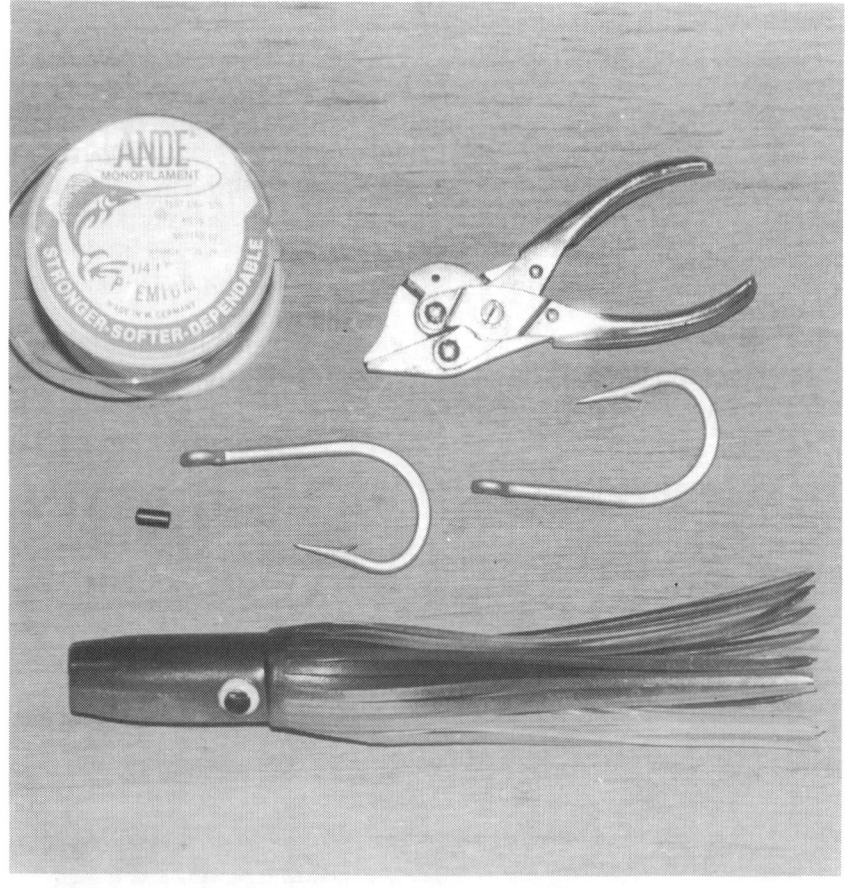

1. **What you need: Mono line for leader, two hooks, crimp or egg sinker, pliers and lure.**

OFFSHORE TROLLING LURES

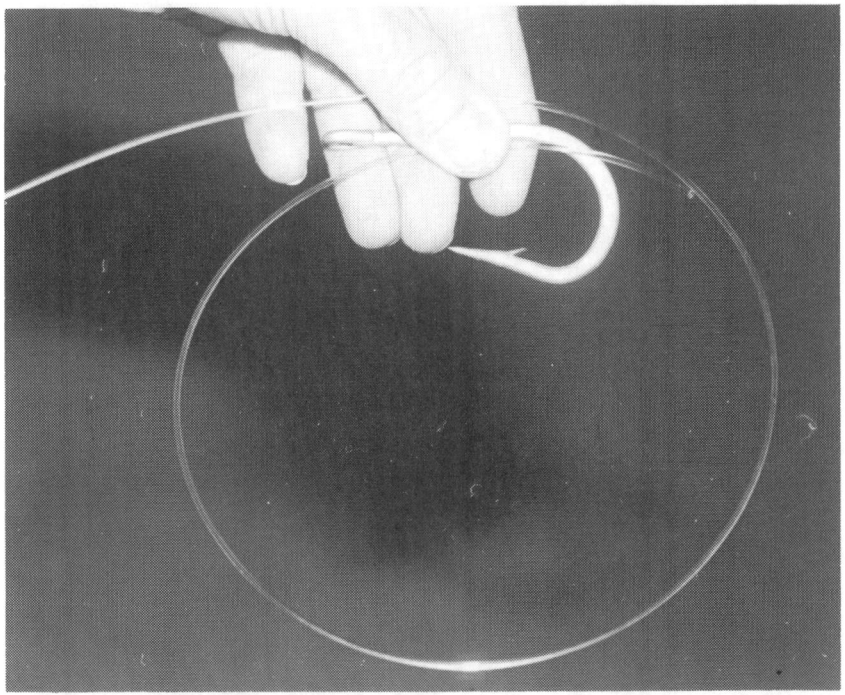

2. Form a loop below the hook, tag end of the leader at the hook bend.

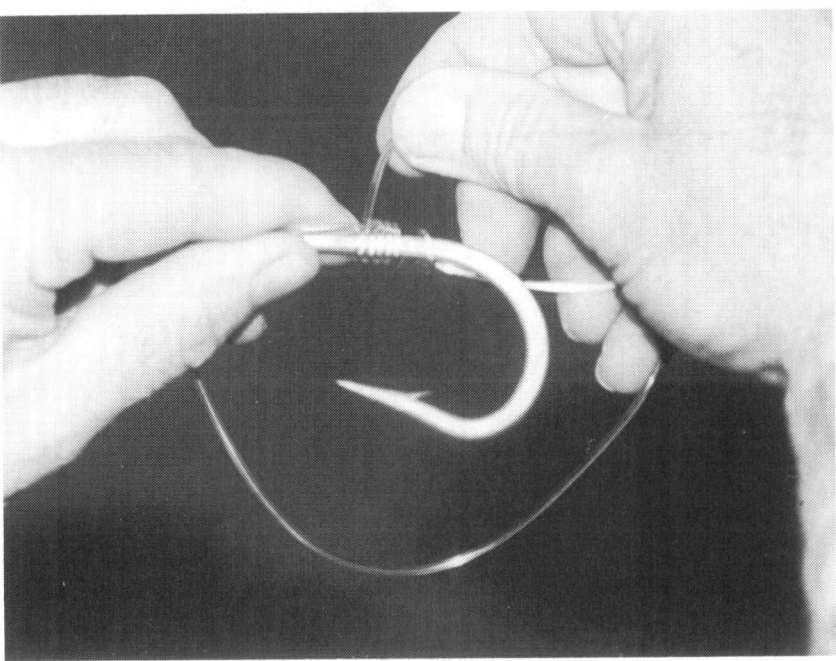

3. Wrap the right leg of the loop in tight coils towards the hook eye.

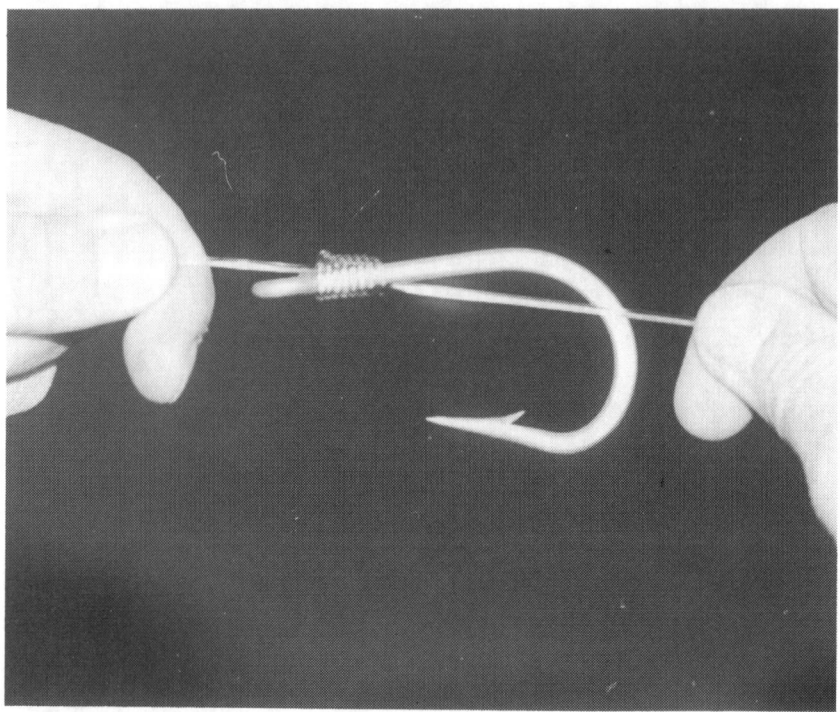

4. Pull the tag end to draw coils tight.

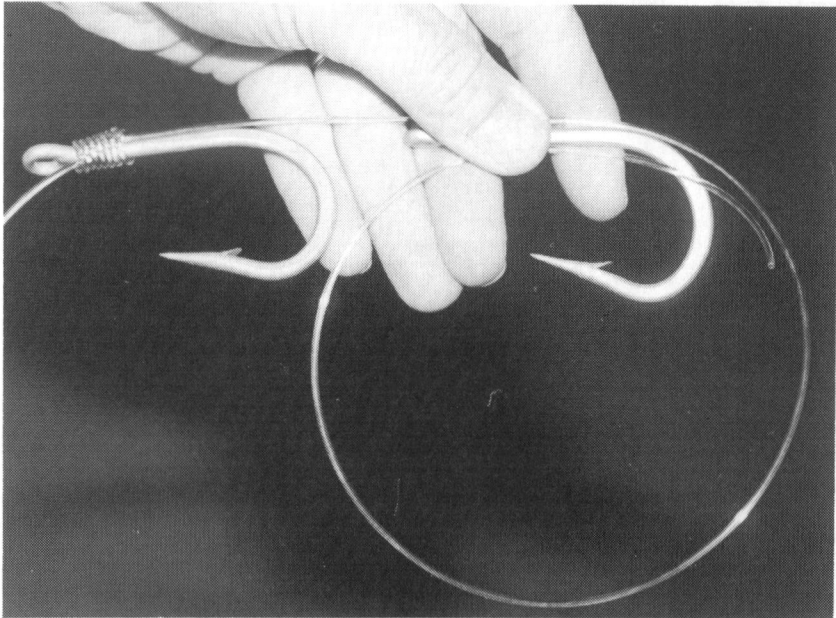

5. Form a loop with the remaining tag end, wrap the right leg towards the hook eye and pull tight. Clip off the tag end.

OFFSHORE TROLLING LURES

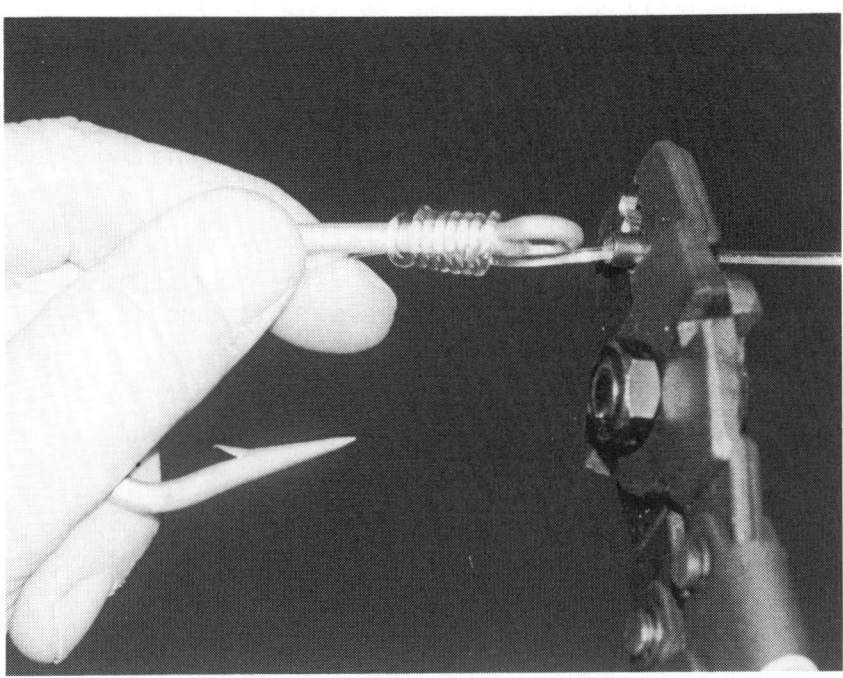

6. Add a single crimp or a 1/4-ounce egg sinker just ahead of the forward hook eye to prevent the hook eye from rubbing on the back of the lure.

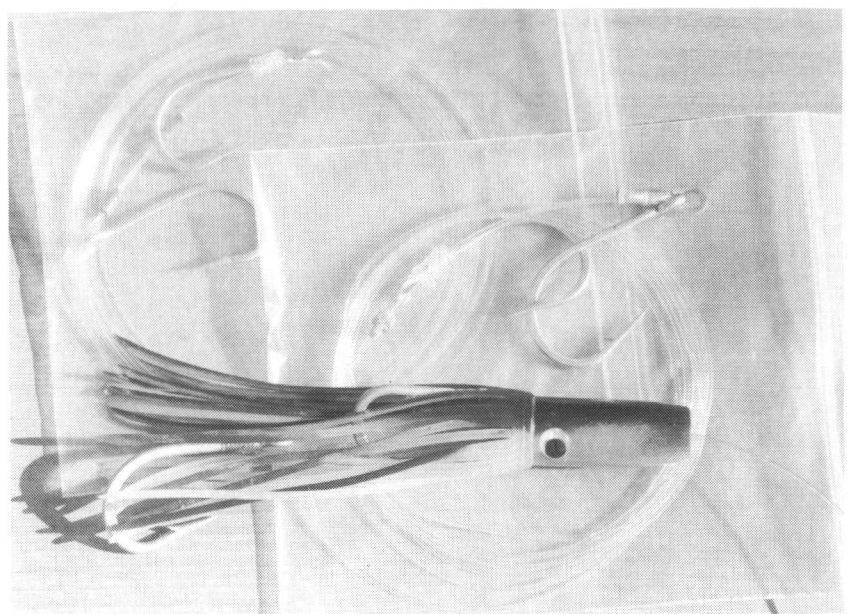

7. The finished lure and some pre-rigged leaders in ziplock bags. Tail hook can also be crimped in place.

Crimp Rig

The majority of offshore trollers use the crimping system to rig their lures. It is more complicated than snelling but it is strong and allows easy variation of the rig to match the hook position to lures with various different skirt lengths.

I position my hooks so the points are 180 degrees from one another since I feel this is best for tuna, but many marlin fishermen position the hooks so they are positioned at 90 degrees from one another.

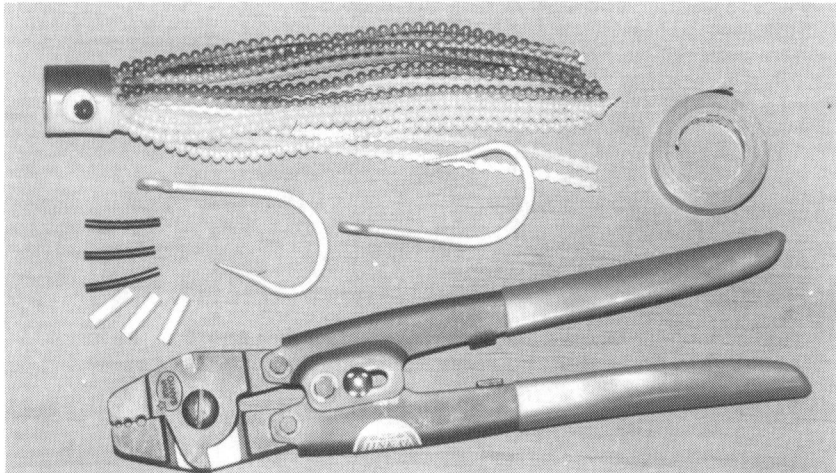

1. What you need: Lure, hooks, chafing tubes, crimps, plastic tape and crimping tool.

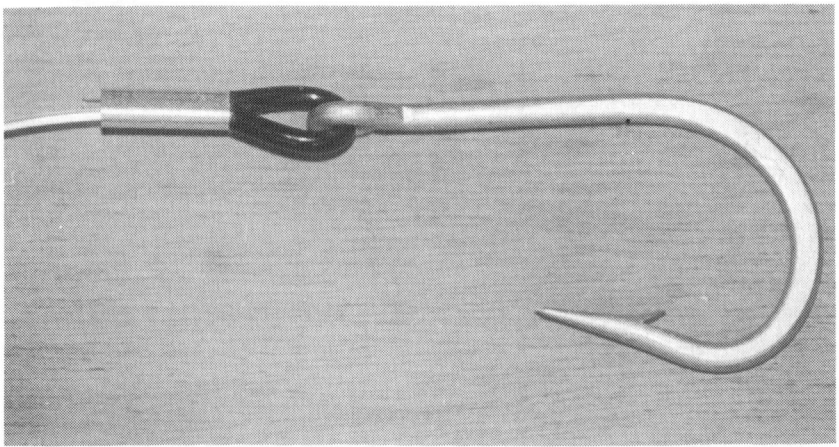

2. Slide crimp and chafe tube onto leader, push leader through hook eye, bend tag end to form a loop around eye and push tag end back through the crimp.

OFFSHORE TROLLING LURES

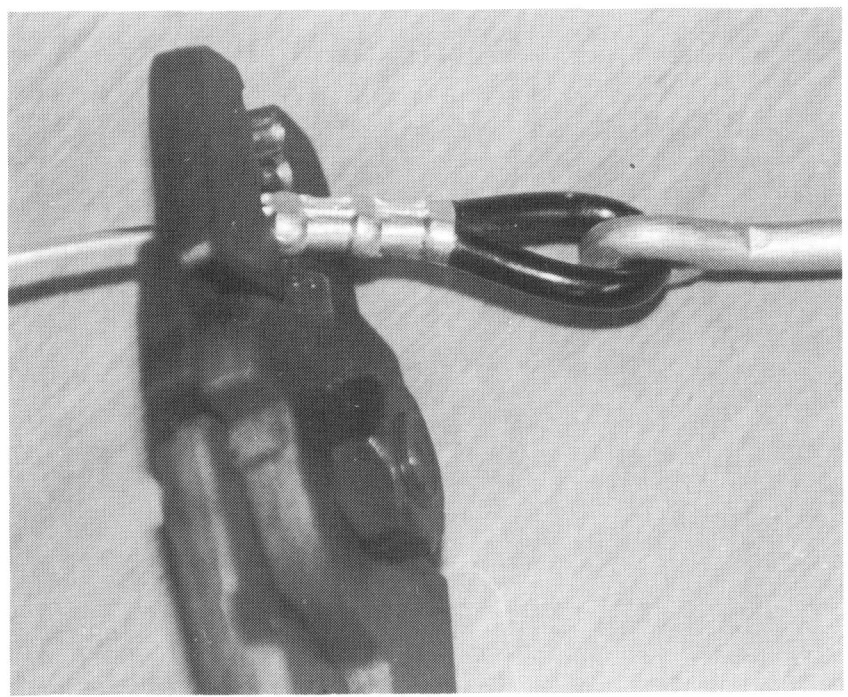

3. Use crimping tool to swage crimp in place.

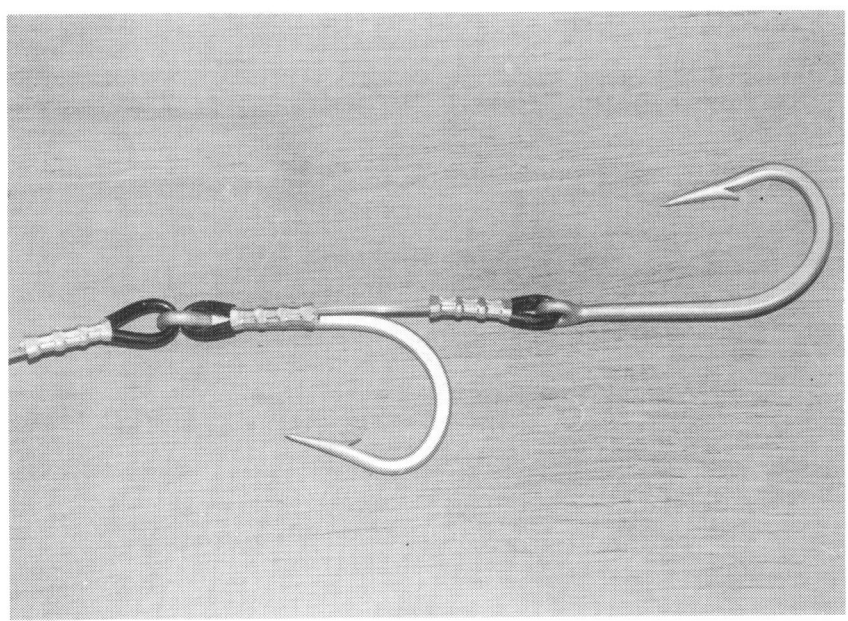

4. Add tail hook on a short length of leader. Crimp in place with chafe tubes at hook eyes in the same manner as above.

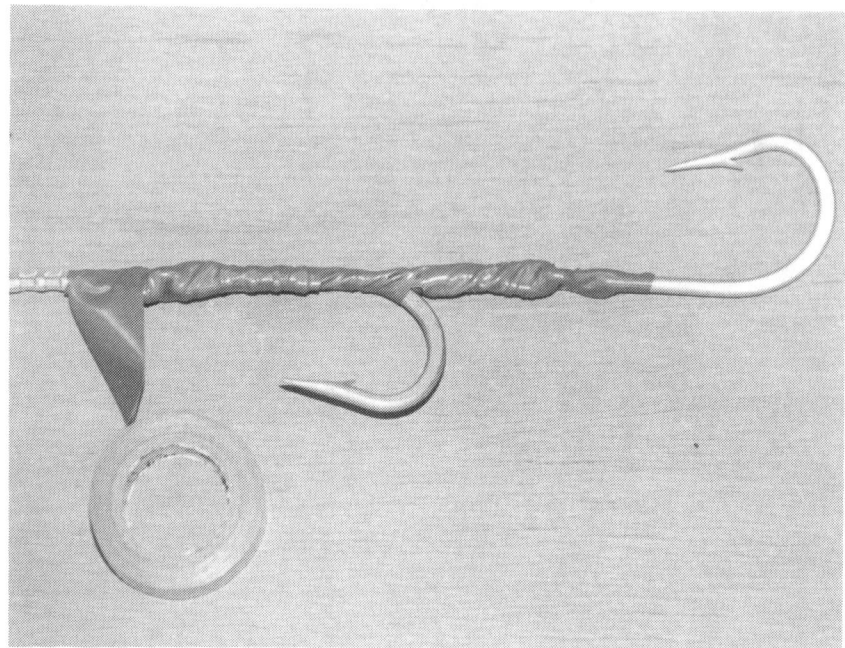

5. Starting at tail hook, tightly wrap plastic tape toward crimp at front hook, then wrap back towards hook bend. Tape stiffens rig so hooks ride perfectly.

6. Finished lure. Note hooks are about same width as skirt, positioned at 180 degrees.

OFFSHORE TROLLING LURES

Double Hook Wire Rig

My son, Rich, showed me a rig he learned while mating on a blue marlin boat in the Bahamas and Virgin Islands. The rig is made with #12 to #19 single strand wire. Once wrapped to the hooks, this double hook rig is super strong and will withstand the punishment of fish in excess of 1000 pounds.

It has the added advantage that once the hooks are positioned at 90 or 180 degrees, they will not vary from that position so a positive hook-up is assured. Captains who use this rig say they get a hook-up to strike ratio that frequently exceeds 50%. Another added advantage is that the wire is somewhat flexible and can withstand some bending when a marlin does its aerial tricks. We lost a nice blue marlin once when using a rig stiffened with a stainless rod. This wire rig is better.

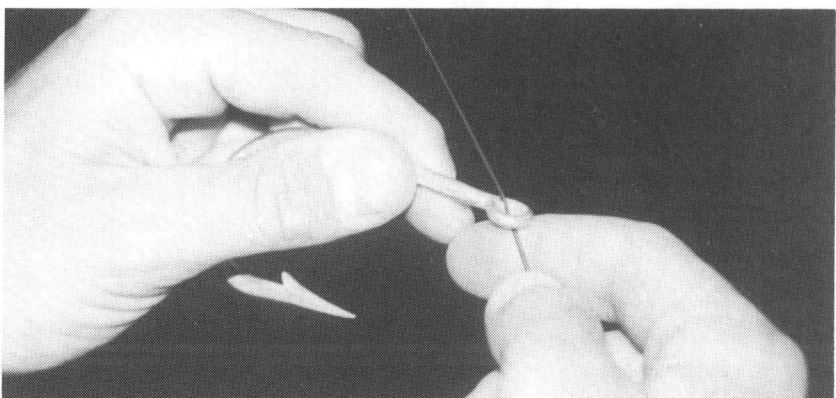

1. With the bend of the hook in the palm of the left hand, push half of a 4-foot length of wire through the hook eye.

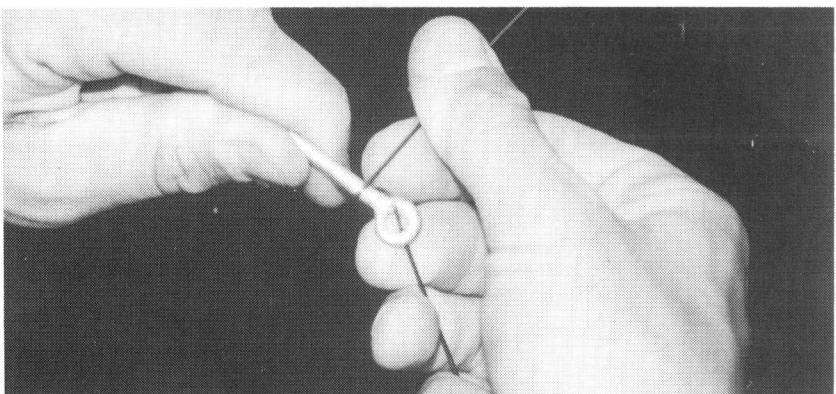

2. Bend the wire over the eye, then under and around the shank to start the first barrel wrap.

FISHING FOR TUNA AND MARLIN

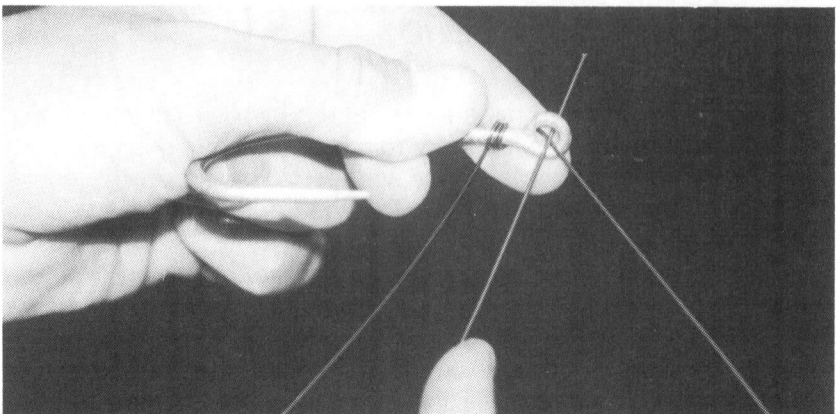

3. Make 3 to 5 barrel wraps, then push the tag end up through the hook eye, opposite the first leg of wire.

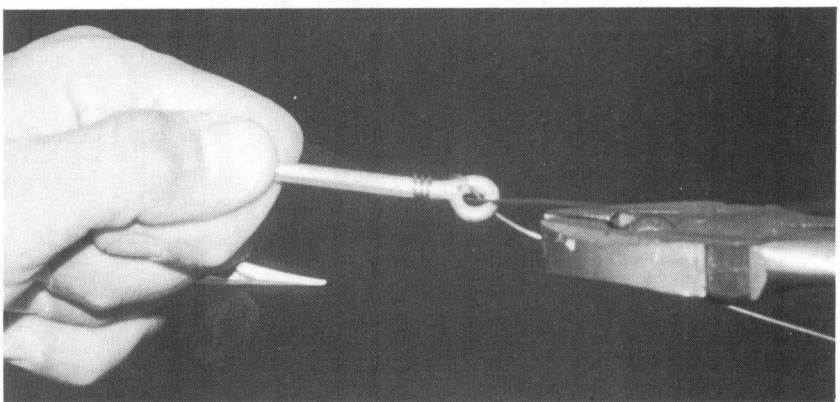

4. Use pliers to firmly pull each leg of wire tight against the hook eye so there is no slack.

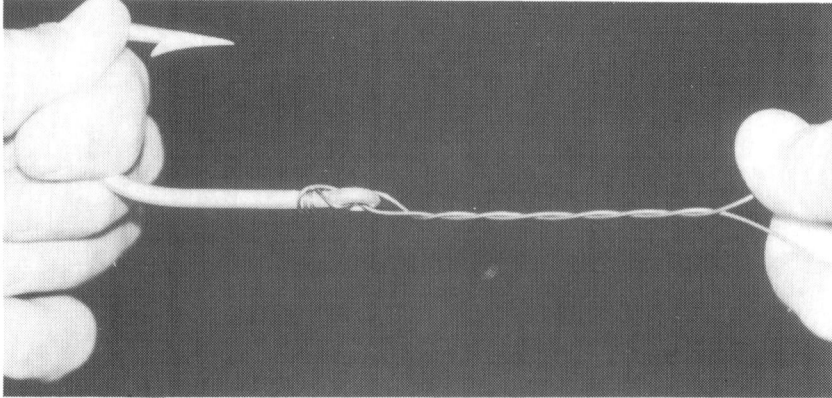

5. Haywire the two legs together for a length of approximately 2 to 4 inches.

OFFSHORE TROLLING LURES

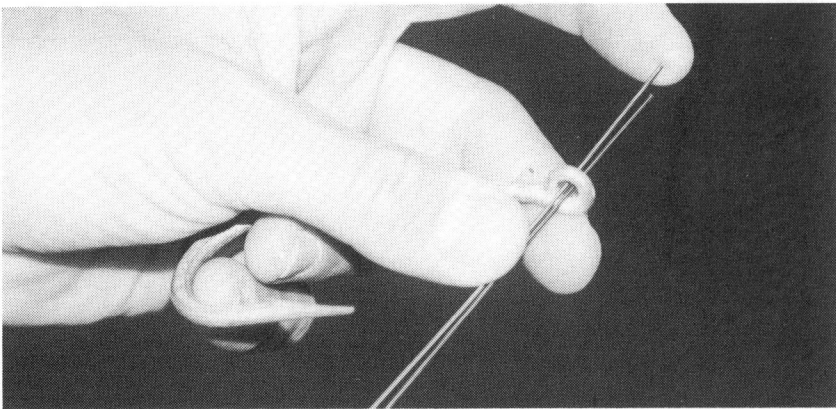

6. Place the second hook in the left hand and push the doubled wire through the eye of this hook.

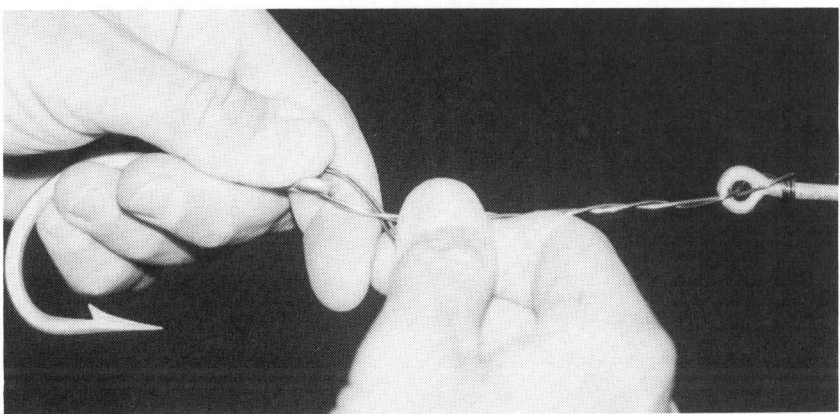

7. Bend the wire back and haywire it down towards the eye of the first hook.

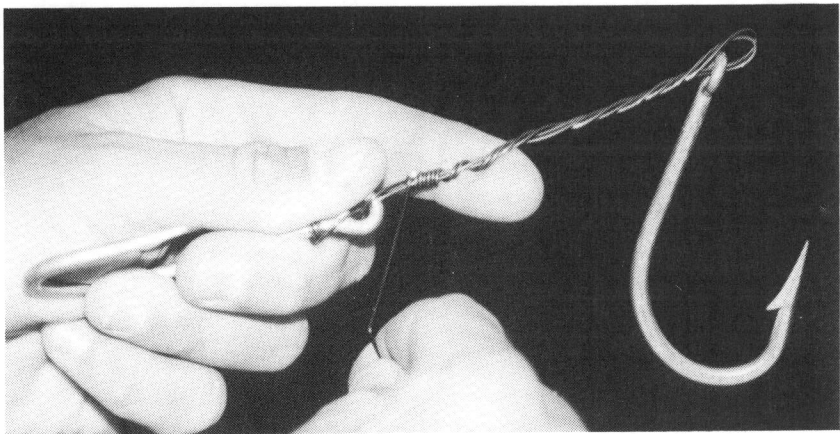

8. Finish the haywire with several tight barrel rolls.

FISHING FOR TUNA AND MARLIN

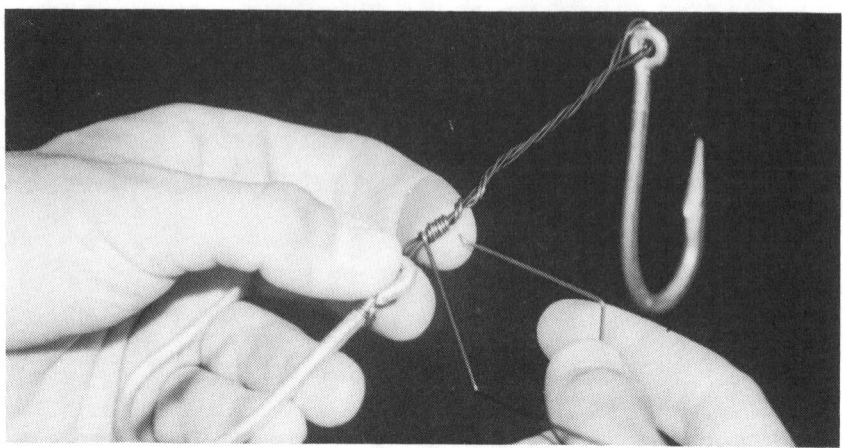
9. With a 90 degree bend in leg, cleanly break off the tag ends.

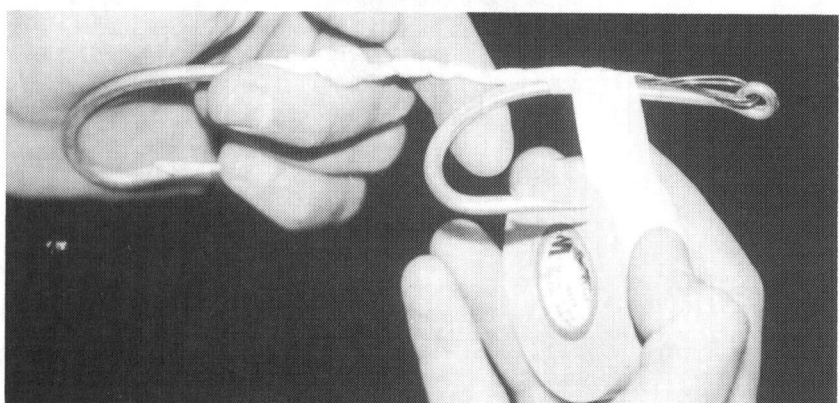
10. Adjust the wire so the hooks lay at 90 or 180 degrees, then wrap with plastic tape.

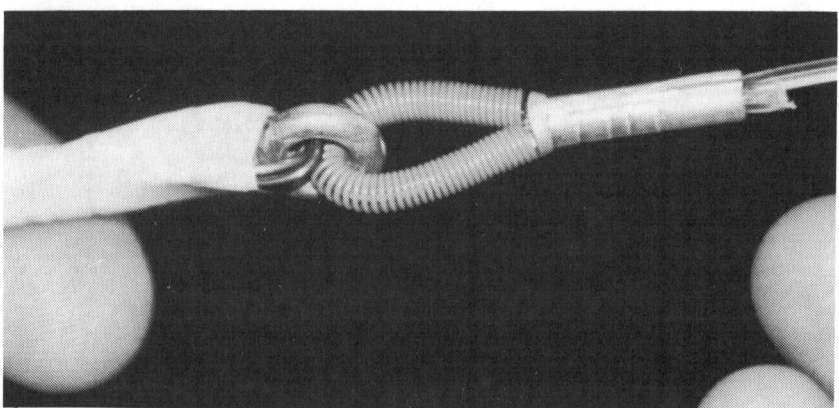
11. Attach the forward hook to 400 or 500-pound mono leader using chafing gear and a crimp.

OFFSHORE TROLLING LURES

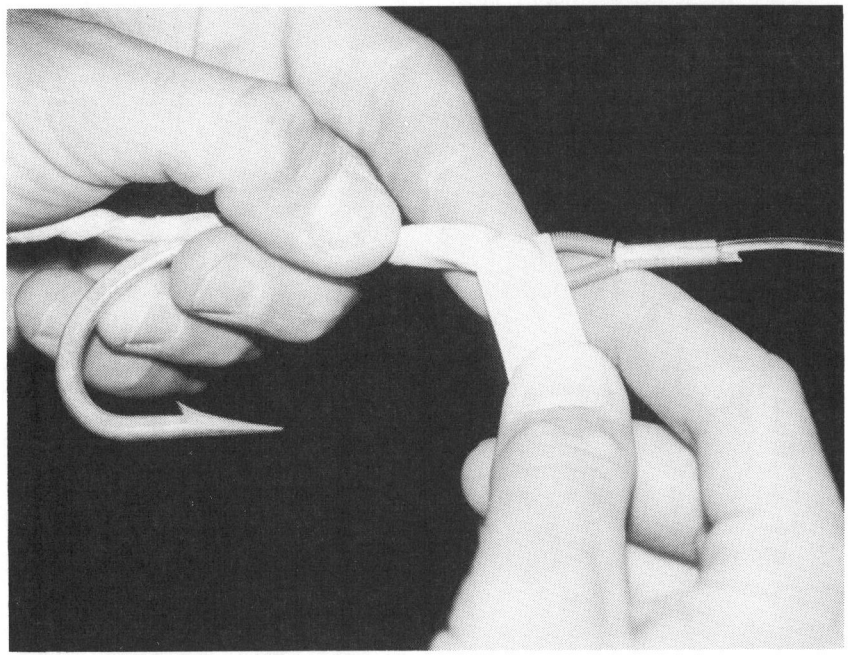

12. Plastic tape wrapped over the mono leader loop and forward hook eye add more stiffness to the rig.

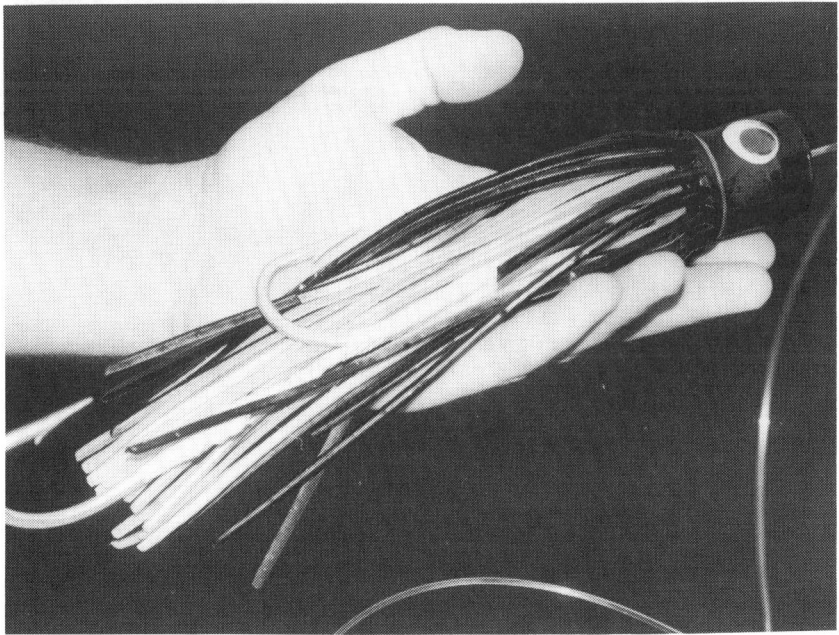

13. The completed lure ready for action with blue marlin.

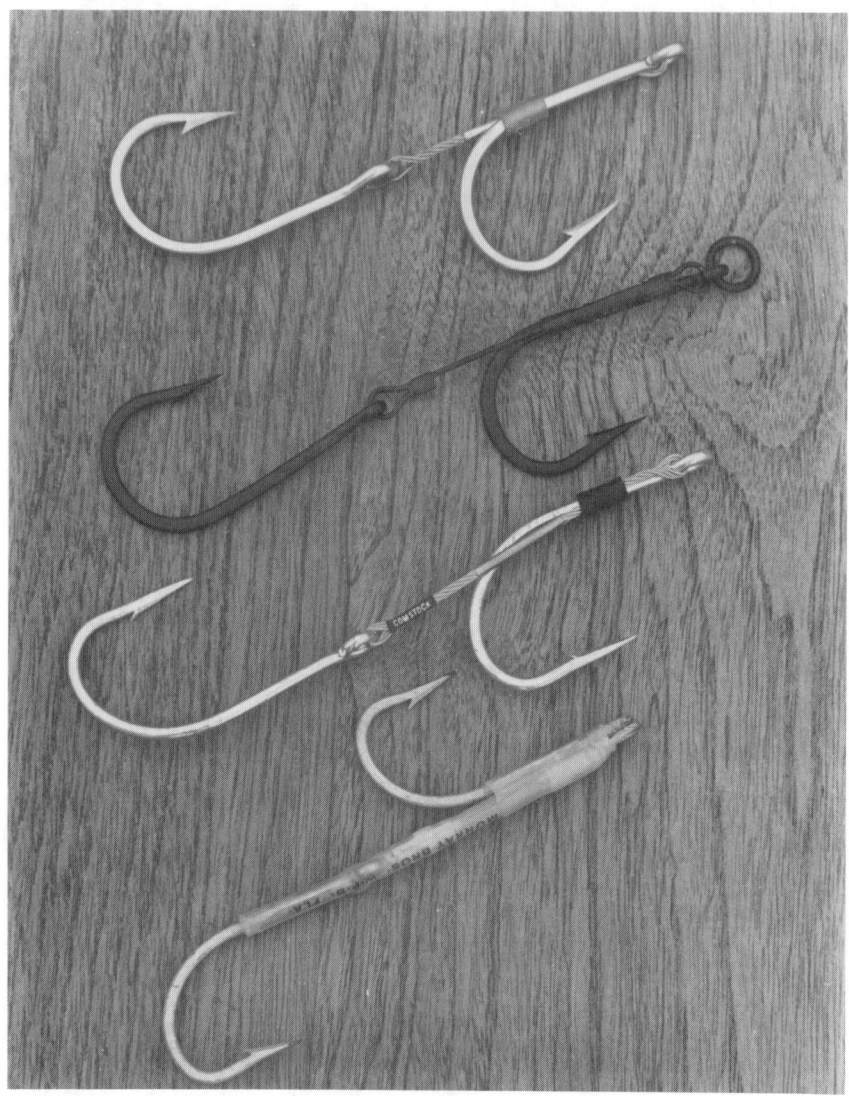

Pre-rigged double-hook rigs are available from tackle manufacturers like Eagle Claw's Comstock Rig, Area Rule and Murray Brothers in various hook sizes and configurations.

Single Hook Marlin Rig

There's always more than one way to skin a cat, and more than one way to rig a lure for giant blue marlin. A popular rig used in St. Thomas, developed by the well-known Captain Red Bailey, uses soft lures, a short length of cable, 400-pound test mono leader and a single 12/0 hook. The effectiveness of this rig has been proven many

OFFSHORE TROLLING LURES

times over and its use is spreading to the Florida Coast and Central America.

This rig is especially effective with soft lures and can be fished much like a natural bait. The reel is fished with a light drag. At the strike, the lure is momentarily dropped back to the fish. As the fish begins to run with the lure, the lever drag is shoved to the Strike position and the fish is struck.

SINGLE HOOK RIG

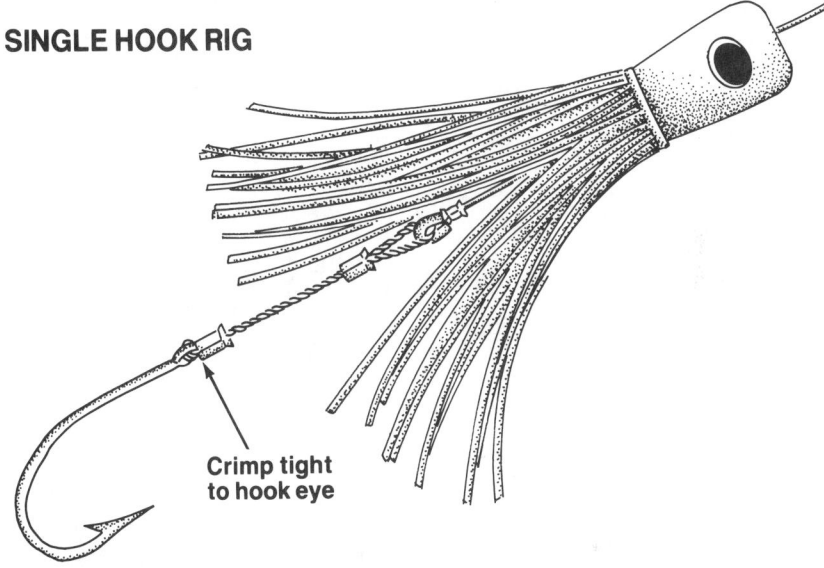

Crimp tight to hook eye

1 - Cut a 12-inch length of Sevenstrand 1 X 7 cable and crimp a 12/0 hook to one end. Jam the cable as tight as possible against the eye of the hook to help stiffen the rig.

2 - Run a 20 to 25-foot length of 400-pound leader through the nose of a Mold Craft Soft Head Chugger, add a small plastic bead to the leader then crimp a stainless thimble at the end to form a loop.

3 - Pass the end of the cable through the thimble at the end of the mono, then form a loop and crimp in place to attach the hook and cable to the mono leader.

The End Loop

The end of the leader needs a loop for attachment to the snap swivel at the end of the fishing line. There are three ways to accomplish this. The simplest uses a crimp and chafing tube, or thimble, for a small, neat loop that wears very well. Also popular is the offshore loop knot, secured by a crimp.

Both systems offer the advantage of adding protection to the leader where it rides in the snap swivel. A single loop of mono, unprotected by a thimble, chafing tube or doubled line could become so worn that it might fail while fighting a fish.

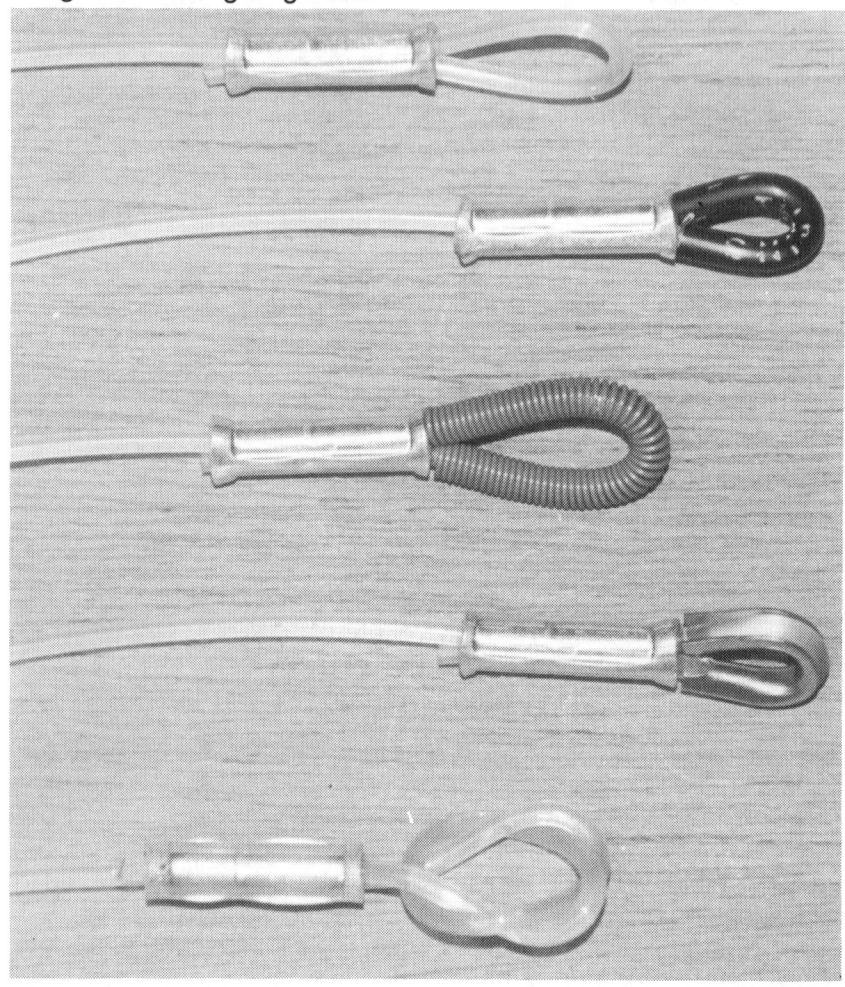

Various popular loops; (top to bottom) single mono loop, tubular chafing gear, coil chafing gear, stainless thimble chafing gear, offshore loop knot.

Daisy Chains

Making a chain is easy. Start with a 12 to 15-foot leader and attach a hook at the bottom end with either a snell or a crimped offshore loop. Stoppers are needed along the leader to hold the lures or squids in place. Use a small egg sinker crimped to the leader with pliers or an aluminum or brass barrel crimp. Crimps come in two styles; the single crimp with one rounded hole and the double crimp with two holes looking much like a side by side shotgun barrel. The single

OFFSHORE TROLLING LURES

crimps work best as stoppers, the double crimps are usually used to crimp two lines together after making an offshore end loop. We'll use double crimps for another variation of the daisy chain rigging in a few moments.

The choice of stopper depends on the lure itself. Lures with solid, hard plastic heads are stoppered with either crimps or egg sinkers. Soft bodied lures, like artificial squids, are best stopped with egg sinkers since the sinkers won't tear through the bodies like a small crimp might do.

After attaching the hook, slide the first sinker onto the leader then the first lure. Get the lure in position so the hook rides at the end of the lure. Crimp the egg sinker in place with pliers, applying only enough crimping pressure to grip the leader without crushing, chafing or pinching the leader excessively.

Slide the next egg sinker and lure onto the leader and crimp in place about 12 to 18 inches ahead of the bottom lure. Continue until you have several lures on the leader. The crimp always goes on the leader first, then the lure.

Use a crimped offshore loop or offshore loop/surgeons knot combo to add a loop that will attach the daisy chain to the snap at the end of the fishing line. The daisy chain is now complete.

This simple chain is effective with both squids and artificial lures but does inhibit the action of squids somewhat. To add more action to squids I use a leader system that uses one long main leader and then adds several short leaders at even intervals along its length.

Again start with a 15-foot leader and attach the hook at the bottom end. Slide the first, or bottom, squid into position just as described above, directly onto the main leader so it covers the hook.

DAISY CHAIN

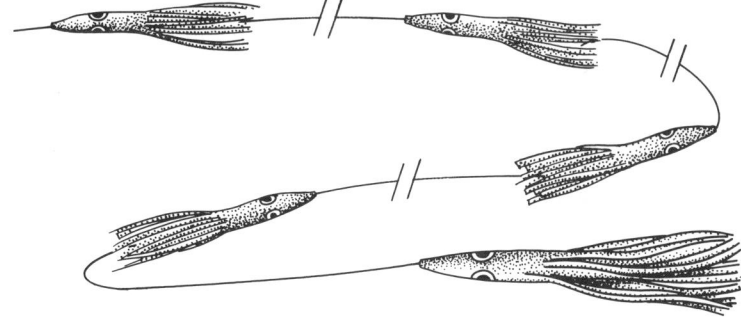

Double-hook rig the last lure on mono leader. Smaller lures are rigged about 18 inches apart, with a single barrel crimp or a small egg sinker crimped in place.

143

Cut several 6 to 12-inch lengths of leader monofilament of the same pound test as the main leader. Slide a double crimp down the leader to a position approximately 18 inches above the bottom squid. Insert one of the short leaders into the other open slot of the double crimp and crimp the short leader to the main leader.

Slide the squid into position on the short leader, followed by an egg sinker and a barrel crimp. Crimp the barrel crimp to the end of the short leader. The squid can now slide down the short leader and into place. The short leader allows the squid much more freedom of movement when trolling.

Complete the chain by attaching the remaining short leaders at regularly spaced intervals along the main leader. Add a loop at the top end of the leader and the daisy chain is all done.

Unlike single lures that run just below the surface and stream plumes of bubbles, squid daisy chains splatter and skip across the surface in the trolling pattern. To make them work effectively you may have to drop the trolling speed slightly. Too fast a speed makes the squid daisy chain jump too much and can actually cause the squids to tear apart from excessive water pressure. Multiple lures rigged on a daisy chain usually require no adjustment to your regular trolling speed.

Daisy chains are one of the most productive lures in my offshore lure box and I rarely put out a spread of lures that does not include at least one multiple lure chain. They have been so productive I just can't fish without them.

Spreader Bar Rigs

Spreader bar rigs are the next generation of daisy chains. They had their beginnings in New England where bluefin hunters rigged daisy chains of squids for these monster fish. It was a natural extension of the multiple bait idea to add a cross bar and double the number of squid or mackerel that could be trolled.

Despite their New England heritage, they do catch fish along other parts of the coast and I know fishermen who have taken bigeye tuna at the Baltimore Canyon, blue marlin at Montauk, yellowfin off Hatteras and sailfish off Stuart and Palm Beach.

The basic spreader bar rig uses a center leader of about 15 feet in length. A cross bar of 3 to 4 feet in width is added about two-thirds the way up the center leader. The center leader can be made of single strand wire, cable or heavy mono. The bar has several loops or swivels spot welded, crimped or holes drilled in place, again depending on the manufacturer, to make it easy to attach the bar to the leader. The center leader is attached to the bar with a crimp and thimble

OFFSHORE TROLLING LURES

much like rigging a lure. The squid on the center leader are kept in place with crimps, the squid on the spreader bar are held in place with short leaders run off the spreader arm, crimped in place. While each manufacturer's rigging may vary, this is the basic rig.

The size of the squid can be varied to suit the species. Murray Brothers use small 6-inch squids for yellowfin tuna, larger 12-inch squids for bigeye and very large 16-inch squids for giant tuna. I've had yellowfin try to eat the big squids while trolling near the Bacardi Wreck for bluefin but I've had more consistent success with the smaller squids for tuna of 40 to 100 pounds.

Color can be varied by rigging different colored squids on the rigs. Small green or amber squid seem to work best for me on yellowfin, but I like the large squids to be black or amber for bigeye. For giants I use only pearl or amber. There are other colors available such as red, yellow, brown and purple. For yellowfin, a rig made by The Reel Seat uses wild colored squids. The rig is nicknamed the Grateful Dead because of the blend of reds, purples, greens and blues that color the squids.

The usual trolling pattern with spreader bars rigged with baits calls for three rigs to be trolled with the rods at the transom, the rigs fished directly off the rod tips. The rigs have a lot of water resistance and are difficult to troll from outriggers as they constantly pull the line from the rigger clips. The center rig is placed on the second or third wave in the wake, the port side at the third or fourth wave and the starboard spreader at the fourth or sixth wave. None are fished off flat line clips.

Artificial squids on spreader bars catch giant bluefin, bigeye and blue marlin. Spreader bars can also be used as teasers to lure in marlin and sailfish.

Ideal trolling speed is about two to three knots depending on the rig, the size of the squid and the sea conditions. Calm water usually allows a slightly faster trolling speed. Rough water and swells make it tough to fish the bars at anything more than a slow crawl. It is important to keep the squid up on top of the water, not diving below the surface. Adjust the trolling speed so the squid are all splashing on the surface. To a tuna this must look like a school of baitfish trying to beat feet away from the tuna, a natural reaction for baitfish. Hopefully the tuna will respond with a natural reaction of a quick chase and a solid hook-up.

Light weight spreader bar rigs marketed by Murray Brothers, Mold Craft and The Reel Seat use thin-walled artificial squids that can be trolled at 5 to 8 knots. I've used them off the Jersey Coast and also off North Carolina for some excellent catches of yellowfin and bigeye. One of these light spreader bars is usually in our pattern at all times, even when trolling with baits, and the light weight bars can be trolled at speeds up to 8 knots.

The light weight spreader bars are gaining popularity as teasers when pulling swimming mullet or ballyhoo for sailfish or white marlin.

Spoon Fed Tuna

Fishing for tuna can be exasperating. Sometimes they bite like mad dogs, striking at anything you put in the water before you troll a few hundred yards. On other days, you can troll until the paint gets washed off the lures and can't seem to catch a cold. These s-l-o-w days can be saved with two techniques that have been proven for decades. One method is jigging, the other is trolling with planers. Both methods use spoons to do the catching. Captain Robbie Robinson, maker of the Huntington Drone spoon lures in Annapolis, gave me some tips on how to get finicky tuna to bite when using these two methods and they've worked real well for me over the years.

Charter boats from New England to Virginia Beach have been jigging school bluefin tuna for many years, since before the 1940s, but many private boats either don't know how to jig or just don't know that jigging works so well. The technique is expanding to other areas and tuna fishermen off the North Carolina Outer Banks and at northeast canyons are jigging with spoons, not only for bluefin, but for yellowfin tuna and longfin albacore, too.

In the summer, it is not unusual to see schools of yellowfin pushing water, but they won't strike a lure. This can be demoralizing, especially if you can troll near the fish and see them while looking down from a tower or fly bridge.

To ease the lockjaw on these fish, use a size 3½ Drone spoon (or a Crippled Alewife, Hopkins, Acetta or Clark spoon) and troll past the tuna. Get the boat up ahead of the school, so the spoons cross right in front of the school, then jig the spoons hard so they pop out of the water and create a lot of commotion. The flashy, splashing retrieve drives tuna crazy. Keep the boat moving slowly, the anglers jigging the spoons with lots of enthusiasm.

Charter captains often keep the boat turning so the spoons settle just below the surface. If the fish can be seen clearly, it is possible to circle the school and stay close to it at all times, jigging constantly and hooking up tuna in quick succession. New England school bluefin specialists used this method for many years to score some terrific catches of tuna years ago before the clippers destroyed the immense schools of fish. The spoons can be dropped even deeper by adding a 2, 4 or 6-ounce drail several feet ahead of the spoon.

Mono leaders that can be cranked right to the rod tip are best. Add a 10 to 15-foot length of 100-pound mono leader at the end of the fishing line with a double Uni-Knot. For bigger fish, use heavier leaders. Since yellowfin may frequently exceed 125 to 150 pounds, I've been using 150 to 200-pound test Triple Fish or Ande leaders. I use the interlocking loop system we talked about in Chapter Three.

The jigging technique works, and it's a fun way to fish. If you see surface tuna that don't want to eat, take a few minutes to re-rig at least two rods to jig spoons. Work ahead of the school so the spoons cross in front of the fish and you should get some intense fishing opportunities.

Planers also work when trolling with spoons. A size #3 is about the best all round size. A 6/0 to 9/0 reel with a firm drag setting is needed to catch tuna and wahoo.

An old captain's tale says "The slower the fishing, the longer the leader." I usually use a 40 to 60-foot leader of 100 to 150-pound test tied directly to the spoon. A swivel tied halfway up the leader prevents a twisted leader if the spoon spins, and a snap swivel on the planer end makes it easy to change leaders and lures. It seems like a pain in the neck to handline a 60-pound tuna 60 feet, but on some days that's the only way to produce fish.

I've used planers at the Hudson and Wilmington canyons, along the inshore tuna grounds in 30 fathoms of water and have fished with charter captains off Oregon Inlet who used planers. Yes, they can be a pain to handline, but they did catch and that's the bottom line. On some real slow days, the planer can steal one or two fish to save the day and make you a hero when other boats are flying the skunk flag.

The best time to use the planer is when you mark fish on the scope. If several passes over the area don't produce a strike, try removing one lure from the pattern and drop the planer and spoon combo in its place. Sometimes it's just the right medicine.

Swimming Plugs

Ed Murray held out a battered and bashed lure. "Take a look at this," he said. "It's the hottest thing for wahoo right now off Bimini. This one caught over 40 wahoo before the captain gave it back to me." It was obvious from the cuts, gashes and chew marks that the lure had gone through some wild fishing. Like any good fisherman, I bought one of Ed's new lures, called the Exterminator and took it home to see if it would fool yellowfin and bigeye. It did and it opened a new world of tuna fishing.

Most of our lures are trolled on the surface. Swimming plugs such as the Exterminator, the Rapala, Braid Grenade (actually a skirted lure but it swims very deep), the Boone Cairns swimmer and others like them, are able to run deeper in the water column and draw reluctant fish up to strike. I've had several experiences when the Exterminator was hit by the first fish to blast the pattern, then one or more surface lures would get smashed moments later.

I've found them to be most effective fished down the center or in close on flat lines. Fishing with swimming plugs is still a new game with lots of experimenting to be done but these lures do catch fish and deserve a try in your pattern.

Swimming lures can be very effective on yellowfin, bigeye and albacore tuna.

The Bird is the Word

What is a bird? It's part of a Japanese handlining system that has been adapted to sport fishing methods. The basic bird is a 12 to 16-inch long slender bodied chunk of wood, plastic foam or soft plastic with short wings, either molded into the bird or attached with screws or epoxy. A lead weight on the belly helps stabilize the action.

And action the birds have - lots of it! They dance and skip along the surface throwing sheets of spray up to four feet in the air while doing a vibrating dance that seems to drive fish absolutely nuts. It doesn't take much imagination to describe the bird's action as like that of a sea bird taking off, legs and feet slapping and skipping across the water. Only the artificial bird never gets off the water, it just keeps on skipping and dancing all day while you troll.

Birds are attached directly to the main fishing line a leader length ahead of the trolling lure. The appearance is much like a fish chasing another fish and in theory it should make a fish catching combination.

There are several styles of birds to choose from. The Boone Bird is constructed of foam with a tough, durable coating that can be colored to look like any kind of fish. A short length of 300-pound mono leader

Birds splash and dance to attract strikes from tuna and billfish. Bird is clipped to the main fishing line, the lure leader is clipped to the bird so lure runs behind the bird.

runs the length of the bird and serves to attach the bird to the leader and provides a loop at the head end to accept the snap at the end of the fishing line and a snap at the tail end to attach to the lure's leader loop.

The Murray bird is made of wood painted in a selection of colors. It gets its action from the aluminum wings epoxied into place at the shoulders of the bird. A lead weight in the belly adds stability and a short 300-pound mono leader is again constructed to hold the bird and to attach it to the leader and main fishing line.

The Mold Craft Soft Bird is injection molded of soft plastic, the wings molded right into the bird. This is the lightest of the birds but you can add as much weight as you wish by placing egg sinkers onto the leader under the skirt before tying or crimping the end loop.

Teasers

"What the heck is that?" asked one of the charter fares as the mate pulled out a string of soda cans laced onto a 3/8 nylon rope. The wild array of colors glistened in the early morning sunlight and the cans clanked as they dropped to the deck.

"These" said Tommy, the mate, "are my secret weapons. Just look at the holes in this can," he demanded as he held up a 7-Up can with a slashing cut through one side. "That was a white marlin; a real mad white marlin that lit up like the fourth of July when he crashed into that teaser string. We hooked him a second later on the flat line."

Tommy said no more as we watched him attach the end of the rope to a small cleat on top of the stern covering board and then dropped the entire mess into the Hatteras Atlantic. I was fishing with three buddies on leave from the Navy base at Little Creek and we hoped to catch a marlin. As the line straightened in the wash the string of cans darted to the left and right, dove under the wake to stream long plumes of bubbles and then burst from the water in a short hop and a splash of blue water. As it danced, the cans tinkled and clinked in the turbulent wake.

Whatever tune it played, white marlin liked it. In less than a half hour the first white knocked the cans into the air slashing wildly with its bill then turning with a violent twist of its purple-sheened body and was gone. "Come on back you snake!" yelled the captain. "Eat my baits." Whether it was the same fish or not didn't really matter, but in a split second the cans were tossed skyward again. This time as the marlin turned to run he blasted the swimming mullet on the flat line and was hooked solidly without even a drop back.

All heck broke loose as the captain and mate shouted commands and threats to one another and the angler tried to keep his cool in the

OFFSHORE TROLLING LURES

Large teasers add to the action of the lure pattern. Run them off the transom on short leaders so they smoke or swim in the clear water of the wake.

midst of a marlin war. "Reel the line you idiot. Don't give him an inch of slack. Reel, reel, reel damn it. Swing the stern. Captain, he's running to port. Watch that other line, get it in quick. Back down, back down. There he goes he's gonna jump! Don't miss that leader. You're pulling too hard. That's it let him run again. OK, ease him in. All right, there's the tag, cut the leader. Good job everyone."

The battle left me, the angler, in a daze. I wasn't quite sure what had happened but I must have been a decent "winder" since the mate and captain both shook my hand and offered their congratulations. Before the day was finished, the Hatteras waters gave up five white marlin to our Navy base crew and probably the soda can teaser helped.

That was about 25 years ago but the message hasn't dimmed with passing fishing seasons - offshore game fish like teasers. Or, maybe they don't like them and are simply taking swipes at a teaser to attack it rather than to eat it. Either way, teasers help draw fish to the boat and to the lure pattern.

Teasers can be made up as chains of hookless squids or lures run off the outriggers and connected to small reels at the hardtop, or they can be single, large lures run directly off a stern cleat. Both styles have advantages and disadvantages.

The outrigger teasers are popular along many parts of the coast and there is no doubt that they help draw fish to the lure or bait pattern, but since they don't have hooks, it can be exasperating to watch a hungry billfish take pot shots at the teaser and never hit a lure with a hook in it. I prefer to fish lures with hooks in them so if a billfish or tuna takes a shot at the teaser he gets grabbed by the hook. I use daisy chains fished from rods to replace the rigger teasers. Some tournaments demand that anglers fish a limited number of rods and in this case the use of teasers is a big plus to add some extra attraction to the pattern. Marlin fishermen who may troll only 3 or 4 rods will also use teasers to put more action in the pattern.

I use mostly single or double teasers fished from a cleat off the transom. My records show that most of our fish are taken from the second to fourth wakes, so the teaser adds a bit of "come on" to the close-in lures. A favorite teaser is a blue multi-mirrored Boone swimmer that darts and flashes in the wake. The first one I had got destroyed by a white marlin that came up and belted the teaser then got bill-wrapped in the teaser line. Something had to give and unfortunately the 300-pound test line that held the teaser gave out before the fish did. I now use heavier braided nylon cord.

Basic teasers have three shapes; bowling pin, Kona head, and flat-face. The bowling pin is one of the earliest teasers and often the first versions were literally real bowling pins "borrowed" from a local alley. The bowling pin's action was ideally suited for trolling rigged baits since it worked so well at slow to medium speeds.

The Kona head fast became popular as the offshore lure craze hit the East Coast. Faster trolling speeds didn't always suit the bowling pin teasers but the scooped faces of the Kona head teasers seemed about perfect. Today the Kona head is still a favorite, especially among marlin addicts.

The latest teasers are the flat-face shapes; huge heads with a diameter of 4 to 5 inches in diameter, like the Mold Craft Giant Hooker. It smokes bubbles like an enormous NASA rocket gone off course. Its side to side action is enhanced by the long smoke plumes that can stretch out up to 15 or 20 feet in length. Tuna can see them from far away and from deeper depths.

Teasers seem to work best when positioned in close to the boat. I like to put mine in the first wake behind the boat. Since each boat throws a slightly different wake, the length of the line to the teaser needs to be adjusted for your own boat. Usually about 25 feet is about right.

Every boat throws a different wake, some are full of white water from props, others are quite clear. The very center of the wake is usually the most turbulent and a teaser placed in this water will not be easy for fish to see. Many offshore captains run the teaser off a stern cleat and out the hawse pipe so it is naturally off center from the foamy water. This makes the teaser do a better job since fish can see it from a far distance.

Teasers are valuable additions to any offshore pattern and attract fish with day-to-day regularity. They are worth the investment.

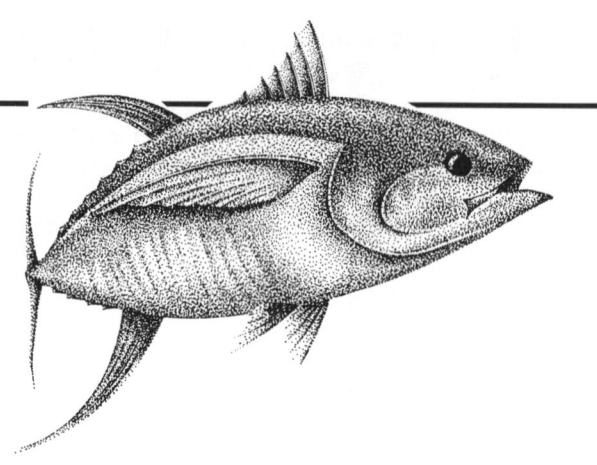

Chapter Six

OFFSHORE TROLLING BAITS

"Ain't nothing like the real thing, Baby," was a line from a popular song and it couldn't describe trolling with baits any better. From Virginia south to Florida, baits are much more in use than lures, and offshore fishermen are skilled in rigging ballyhoo, mullet and mackerel to fool everything from dolphin to sailfish and marlin. Each area of the coast has developed its own rigging techniques, but the basics are still the same from one port to another.

Wire leaders are the standard in Florida while the Outer Banks of North Carolina sees a lot of mono leaders used. Marlin fishermen often spend extra minutes making sure a bait is rigged just perfect, while tuna fishermen, who may experience repeated blasts of multiple hook-ups don't see the need to get too fancy with the baits because the fish are so numerous.

Many northern offshore anglers are also avid fans of trolling baits and I've met fishermen from Snug Harbor, Rhode Island to Cape May, New Jersey who disdain lures and primarily fish with baits. So, depending upon where you live, trolling with baits is either the "only" way to go, or it's something only a few captains use.

In this chapter, we'll cover rigging several of the most popular baits, but it is not my intent to cover every rigged bait. Instead I'd recommend readers be sure to get a copy of *How to Rig Baits for Trolling* from Penn Reels and *Secrets of Successful Big Game Fishing* by Captains Samuel A. Earp and William J. Wildeman, published by Little, Brown and Company. Both books are excellent guides to rigging just about every kind of bait in every kind of way. If you are an offshore fisherman, these two books ought to be on your library bookshelf. I keep an extra copy of both books on my boat for handy reference.

Getting Bait

Most fishermen simply walk up to the counter of their favorite offshore tackle shop and say, "Give me three dozen bally" while plopping down some cash on the counter. The best tackle shops take the time to order prime baits, carefully prepared by professionals so the angler is assured of purchasing a quality product. Those of us who use a lot of baits will buy ballyhoo, mullet and mackerel in bulk quantities, or flats, so we have a ready supply on hand at all times.

You can also catch your own bait, sometimes, by using chum to draw the fish to the boat and then baiting them on tiny hooks. This works well with ballyhoo over reefs where the bait schools up. I've done this many times in the Keys and while it does get you a supply of the freshest bait possible, with little expense, it is time consuming and takes away from fishing time. A cast net is the way to go if you are serious about getting quantities of your own bait.

Other baits, like eels and mackerel, can be obtained from local fishermen, or as some offshore fishermen do, they look for some local fishing kids to catch a supply of bait. Some offshore fishermen even admit to having a good time catching their own mackerel on light tackle on a family day of fishing.

But, for many fishermen a visit to the bait and tackle shop is the way to go. The shop may have fresh or frozen baits. Fresh is always the best if the baits are clean and not battered and bruised with scales missing. Frozen is okay if the baits were prepped well before freezing. The best baits will be washed in a baking soda rinse and packed in air-tight vacuum bags to avoid freezer burn.

Prepping the Baits

Prepping the bait for fishing starts with a rinse of clean saltwater to remove excess slime, milt and roe and any loose scales. Fresh baits are ready for rinsing immediately, frozen baits should be thawed slowly, overnight if possible, while still on ice so they don't get too soft.

If you plan to use only a small number of baits in a short time, such as when fishing only a few hours in the morning, the baits can be neatly stacked on top of a layer of ice. Chances are you will use the baits up so quickly that they will keep just fine for this half day of fishing.

More care is required if you plan to fish all day, travel a long distance or use a lot of bait during the day. I use a 48-quart cooler with a 10-inch layer of crushed ice in the bottom, smoothed level and coated with a layer of kosher salt. A wet towel is laid over the ice and the baits are laid on the towel so they do not come in contact with the ice. By using several towels, I can layer several rows of baits. If the baits are very juicy or still slightly unthawed, a light sprinkle of kosher salt will help reduce the wetness and toughen them up.

You can be assured of a tougher bait by first pickling the baits in a solution of salted sea water with a touch of pickling lime, available at many grocery stores, or a few ounces of formaldehyde, available at drug stores.

To avoid an excess of sloppy water inside the cooler, leave the drain cap open. A soupy mess of water, salt and mixed up baits does not make for an efficient running cockpit. Be sure to wash down the dribble of juice that drains from the cooler so the deck doesn't become slippery.

Bait Rigging Equipment

The following equipment and supplies will be needed to rig baits: Manley or Sargent 5-inch pliers, small bait knife, fillet knife, sharpening stone, rigging needles in several lengths, waxed rigging thread, wire leader coils in sizes 5 to 9, coils of mono leader in 125 to 300-pound test, crimps, crimping tool, egg sinkers in 1/4 to 3/4-ounce weights, hook file and sharpening hone, de-boner, copper rigging wire, plastic bucket and towels.

Hook Styles and Sizes

Among the most popular bait rigging hooks are two VMC 9730PS, VMC 9255PS, Mustad 7731, Mustad 7691 and Eagle Claw 254. Hook sizes will run from 6/0 to 14/0 depending ont he size of the baits being rigged and the targeted species. The VMC hooks are a big more expensive, but well worth the price. You can save money by purchasing hooks in quantity and all three manufacturers package hooks in various multiples of 5, 10, 25 or 100 hooks per pack.

Larger baits, such as Boston and Spanish mackerel, meant for blue marlin and giant bluefin will need 3X strong hooks like the Mustad #7690 needle eye and #7691 brazed ring eye Southern Tuna Hook. These are available up to 16/0 size and have a reputation for extreme strength.

Leaders

There are two preferred types of leader; wire or mono. Braided cable leaders are not usually used. Wire leaders are sold as tinned wire, also called music wire or piano wire, coffee-colored stainless wire and plastic coated stainless wire. Wire sizes of #5 to #9 are most commonly used, sometimes #12 or #14 for blue marlin.

The following can be used as a guide to wire selection for offshore trolling:

School tuna	#5 to #7	fish to 50 pounds.
Yellowfin	#9 to #12	fish to 150 pounds.
Bigeye bluefin	#14 to #16	fish to 300 pounds and to 1000 pounds.
White marlin Sailfish	#5 to #7 #9 or #10	use when fish might be leader shy. use when blue marlin may crash the baits.
Blue marlin	#10 to #14 #16 to #19	fish to 250 pounds. fish to 1000 pounds.

The only good way to attach hooks to wire or to put a loop in the tag end to clip to the snap swivel is with a haywire twist.

Monofilament leaders can be made with standard mono (the same stuff you use to fill your reel), or by purchasing special mono with a hardened finish that resists fraying. It is often spooled in 50 to 100-yard coils. Some manufacturers make their leaders with a unique formula to make the outer surface less susceptible to scuffing from a marlin bill while still keeping the mono somewhat soft and supple so it is easy to handle. A surface that is too hard may well resist scratches but it may also be so brittle that it will break rather easily under the intense force from the impact of a striking fish.

Depending on where you live, you'll find most of your neighbors using either wire or mono, usually not both. It's typical to see more wire used to the south and in Florida, mono used from Hatteras north to New England. Some fishermen use a mix of both by using a short length of wire to rig the bait, then snap on a longer length of mono as the main leader. These short, 4 to 10-inch wire leaders require no coiling while storing the rigged baits in a cooler and are faster to grab on to, with no tangles as with coiled leaders, so placing a new bait on the leader is easier and much quicker.

Rigged Ballyhoo - Wire Leader

This is a universal bait used nearly everywhere in the world. It is simple to rig and even a novice can learn to rig a ballyhoo with only a few minutes of practice time. Captain "Spider" Halperin of the Marker 32 fishing out of Sailfish Marina showed me his way of rigging ballyhoo and I've been using it ever since.

"Twelve pack" ballys are about the right size for most fishing purposes where tuna, white marlin and sailfish are the target species. Blue marlin may want a bigger bait, like the so-called "six pack" ballys or the super large "horse" ballyhoo that you buy one at a time.

The bait must always be prepped before it is rigged on the hook. Take the bally in the left hand, belly up, bill pointing to you, tail away from you. Push the right thumb down the belly from the gills to the vent to squeeze out the stomach contents. Keep a bucket of water handy to wash each bait so it is clean of any residue. Hold the bait by the head in one hand and tail in the other hand and work the body into "S" shaped bends to loosen the bait up so it will swim better.

With the bait in the palm of your left hand, bill pointing away from you, lift the right gill flap with your thumb and insert the hook point. As the hook is pushed into the bait, bend the bait to follow the curve of the hook until the point exits just behind the pectoral fins. Push the small wire pin through the nose of the bally and use a rubber band or a length of copper rigging wire to secure the nose and bill to the leader. Break off the end of the bill. Slide the skirt into place and you are ready to troll.

It's best to make up a few wire leaders ahead of time so you have several dozen ready to go. The rig can be fished "naked" or color can be added by sliding a Sea Witch onto the leader. This is a favorite of many captains and they are found in a wide variety of colors. Sea Witches are the nylon haired trolling lures with the longer hair of the lure facing forward. When the rig is trolled the hair folds back over the head of the lure and bait, pulsating in a breathing rhythm. Small vinyl skirts can also be added or small lures like the Mold Craft Hookers, Iland lures, feathers or Tuna Clones.

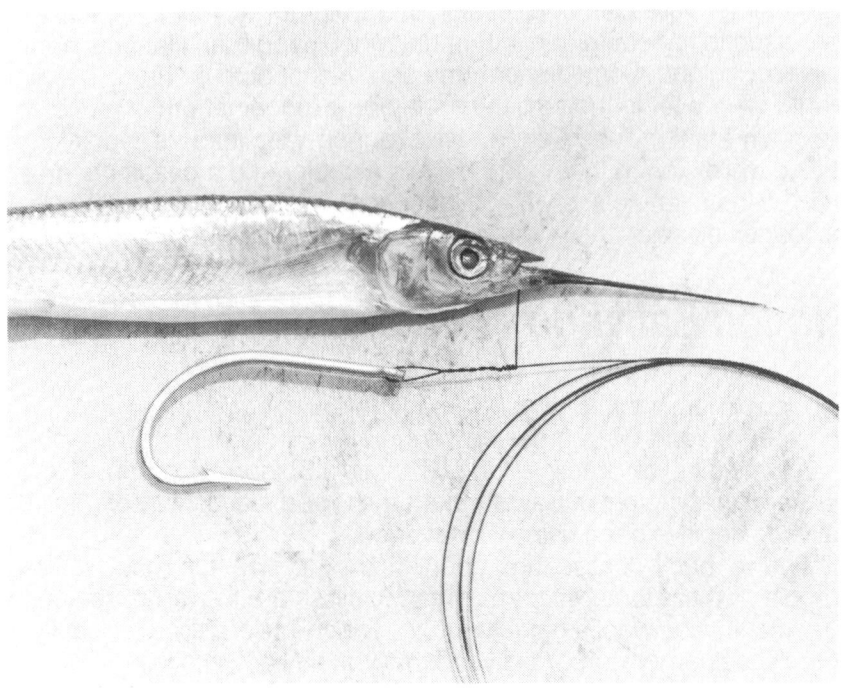

1. Lay leader and hook next to ballyhoo to check hook position. Use hook point to poke a small hole in belly where hook will lie.

2. Lift gill flap and insert hook into body cavity.

OFFSHORE TROLLING BAITS

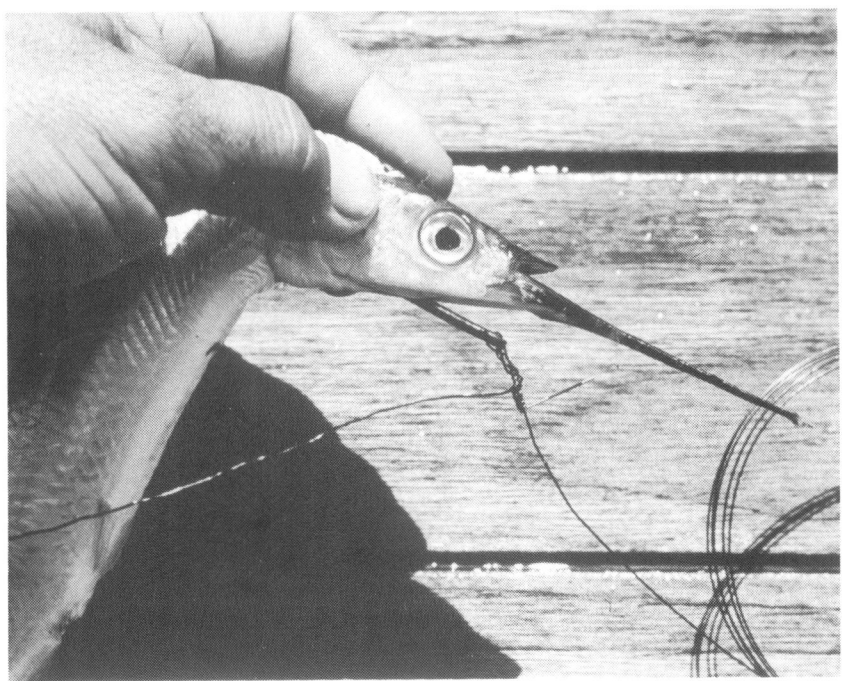

3. Bend ballyhoo while pushing hook until hook is in position in belly of bait.

4. Push wire pin through nose of ballyhoo.

FISHING FOR TUNA AND MARLIN

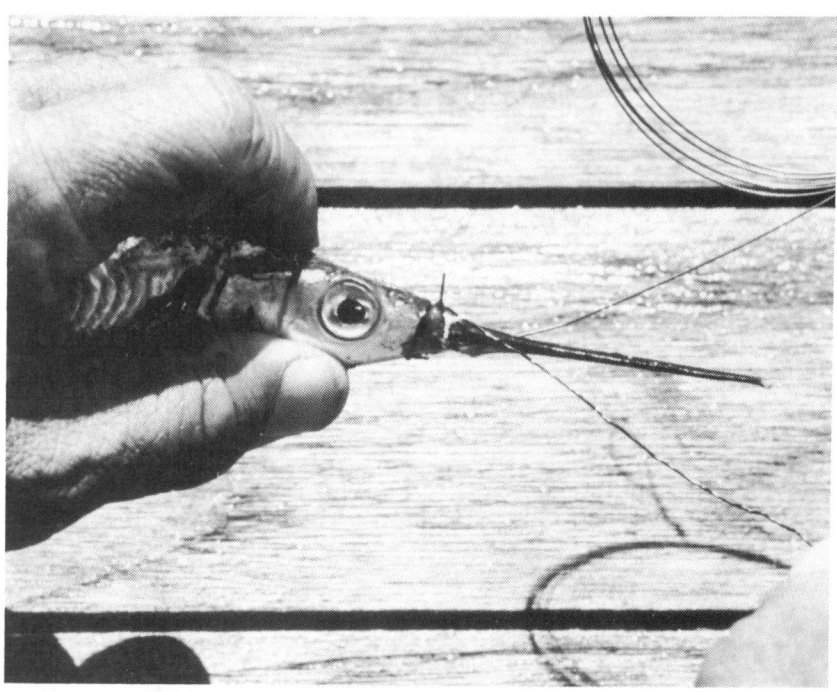

5. Wrap rigging wire around nose of bait, alternating wraps behind and in front of the pin. Finish by breaking off the bill an inch above the jaw.

6. Slit belly to allow hook movement. Skirts add color and action.

OFFSHORE TROLLING BAITS

Rigging a few dozen baits ahead of time, before you head offshore, will save valuable time while you are fishing. Store the baits in a small cooler half filled with ice. Lay a towel or a folded newspaper over the ice then lay the rigged baits on the towel. Sprinkle with kosher salt to toughen the bait and the silver bullets are ready to fool tuna and billfish.

Critical to good tracking in the wake is a slit in the belly to allow the hook to swing free. A hook, cocked at an angle, may make the bait run with an odd action, or make it spin.

Ballyhoo rigged in this manner, with no weight are usually fished at fairly slow speeds, splashing on the surface. It is a dynamite bait for sailfish, white marlin and dolphin.

Swimming Ballyhoo - Mono Leader

Swimming ballyhoo baits have become a mainstay in our offshore bait offerings after Chris Hall, former mate on John Bayliss' Tarheel out of Oregon Inlet showed me some tricks that makes rigging this bait a breeze. I like the mono leaders because they last a long time, even after repeated hook-ups with tuna, and I feel the mono is easier to fish with.

To make mono rigs, you need 7/0 or 8/0 Mustad #7731 round eye hooks, 125-pound test mono, 1.2 mm crimps, #7 wire, 3/4-ounce egg sinkers, crimping pliers, rubber bands or copper rigging wire. For tuna, substitute 200-pound test mono and Hi-Seas 1.8mm crimps.

Begin the rig by pulling off 15 feet of leader. At one end, slide on a crimp, then the egg sinker and then the hook. Fold the end of the leader back over itself and push the tag end through the egg sinker. Slip the crimp onto the tag end and slide the crimp and sinker toward the hook until only a small loop is left at the hook eye. Before crimping the sleeve, cut a 1-inch length of #7 wire and bend it to form an "L". Slide one end of the "L" into the crimp so the exposed part of the wire forms a point at 90 degrees to the hook eye. Crimp the sleeve.

Secure the bait to the leader with a rubber band or length of copper rigging wire as described above for rigging a bally on a wire leader. The sinker shoiuld ride just below the gills. Be sure to check the ballyhoo to see that it swims correctly. Hold the leader just ahead of the bait and let the bally hang at eye level. If the hook is pulling on the belly making the bait form a curve, slit the belly.

Tuna seem less selective than white marlin and rubber banding the nose of the bally works just fine. The finicky white marlin will hit more readily when the bait is rigged with copper rigging wire run through the eye sockets, then wrapped around the nose and leader. The bait is then pulled directly from the eyes and will run better.

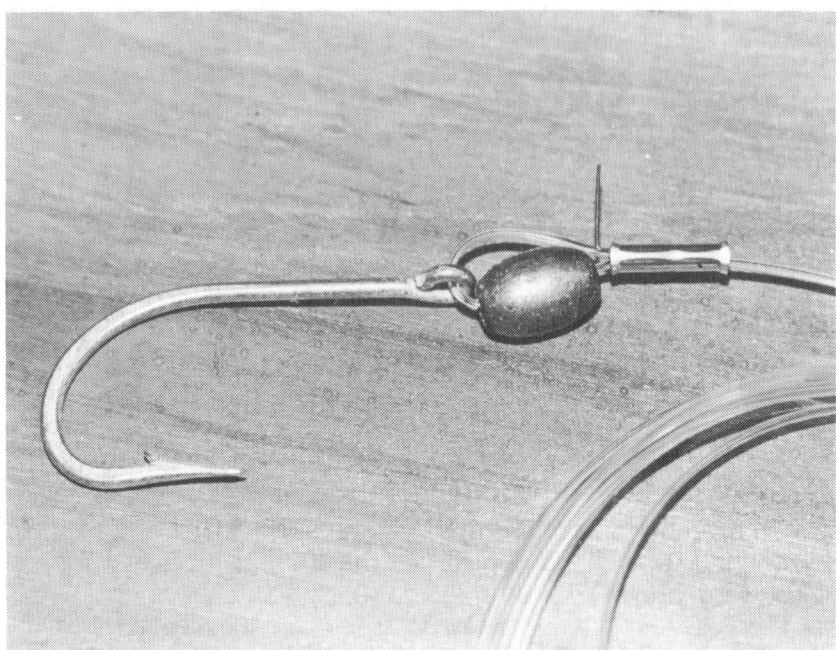

Slide a crimp, egg sinker and hook onto the 100 to 200-pound test mono leader. Insert a short wire, bent to 90 degree into crimp, then push tag end into crimp. Use crimping tool to swage the crimp in place.

Insert hook into bait so sinker is positioned below the chin. Finish with wire wraps to secure the nose pin.

OFFSHORE TROLLING BAITS

Finished bait with chin sinker and skirt has seductive swimming action.

Weedless Ballyhoo

This slight variation of the mono rig places the hook point inside the bait so it cannot snag weeds. While not recommended for use on a daily basis, this rig is very helpful whenever you encounter large quantities of weed that is scattered and spread out over a wide area with no clearly defined weedline. The constant snagging of weed on the bait hooks makes fishing almost impossible unless the hook is buried as shown.

Hook in ballyhoo belly makes the bait weed-free. Note that the nose pin is on same side of leader as hook bend for this rig.

Swimming Mullet

The accompanying photos show how I rig a simple swimming mullet. It is effective and catches fish real good, but many mates who fish "meat" most of the time in their spread, have developed special techniques to rig swimming mullet that are like works of art. Ed Murray produced a video, titled *Rigging Natural Baits* that shows the tricks of "Split Tail" Charlie Hayden, one of the all-time greats of bait rigging. If you want to go further than my plain vanilla rigging, I highly recommend this video.

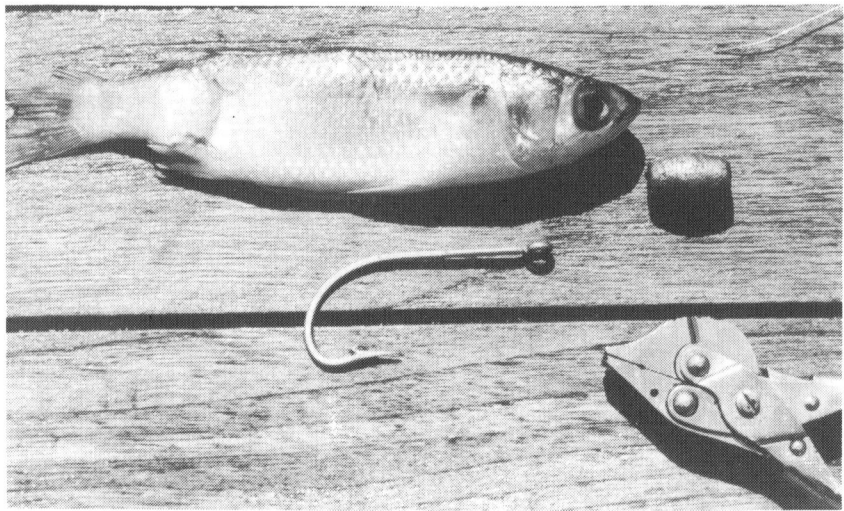

1. You need split-tailed mullet, hook, egg sinker, wire leader and pliers.

2. Use hook point to poke a hole through the hard nose of the mullet.

OFFSHORE TROLLING BAITS

3. Insert hook so the eye is in line with the nose hole.

4. Push a 12-inch length of wire through the nose and through the hook eye.

FISHING FOR TUNA AND MARLIN

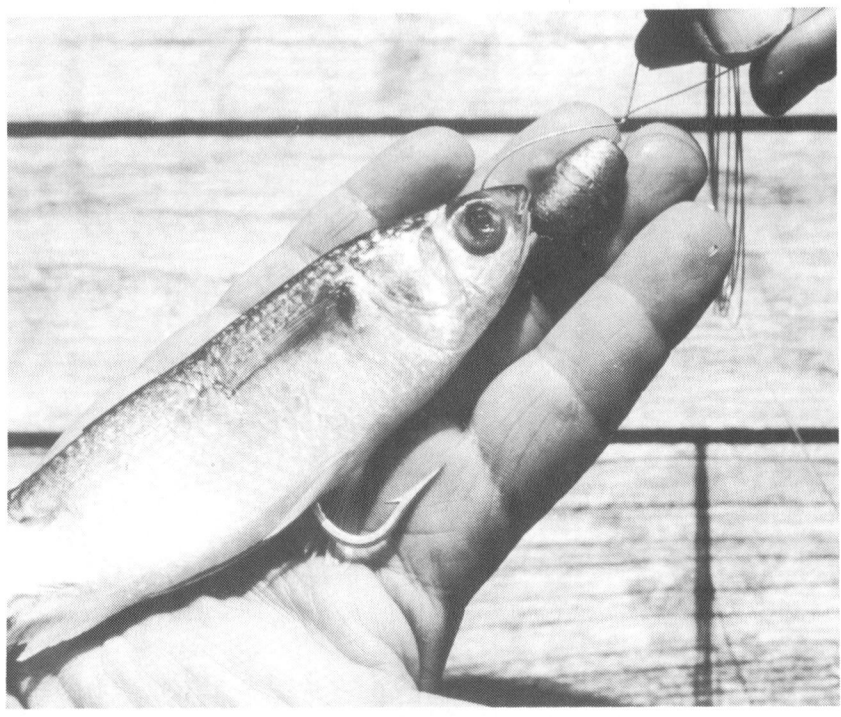

5. Form a loop and add the egg sinker on bottom of loop.

6. Finish with a haywire twist ahead of the sinker.

OFFSHORE TROLLING BAITS

Mullet and Ballyhoo Daisy Chains

Superb teasers can be made by rigging a string of mullet or ballyhoo on a single 15 to 20-foot leader. Since they are meant to be fished as teasers, none of the baits have hooks in them, not even the tail-end bait.

One of the slickest ways I ever saw to rig a daisy chain with natural baits used a long center leader of 200-pound test mono with loops crimped into the leader at 18-inch intervals. Each loop held a small snap swivel. The mullet and ballyhoo were rigged on short, 6-inch leaders, prepared much like a hooked bait, but without the hook in place, and the loop at the forward end of the leader was clipped to the snap swivels. Damaged baits could be changed quickly when a supply of teaser baits was kept on ice ready for instant use.

Depending on your trolling speed, the teaser rigs may need 1-ounce trolling leads (egg sinkers) crimped to the short leaders just ahead of the baits. With no weights, these teasers will jump all over the water at speeds meant for trolling swimming ballyhoo and mullet, but will work just fine at sailfish trolling speeds when unweighted bally are used.

The length of the daisy can be modified to use only a few baits or to present up to nine baits at once. The spashing and commotion that the teaser makes calls in many a wary marlin or sailfish.

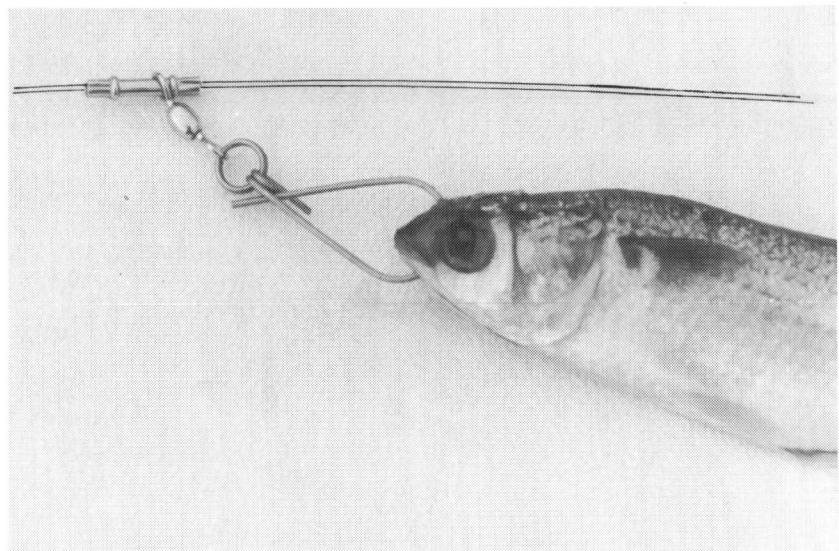

Base line snap swivels are available with bait snaps (shown) to clip baits through the nose, or with standard snap swivels, which is the preferred choice for attaching swimming mullet rigged on short leaders with egg sinkers at the chin.

Rigged Mackerel

A whole mackerel is a relatively easy bait to rig. Placing a big bait like this in the trolling pattern does wonders for your dreams of catching a huge fish and there's no doubt that some huge billfish and bluefin have been taken on whole baits. If you fish from Ocean City, Maryland south through Hatteras, South Carolina, Florida and the Bahamas, a whole bait is a must if you expect action with blue marlin.

The bait is first prepared by slicing the belly and removing the entrails. A 10/0 to 12/0 hook is slide into the body cavity so the hook eye rests inside the mouth of the bait. The tag end of the #12 to #15 wire leader is pushed from the lower jaw through the eye of the hook and out the top of the nose, then folded back towards the leaders to form a neat loop. The loop is haywired into the leader forming a strong connection that allows the bait to have slight movement.

With a small rigging needle and 3-foot length of Gudebrod Waxed Rigging Floss, the gill flaps and stomach are sewn closed with criss-cross stitches to prevent flowing water from tearing the bait apart.

Rigged mackerel are especially good for marlin. Gut bait, sew belly with bait rigging thread or floss. Some trollers also sew mouth and gills.

Strip Baits

Overlooked by many fishermen, strip baits can be dynamite fish catchers. I've used strip baits for football blackfin tuna at the Hump off Islamorada, for sailfish, white marlin, school bluefin and yellowfin.

Strip baits are generally made from the belly sections of small tuna, like bonito or little tunny, or dolphin, mackerel or school tuna. I find it helpful to cut the bellies from fish as I catch them, prepare the strip baits and place them on ice. Any unused strips are frozen, packed in zip lock bags so they are ready for use on a future day of trolling. A small amount of salt in the bag helps to toughen them up and removes excess moisture that may cause the baits to spoil. In a pinch, the sides and back of small tuna can also be used from fresh-caught baits. This meat is not at as tough as the belly strips but it will catch fish.

If I have a lot of belly strips left over, I use a vacuum bagger to remove all the air from around the strips so they can be frozen for long periods of time without loss of quality.

A number of companies now make artificial belly strips and they often work just as good, without the hassle of freezing and prepping. Turbotails is one brand that I've tried and they are reinforced with a nylon webbing inside the bait and will last a long time. I've only seen them at tackle shops around the south Florida area, like Beach Bait & Tackle in Fort Lauderdale, and they may not be readily available along the entire coast.

Like ballyhoo, strip baits can be fished naked or with a skirt. I've also rigged them with a 1/2 or 3/4-ounce lead under the skirt so they dig into the water a foot or two.

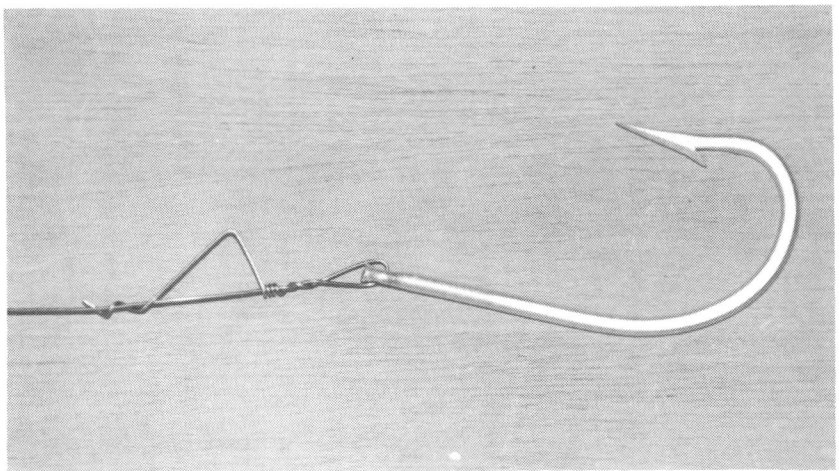

1. Tag end of haywire is bent to a safety pin shape for a strip bait rig.

FISHING FOR TUNA AND MARLIN

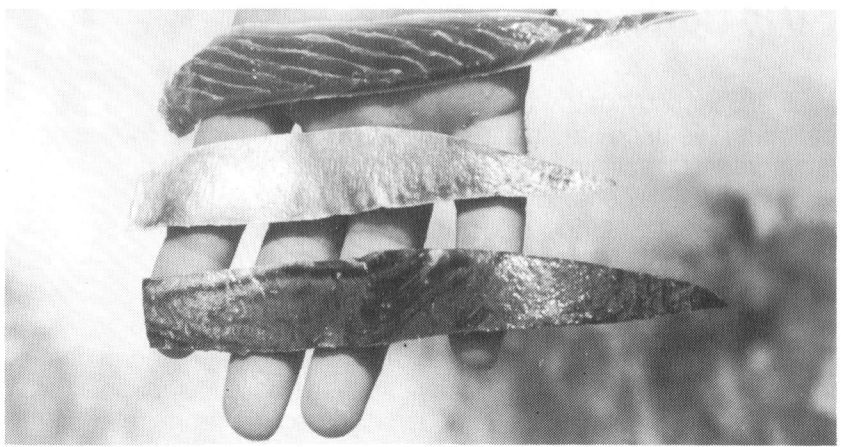
2. Strips are cut from the belly of bonito, skipjack or other small tuna.

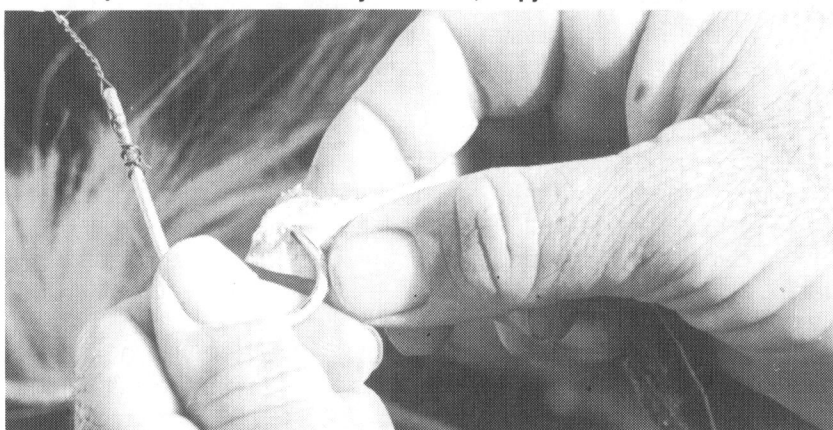
3. Use hook point to poke hole at front of strip bait.

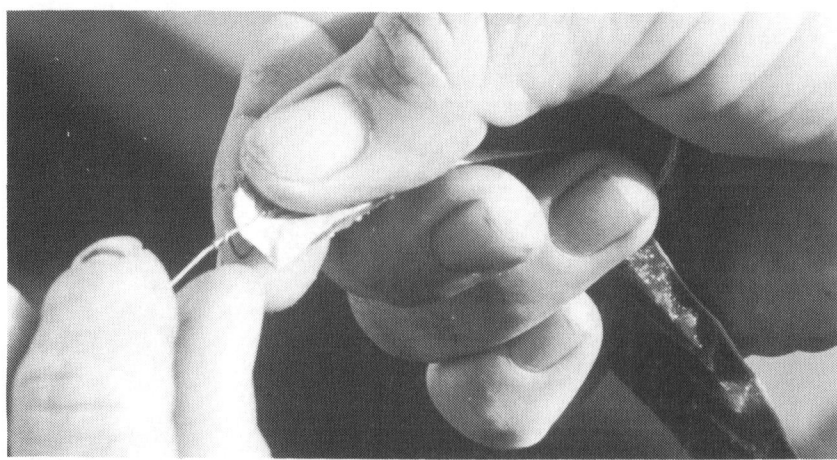
4. Slip safety pin latch through the hole.

OFFSHORE TROLLING BAITS

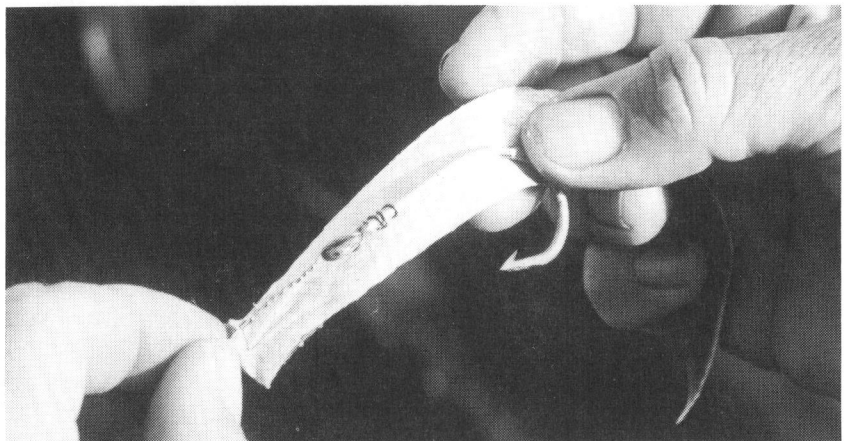

5. Lay hook next to the strip bait to check hook position.

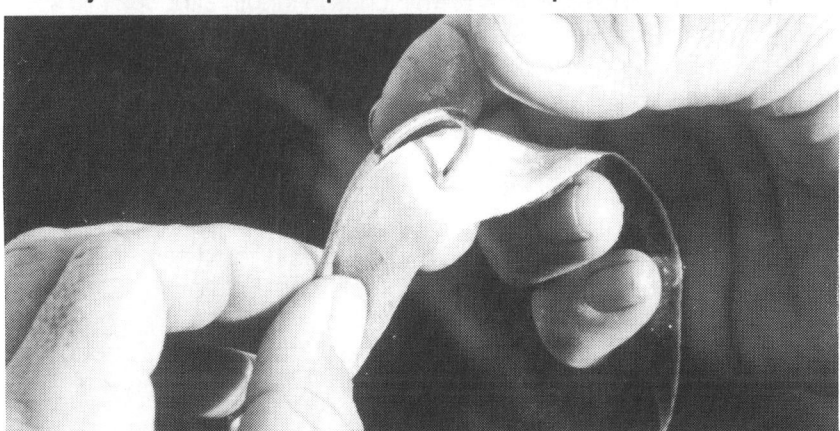

6. Push hook through strip bait from skin side.

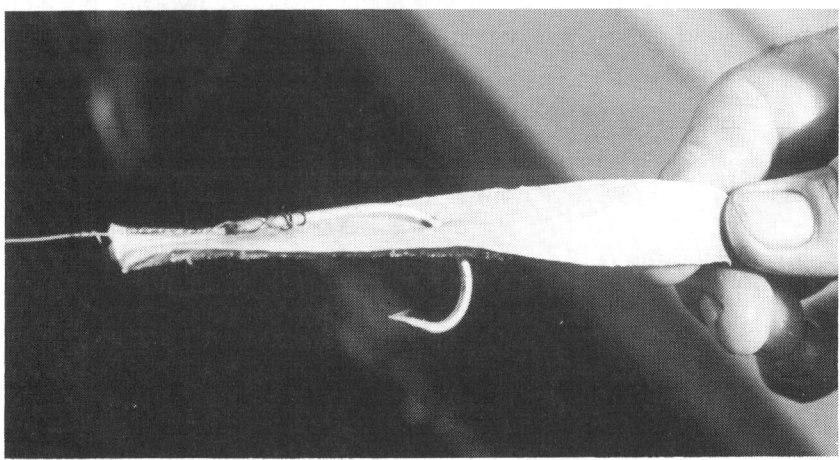

7. Finished bait. Note skin side lays next to hook shank.

Red Hot Eels

An excellent bait for white marlin that often gets overlooked is a rigged eel. While not as popular as bally and mullet, many a white marlin fanatic considers the eel to be the ultimate bait, and eels catch tuna, too.

Some tackle and bait shops along the coast sell pre-rigged eels. The best are fresh-frozen and vacuum bagged to keep indefinitely, and they are rigged with quality hooks. You can also easily rig your own. If you live close to the coast, you can probably pot your own eels, or enlist the aid of a local dockside, future marlin fisherman to catch some eels for you. Eels can also be bought live, or fresh frozen at many tackle and bait shops.

The eels should be about 14 to 18 inches in length although I've seen some "gigundo" rigged eels of 24 inches or so rigged for offshore fishing. It's best to rig several eels at a time. They store well and can be used more than once if re-frozen in a salt brine solution.

Wash the eels thoroughly to remove the surface slime, then wipe dry. You'll need a 12 to 18-inch rigging needle, #6 wire, Mustad #7731S needle eye hooks in 6/0 to 8/0, small barrel swivels, pliers and a cotton glove.

Haywire a 24-inch length of wire to the hook being sure the loop in the haywire is compressed to a small, tight bend. Fold an inch of the tag end back over itself and insert this into the eye of the rigging needle. Push the needle through the anal vent and work the needle through the eel and out the mouth. Pull the needle and wire until the hook is firmly seated in the eel. Remove the rigging needle.

Lay the eel on its side so it lays naturally with no body bends. Slide the head of the eel back on the wire about an inch or two, and put a 90 degree bend in the wire where the inside of the eel's mouth was positioned before you slide the head back. Haywire a #3 barrel swivel to the wire.

Slide the eel's head forward and over the barrel swivel, then use a length of copper rigging wire or waxed rigging thread to secure the barrel swivel to the eel's mouth. Run the wire or thread through the chin, through the aft swivel eye and out the top of the mouth, taking several wraps around the nose. This prevents the eel from slipping down the wire as the bait is trolled.

A 125-pound test monofilament leader is attached to the forward eye of the barrel swivel. Some fishermen use a Uni-Knot, others use a small Hi-Seas or Jinkai crimp and a short length of plastic tubing as chafing gear. Eels to be fished tomorrow are laid on ice, covered with kosher salt to toughen them up. Eels to be frozen are first laid in salt to get the tough guy treatment, then vacuum bagged.

OFFSHORE TROLLING BAITS

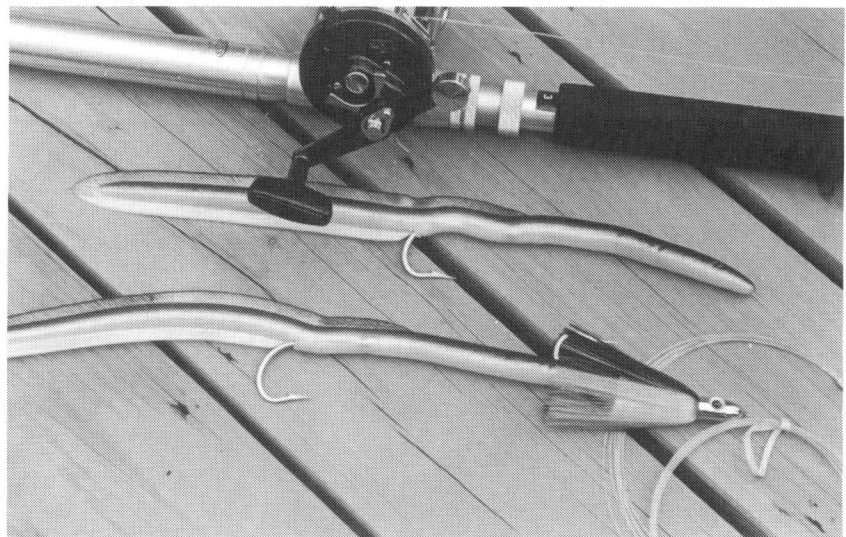

Natural or artificial, rigged eels are a prime white marlin bait.

Rubber eels can work just as well as fresh eels and will appeal to the those fishermen who don't have access to eels or can't keep frozen baits on their boat. I've been using the J & J Tackle eels and they rig easily, store with no problems and most important, they catch fish.

I rig the fake eels with a second hook in the head. The tail hook is placed in position just as with a real eel. Once the wire is in place, I add the second hook, a Mustad #7731 with a round eye, by inserting the point into the nose, then bending the eel to work the hook until it is in position with the eye of the hook just protruding from the nose. I haywire the tail hook to the eye of the front hook. The mono leader is attached with a crimp.

Color and flash can be added to the real McCoy or the artificial eels by slipping a Sea Witch, a small skirted lure or a vinyl skirt down the leader until it drapes over the head of the eel. Weight can be added by using a weighted lure, or by sliding an egg sinker (trolling lead) down the leader before adding the skirt.

The rubber eels are handy because you can store a few in a tackle locker so they are ready for instant use with no freezing or refrigeration. They are so handy that the shorter life of a plastic eel is not always so important.

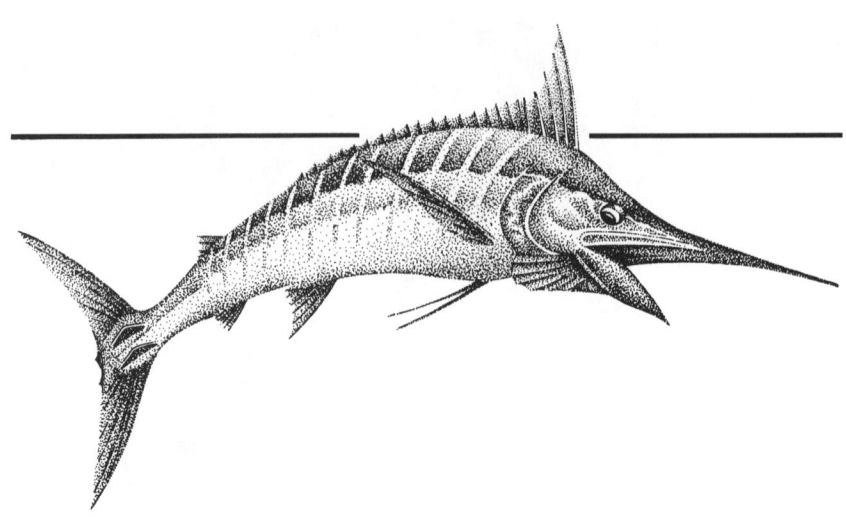

Chapter Seven

LIVE BAITS AND CHUNK BAITS

For many offshore fishermen, the drone of the engines, the splash of the lures and the anticipation of a crashing strike is the very essence of offshore fishing. There's no doubt that trolling is a good way to fish, but as fine a fishing method as it is, trolling is not always the most productive way to catch fish. There are times when power drifting or kite fishing with live baits; or anchoring, drifting, or chunking with fresh dead bait will be superior methods to make a good catch of fish.

Live bait is the favored method for sailfish in many Florida ports. Live baits fished for blue marlin are famous for fooling some impressive billfish in many parts of the world, not just Florida. With swordfish numbers down from what they were 20 years ago, baitfishing is just about the only choice now available to catch the wary broadbill. Each season sees a few white marlin and blue marlin that get fooled by a properly presented squid meant for a swordfish, or a chunk bait meant for a yellowfin tuna.

When the action is good, fishing with bait can provide fast, intense fishing unlike anything experienced while high-speed trolling. It is a rare fisherman indeed who doesn't get a case of the knee knocks when a 150-pound yellowfin glides past the transom only a scant few feet from the rod tip with its mouth open to suck down a butterfish bait, or who doesn't get excited when the clicker sings out "fish on" as a sword moves off with a rigged squid.

Let's take a look at the different ways to fish with live baits and chunked baits. Each method has its own special techniques to catch fish and special rewards for those who learn how to effectively practise this added dimension to offshore fishing.

Live Baits for Marlin

Fishing live baits for blue marlin is most popular along the Florida Coast, yet I know of a blue marlin taken at the Wilmington Canyon off Delaware on a live squid and of a white marlin caught on a live snapper blue not too far from Block Island. The squid was intended for a yellowfin or bigeye tuna, but a 200-pound blue one ate it and the angler successfully brought it to the boat where the fish was tagged and released. The snapper blue was also meant for a tuna, yet the billfish ate it with gusto. It illustrates that perhaps mid Atlantic and northeast offshore fishermen should consider trolling live baits if the opportunity arises. It is unusual to see anyone trolling live baits for marlin north of Jupiter or the Palm Beaches.

Some white marlin specialists have been using live baits, like snapper blues, off Martha's Vineyard and Nantucket with varying results. Some seasons the fishing is exceptionally good, other years it's not so hot, perhaps due to the fact that so much live bait is available to the schools of game fish.

The little tunny, called bonito in Florida, is the primary live bait used for blue marlin, but I've seen blackfin tuna and skipjack used in the Keys with equally good results. Any small member of the tuna tribe is a good bait and in a pinch, blue runners, goggle eyes, mackerel and small dolphin can also be used. If you decide to fish with live mackerel (the Spanish kind), be sure the size of the bait exceeds federal or state minimum sizes.

Baits are obtained by trolling feathers, small skirted lures or spoons near the edges of reefs and drop-offs. The first bait caught is then quickly rigged to the marlin tackle. A good bait-catching rig uses a small Drone, Crippled Alewife, Clark or Reflecto spoon trolled on a 15-foot leader with a 4 to 8-ounce lead drail to take the spoons a few feet below the surface. When a bait is hooked, it is brought to the boat quickly and impaled on the hook already attached to a much heavier rod and reel meant for marlin.

Goggle eyes and jacks are fairly hardy, but some tuna can quickly die if not handled quickly during the rigging process. To help keep a tuna bait alive and healthy while the hook is being positioned, hold the bait in one hand, belly up, and use the saltwater wash down hose to gently flow water through the bait's mouth. A second mate or crew member does the rigging. Some baits just won't hold still, so I use a

LIVE BAITS AND CHUNK BAITS

HOOKING LIVE BAITS

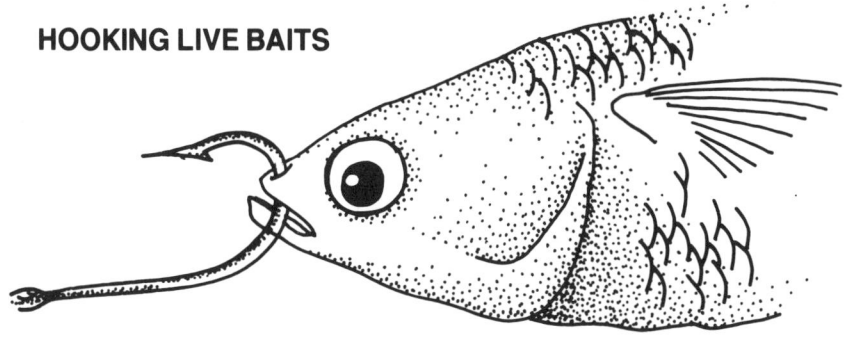

Through roof of mouth, out the nose.

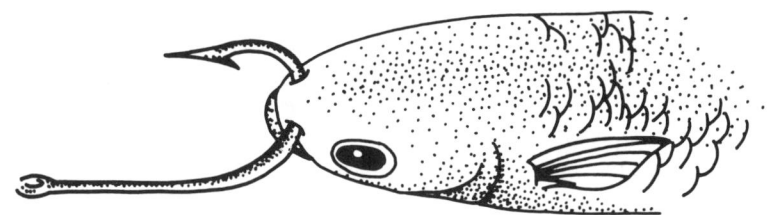

Crossways through nose.

wet towel to hold the fish down on a rigging board or tray. Covering their eyes sometimes helps to calm the fish down.

The quickest rig simply has the hook pushed through the fleshy area of the bait just ahead of the dorsal fin and behind the eyes. Another quick method places the hook through the upper jaw and out the nose of the bait. While fast to complete, most live bait pros prefer to sew the hook in place or loop the hook to the bait because sewing does less damage to the bait and the hook is completely exposed for a solid hook-up.

Use cotton rigging thread sold in most offshore tackle shops and a short, stainless rigging needle to complete the rigging. A short, but razor-sharp rigging knife should also be handy. Cotton rigging thread or Gudebrod Waxed Bait Rigging Floss are the two choices for rigging and each has its proponents. It's a matter of personal choice since both threads work well. I like the sticky finish of the Gudebrod thread and knots tied with this material do not come undone very easily.

There are two primary ways to rig live baits with stitched hooks. The first method uses an "X" shaped stitch across the back of the bait, just ahead of the dorsal and behind the eyes. The cross stitches

TROLLING LIVE BAIT

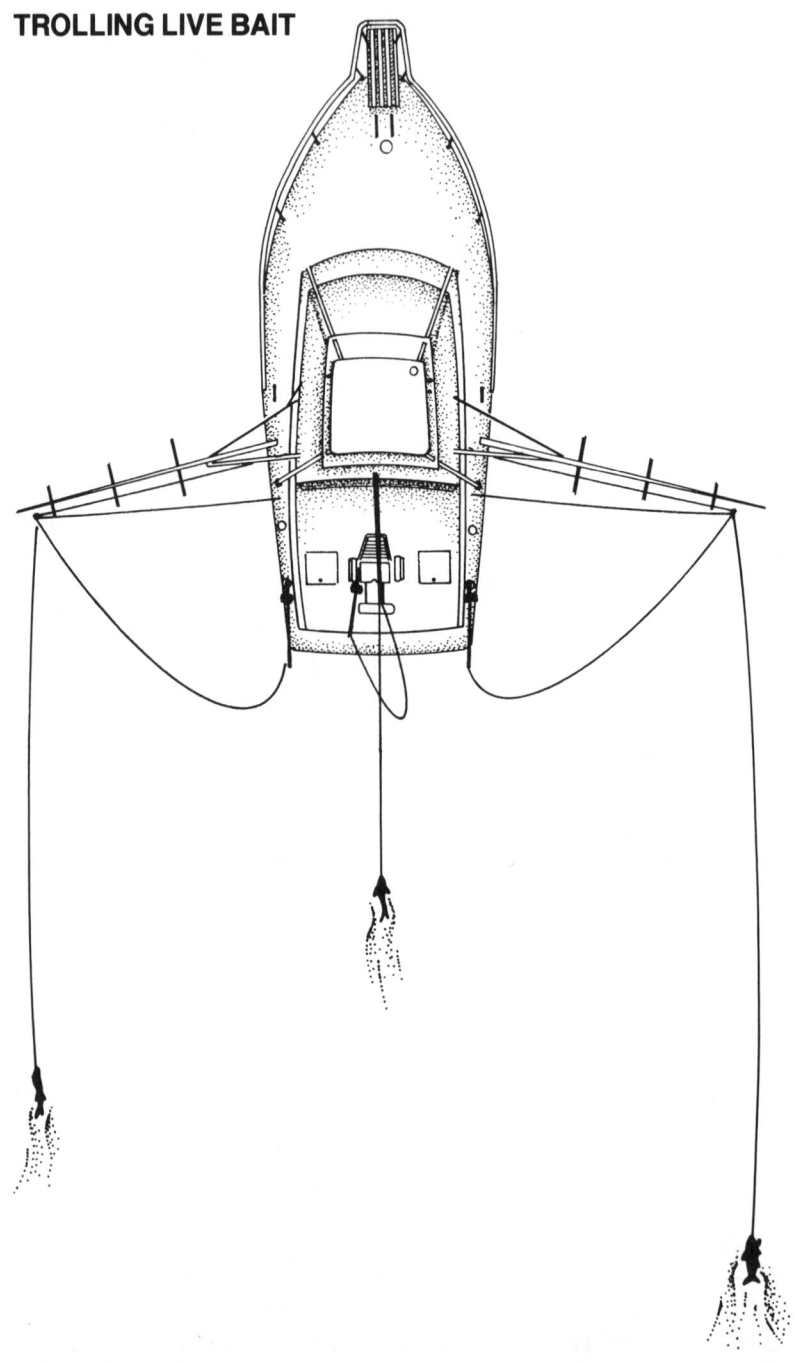

A basic set up for slow trolling (power drifting) with live baits. Marlin trollers may fish one or two baits, sailfish troller may use two or more baits.

are made from left to right at 45 degree angles so the stitches look like the letter X. The hook is slipped under the thread so the center of the bend sits in the center of the X stitches. Take the tag ends of the thread and tie them tightly across the hook.

The second method uses the same rigging threads, but stitches the hook directly to the nose of the bait. Make the stitches in the upper jaw only, through the nose so the bait can continue to move water through its gills. It must be lively and frisky when a blue marlin comes sniffing around. A nearly dead, lethargic bait may get passed right by.

A second hook can be added to the rig on a short wire or mono leader. The trailing hook should also be stitched to the side of the baitfish so the hook doesn't dangle free. In the interest of speedy rigging which helps keep the bait alive, some fishermen use a small rubber band to keep the trailing hook in place.

The game plan is to power drift, moving the boat at a slow speed so as not to damage or lose the bait. The captain watches for signs of life, such as bait, weed lines, and color and temperature changes while shifting one or both engines in and out of gear. The live bait is moved slowly towards and across good bottom structure, color changes and near weed lines.

The trolling speed is so slow that it can be hard to catch additional baits, but the mate might get another tunny by jigging a spoon in the prop wash with about 50 to 75 feet of line in the water. The erratic speed up and slow down of the lure may get some interest and a second live bait can then be fished in the pattern. One bait is fished long about 250 feet aft, while the second bait is placed about 150 feet astern. They are best fished from outrigger clips so the spread of the outrigger poles keep the baits apart. A honeymoon for the baits means tangled lines and lots of lost fishing time.

Hefty tackle of the 50W or 80-pound class gets the nod for this fishing. Tackle this heavy may overpower the smaller marlin that may take the bait, but it will assure success when a big boy of 500 to 600 pounds slurps the bait down.

Live Bait Sailfish

Late fall, winter and early spring in Florida, from Palm Beach to the upper Keys, is prime time for live bait fishing for sailfish. Does it work? You bet it does and it works so well that during some tournament weekends, live goggle eyes will sell for over $100 a dozen and fishing boats stand in line to get their ration of bait from the local bait boats!

If your pocketbook can't withstand that kind of punishment, many other baits can be caught off the docks that will work just as well, such as lookdowns, jacks, blue runners and grunts. Runners are often relatively easy to catch just off the beach over reefs and rocky bottoms or near waterway marker pilings. Use a jigging rig that has several tiny feather or quill jigs attached along the leader. The feathers are spaced about 12 inches apart on a long leader with a bucktail or jig at the bottom end for casting weight. Small white or silvery feathers with tiny hooks on short leaders can catch plenty of runners for a day's fishing.

In the Keys, the primary baits are ballyhoo and cigar minnows chummed within cast netting range along the coral patches inside the drop-off at the big reefs. I was never too handy with a cast net so I used tiny wire hooks to catch bally at the patches one at a time. It usually took no more than a half hour or so to catch a day's supply to then troll along the reef.

Ballyhoo are hooked through the lower jaw and out the top of the upper jaw with the beak broken off. Goggle eyes and most other baits are hooked with a short length of cotton rigging twine run cross ways through the eyes, or cross stitched across the top of the head.

Most small baits are reasonably hardy when kept in a circular built-in live well or an above-deck tank. Built-in, below-deck live wells are exceptionally handy since no deck space is lost. The downside is the generally small size of many built-in tanks. Some custom boats, however, that spend a lot of time on the sailfish grounds, may have a huge tank built in under the deck.

One of the nicest above-deck bait tanks is the doughnut shaped style that slips over the fight chair or rocker launcher stanchion. It is out of the way so little deck space is lost and it can keep several dozen baits alive and frisky. Another good choice is the 30 to 50-gallon barrel-shaped tanks. This is the style that I use, tied to a tower leg so it doesn't move in choppy seas.

The more water that can flow through the tank, the better it will be for the baits. I've had great success with the SHURflo #2088 bait tank and wash down pump. This pump is actually rigged as my saltwater wash down system. I add a Y-valve so one hose goes to the 40-gallon bait tank, the other to the wash down hose. The momentary, slight loss of water flow when the wash down hose is used doesn't bother the baits. I've kept baits alive in this tank for several days with no problems.

The best tanks are always circular. The intake hose should enter the top of the tank and curve along the inside of the tank until it reaches the bottom. When the pump is activated, the water current will swish in a circular motion so the baits can swim against the current. This is essential for healthy baits. If they nose into the corners of a square-shaped tank, they may suffocate even though lots of water is being pumped through the tank. It is always best if the baits are actively moving all the time.

LIVE BAITS AND CHUNK BAITS

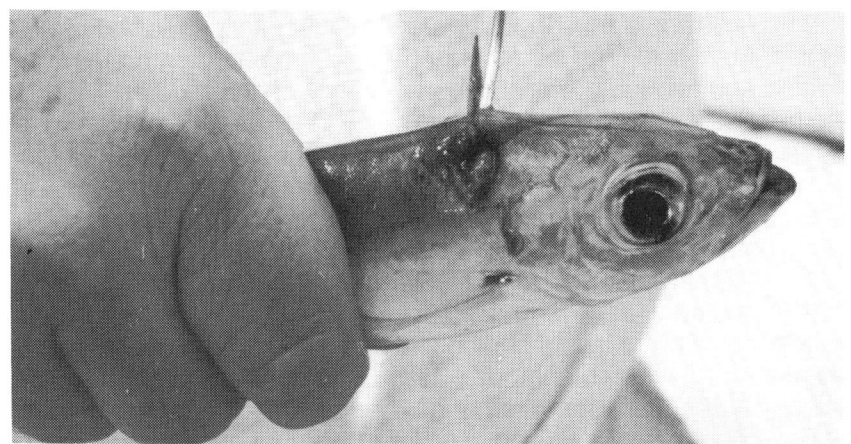

Goggle eye hooked just ahead of dorsal fin. Jeff Merrill Photo.

Ballyhoo hooked through lower jaw.

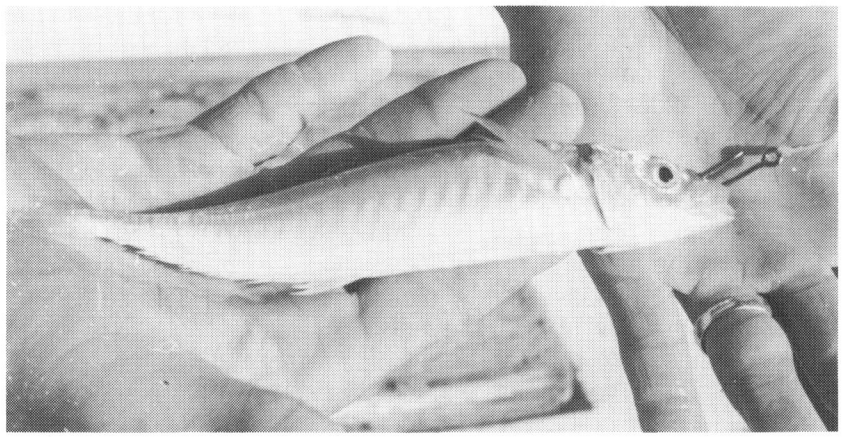

Cigar minnow hooked through mouth and out the nose.

Baits are hooked in the same manner as described for marlin fishing. Four baits can be fished at the same time, two off the outriggers and two more off flat lines or directly off the rod tips. Placing the baits at 50, 75, 125 and 200 feet behind the boat will cover a wide range of water. The boat is power drifted across the edge of the reef or drop-off by alternately shifting one or both engines in and out of gear to slowly pull the baits from the shallow water to the deep, or along bottom structure that has held sails in the past.

Water depth, water color and water temperature can be critical so it pays to keep an eye peeled to the electronics that show the changes in surface temps and bottom depths. Fishing off Palm Beach one February we had some fair action with sails in 90 feet of water, releasing three fish that afternoon. The next day we caught nothing until we began power drifting in water of 240 feet of depth where the water was a deeper blue and a full degree warmer than the inshore water.

High on Kites

Kites are used extensively by Florida fishermen and they are used with telling effect. The method keeps live baits right near the surface splishing and splashing in a dance that drives sailfish wild. Kites are not just for sailfishing, however, and a growing number of offshore fishermen are beginning to use kites for tuna, marlin, wahoo and dolphin. I watched Captain Barry Dudas on the charter boat L & H, catch yellowfin tuna while lying at anchor in the midst of a bluefin tuna fleet off Block Island. We were two boats away from the L & H and needless to say we were frustrated at Barry's success and the lack of ours, but we sure enjoyed the show of how well kites can work. Fred Lane, who fishes out of Ocean City, Maryland, told me of the exceptional success he's had with yellowfin tuna by fishing live spot or snapper blues from kites. Barry and Fred may be the exception today, but as more anglers realize how good kite fishing can be, this method may become more common in mid Atlantic and northeast waters.

Kites are available at most southern fishing tackle shops or they can be ordered through the mail from places like Murray Brothers in Riviera Beach or Custom Rod and Gun in Pompano Beach. The Bob Lewis kite is the best known and it is available in several versions for light, medium and heavy winds, along with a variety of kite fishing accessories including special kite reels and lines.

Factory-made kite rods and reels, use a large wooden or plastic reel spool to hold the kite line and allow for the letting out and taking in of the line. Fancier custom rods, only 2 to 3 feet in length are also used and can be wrapped to match the boat's fishing tackle. If a

LIVE BAITS AND CHUNK BAITS

FISHING WITH KITES

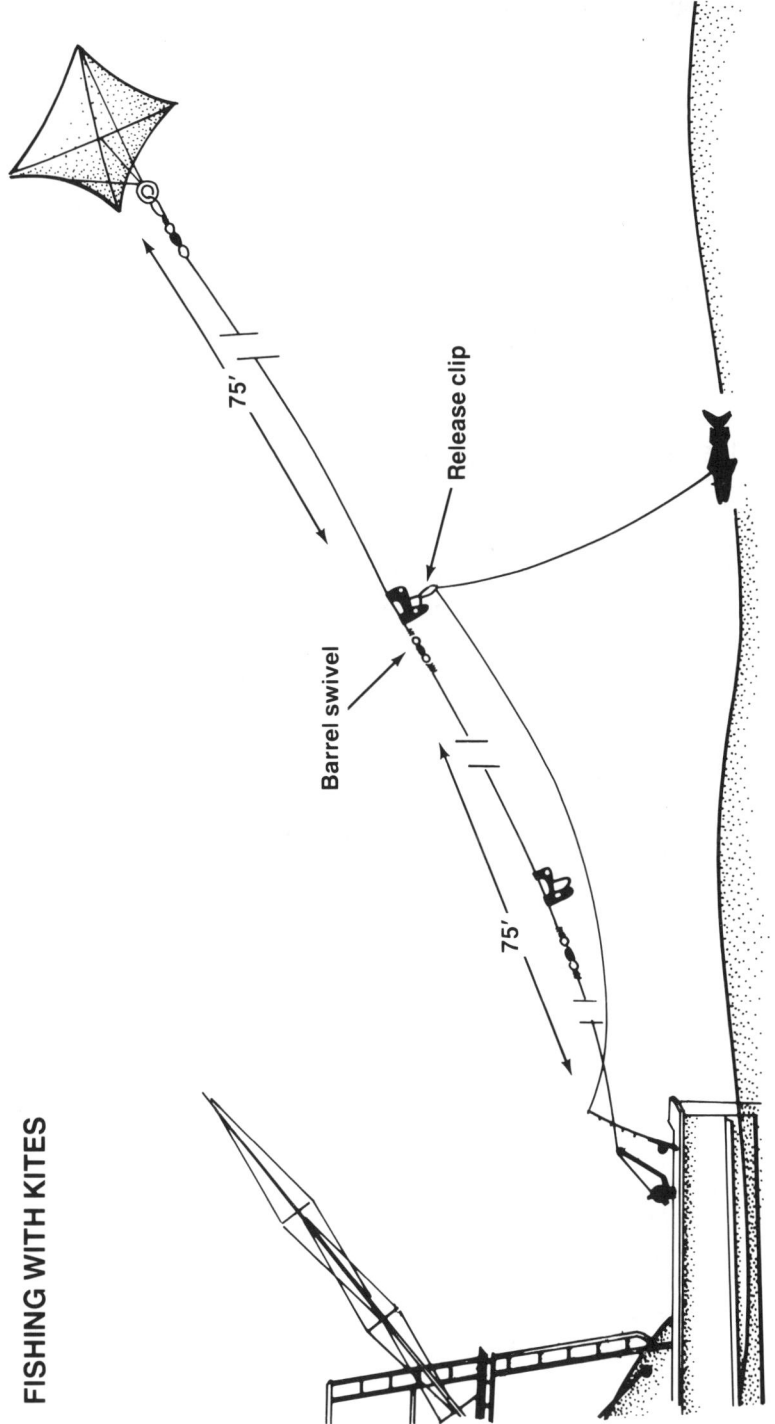

185

custom rod is employed, a star drag reel like the 112H or 113H is perfect for holding the kite line. The fanciest of kite outfits use electric reels to work the kite line.

Dacron is the line of choice for the kite, although some fishermen do use mono. The Dacron is light in weight so it flies well with the kite and it has no coiling memory like mono. The coiling line can be a minor annoyance when first letting the kite out when there isn't much pull on the line as when the kite is fully deployed.

The basic kite outfit is rigged with a snap at the end of the line to attach to the kite. A release clip is slipped onto the line above a small barrel swivel that is tied about 75 feet from the snap. An optional second release clip can be installed on the line but it must have holes in the clip that are large enough to allow the clip to slide over the first, or upper barrel swivel. To prevent the second release clip from sliding down the Dacron line, a large barrel swivel is tied about 75 feet from the first swivel.

The line from the fishing rod and reel is slipped into the release clip and the kite line and rod and reel line are pulled out by the kite as the wind lifts it away from the boat. The fishing line can be adjusted in length so the bait splashes on the surface of the water. Too much line will allow the bait to swim deep into the water, while too little line will keep the bait airborne. The length of line to the bait will have to be fine tuned during the day as the boat moves and changes direction to the wind, or as the breeze freshens or slacks off.

While it is possible to fish two kites at the same time, one kite is the best bet. Use the second release clip to add a second bait, rather than deploying another kite to get more baits in the water. I know from experience that a pair of kites can cause unbelievable problems if they get crossed and tangled.

With the rod and reel in a rod holder in the cover boards, the strike of a fish is easy to play out for a high percentage of hook-ups. The reel is in free spool, or with a slight amount of drag to avoid an overrun or backlash. At the strike, the angler picks up the rod and reel from the holder and points the rod tip towards the fish. The lever is shoved to the Strike position, or the free spool lever is engaged, and the reel is cranked to remove any slack line. As the line comes tight, the angler lifts the rod tip smartly several times to set the hook.

The natural delay as the rod is pulled from the holder, the line is reeled tight and the rod tip lifted is about perfect for assuring a good number of hook-ups. However, a number of top-notch sailfish addicts recommend a slightly longer drop back to the fish. The drop back should rarely be more than 5 to 7 seconds. If the fish drops the bait, jigging the rod tip may make the bait look enticing for a second look from the sail.

Once the fish is hooked, the fishing line is automatically snapped free from the release clip as the line comes tight against the battling fish. The kite is reeled in and the fish is fought directly from the fishing rod and reel.

Baitfishing for Tuna

Baitfishing techniques to catch tuna have been around for many years under many different names. In Australia they call it burleying, in America we call it chumming. In Bermuda chumming means dicing up little tunny and tossing the slivers into the rich waters off the Challenger and Argus banks to catch yellowfin. Along the East Coast butterfish are sliced into pieces for bluefin and yellowfin and it's called chunking. No matter the name, or the slight variations to fine tune the technique, it is baitfishing at its finest and it frequently catches tuna like crazy.

This style of fishing probably got its start decades ago when northeast and mid Atlantic inshore bluefin tuna anglers chummed with ground menhaden and baited with tinker mackerel, butterfish or chunks of menhaden. The largest baits were cut up into chunks and tossed into the chum slick to spice it up with added fish scent, flash and dining appeal for the tuna. Handfuls of sand eels, spearing or smelt were also added to further juice up the slick.

A heavy chum slick often called excessive numbers of bluefish into the baits, a less than desirable fish if the target species was exclusively bluefin. To avoid bluefish attacks, many anglers simply chummed by cutting the butterfish or bunker into small pieces. Ladled into the water in batches of 5 to 15 chunks, the slick was not so heavy to attract the voracious, but pesky bluefish, but it was still very effective on tuna. It became a favorite method of party and charter boats.

Back in the late 1970s, as the smaller sizes of bluefin declined dramatically, yellowfin moved closer to shore to take up residence in areas previously held by bluefin. Chunking with butterfish proved to be a deadly effective way to catch the yellowfins consistently and it wasn't long before chunking became widely used in the Canyon areas from New England waters to south Jersey. Today, the technique continues to expand and variations of this cut bait technique are used from Key West to Virginia and in the traditional grounds from Delaware to Massachusetts.

Chunking seems to work the best during mid summer through early fall when surface water temperatures range between the mid 70 degree and 80 degree mark. A careful eye on the color scope while trolling in August or September will usually show tuna holding 5 to 20 fathoms below the surface in the daylight hours. Once the sun goes down, the fish will often rise to the occasion and readily take chunk baits, sometimes with abandon. On the inshore grounds the best action is often at dawn and dusk, but can continue through the daylight hours. Cloudy, overcast days may have non-stop action all through the day.

Catches of 20 to 30 fish per night at the edge of the Continental Shelf are not at all unusual when the tuna are on a good feed and there is plenty of bait around. Chunking isn't a guarantee on every trip however, and cool water, lack of bait, moon phase and weather can all throw a glitch into the good fishing.

Look for the invasion of a warm eddy into a particular canyon which may assure good fishing. The presence of whales and porpoises, hordes of squid and mackerel, and clear blue water are also good signs that tuna will congregate in an area, signaling good fishing.

Tuna fishing is always exciting but chunking offers the chance to stand toe to toe with these amazing fish. Being able to feel the determined pick-up of the bait, the yank of the fish as it pulls the line from your grasp, and then the power of the fish as the rod tip is lifted to set the hook is unlike anything ever experienced while trolling. You are in much closer contact with the fish and there lies the reason why chunking is so popular.

Depending upon where you actually fish, inshore or offshore, it's possible to use this method to catch yellowfin, bigeye, bluefin, long fin albacore and occasionally even billfish such as white marlin and swordfish, plus dolphin. Chunking is a very effective way to catch offshore fish.

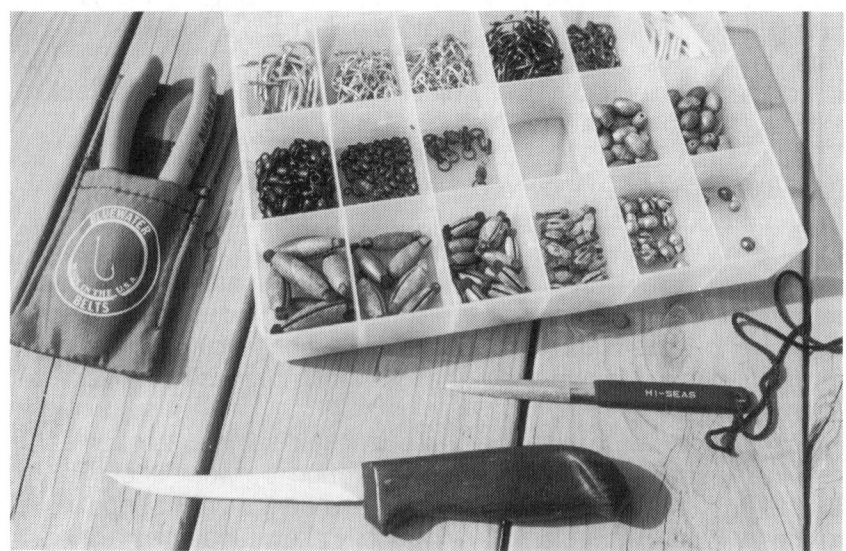

Chunking equipment is minimal; hooks, sinkers, swivels, pliers, knife and hook sharpener.

Tackle Tips

From spinning reels to lever drag reels, tackle runs the gamut from relatively light equipment to heavy duty stuff that can put the boots to big fish. Unfortunately, many fishermen use tackle that is far too heavy for the fish they intend to catch. Hefty rods and reels capable of handling 100 to 200-pound test line will usually "kill" the angler long before the fish is even beginning to tire.

On the inshore grounds where most tuna will range from 15 to 75 pounds, 30 or 40-pound test tackle is ideal. In deeper water, 50, 60 or 80-pound tackle is usually preferred for the tuna running from 75 to 200 pounds.

Bigger fish can be brought to the boat in less time when fought with 2-speed reels. Rods with short lower butts and long grips ahead of the reel have replaced standard trolling tackle which is usually unsuited for stand-up fishing except in the light tackle range.

As discussed in Chapter Two, the very short West Coast rods are giving way to slightly longer East Coast style rods that have a bit more power in the butt section, yet still have a light tip action. Very short 4½ to 5-foot rods provide great leverage to lift big fish from deep water but offer no defense as tuna try to tangle lines around an outboard lower unit or inboard props and rudders. The best choice for East Coast tuna action are rods of 5½ to 6 feet to gain slight extra length to work the fish with maximum control.

Smaller tuna, like school bluefin and yellowfin, false albacore, skipjack, blackfin tuna and bonito will sometimes frequent the same waters as bluefish, snake kings and dolphin. They offer a perfect light tackle opportunity. Hook into a 10-pound school tuna on a one-handed spinning outfit and you'll be busy for quite a while. Spinning gear can be used for bluefin and yellowfin up to 40 pounds and is very effective for these smaller fish when they are extremely leader shy.

Rigging Up

How to rig for chunking will change with water clarity and whether or not the fish are extremely spooky or if they are very aggressive. Chunking in the daytime may call for lighter, less visible leaders than chunking during the night shift. Most chunkers would prefer to add a heavier leader at the end of the line but when the fish are line-shy this isn't possible. Therefore, there are two choices; tie direct with no leader or add a leader to protect against cut-offs in battles that may last 15 to 45 minutes. Tuna can be notoriously line-shy so there are times when no leader can be used at all. I sometimes go down to 20-pound test, tied direct to the hook, to score with line-shy tuna. Most

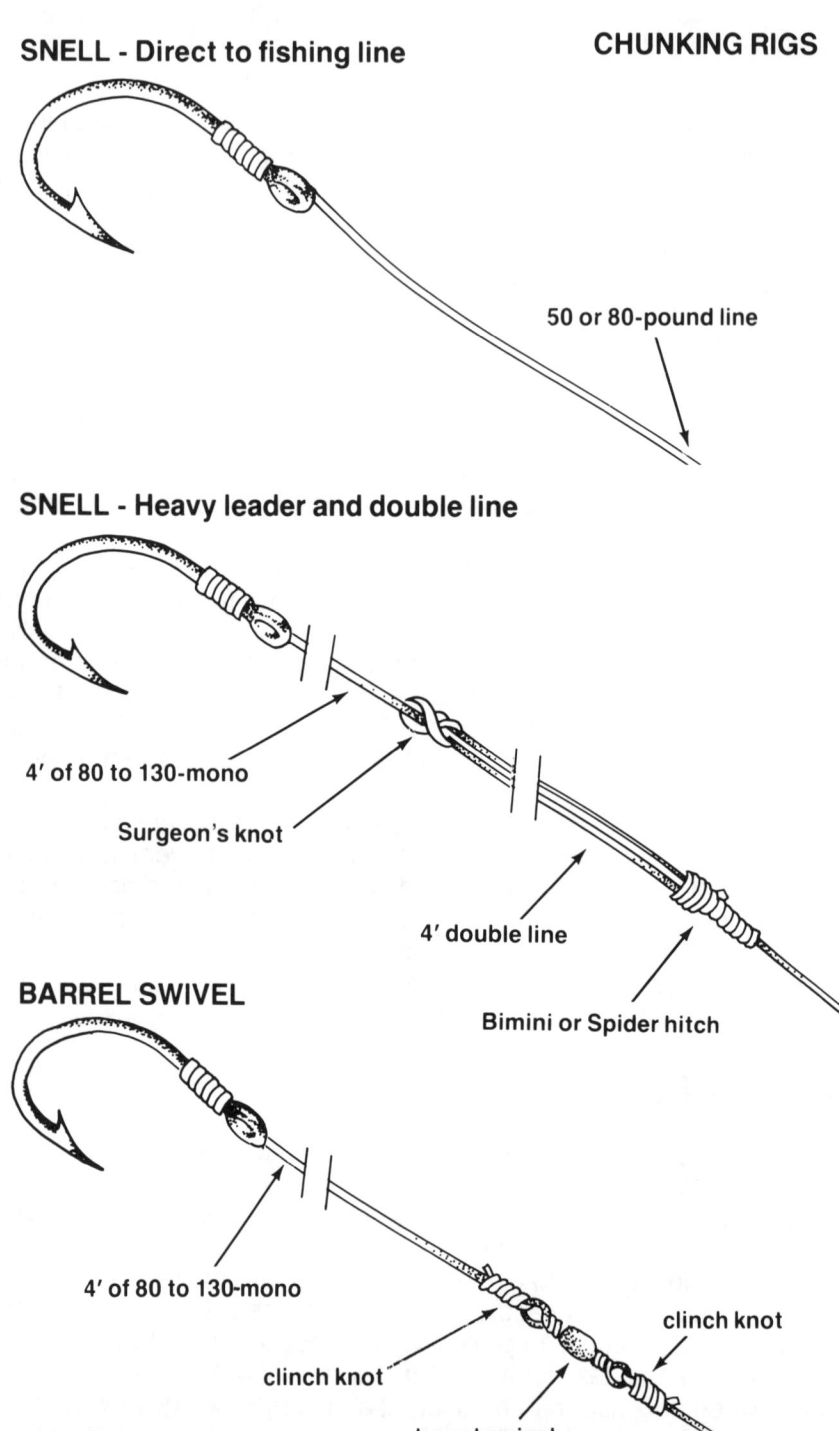

chunkers select leaders about twice the strength of the main fishing line. With 30-pound line use a 50 or 60-pound test leader. With 50-pound line use an 80 or 100-pound test leader.

The leader can be added in either of two ways. The first method uses a short bimini twist to make a 2 to 4-foot double line, then joins the leader to the double line with a surgeons knot. With this method the leader can be up to 10 feet long. The second method adds a ball bearing swivel between the fishing line and the leader. A clinch knot secures the main line and leader to the swivel. In this case the leader should be 4 to 6 feet in length so the barrel swivel can be reeled right to the rod tip, placing the tuna within tagging or gaffing range without the need to handline any part of the leader. The swivel prevents line twist from spinning baits.

Several hook styles work well, including the Mustad #9175, #9174 and #94150; and the Eagle Claw #188. Use either bronze or silver finish hooks, sharpened to razor points. The size hook to choose depends on the size of the bait, not necessarily the size of the fish. Small chunks of butterfish work best with 3/0 to 5/0 hooks while a whole butter may get more hook-ups with a 5/0 to 9/0 size hook.

Hooks are attached to the leader or directly to the line with a palomar, improved clinch, or Uni-Knot. For bigeye tuna when heavy leaders are used, some fishermen prefer to use a small crimp to add the hook to the leader instead of a knot. To save rigging when the action is fast paced, I make up groups of 10 leaders and store them in zip lock bags. They stay dry and can be stowed handily in the tackle locker or a ditty bag ready for instant use. When the bite is red hot, every second counts.

Chunking requires several sharp knives, cutting board, several 5-gallon buckets to store chunks and baits, two or more long handled gaffs, tail ropes, tuna bag, ice, boxes of hooks, coils of leaders, pliers, box of barrel swivels, split shot, egg sinkers, rubber core sinkers, anchor and line, leadering gloves, charts, note pad, tags, saltwater wash down to clear decks and towels to keep hands dry.

Bait Choices

Butterfish, cut into chunks or fished whole is the bait most often used but bunker (menhaden), ling, whiting, large spearing and sand eels are also used. To hook a whole butterfish, insert the hook through the mouth and out the gill plate. Push the hook point cross ways through the body of the bait about 1/3 down the side of the butterfish. The leader should lie underneath the gill plate, the hook pulling against firm meat so the bait doesn't bend and the hook point is exposed.

While whole butterfish are used as hooked baits, the chunk slick is made from sliced chunks of butters, bunker or sand eels; hence the name of the game - chunking. Depending on the size of the butters, three to five chunks can be cut from each fish. Butters are usually purchased frozen in 25-pound slabs packed in flat boxes. Each flat will last from one to two hours depending on how heavily the angler chunks. I prefer to chunk lightly but occasionally toss in a large handful of bait if the action is slow. The idea is to attract the tuna to the boat where they can eat the baited hooks. Too heavy a chunk slick keeps the tuna far back and away from the boat and out of range of the hooked baits. When tuna show in the slick and boil behind the boat, it can pay to toss extra chunks to get a feeding frenzy started. Any hooked bait tossed into the slick at this time will usually get smashed immediately.

On a boat with three fishermen, two anglers will fish while one will chunk. The chunker should toss several chunks in a pattern around the boat watching to see how the chunks drift with the tide or current. As the first set of chunks disappears from view into the water, another set of chunks is presented. The rhythm is continued until tuna invade the slick and attack the baits.

For school tuna, small fish such as spearing or sand eels on small hooks of size 1 to 2/0 hidden in the baits and tied directly to the mono line. A little weight may be needed to sink the offering so it stays in the slick level. Small split shots of 1/4-ounce rubber core sinkers do the trick to get below the surface layer. When fish are active in the slick they will sometimes hit diamond jigs or butterfish jigs.

Live Bait Tuna

Cut butterfish catch tuna so well that few fishermen try using live baits, yet there are times when the fishing can be exceptionally slow and a fresh, frisky snapper blue, spot, menhaden, mackerel or squid, can turn slow chunking into unbelievably fast action.

Snappers, spot and menhaden must be caught back at the dock or in local rivers and tidal basins leading to the inlets. The baits are transferred to a live well. Any baits that may be bleeding slightly should be taken from the tank and placed in the cooler for possible use when the live ones run out.

Squid and tinker mackerel can often be found in huge numbers offshore, zipping through the chunk slick every few minutes, feeding on the tiniest pieces of bait. A squid jig or small piece of butterfish on a tiny hook will catch these baits with regularity so they can be drifted back into the slick to catch a tuna.

Small live baits fished in the Keys at seamounts like the Hump, are simply hooked once through the flesh just ahead of the dorsal fin and cast gently away from the boat. Blackfin eat 'em up like kids grabbing for candy.

Yellowfin will come within a few feet of the transom when feeding aggressively, and it's an awesome sight to see 100-pound tuna chasing a live bait. They make quite a commotion and forget all about caution as they focus on trying to capture the bait as it zips right and left trying to avoid becoming an hors d'oeuvre.

Working the Tackle

Whether fishing for school tuna or bigger offshore tuna, the tackle is worked in essentially the same manner. The rod is placed in a flush mount gun'l rod holder, the reel is in free spool with only slight tension on the spool to prevent a backlash at the strike. The angler stands along side of and slightly ahead of the rod and reel. Line is pulled hand over hand, a foot or two at a time so the bait drifts back into the slick with no resistance from the line but not too fast to cause excess slack line.

After 30 to 100 pulls with no strike, the bait is retrieved. A fast retrieve may cause excessive line twist, so go easy. A favorite trick of ours is to retrieve the bait with just enough tension on the reel spool to allow the line to be slowly wound on the reel. Sometimes tuna attack these backward swimming butters.

At the strike, the angler turns to the rod and reel, lifting the tackle from the rod holder with the left hand ahead of the reel, the right hand on the butt below the reel. The right hand guides the rod butt into the gimbal belt, the left hand keeps the rod tip parallel to the water. The right hand slides the lever forward putting the reel into gear then reels until the line comes tight. The left hand lifts the rod tip smartly to set the hook. At the strike both hands are needed to hang on! With practice this takes a scant two to three seconds to work the strike smoothly and with a positive hook-up. Too much delay may cause a lost fish.

For truly big fish that may take more than 10 to 15 minutes to land, a buddy should help the angler get into a kidney harness that attaches to lugs on the reel and provides support across the angler's back. By rocking back and forth and using legs and lower back, the fisherman raises the rod tip to lift the fish and lowers the rod tip to reel in line. This pumping action gains line quickly with little strain. Especially tough fish are short stroked with a rapid rocking motion gaining line a few inches at a time by putting the fish off balance.

Gaffing Tips

Tuna caught while chunking are notoriously "green" when brought to the side of the boat. Their power is amazing and many captains have stories of gaffs ripped from strong deck hands as tuna tried to escape. Tagged fish should be estimated in length, tagged near the dorsal fin and the leader cut close to the mouth quickly with a sharp knife, not pliers.

Fish meant for the table should be gaffed near the head to save the most meat. A 6 to 8-foot gaff with a 4-inch bite of 5/16-inch diameter stainless is about perfect. Heavy fish can be lifted into the boat with the added help of a tail rope. Once on board, a tap in the noggin with a billy club calms the fish as it's slid into the ice bag or cooler. Decks should be cleaned right away to get back in action quickly.

It is vital that the chunker must continue chunking all through the battle and boat side antics. If not, a new slick will have to be started causing a delay in the action.

A 100-pound yellowfin taken on stand-up gear is an experience to remember.

LIVE BAITS AND CHUNK BAITS

Anchoring VS Drifting

Many northeast offshore fishermen have become obsessed with lobster pots. That only sounds strange to those who don't fish the northeast. Lobster pot markers were once thought to be an ideal tie-off point to keep a boat stationary during a night of baitfishing. Actually lobster pots are both good and bad. They are bad if the current is running against the wind causing the lines to run under, not away from, the boat. They are good on a rough night since tying off keeps the bow pointed into the wind and sea making for a more comfortable lay over. They are bad news, however, if the fish never come near the spot where your boat is tied off and this is why many of the most successful chunkers prefer to drift rather than tie off.

An often overlooked point is the position of the commercial fisherman who owns the lobster gear. Tying off incorrectly, can cause the gear to tangle or possibly to bounce on the bottom ruining any chance for a good lobster catch. This causes lobstermen to get justifiably angry at the "sporties". This is private property and no one but the owner of the gear has a right to use it.

I have done so much better when drifting instead of tied off, that I never bother with tying off any longer. Tuna must swim constantly to stay alive, so they are always on the move. Drifting allows the boat to move with the fish so the crew can catch fish after fish, often all night long.

It is impractical to anchor along the deep edge of the canyons where the water depth exceeds 100 fathoms, but it is possible to anchor in 50 fathoms or less with relative ease. To grab the bottom with no chance of sliding, use an extra heavy anchor and a 20-foot length of chain. The anchor line should be long enough to be two to three times the depth of the water. That's a lot of line but we'll discuss a neat anchor retrieval system in a few more pages.

For inshore fishing, I have two anchor lines prepared and take the one I need with me depending on where I'll be fishing. The 300-foot rode is used to anchor in water of 120 to 180 feet and a second line of 600 feet for deeper water of 250 to 350 feet of depth. They are stored in large laundry baskets and washed after each trip.

Although lobster pots are private property and should not be disturbed, many fishermen do get on the pots all the time. On a calm night with no rough sea, there is probably no adverse affect on the gear and it may be okay to "get on the ball" for the night's action. If you must do this, use a long tag line to attach to the high flyer marker. Attach the line with a large stainless snap below the float at the bottom of the high flyer. Use a line of at least 200, preferable 300 feet in length to dampen the rocking action of the boat against the lobster pot line.

Anchor Retrieval System

Anchor float balls had been used by giant tuna fishermen for many years, but I first saw the float ball system used when fishing in the Florida Keys. Charter captains anchoring in places like the North Hole off Islamorada for school kingfish needed an efficient, fast way to haul a 22-pound anchor aboard. The seas were sometimes choppy at the edge of the drop at the reef and it was no fun for a mate to struggle with a bulky, flopping anchor.

Local Keys captains had been using the float ball system for many years and it sure made anchoring life a lot easier. Captain Ted D'Esposito of the charter boat Sump'N Special gave me the split ring I needed to make up my own float rig and the next season, back home off Manasquan, I started using the float rig on my own boat.

The rig is simple. It consists of a Norwegian style float ball with a short length of 1/2-inch line eye spliced to the ball. At the other end of the short line is a brass or stainless snap, also attached with an eye splice. The key part is a stainless steel loop that gets slipped over the anchor line and is clipped to the float ball with the snap at the end of the short line.

All the parts are readily available from marine supply stores from Maine to Key West although you may have to search a bit for the stainless steel split ring. If your dealer does not have the ring in stock, ask him to try Sea Bright Stainless, Captain Vic's Enterprises or Reliable Gaff. Mail order sources like Fisherman's Paradise, Outer Banks and Fisherman's Headquarters also have the split rings.

Some fishermen are skeptical when they see the system work for the first time because it looks like the anchor line is going to get chopped to smithereens by the props. The trick is to check the compass heading toward the anchor line as it lies off the bow while you are still anchored.

Get the float ball ready by unsnapping the ring from the brass snap. Slip the ring over the anchor line, then re-attach the brass snap so the anchor is now trapped inside the ring. Toss the ball off the bow into the water. The end loop of the anchor line is still attached to the bow cleat.

As you start the retrieve, run at 90 degrees to the line for a distance of about 25 feet. Once clear of the line, as shown by the ball as it slides past the side of the boat off to the stern, you can run the compass course up the anchor line. The line will lay along the side of the boat, the float ball slides down the anchor line. Once over the anchor, the float actually lifts (or floats) the anchor free of the bottom. You'll see a large splash as the anchor shank slides through the ring and you know the anchor is now on the surface.

The various parts can cost up to $100, a fat piece of change, but the

LIVE BAITS AND CHUNK BAITS

TOP VIEW - ANCHOR RETRIEVE

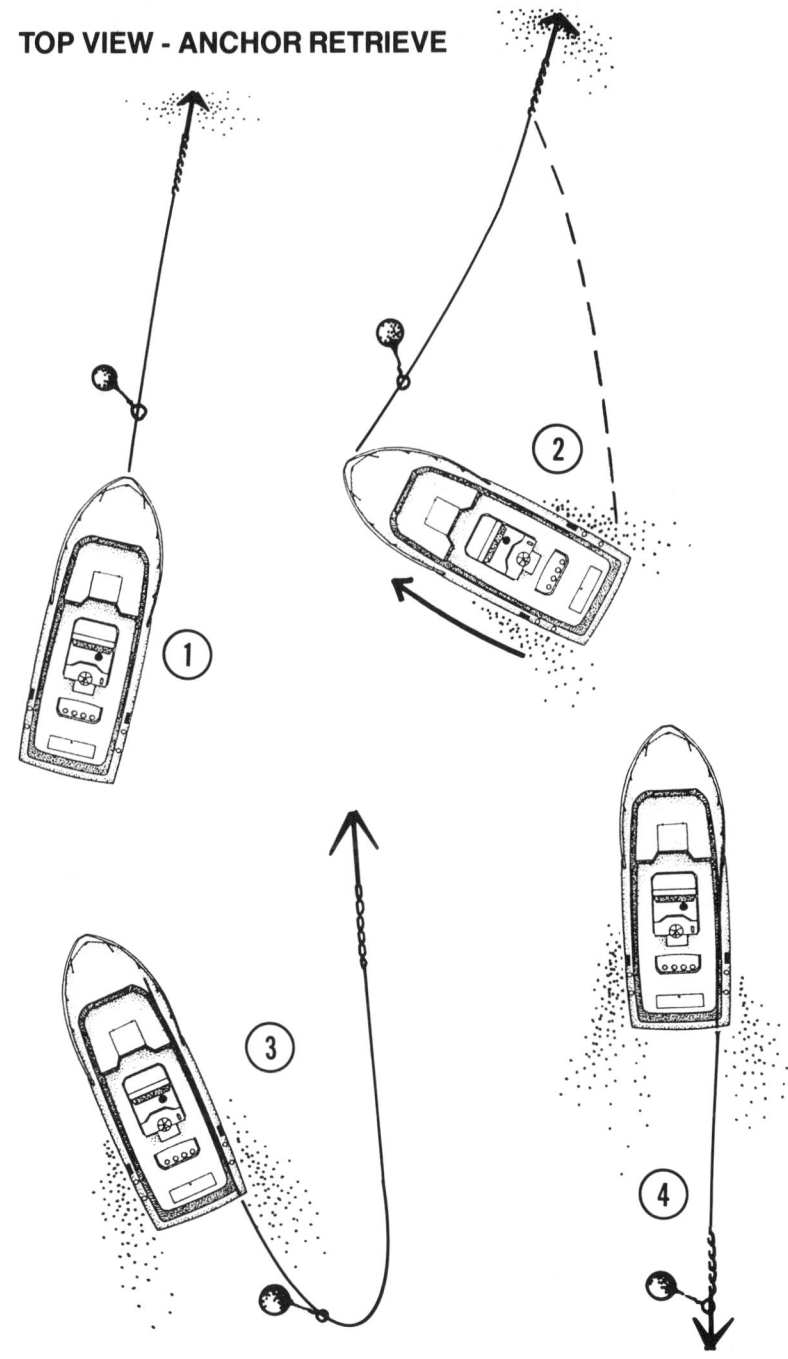

(1) Check compass heading to anchor line. (2) slowly run at 90 degrees to anchor line for 25 feet, then (3) run the compass course up the anchor line until (4) the anchor floats free of the bottom.

FISHING FOR TUNA AND MARLIN

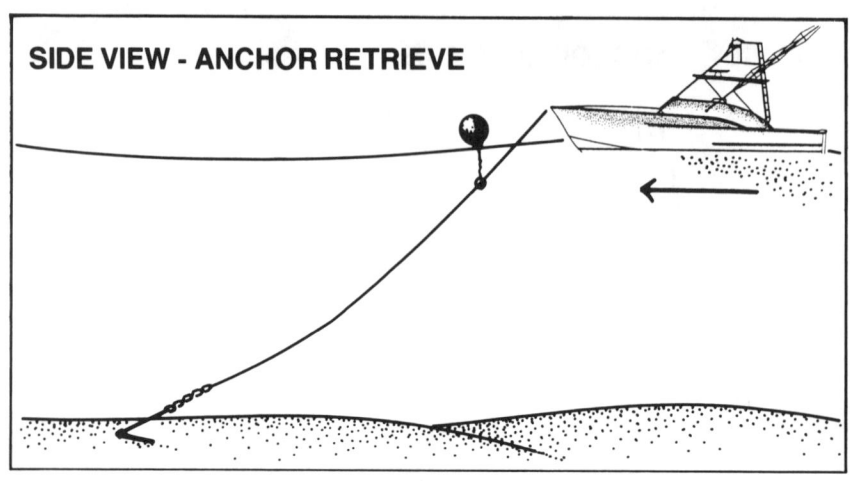

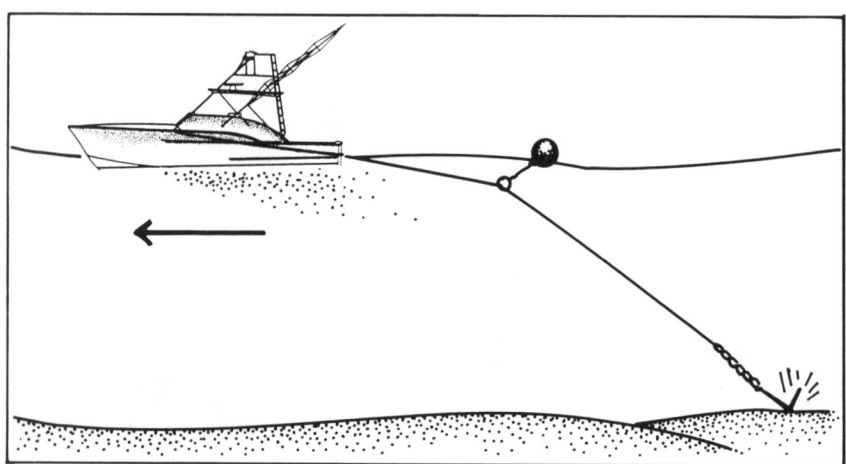

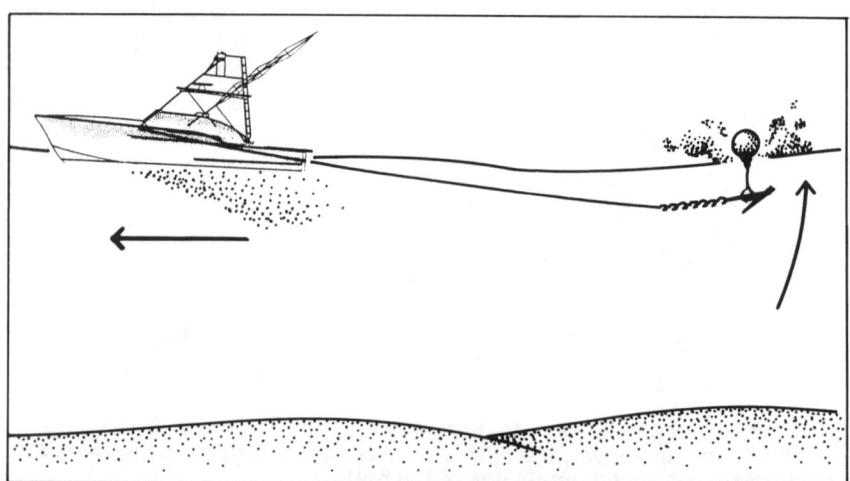

LIVE BAITS AND CHUNK BAITS

Float ball is attached to a brass snap on a short length of 3-strand line. Stainless ring locks over anchor line when brass snap is in place.

system will last for years. I've been using my ball, ring and snap for 16 years. It cost me $60 back in 1975, and put a sizable dent in my wallet, yet if I divide the number of years I've used the anchor lift, it comes out to less than $4 per year. It's still declining in cost as I continue to use it.

Once you have the parts; the float ball, brass snap, 1/2-inch line and the split ring, it's an evening's work to do the splices and get the rig ready for next season. Your back will love you for it.

Drifting for Swordfish

Before the overexploitation of swordfish by commercial longliners, it was a relatively easy thing to catch a trophy broadbill off the East Coast. From the Florida Straits to the canyons that nicked the Continental Shelf from the Norfolk north to the Atlantic Canyon, hundreds of boats drifted at night for these secretive, but highly prized trophy fish. Swordfish were in better shape, safe from the longliners, when they were believed to have high concentrations of mercury in their flesh. Unfortunately for the fish, this was later proved erroneous and the relentless pressure to deliver swordfish steaks to the market never let up. Today, few boats catch swordfish, but it not impossible to catch one of these great game fish.

FISHING FOR TUNA AND MARLIN

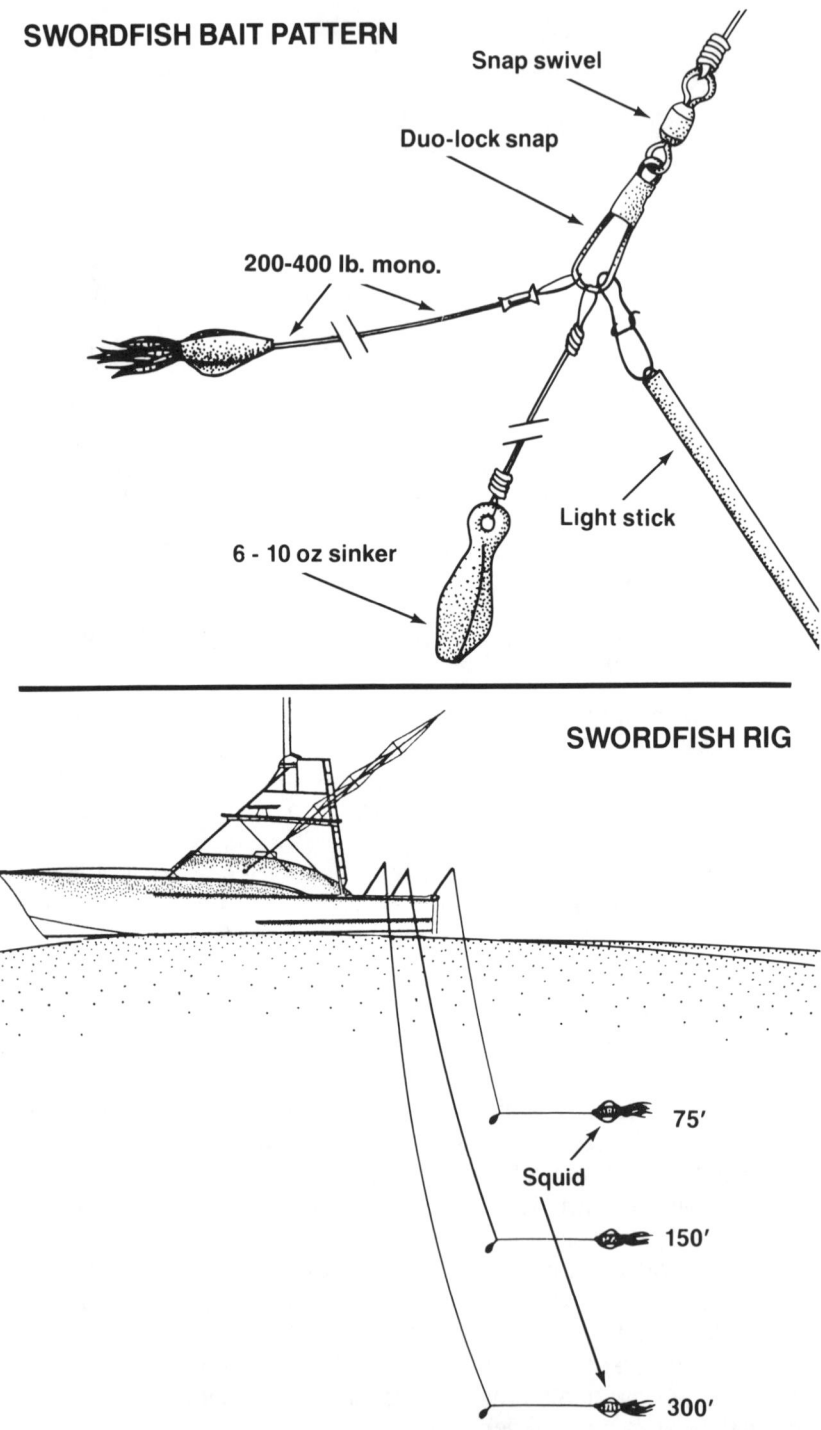

They are primarily nocturnal feeders, roaming the dark waters for squid and other bait. During the daylight hours, swords used to be seen lazing on the surface, half asleep it seemed, sunning themselves. Rarely do we see swordfish basking on the surface, during the day, their distinctive dorsal and tail fins cutting through the water.

If you are fortunate enough to spot one, the fish can only be approached cautiously to present a rigged bait. Run the boat beyond the fish then make a shallow turn to bring the bait directly in the path of the fish as it swims lazily along. Whole natural baits are preferred, such as a large squid, mackerel or small skipjack or bonito rigged on a double hook rig; one hook forward and the second in the tail.

Should the fish sound, it doesn't necessarily mean that it's not interested and the fish may come back to slash the bait with its broad, flat bill. Sometimes the fish do get spooked quickly and they dive out of sight paying no attention to the juiciest of baits. Fishing for swordfish on the surface can be extremely frustrating but for a number of sportfishermen who seek the highest angling challenges, a surface baited swordfish is the ultimate catch.

Fishing at night, however, is another story. Canyon anglers who drift after dark and fish squid baits at several depths, with cyalume light sticks clipped to the line, still catch some swordfish, although this method, too, is not as successful as it once was. Up until 10 years ago, drift boats off Miami and Palm Beach, at the Washington and Norfolk Canyons and off Block Island did fairly well with swordfish. Many fish exceeded 250 to 350 pounds and were truly trophy catches. The rape of swordfish by commercial longliners has been very thorough along the East Coast and few fish above 50 to 100 pounds are now caught.

Night swordfishermen usually fish three weighted lines. One is set with the bait at 50 feet, another at 100 and the third down 150 to 200 feet. A Cyalume light stick is tied to the swivel with thin line or a rubber band that will break after a fish is hooked. The light stick glows and acts as a beacon for wandering fish. Leader length is 15 to 30 feet of heavy monofilament. Swordfish have very soft mouths so large hooks are used; 12/0 or 14/0. The bait may be a large, whole fresh squid, whole bonito or other small tuna, a skipjack fillet strip bait or a live bait.

Reels are left in free spool with the clicker on while the boat drifts. The rods are in holders and all the angler does is sit back and wait for that electrifying sound of line being pulled off a reel. As in any kind of baitfishing, the lines should be checked occasionally for weeds and the baits replaced every hour or so. The simple act of changing a bait may get the strike as the fresh, new bait moves into position below the boat.

Chapter Eight

LOCATING FISH

Finding fish can be real easy on some days, frustratingly hard on others. Weather and sea conditions combine with water color, water temperatures and finicky fish to make or break a day on the water. The best fishermen become Columbo-like in their approach to fishing as they first try the obvious places to find fish and then begin eliminating the variables as the day progresses until they score a good catch. Sharp eyes on the depth finder to watch the changing bottom contours and on the water's surface for tell-tale signs help locate the best fishing spots.

The most important factor is usually the underwater bottom structure, the contours of the sea bed as it rises and falls in steep drop-offs, deep sloughs, humps, and finger-like ridges. The configuration of the bottom structure provides the "highways" that fish follow as they move from one area to another in search of food, safety and comfort. Most times, if you find the bottom structure, you'll find the fish.

Bottom structure isn't the only variable in the fish finding puzzle. Rips, color changes, temperature changes, weed lines, slicks and thermoclines also help locate or hold fish in certain areas. The best offshore captains are constantly searching the water for these vital signs that signal good fishing.

Bottom Structure

For fishing purposes, structure is any significant change in the bottom contour such as a ridge rising from 150 feet of water depth to a peak 120 feet from the surface, or a sharp drop-off into a deep hole or a stretch of irregular bottom with sloughs and ridges. Some structure can be very large like the Hudson Canyon off New Jersey and New York that covers about 200 square miles of fishing potential while others are very small like the Hump off Islamorada, Florida which is only a hundred yards or so in diameter.

The bottom contours are already marked on navigational charts sold by the government as NOAA charts and on many privately produced charts from a variety of local printing companies. The standard NOAA charts can be converted to excellent fishing charts by tracing over the bottom contour lines with a fine permanent marking pen to enhance the pale gray lines already printed on the chart.

Another excellent chart just starting to make an impact with offshore fishermen are the new bathymetric charts offering far greater bottom detail than previously available on the standard NOAA charts. Unfortunately these charts give depths in meters, but it only takes a

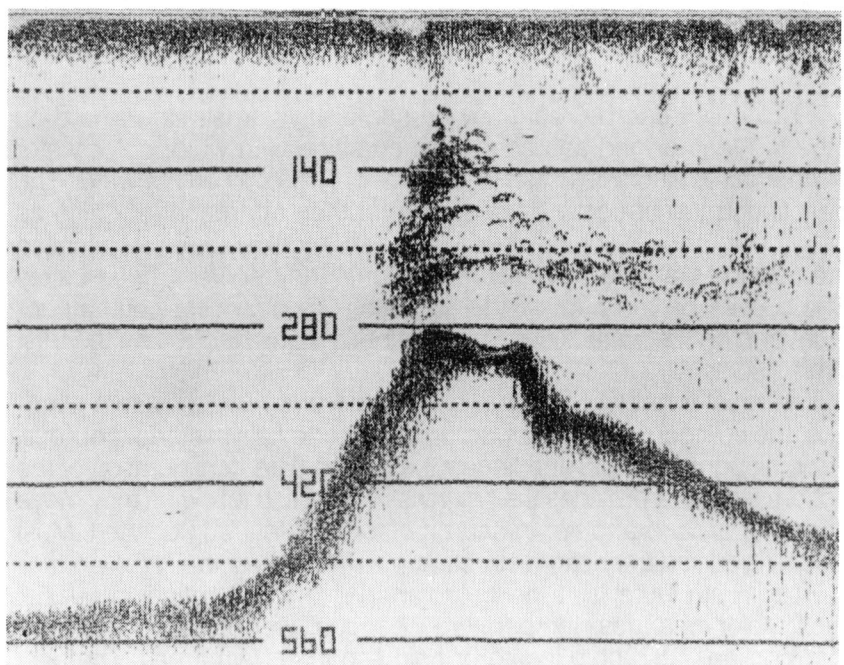

The Hump off Islamorada is a classic example of offshore fish-holding structure.

short time to get used to converting meters to fathoms or feet to get a good idea of what is on the bottom. Many depth finders meant for offshore use can provide depth readings in meters with just the flip of a selector switch.

NOAA and bathy charts are printed on paper that doesn't stand up well to water and they are usually too large for daily fishing use. I find it handier to cut the chart down so it fits into a zip lock style plastic cover. These are available at many boating supply, stationary and office supply stores. They last a long time and keep your charts bone dry. I have several offshore charts that cover areas like the Hudson Canyon to the Lindenkohl, Wilmington Canyon to Norfolk Canyon, the North Carolina Outer Banks, the Florida Straits and Bahamas, and the Florida Keys. They are readily storable and once marked with the contour lines, make ideal fishing charts. I also trace over the best pair of loran lines so these are also enhanced for greater visibility.

Birds, Rips, Weeds and Slicks

Most captains will fish along known structure lines but once on the edge of the structure, they follow their eyes to find specific good spots. The visible surface signs such as rips, birds working over bait, weed lines and bait slicks are also valuable markers that say "This is the spot!"

Birds can give away the location of a school of fish, but a lot depends upon the bird. The large and graceful frigate bird, also called the man-o-war, may hover over large bull dolphin and occasionally mark a marlin but they rarely indicate the presence of tuna. Shearwaters are more numerous than frigate birds and since they like the clean, blue offshore waters, they are good signs that you are fishing in good water. Shearwaters are good indicators of schools of bait which will usually attract both billfish and tuna. The little petrels, nicknamed Mother Cary's Chickens, that flit and dance on the surface often give away schools of tuna. The petrels feed on the small bits of baitfish that the tuna schools have ravaged.

On a trip to Chub Cay in the Bahamas a few years back, Bruce Huppert and I were trolling in his Mako, the Bru-Ry, off the Jolters and we noticed some birds working off to the deep of where we trolled. We ran a set past the dipping diving birds and hooked a blue marlin, Bruce's first, and therefore a memorable fish. We had been snake bit for three days while we heard of other boats in this Mako Marine tournament taking a blue one or a white one every day. The birds finally helped us score on that trip.

Another time at the Spencer Canyon, off New Jersey, we had large schools of longfin crashing bait in a frenzy. A keen eye with the binoculars disclosed the wheeling, diving petrels. Only when we got closer to the massive feeding attack did we see the splashes of the albacore. Birds again were the give away to good fishing and we had repeated blasts of albacore in the pattern, often with four to five fish on at once.

Rips can give away the location of fish, too. An unsuccessful morning several years ago just inshore of the Norfolk Canyon was shattered dramatically when we came upon a tremendous rip with white water waves churning up 2 to 4-foot seas. Pulling our spread of lures through that rip paid off with a 300-pound class blue marlin blasted the lure dropped way back off the center rigger. The rip held schools of skipjack, dolphin and at least that one blue marlin.

Rips form when two currents rub against one another in opposite directions causing swirling eddies, or where underwater currents are pushed to the surface by bottom structure, such as high ridge or hump. In either case, rips will often hold quantities of bait and provide a ready dining table for game fish. White marlin, in particular, may laze near rips waiting for the right meal and I've had several occasions where school yellowfin and longfin albacore worked a rip providing steady fishing for several hours.

Off Ocean City, Maryland just beyond Jacks Spot we found a huge rip that turned out to be a super producer of white marlin. The rip stretched for several hundred yards and we trolled skirted ballyhoo over the rip. Several small skipjack were an annoying diversion but not the trio of white marlin that crashed the baits. One was lost after a few jumps, a second bill-wrapped fish was lost near the boat when the light leader frayed and the third was released after being tagged.

In deep water, weed lines are usually made up of sargasso weed, picked up by the Gulf Stream and given a ride along or near the Continental Shelf. On the inshore grounds, eel grass and other types of vegetation may form in long strings of weed lines. The weed lines are actually formed by wind blowing the weeds into clumps, then into long strings of weeds as the wind stays steady from one direction. Should the wind change its course, the weed lines may get broken up, only to reform again as the new direction of the wind remains steady for several hours or several days.

Dolphin are notorious for holding under weed lines or floating debris. One tuna trip, trolling at the Wilmington Canyon, we found a weed line that stretched for miles. It held a big mess of 5-pound dolphin and we scored on several dozen of the prized gourmet fish. We ate dolphin all through the winter from that catch!

One of the largest dolphin I ever caught, however, came from beneath a floating copy of a newspaper. We picked a few small grasshoppers from under its wet pages by casting with spinning tackle. Suddenly a big ol' bull dolphin smacked a bucktail and did an

A roaring rip, like this one at The Point off Oregon Inlet, often holds billfish and tuna.

aerial dance for 20 minutes before he was boated. It weighed 46 pounds; a neat fish on 12-pound line, and it was caught from under a piece of debris only 2-feet square.

Oily looking slicks on the surface usually indicate schools of baitfish below. Intense, heavy slicks may mean tuna or billfish have been on a rampage, feasting on bait and the pieces of those that didn't get eaten entirely float to the surface where petrels and other sea birds feed on the remains.

Slicks are always worth a few passes as a "look see" to investigate if any fish are in the area. Slicks don't always mean fish are present at the time you troll past them, but something must have happened a relatively short time ago to cause the slick. Tuna can crash into schools of bait and wreck havoc on the smaller fish. The smashed and wounded bait leave a slick that can often be seen from quite some distance away.

I once came across a huge slick of several hundred yards in area, but several passes didn't get a sniff. Writing the TDs down in a notebook I keep at the helm, we returned to the slick later in the day and caught longfin albacore until our arms fell off.

Temperature Fishing

Water temperatures have a marked affect on where tuna or billfish may be located. On our runs to the offshore grounds we always keep an eye on the surface temperature gauge. Typically we arrive near the canyon edge after running for several hours in darkness. The damp morning air can be chilly and steamy hot coffee keeps us warm. At first light of dawn, the throttles get pushed forward a few hundred rpms to make better speed as the light improves and we can see the water ahead clearly.

As we near the edge of the shelf waters, Richie will be sorting through the lure box selecting winners from past offshore battles and Jeff is readying the cockpit to be sure everything is well organized and in its proper place. I'll be checking the chart and eyeballing the electronics. Anticipation is always in the air as we approach the edge.

Many mornings we get surprised by the alarm on the Dytek, as it buzzes its announcement of warmer, or cooler, water. If we hit a pocket of changing water temperature, even if we are short of the structure edge of the canyon, we may still fish that spot to see if fish are present. And, many times a quick stop on a temperature edge results in the cry of "Fish on!" as we hook-up on the first fish of the day.

Offshore species, like this sailfish, are strongly influenced by water temperatures.

LOCATING FISH

A red-hot boat, custom tackle, top notch crew and the sexiest, fish catchingest lures do not guarantee success at the canyons. A cockpit full of gold reels and diamond wrapped rods are all for nothing without a $200 to $300 temperature gauge to help you locate warm water eddies and smaller warm water pockets.

Longliners have known about warm eddies for years and have been specifically fishing the eddies with telling success. Sport fishermen began to realize the importance of fishing the edges of temperature changes several years ago and many captains do not run offshore without the latest fax print-out showing the location of the Gulf Stream and any nearby eddies.

Some anglers rely on word of mouth reports from dockside conversations as they compare notes with fellow canyon runners to plot the locations of temperature edges. Word of mouth reports are only as good as the captain passing along the information, so many canyon fishermen are investing in the services of companies that publish temperature charts, fishing reports and predictions of where the fishing is likely to be "hot" in the coming days.

For information on these services write or call:

OCEAN IMAGING
201 Lomas Santa Fe Drive, Suite 370, Solana Beach, CA 92075
(619) 792-8529

OFFSHORE SERVICES
Captain Len Belcaro, Rt 70, Manasquan Park, NJ 08732
(908) 840-4900

ROFFS
Dr. Mitch Roffer, 8542 SW 102 St, Miami, FL 33156
(305) 274-5759

When fishing warm eddies, we are basically looking for the bluest, cleanest water to be found in the oceans, known as Gulf Stream water. Inshore shelf water is usually greenish in color and while it can hold fish, it is less than ideal for maximum success. It is the most inshore of the water classes. Slope water is more blue and is usually found along the edge of the 100 fathom curve. Gulf Stream slope water is bluer yet and is a mix of the pure Stream water with the slope water.

WARM CORE EDDYS

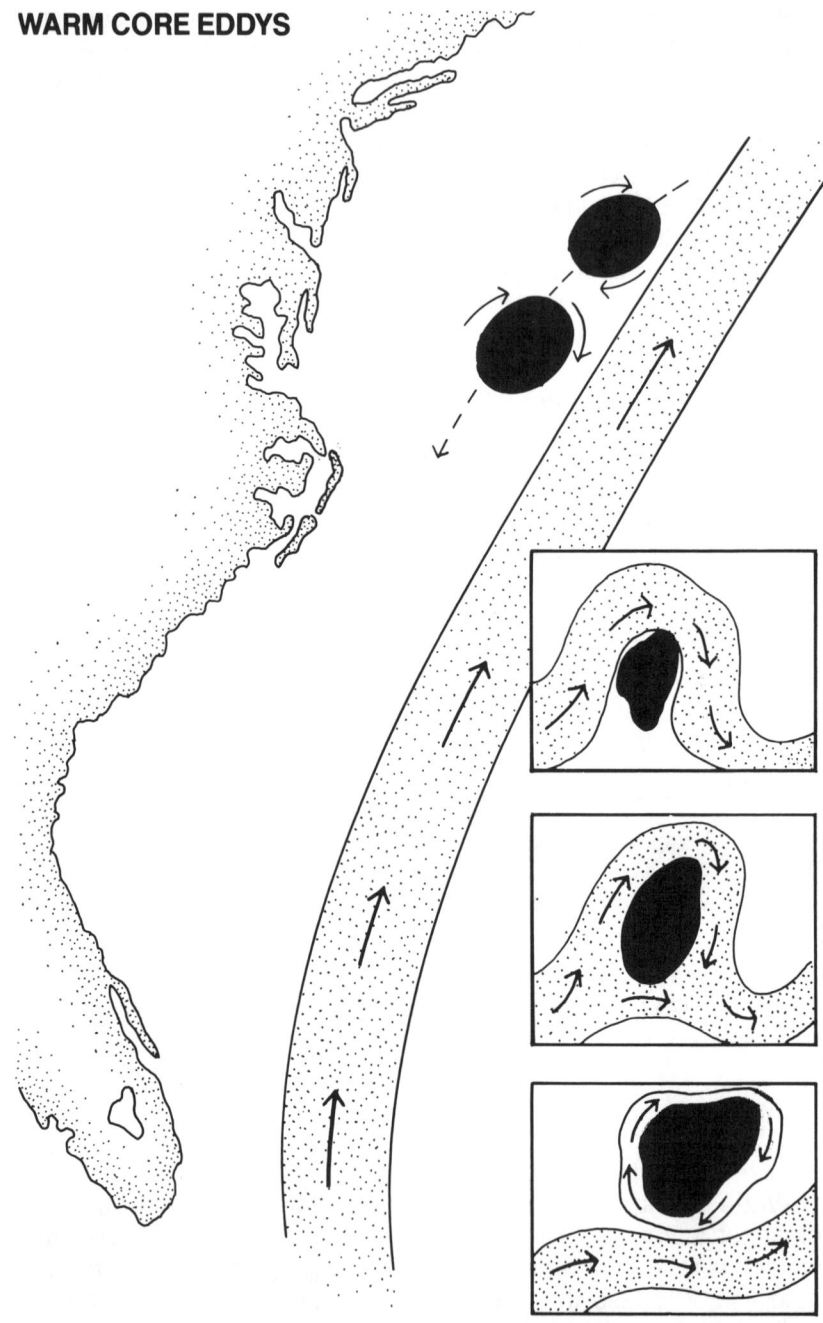

As the Gulf Stream moves northward, bottom along the edge of the Continental Shelf, eddys may break off the main stream and move inshore, bringing excellent tuna and billfish action. The eddys move in a southerly direction.

The ideal fishing situation is to catch the edge of a Gulf Stream eddy with its pure blue water, ideal temperatures and fish life. The eddy spins in a clockwise direction and many anglers feel the northeast edge is by far the best area to fish since it offers the most dramatic change in water temperature and water gradients. Others feel the south and southwest edges are better because these areas are pulling in more Stream water and are bluer and cleaner.

In actual day to day fishing, since the eddy tends to bump along the edge of the shelf and can extend to way over one hundred miles offshore of the coast, the northeast edge is generally closer and therefore more fishable to most tuna and marlin anglers.

If you don't subscribe to the temperature services you can still find the warm water but it takes a lot of time and it depends a lot on luck. Keep your eye on the temperature gauge to signal an increase in water temp and on the color of the water. Any transition from greenish to bluer water usually means you are approaching the edge of slope water, Gulf Stream slope water or pure Stream water; all of which are usually better producers of fish than the inshore green shelf water. Fishing this edge by trolling a zig zag pattern from warm to cool water can be very productive.

Eddies are generally large in size and can cover hundreds of square miles but sometimes you may find smaller pockets of warm, and clear, blue water. I've fished pockets that covered only a few square miles and had excellent action for several hours before the water currents caused the pocket to disperse or we simply had to head back to port.

In an ideal year, several eddies will bump along the coast. Fishermen along the New England to Virginia Coast see this as a southwestward movement. During the summer months of prime canyon fishing we will be lucky to see more than two eddies travel through and influence the canyon areas in this region. Areas to the south, depend less on eddies and more on the location of the Gulf Stream.

It is possible to catch tunas without the presence of a warm eddy but the movement of an eddy into an area will dramatically improve the tuna fishing. Marlin on the other hand are much more dependent on warm eddies and the Gulf Stream water. Few whites or blues are taken in slope water and the best billfish action will always come on the edge of an eddy.

While it may sound too high tech to some anglers there's no doubt that plotting and locating warm eddies with their temperature and water quality gradients can mean outstanding success or dismal failure. Check the scuttlebutt at your local marinas, especially those catering to canyon fishermen, or subscribe to the temperature services. You'll be amazed at how warm eddy fishing can improve your catch of both billfish and tunas.

LOCATING BAIT

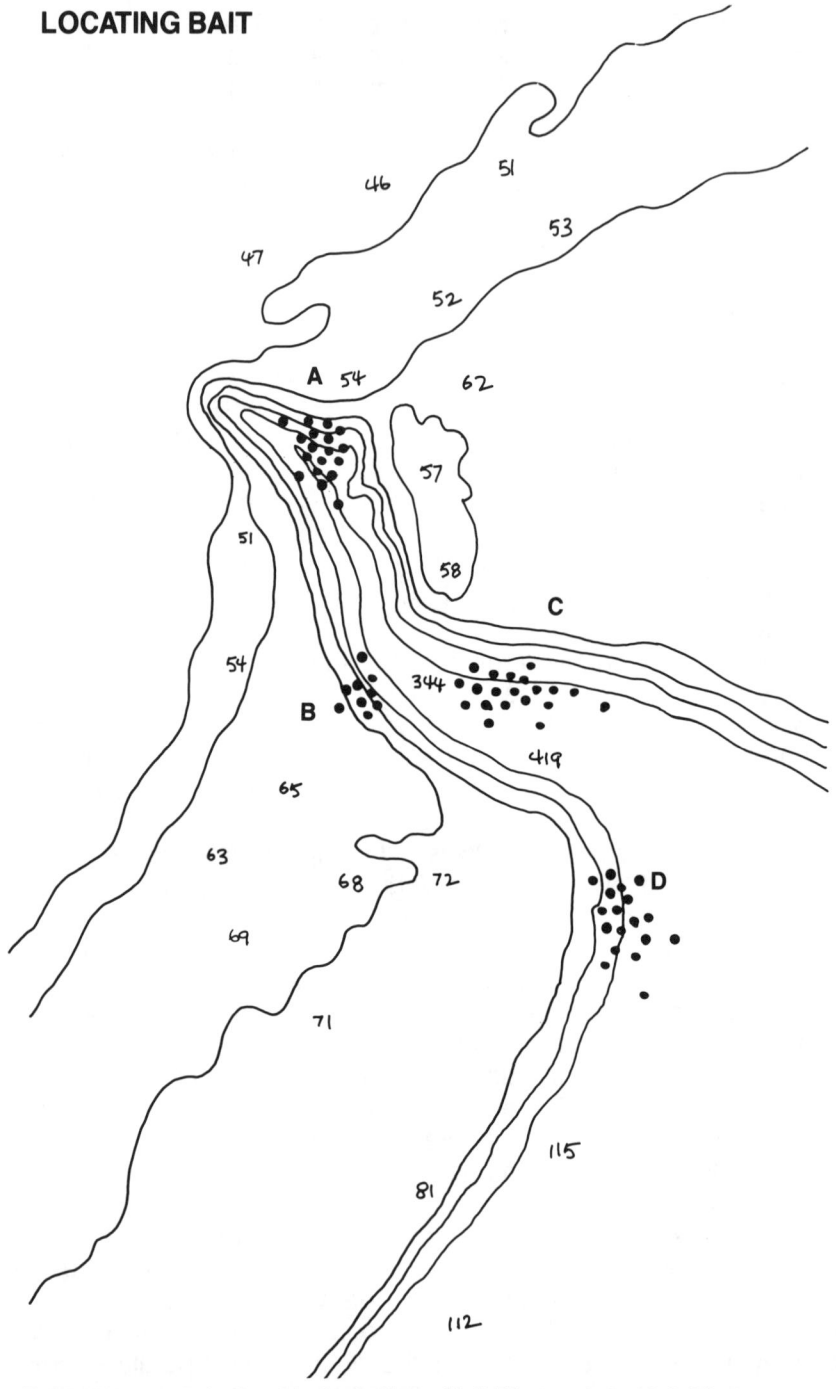

Bait may concentrate at indentations (A & B) or points (C & D) along the edge of the drop-offs.

LOCATING FISH

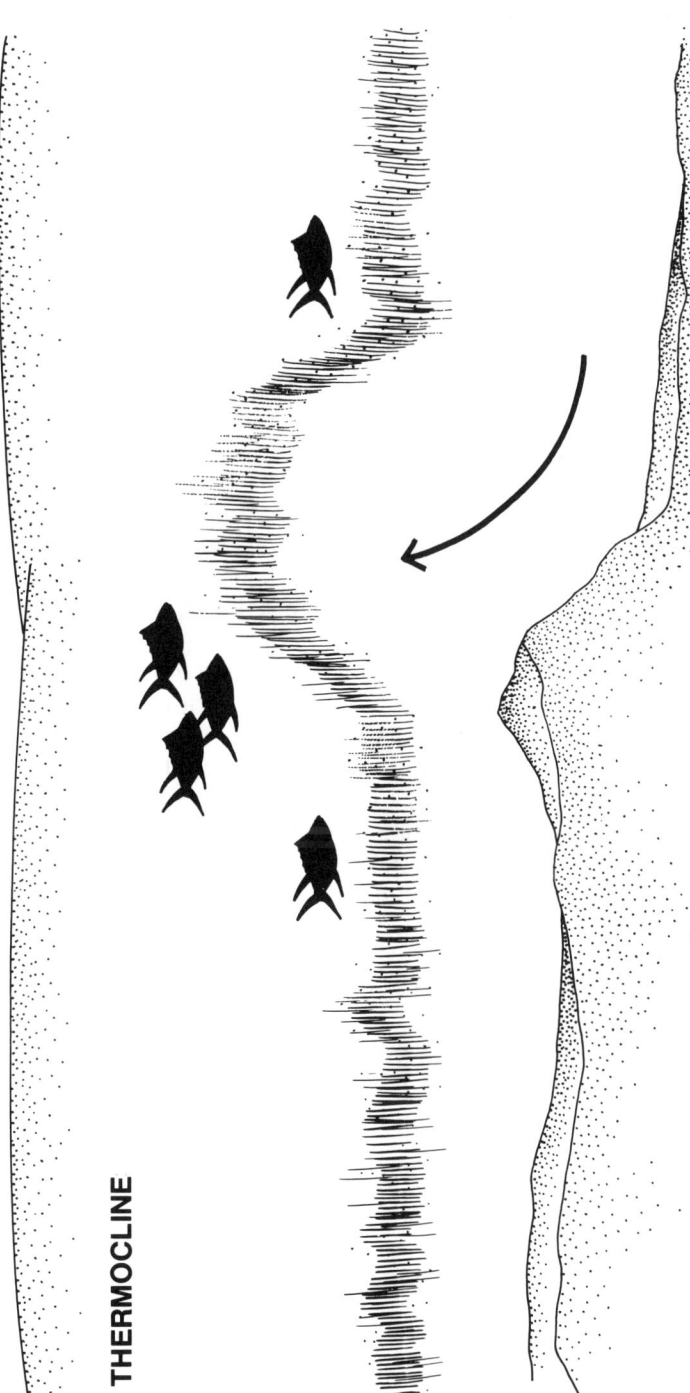

Tuna and billfish usually stay above the thermocline, a cooler layer of deep water. Currents that upwell from the deep at a drop-off may push the thermocline to a higher level, moving the fish closer to the surface.

The Color Scope

Color scopes are one of the most important electronics items to have on an offshore boat. Since they don't use rolls of paper like a graph recorder, they can be used all day long at no expense. More importantly, they visually show the bottom contours, the presence of bait, the presence of game fish and the underwater temperature thermocline.

Before I installed my first color scope, I used only a digital depth finder to watch the changing numbers that indicated the relative ups and downs of the bottom structure. The color scope was so far superior it was like a blind man being able to see again. The color scope added a lot of fish to our take, not so much for the pretty pictures it painted of the bottom, but more for the bait and game fish it clearly showed.

Prior to using the scope, I never knew if I had trolled over a pod of bait or a school of tuna. There were surely many times when I crossed over productive water but the bait or game fish were holding down deep and so I never saw them and never got a strike to hint that success was below the boat. Now, when I troll across a pod of bait, I jot down the TDs and make a second or third pass over the bait and on many occasions, these repeated sets across water that holds bait will get us a strike from a tuna or billfish.

I often see bait, marked as large blobs of color, and nearby will be smaller individual marks of tuna. On many trips I've watched the scope mark tuna at, let's say 15 fathoms, then 10 fathoms a few sets later, then 5 fathoms and then on the next pass we'll get one, two or more fish to crash the lures. Without the scope I'd never have seen the fish marks, never have seen the fish rising in curiosity to finally hit the lures.

Color scopes can also show a thermocline, the underwater layer of cold water that tuna, and bait, won't go below unless trying to escape danger. Cold water is more dense than warm water. By increasing the Gain control, most scopes will show the thermocline as a shady line somewhere between the bottom and the top. The thermocline may rise and fall, snake-like, as the underwater currents cause it to change depth, much like a water-borne jet stream. An uprising of the thermocline may indicate game fish and bait being pushed to the surface where they will be closer to your lures or baits.

A good example of distinct thermocline uprisings can be seen at the Hudson Canyon, a 15 mile wedge-shaped cut into the Continental Shelf located SE of Montauk. This area often holds bait and game fish when the thermocline rises, sometimes to within a few fathoms of the surface.

Other Things to Look for

Whales and porpoises are a sure sign that tuna may be present. Whales need to eat huge quantities of food and they won't be found in any area where there isn't a generous supply of small fish, squid and plankton.

Sighting whales on the offshore grounds is a special thrill all its own and they sometimes put on quite a show for fishermen, breaching in huge splashes of water, their gigantic bodies nearly clearing the surface. Some of our best days spent at the offshore canyons have occurred when herds of whales were nearby. It's a time to get out the video or 35mm camera and get some incredible footage of these unique animals. We once were able to get right in the middle of a herd with about 30 whales, including small young of the year whales. As they rose to the surface and blew off, the spray would come down on us. Exciting, but believe me, some of those whales needed a breath mint!

Commercial boats, trawling for squid or dragging for bottom fish, may also draw game fish, especially tuna. The tuna may not always be at, or near, the surface since the huge nets and underwater gear may spook them, or they may just be holding in deeper water because that's where the spillage from the net is the most abundant.

Watch the color scope when trolling near the squid boats to see if tuna are nearby. If fish are marked, it may pay to stick it out and work repeated sets near the boat. You may be surprised to see that a number of the tuna will not be holding close to the boat, so it is not always imperative to troll up close to the commercial boat. Ranging the nearby waters can be more productive.

Every day on the water is a new day. What worked yesterday may not work today. Yesterday's oasis could be tomorrow's desert. What makes or breaks most offshore fishing trips is the captain's ability to keep a watchful eye on the natural surroundings, like rips, weed lines, birds and slicks and to blend them with the information from the temperature gauge and color scope. It's a new situation every minute and you have to keep alert and use the information being presented to you. That's the challenge of the blue water world.

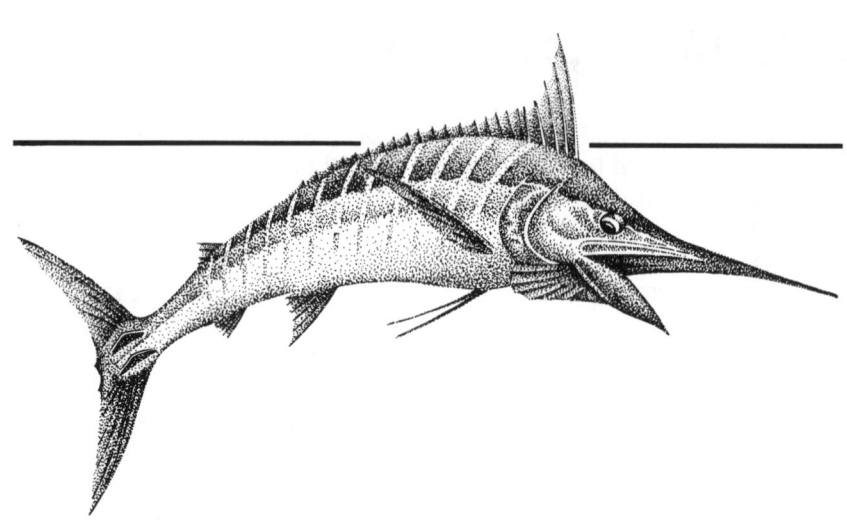

Chapter Nine

THE TROLLING STRATEGY

Trolling for tuna and billfish is exciting. The smell and drone of the diesels, the lures dancing in the sparkling wakes, the nearby whales and porpoises and the anticipation of a strike that can quickly shatter the tranquility of the blue water make offshore trolling challenging and fun.

As enjoyable as it is, it still takes a lot of work to troll if you want to do it "right". The angler who lazily trolls with no thought to lure colors and sizes, trolling speeds, lure patterns and structure will never be a consistent fisherman - lucky, maybe; consistent, never. He may luck into a big fish, or a good day's catch, but day in, day out, the haphazared offshore troller will not be as successful as another angler who puts more effort, thought and planning into the day's opportunities.

Trouble is, just when you think you have 'em figured out, the fish start to do something different and you have to start all over again developing a new strategy. But then that's the fun of it; that's what keeps us on our toes looking for new ways to outsmart these blue water rockets. The ability to modify a trolling pattern, lure selection, trolling speed and lure colors to meet the ever changing movements and preferences of tuna or marlin is what trolling is all about.

The following trolling tips are offered as starting points to build an overall trolling strategy that is flexible and effective. The thoughts are gleaned from the experiences of many charter captains I've been priveleged to fish with and from experiences and trial and error on my own boat.

At the Dock

Whether it's a tournament, a charter trip or a fun trip with a few buddies, the strategy begins at the dock before you even fire up the engines. So I don't forget anything, I use a list as a reminder to check that lures, baits, ice, tackle, food, electronics and extra gear is on board. Each rod and reel has its drag checked with a pull scale, the terminal end of the line is re-tied, re-crimped or checked for any nicks or abrasions. The engines are checked for fluid levels, spare oil, spare water and that all systems are okay.

The latest weather report is reviewed, temperature charts are compared, and a passenger list is drawn up. Before we pull away from the dock, every small detail has been gone over and checked that it is properly prepared, that it works and that back ups are on board if needed.

The ride to the fishing grounds can be short or long, but it can also be time well spent. The hooks on the lures or bait rigs that will be used for the day are sharpened to fine, rounded points. Gaff hooks are sharpened, baits rigged and placed in the cooler or chill box, covered with salt.

Setting Up the Boat

In Chapter four, we talked about boats for offshore trolling. This chapter will bring all the parts of the boat and its systems together as a fishing machine. Whether it's a 25-foot center console, a 30-foot raised helm or 46-foot fly bridge style, the basics are similar.

The captain should have clear visibilty to see his electronics, his crew and the angler at all times. An elevated position is best to gain maximum visibilty of the baits and signs of fish such as rips, weedlines and breaking fish. This can all be accomplished with ease on a fly bridge or raised helm boat, or with a small tower on a cuddy cabin skiff or a center console. The downside of a tower on a small boat is that the captain cannot use his electronics to advantage. There just isn't space enough to put everything needed in the tower. A tower can be very helpful on a larger boat, too, and a small tower control console will handily hold a second loran, a digital depth finder, a temperature guage and a VHF radio.

A neat, tidy cockpit is essential. Coolers should be carefully placed against the forward bulkhead, a wet towel under them so they don't slide around. The fight chair should be adjusted and ready for action with no excess cushions, tubes of suntan lotion or sodas lying in harms way. If anglers wish to use stand-up gear, the gimbal belts and kidney harnesses should be handily stored so they can be gotten to in a moment, not buried under piles of duffle bags in the cabin.

Depending on the size of the boat, gaffs can be stowed under the cover boards, strapped to a bow rail or tower leg. On my latest boat, a special compartment was built into the side of the engine room with an access door into the cockpit. The gaffs are slid into 6-foot long tubes, hidden behind the small door that keeps them out of the way yet ready for instant use when needed.

Tackle can be stowed in a variety of ways. Larger boats have built-in tackle lockers against the aft salon bulkhead to hold lures, charts, small rigging items, bait rigs, extra hooks and the hundred other small tackle items. Center console and cuddy cabin boats make good use of a combination rocket launcher, tackle locker to keep these same items handy yet out of the way when not in use.

Extra rod holders to hold rods and reels while cruising to and from the fishing grounds, or to keep rods and reels safely out of the way while fighting a fish can be added along the back edge of a hard top or T-top, on tower legs and across the side-to-side bracing of towers.

A place for everything and everything in its place. Tackle storage is a must on an offshore boat.

Outriggers

The famous, and innovative, Captain Tommy Gifford, is generally credited with being the first fisherman to use outriggers back in the 1930s. His early bamboo poles eventually developed into the beautiful aluminum riggers made today by Lee's, Pipewelders, Rupp Marine, Rybovich and Schaefer.

Outriggers have two primary advantages; they spread the lure pattern over a wider area and they allow an automatic drop back, or pause, when fishing with baits. Once the outriggers are laid down into the fishing position they become much more than a pretty accessory that makes a boat look racy or sharp. Outriggers play an important role in making lures work like they are alive, and in giving baits enough time to get swallowed by a white or a sailfish.

Most skiffs under 27 feet will be rigged with single halyards but longer riggers used on larger boats can be double rigged with two halyard lines, one long and one short, on each rigger pole thereby allowing two lines to be fished off each rigger. My preference is to fish lures or baits that splash and dive from the outriggers, and fish the divers or sub surface lures on the flat lines.

The outrigger halyards can be made of monofilament or braided cord and both have advantages. The mono is softer and easy to rig requiring only simple crimps to secure each end of the halyard to the outrigger clip. Mono, however, stretches and the rigger halyard may have to be shortened several times after a new mono halyard is installed. The new mono will eventually stretch to its maximum length and no further adjustments need be made. The braided halyard does not seem to slide so smoothly through the outrigger eyes and the braid is best secured with a hangman's type sliding knot for good knot strength. However, the braid seems to be much more durable than the mono halyard.

Outrigger line clips are available from several manufacturers like the simple Black's Marine with a hook shaped clip, to the AFTCO and Rupp roller guide clips. While the roller guides assure long line life and virtually no fraying, some fishermen prefer the simplistic line clip. If you are worried about line chafing on the simple clips (with no rollers), a loop of Gudebrod Bait Rigging Floss can be adlded to the line at the point where the line would usually be attached to the rigger clip. The floss slips through the rod guides with no problem and takes only a few moments to add to the fishing line. Use the same rod and reel for that rigger each time so you don't have to re-measure or tie a new floss loop each time you troll. A squirt of spray oil after each trip will keep any clip working like new for an entire season.

An ideally mounted outrigger would have each support leg of equal

DOUBLE HALYARD OUTRIGGER

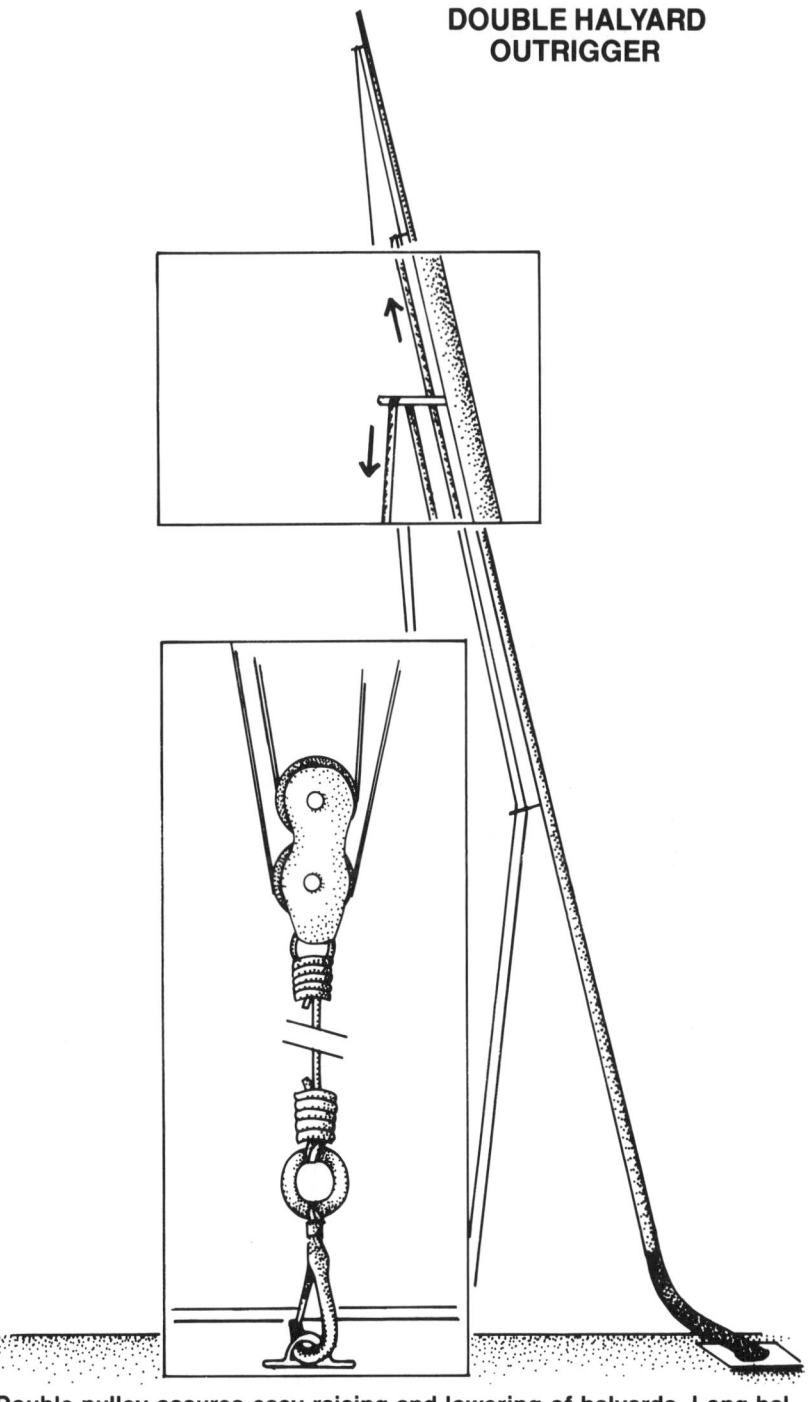

Double pulley assures easy raising and lowering of halyards. Long halyard runs to tip ring of outrigger, short halyard only runs to second ring.

FISHING FOR TUNA AND MARLIN

OUTRIGGER LINE SPREAD

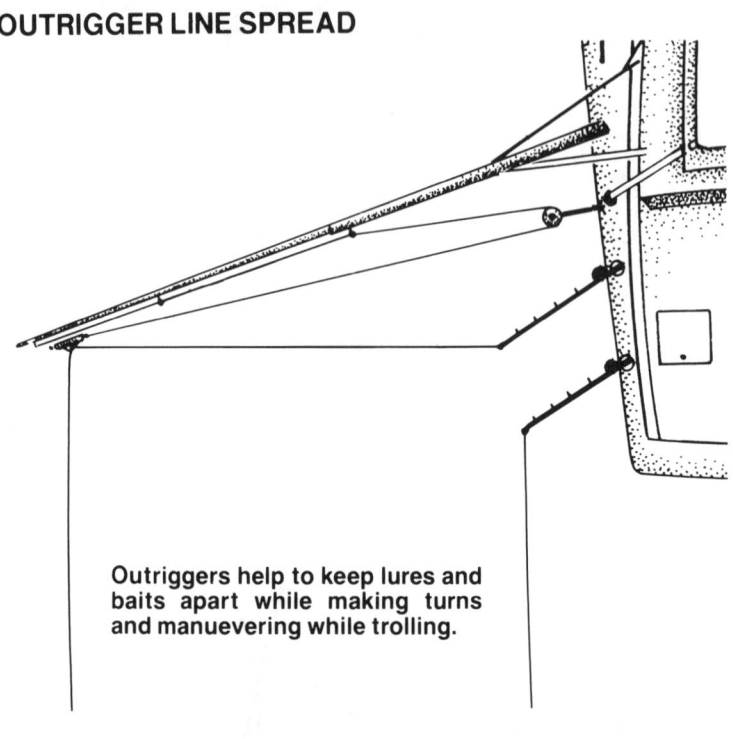

Outriggers help to keep lures and baits apart while making turns and manuevering while trolling.

OUTRIGGER TAG LINES

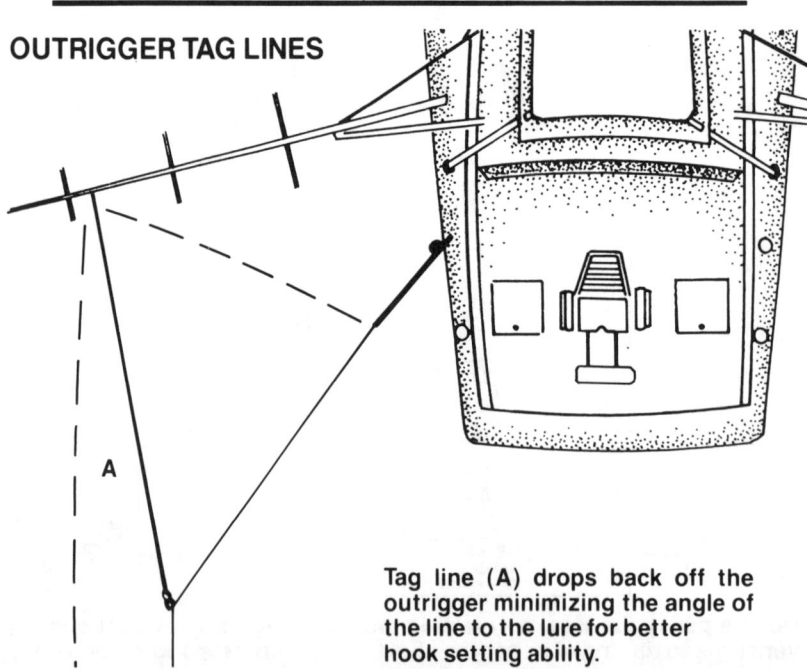

Tag line (A) drops back off the outrigger minimizing the angle of the line to the lure for better hook setting ability.

length and in the same plane as the rigger halyards so when the riggers were dropped into the fishing position, no adjustment would be needed to the rigger lines. In the real world, this rarely happens and some slight adjustment in the length of the halyards is usually needed. Many boats have elastic bunji cords to take up the slack line, but these cords look horrible after a short time and are not as neat looking as a slip lock system tied into the halyard itself. The accompanying diagram shows how to rig this quick system.

A high grade pulley mounted on a short line just above the cover boards will make running the halyard lines up and down the rigger much easier and will add life to the halyard lines. These are sold in marine supply stores for sailboaters and from companies like J-Mar Tackle in Melbourne, Florida and Rupp Marine in Stuart, Florida.

There's no "law" that says the fishing line must be run all the way out to the end of the outrigger. Often, lures will run, or track, better in the pattern with the halyard line run only part way up the rigger, not necessarily all the way out to the end. Depending on sea conditions, the amount of wind and the trolling speed, the lures or baits may work the best only when run partly up the halyard. What is most important is to get the bait tracking right regardless of how far up the rigger the line is.

One of the major advantages of outriggers is the spread they give to the lures so quick, responsive turns can be made. The boat can be nimbly turned to approach a floating clump of weeds that may hold fish or to turn towards breaking fish, a lobster pot marker, a slick or a bird diving to pick up bait.

On every turn, the outside lures will speed up slightly and change their action, while the inside lures will slow down slightly, also changing action. This speed up or slow down of the lures can entice fish to strike and gives a clue about how the fish want their "dinner" that day. If the fish are always hitting on the inside lures as the lures slow down, this is a strong message to slow down the trolling speed. If the fish are striking on the outside, faster lines, the message is to speed up slightly. A small increase in speed, 25 to 50 rpms up or down on the tach, can often make the difference in whether a day is successful or not.

Flat Lines

Flat lines are vital to our fishing success. Their importance was impressed upon me on one particular trip for inshore school bluefin tuna. The 5-foot seas and gusting winds made for a rough ocean and the crew weren't the only ones getting tossed around. The boat was getting kicked about like an old pair of jeans in the washing machine. It was definitely a foul weather gear day but the school tuna action was superb.

Even the one crew member who kept calling for his Irish uncle, Ralph O'Rourke, said, "Let me catch just one more before we head back in." In spite of the weather no one wanted to give up. It was a day to remember in more ways than one. Somehow the awful sea conditions don't seem so bad years later, but the terrific catch of school bluefin is still fresh in my memory. We boated 10 fish and released another 26 bluefin, all in the 35 to 40-pound range and caught on 20-pound gear. What a day!

A large part of our success was due to a small tackle item often overlooked but which can be of vital importance while trolling; the flat line clip. The type I preferred at that time was the proven Black's Marine with the small lever arm that firmly held the line in place until a fish hit and the arm snapped out of its clip. A pair of stainless screws mounted each of three clips; one at each transom corner and a third atop the outboard engine cowling. I could fish three lines down tight to the water so the lures pulled straight and true, unaffected by the turbulent water in the prop wash.

The lures were usually cedar plugs, lead-headed spoons or small feathers. The extremely rough wake thrown up by the outboard made it all but impossible to troll lures close in to the stern on the first and second waves in the wake. Since these close in waves were the favorite spots for school bluefin to ambush the lures, these were obviously the best place to set the lures. The problem was the violent water action, the solution was the flat line clips that gave the required line control to allow the lures to ride the rough water. The tuna did the rest.

My tuna fishing at that time was limited to the 20 fathom water 15 to 30 miles from the coast and we often found good action, mostly with little tunny, bonito, sometimes a few school bluefin and occasionally some dolphin. Later when I was able to move up in boat size, the flat line techniques worked just as well on the deeper water tuna grounds. In fact, when I fished outboard boats I often fished only a pair of lines on outriggers, the other lines were on flat lines to maximize lure action.

Even bigeye sometimes hit so close to the transom that they can leave you speechless. While fishing The Point off Oregon Inlet with Captain John Bayliss on his Tarheel we had a bigeye attack a bait positioned on a flat line on the first wake behind the boat. The enormous dark shadow was almost scary as it came at the bait like a submarine. It missed the first time but came back around and waffled the bait. A half hour later, the citation-sized fish was slid in the tuna door.

Flat line clips also prevent lines from getting tangled around rod tips. On rough water days, those rods that have the lures dropped back

THE TROLLING STRATEGY

several wakes and that usually work well with lines run directly off the rod tips, may still get to bucking and bouncing around so much that slack line will take a wrap around the tip. Another bigeye, but a different day, announced its presence with a walloping crash at a lure but when the line came tight and the rod tip bent over, the wrap tightened fatally around the roller. The line parted like a pistol shot. Good-bye fish, hello another fishing lesson.

On very rough days I fish any line not already in an outrigger clip from a flat line clip. My preference now is for the AFTCO Roller Troller clips modified by removing the usual rigging and mounting wires so only the clip remains. A short length of braided outrigger line (about a 10-inch piece) forms a loop that is interlocked into "U" shaped strap cleats on the transom rub rail. While not fishing, the clips ride against the rail and do not rub or scuff gel coat or a paint finish. They are ready for instant use at all times. I can fish up to six flat lines if needed.

A handy temporary flat line can be rigged with a #64 rubber band. I buy them by the big box full from our office supply company (oops, hope the accountant isn't reading this) and use them for rigging temporary flat lines, shark floats, line clips, bait rigs and a dozen other little jobs. To use the rubber band for a flat line, pull line from the rod tip down to the level of the lowest guide. Wrap the rubber band from one side of the guide, around the line, around the blank and around to the other side of the guide. The tension of the lure in the water stretches the rubber band and pulls the line away from the rod. There's no danger of tip wrapping or tangling, and the band breaks away at the strike of a fish.

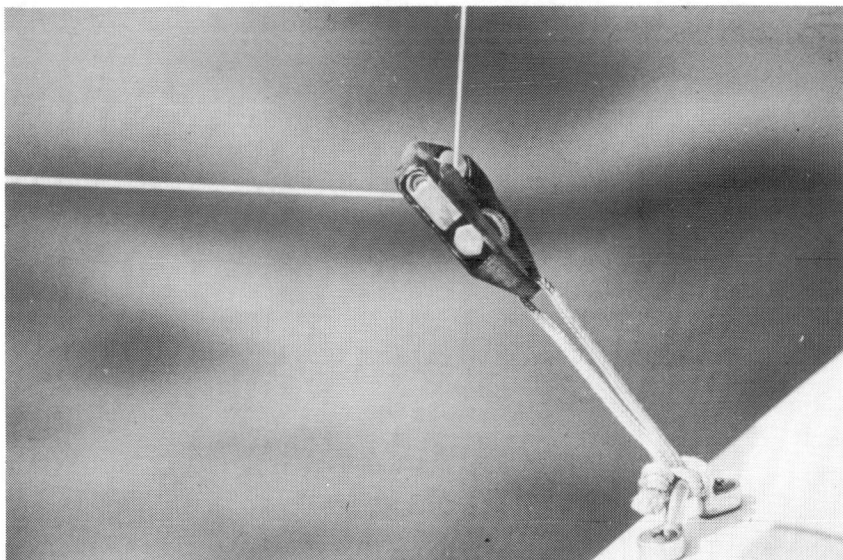

A handy flat line clip can be made by removing rigging wire on AFTCO outrigger clip. Short length of nylon line is looped to a cleat on transom.

Trolling Speed

There is no set "best" trolling speed. I often hear fishermen talking back and forth on the radio, swapping info on trolling speed and while it may be helpful on special days, the reading on the tach is almost irrelevant when comparing one boat to another since every boat handles just a little bit differently than every other boat.

The best trolling speed is that speed which makes the lures work with those long smoke trails. Put the lures out, watch the lures and adjust their position until they are working right, *then* look at the tach. The rpms may change each time you change direction, each time you head into or away from the wind or as you work the edge of the structure where one side has more current than another side. To blindly troll by the tach is a bad strategy. Your eye on the lures is your best guide to trolling speed.

Most tuna trollers agree that the optimum trolling speed is from 5 to 8 knots for tuna, 7 to 10 knots for blue marlin and 4 to 6 knots for white marlin. Naturally there is always the exception to the general rule, but these speeds seem about right most of the time. The best all round speed is 7 to 8 knots.

Sea conditions can throw the best trolling speed right out the window

Optimum trolling speed for flat-face lures will make them smoke long plumes of bubbles to attract fish.

so variation can be important. A rough sea calls for a slower speed and makes high speed trolling very difficult so the fisherman who always runs at 8 knots may not consistently do very well. A change in game plan would drop the speed down to about 5 to 6 knots.

Calm seas allow slightly higher speeds. Trolling with the wind as opposed to trolling against the wind can call for a change in boat speed. So can running against the sea or with the sea, or quartering the sea. A slight change of 25, 50 or 100 rpms to adapt to changing conditions can make all the difference in the world to the success of the day.

The best indicators of the correct trolling speed are the lures themselves. Bullet head lures should be splattering and splashing on the surface and occasionally diving a few inches. Flat-face lures should be diving with long jet streams of smoking bubbles. Forget the tachs, forget the text book trolling speeds - the lures tell it all.

If the lures are jumping clear of the water and tumbling, the speed is too high. If they are staying under water all the time and not smoking bubbles or splashing, the speed is too slow. Most boats get a narrow range of engine rpms that make the lures work well, but that range needs to be fine tuned on each day and as sea conditions change.

As you set your trolling speed, it will become obvious when you have a lure that doesn't fit your pattern as you try to adjust the speed so all the lures work correctly. The odd lure will either not trail smoke because

A spreader bar is trolled slowly, making a commotion and looking a lot like a school of bait.

it is too heavy to catch the surface every so often to gulp air or it may be too light and so it dances all over the top of the water, tumbling and tangling on the leader.

Try placing the odd lure in another position - off the rigger, or on a flat line in the first wake. It may work better there. This tuning of the lures is a critical part of tuna trolling. Once you get a good lure pattern, lock it in your memory bank. The pattern that worked today with the right colors, actions and sizes will most likely work again on your next trip, too.

Ninety-nine times out of l00, the lures should be positioned on the face of the wake so you can see them clearly and adjust position and speed as the seas change. Sometimes trolling into a large head sea with large swells, the lures will fly out of the wake as you sleigh ride off the swell. To avoid this, place the lures on the back side of the wake. This is not recommended any other time because you can't see the lures and work them properly, but it does save a bad sea approach.

Trolling Pattern

The two most successful lure spreads are the V and the W patterns with each having strong and weak points. The V pattern will put a pair of lures on the outside edges of the 2nd, 3rd, and 4th wakes and allows a single lure to be positioned in the center of the spread held in close or dropped way back onto the 5th or 6th wake. The V pattern covers a lot of water and generally does better at picking up single fish on those days when the action is a slow pick and the fish are not aggressive.

The W pattern will put four lures on the second wake (two in close and two out on the edges), two lures on the third wake and a center lure positioned close in on the fourth wake or the back further in the fifth or sixth wake.

Trolling is generally easier with the V pattern in crowded areas where maneuvering gets tricky. The W pattern does much better with aggressive fish gaining the advantage of more numerous multiple hook-ups. It doesn't usually work as well on the slow pick days. Sea conditions can dictate which pattern you use. A strong breeze can push the lures on the windward side a few feet across the wake so they work too closely to the lee side lures. This may cause tangled lures as you turn. Oily calm seas sometimes see the fish get skittish and they will only hit on the distant or widespread lures, so the V pattern often gets the nod as the best approach on calm seas.

An alternative to both patterns is to offset the pattern and shift one side of the spread back one wake. By staggering the lures the spread can be lengthened to add a lure on one or two wakes further back behind the boat, covering more water.

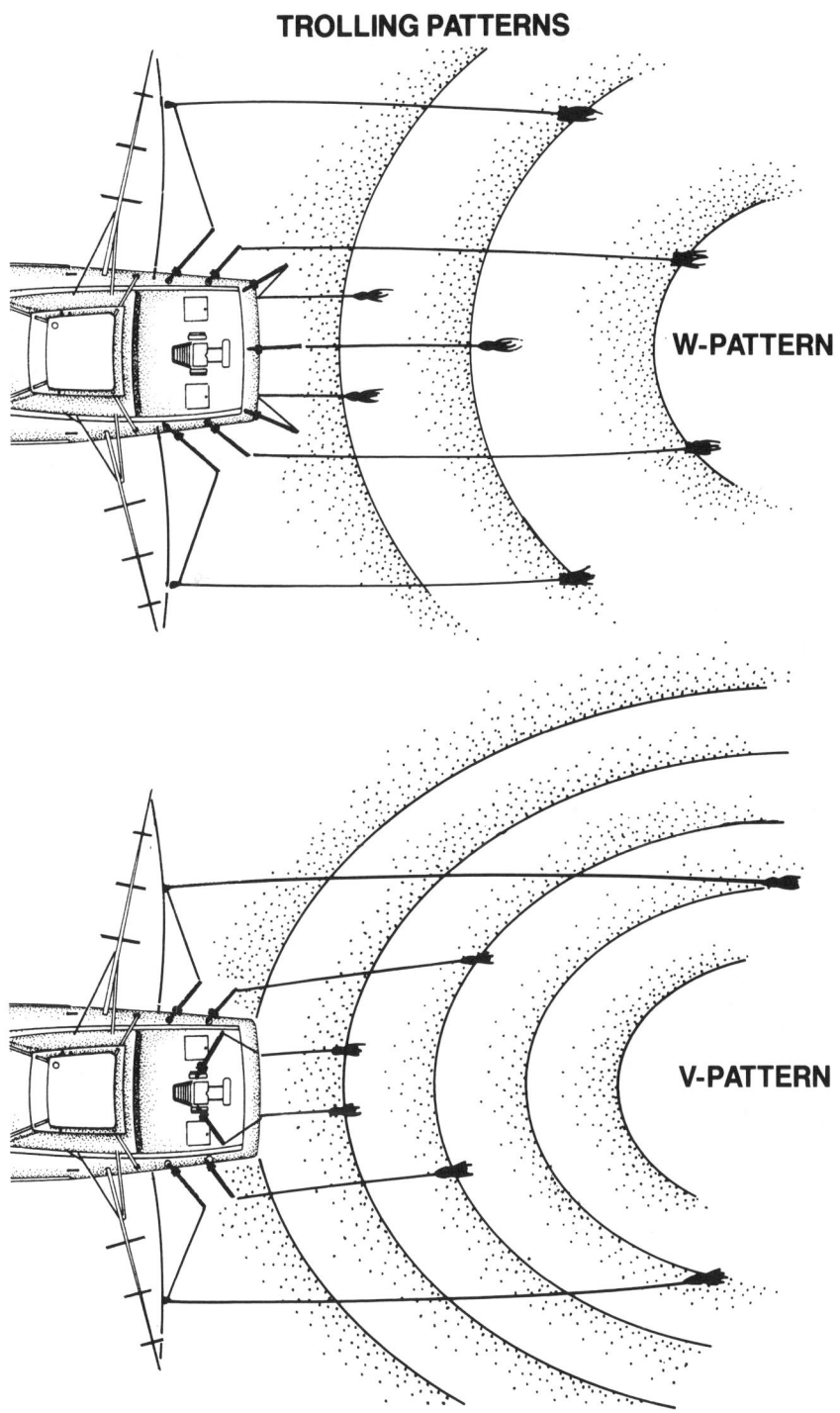

FISHING FOR TUNA AND MARLIN

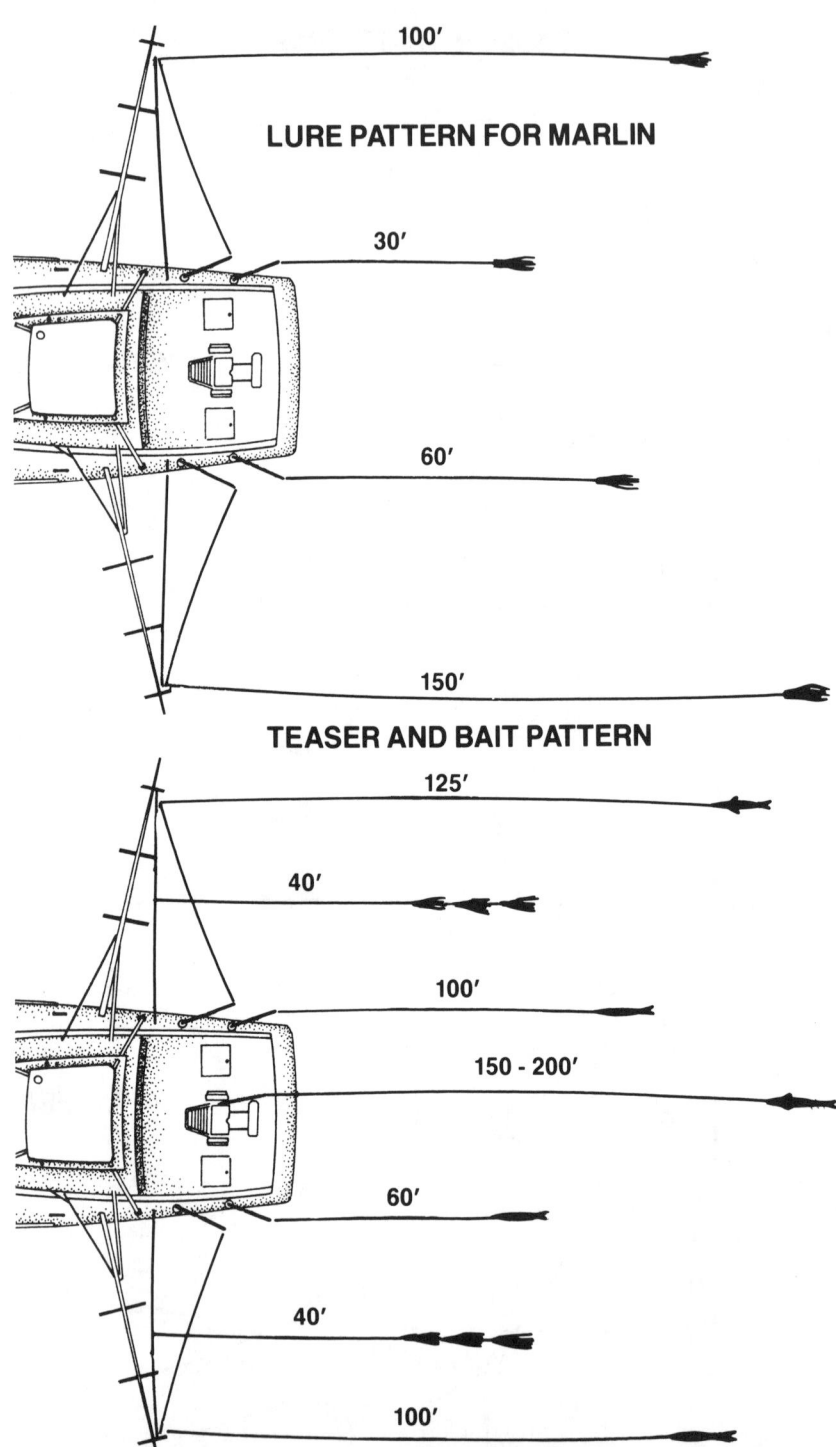

Search Pattern - Working the Structure

A graph recorder or color scope proves that baitfish and game fish hold near the edge of some structure, like the edge of a deep hole, the shelf or along a ridge or bank. Aimless trolling in a haphazard pattern will catch fish only when the boat happens to "luck into" the structure edge.

A digital depth finder is a great aid to trolling tuna as it indicates the rising and falling bottom. It won't mark fish but it makes it easy to zigzag an edge by watching the depth numbers change. By matching the digital depth finder to the loran TDs of your present position, it's easy to work a north to south, east to west trolling pattern that takes the lures back and forth from the shallow edge to the deep edge.

Marking down the loran numbers for each fish and marking a master chart will show the locations that time and again give up tuna. Knowing the most productive spots will save you time by eliminating the unproductive spots.

The standard offshore trolling lure pattern is the V pattern. It keeps the lures spread away from each other, avoiding tangles, allowing tight turns as you maneuver to work a small area or to avoid other boats trolling nearby. Another pattern popular with fishermen who want to troll more than four or five lines is the W pattern. It requires a wider turning radius, but some trollers feel it gives a better spread to the lures and that it gets more multiple hook-ups.

Marlin fishermen will troll three to four lines. Tuna fishermen may troll from four to five and occasionally you may meet a charter skipper with a well trained crew that can handle up to seven rods, especially when seeking smaller tuna like blackfins. I like to fish with five lines so that lures are put on the second or third to sixth or seventh wakes.

The top of the ocean may look flat, but down below there are canyons, mountains, ridges and fingers that provide avenues for the tuna to move along. To catch the best you have to be trolling these structure edges to intercept the fish as they move along their "highways".

With a loran it is easy to run to an offshore spot and by watching the digital sounder and the changing loran numbers you can plot a course to criss cross the structure edge taking you from the high ground into the deep and back again. With the loran you can still do it by trolling with your eye on the compass and by watching the depth read-out.

Aimless straight trolling only gets you into a lone kamikaze fish intent on hitting anything you dragged across its nose. Consistent success is dependent on working the structure edge with a careful pattern. Veteran marlin trollers like Rich Price of Big Pine Key will work an area like the Wall crossing back and forth from the high ground into

ZIGZAG SEARCH PATTERN

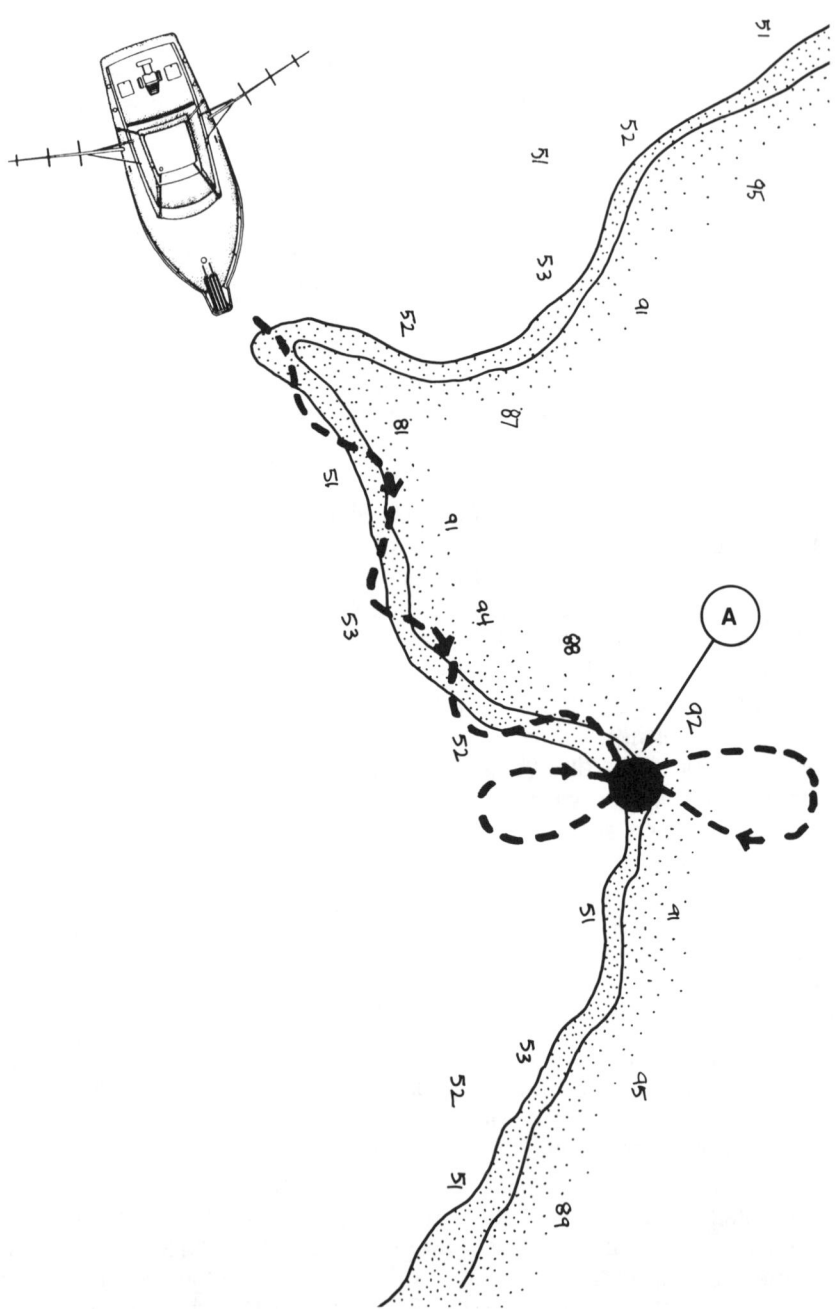

A zigzag searching pattern from shallow to deep water usually works best. Switch to a figure 8 pattern once fish or bait are located.

THE TROLLING STRATEGY

DOWN SEA SEARCH PATTERN

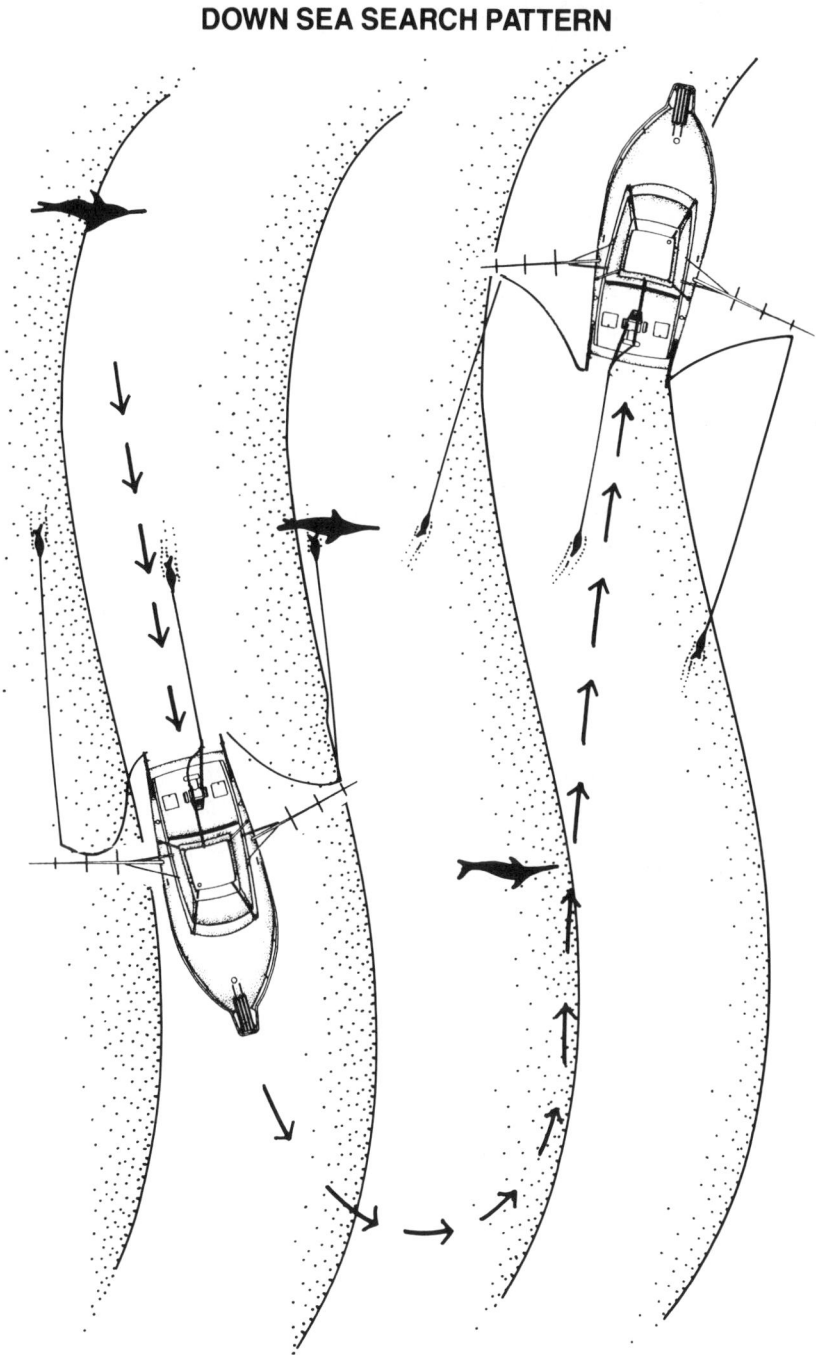

Sailfish and marlin often swim down sea, so a pattern that criss crosses the swells intercepts more fish.

the deep, high ground into the deep all day long until they find fish.

A temperature gauge is very helpful. There are days when a few tenths of a degree will make the difference in a few fish and no fish. The edge of a warm water core works just the same as a bottom structure and fish may hold along the edge of the warm water.

Team Work

We fish to have fun and the day's rules should be flexible enough so everyone can do his or her thing for a memorable trip. However, if everyone doesn't know their job as part of the team, a big fish, or the winning of a tournament can be lost because of confusion. The boat can only catch a lot of fish if the team works together in unison. The captain is no more important than the mate who is no more important than the angler. Everyone has a job to do and if one person on the team fails, the entire team fails. Even when I fish with friends, there is always one person on the team who serves as mate, because he has fished with me a lot or because it's his nature to be sure everything is well organized.

The captain is responsible for watching the water for fish signs, the scope, the loran, the temperature guage and the boat to be sure all is working as it should. The mate should be watching the lines, the baits or lures, the wake and anything that happens in the cockpit. The angler should be planning in his mind what he or she will do when the cry, "Fish on!" splits the air, concentrating on handling the tackle, the fight chair, remembering the techniques of working the lever drag and the rod for maximum power against the fish.

It doesn't have to be so serious that the fun of the day is lost, yet it cannot be so lax that mayhem is the result when a fish strikes. When everyone is focusing on their job, the day will feel relaxed, with just enough tension in the air to keep the team on edge, waiting, expecting the strike of a great fish. A well-organized team can add to the experience of the fishing trip, rather than take away from it, as can happen when no one seems to know what to do or when to do it.

To Roam or Not to Roam

Offshore fishing is by its nature a day of discovery, of searching for fish or signs of fish until the fish are eventually found. Many offshore anglers or captains get the urge to see what's over the horizon even when things look good right in front of them. It's called the Grass is Greener syndrome or Analysis Paralysis. By either name it makes smart folks become stupid folks.

Never leave fish to find fish. Once you've found a spot with good water color, good temperature, with bait showing on the scope, don't leave if the fish don't show right away. Work that spot until the fish can't take it any more and they blast the lures to get rid of the annoying things circling over their turf. An ounce of patience can be worth more than a pound of curiosity to see what lies around the corner.

One trip to the Wilmington Canyon off Cape May, we found good water and the scope showed signs of masses of bait holding some distance below the surface. No tuna, however, showed any sign of interest in the lures. For more than an hour I worked that spot to no avail and decided to move on to another spot. I radioed a buddy in a nearby boat to let him know what I had in mind.

"Okay," he said, "but I'll stay here. These fish have to show any time now."

I veered off to head to the 500 fathom deep, but had gone no more than a mile when I received a call to come back. "I have four on!" the other captain shouted into the radio, "Get your butt back here."

Luckily I had not gone too far and by the time I made it back, I did get in on the action with a few fish. If I had left the spot sooner, I would have been too far away to get back and cash in some good fishing.

Likewise, if you don't find the right combination of water color, temperature, bait and other signs of fish, it doesn't pay to spend a lot of time hoping for something to happen. If there are no signs of fish, it's better to keep searching until a better location is eventually found.

The major advantage of the temperature services mentioned in Chapter Eight is their ability to narrow down the variables and to predict or indicate where the better areas should be. It's a huge ocean out there and if you can eliminate the fishless water before you leave the dock, it makes it that much quicker to find fish once on the fishing grounds.

Diamond Jigs

A well-placed diamond jig, dropped back into the pattern after the strike of a fish may add an extra tuna to the day's catch. Many fishermen don't bother with jigging an extra fish or two, but it can be fun. One of our charters showed us how to do it a few years ago. Barry Saunders had been to California and had a bad case of "In California they do it this way." He offered advice on everything we did as we trolled for yellowfin tuna at the canyon edge. New ideas are great but the guy was getting on everyone's nerves. With several yellowfin already iced down we were having a good day and even Barry's buddies were getting itchy over his constant chatter.

BREAKING FISH

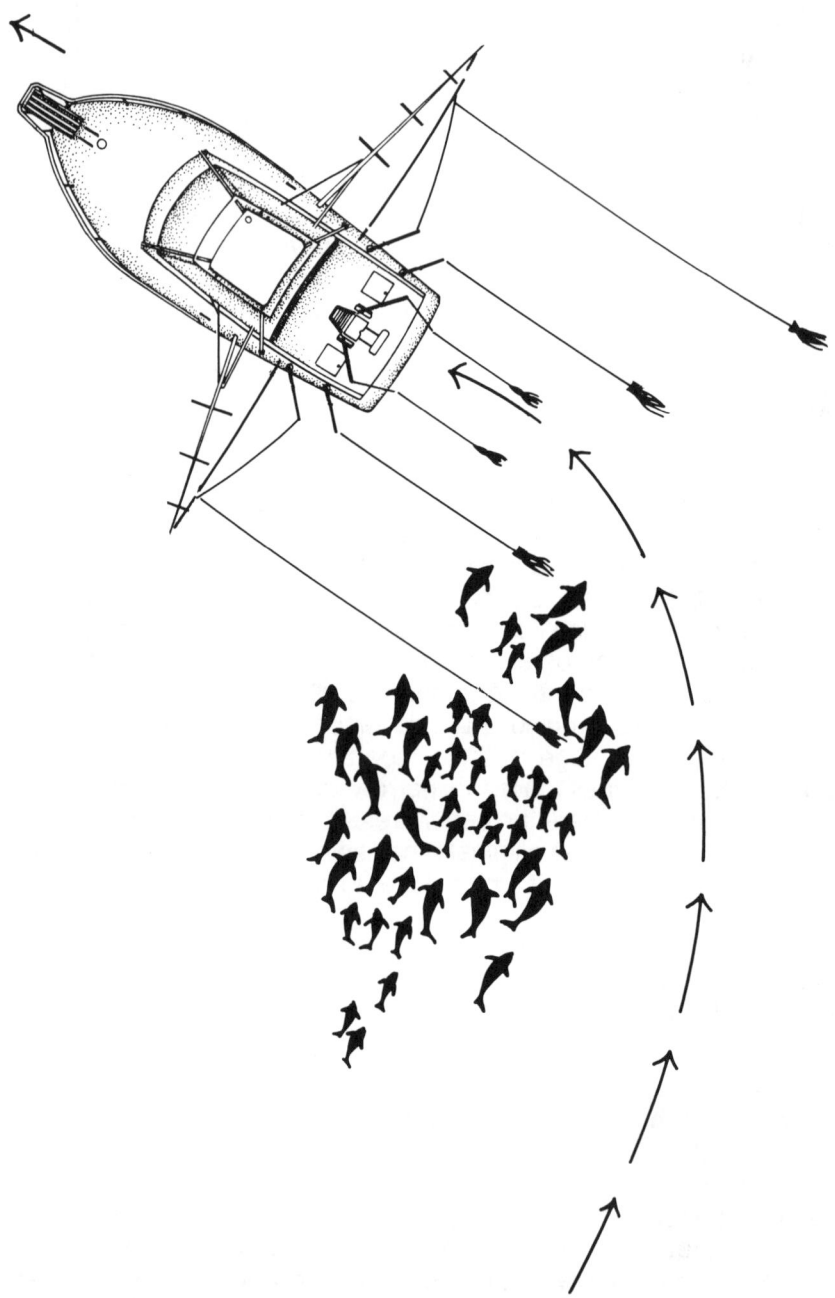

Approach a surface feeding school of tuna by moving alongside, then ahead of the fish. Make the turn so the lures, not the boat, move through the school.

THE TROLLING STRATEGY

SPOON JIGGING

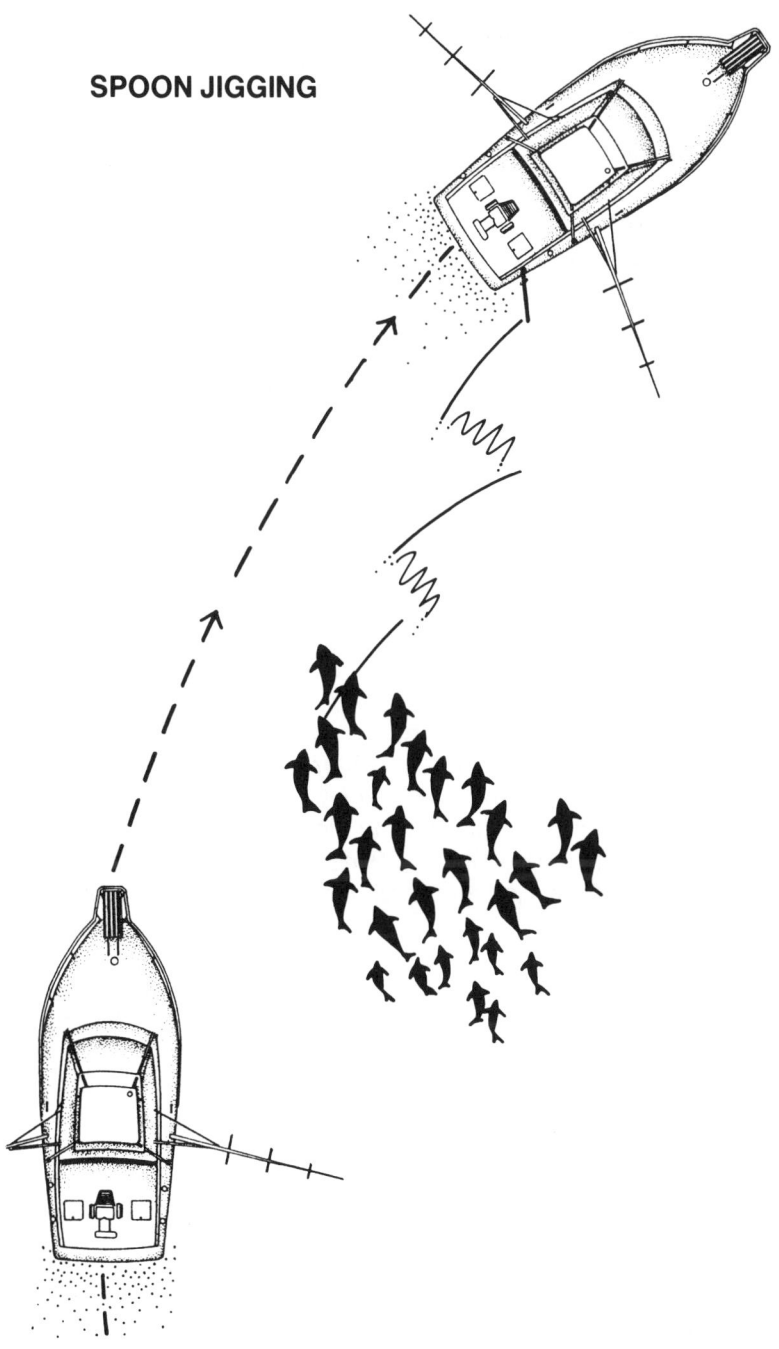

Surface feeding tuna can be hard to fool. Jig a #3½ Huntington Drone spoon in front of the fish with long sweeps of the rod tip. Tuna hit as the spoon flutters below the surface in between the jigging action.

"Hey, captain. You mind if I throw this jig when we get the next hook-up?" He held a stand-up rod in his hands with a 6-ounce diamond jig tied to the end of the line.

"Sure thing. Just don't get tangled up in the lines." This would be a sight to see I thought and it wasn't long before we could see Barry get his chance at diamond jigging a yellowfin tuna.

As we trolled past a lobster pot marker and the scope marked the bottom falling away into the abyss of the canyon, two trolling rods went off. Instantly two of Barry's friends grabbed the rods while Barry winged the diamond jig back into the wake. Somehow he missed the other lines and he quickly cleared a slight birds nest as he let the jig settle deeper in the water. The boat slowed to a crawl so we could work the two fish already hooked.

I watched Barry from the corner of my eye and saw him spin a few cranks of the reel handle before a yellowfin blasted his lure. Somehow he held onto the rod even though he stumbled from the strike, sliding to the stern of the boat. The shock of 20 pounds of drag yanking back so sharply nearly put him on his knees! Barry was into a fish and announced it to the world, "Yahoo! I'm in. Oh boy what a fish." The jig worked!

He even beat his buddies in bringing the yellowfin to the boat, a small 30-pound fish that he released. From the tower I could look down and see several other tuna following the antics of the two fish we were still hooked up to. "Hey, Barry. Drop that jig down again. There's three or four fish right under us."

As the jig flip-flopped its way to deeper water, one of the tuna rushed the jig and inhaled it only 20 feet below the surface. Barry was surprised but quickly got control of the situation and started working on his fish. It, too was a small one, but on the stand-up gear it gave a good account of itself before being released.

We all had to admit that the diamond jig did work and while it irked us to keep hearing, "See, that's how they do it in California," Barry didn't rub it in too badly. Diamond jigging had made a big impression on me. I knew we'd use the technique again.

A more common approach to jigging is to use jigs when schools of tuna are marked holding well below the surface. When the first fish is hooked, the boat is turned at a 90 degree angle to the fish, and a heavy jig is dropped down about 50 to 100 feet. With the reel in gear, the angler jigs the rod tip and waits for the strike. Depending on the size of the fish, the strike can be wild indeed! When a good school of bluefin or yellowfin is located like this, the boat can be run in a circle over the fish for repeated hook-ups.

Some jigs are available from the manufacturers with adequate, strong hooks but many others need some doctoring before they can stand up to a yellowfin. Many first timers are surprised at how strong a tuna can pull against 20 to 30 pounds of drag and flimsy hooks are quickly destroyed, the fish is history.

After removing a flimsy hook and split ring, add a larger, stainless steel spilt ring and an 8/0 to 10/0 brazed eye hook like the Eagle Claw #9014 or Mustad #7731. There are other good hook styles available. Look for a 3X strong shank, brazed eye and no offset to the point. Open eye hooks are verboten, so are thin wire shank hooks.

Spreader Bar Rigs

The usual trolling pattern with spreader bar rigs calls for three rigs to be trolled directly off the transom. The rigs have a lot of water resistance and are sometimes difficult to troll from outriggers as they constantly pull the line from the rigger clips. The center rig is placed on the second or third wave in the wake, the port side at the third or fourth wave and the starboard spreader at the fourth or sixth wave. None are fished off flat line clips.

Ideal trolling speed is about 3 to 5 knots depending on the rig, the size of the squid and the sea conditions. Calm water usually allows a slightly faster trolling speed. Rough water and swells make it tough to fish the bars at anything more than a slow crawl. It is important to keep the squid up on top of the water, not diving below the surface. Adjust the trolling speed so the squid are all splashing on the surface. To a tuna this must look like a school of baitfish trying to beat feet away from the tuna, a natural reaction for baitfish. Hopefully the tuna will respond with a natural reaction of a quick chase and a solid hook-up.

Lures can also be fished on spreader bars. Frank Johnson of Mold Craft has experimented with blue marlin while trolling the spreaders with various sizes and styles of his lures. His primary purpose for the spreader is to develop a teaser system using his molded squids.

New light weight spreader bar rigs from The Reel Seat and Murray Brothers Tackle that use hollow squids with little water resistance are now available. I've used these rigs from the Hudson Canyon to North Carolina and have taken yellowfin, bigeye and bluefin with them. Others I've talked to have had good success with the bars on blue marlin. These lighter bars can be trolled at speeds up to 7 knots, even more, and fit well into any lure pattern.

The spreader bars can be tremendously effective when trolled over concentrations of fish, as when tuna are schooled tight around masses of squid and mackerel at the edge of the shelf.

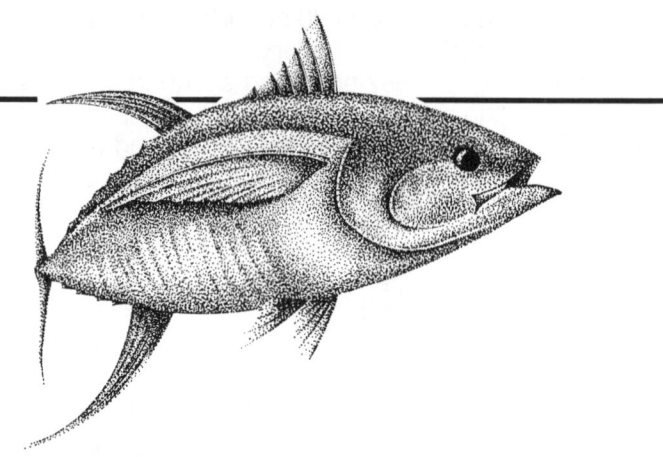

Chapter Ten

ATLANTIC BLUEFIN TUNA

Back in the 50s and early 60s, if you said you were fishing for tuna, you meant bluefin tuna. Catches of yellowfin were unusual, if not rare, and most East Coast fishermen never even heard of yellowfin tuna unless they read a magazine story or book about fishing in Hawaii, Bermuda, the Bahamas or some other exotic place. Fishing at the edge of the Continental Shelf was still a dream and the canyons were therefore unknown to the average tuna troller. Most tuna fishermen plied the waters near the coast searching for bluefin, usually within sight of land and in waters of 15 to 30 fathoms.

The bluefin was once very abundant, before the decimation of the schoolies by the commercial purse seiners. It was not uncommon to see acres of school bluefin, fish of 10 to 30 pounds, breaking water and crashing bait a few miles off the summer beaches of Cape Cod, Block Island, Montauk, Brielle, Cape May, Wachapreague and Rudee Inlet. Party boats, private boats and charter boats all plied the waters and had a relatively easy time catching good numbers of fish of all sizes. A 100-pounder bluefin was not an exceptional fish, especially in the spring and fall and there was always the chance at catching a giant, a fish in excess of 300 pounds, possibly a fish exceeding the magical 1000-pound mark.

For nearly 100 years, the bluefin of the East Coast was primarily a sport fish. Charter and private boat fleets flourished from Cape Cod to New Jersey for summer and fall fishing. In 1915, Jacob Werthiem caught a 286-pounder off Sea Bright, New Jersey that stood as the world record until 1923 when Christian Feigenspan fished the same area and boated a 407-pound bluefin. Ten years later, Sea Bright yielded another record, a 705-pound Atlantic bluefin for Francis Low. Later, Bimini became the hot spot, then the Canadian Maritimes.

Today's world record stands at 1496 pounds, a huge fish taken by Ken Fraser off Aulds Cove, Nova Scotia.

When I was in college, a bunch of us would get together for a day on one of the many New York or New Jersey party boats in hopes of catching bluefin. It was not much effort as the ocean seemed full of school fish and more than enough bigger fish to 200 pounds to delight us. That was 25 years ago; today the acres of tuna have been replaced with thin schools of bluefin. There are so few giants that they can be individually counted by biologists in spotter planes. Like the buffalo, bluefin may be on the verge of extinction.

The conflict between commerce and sport, big dollars and big angling challenge has been severely tested in the last 20 years. In the late 1960s, purse seiners began to exploit the Atlantic bluefin. At first the small school fish were taken in enormous numbers, then the giants as the prices soared. The Atlantic bluefin tuna population declined dramatically. According to biologists, today's bluefin population is a meager 10% of what it was before the seiners did their damage.

Atlantic bluefin tuna bring up to $30 a pound, or more, from Japanese fish buyers, so the fish must be boated and prepared with care. The fish are quickly bled, gills removed and the fish is chilled, if possible, during the run back to the dock. A Japanese buyer takes a core sample of the flesh as the fish is weighed, classifies the quality of the meat and a sale price is agreed upon. The fish is headed, gutted and chilled in a brine to wait quick shipment to Japan's wholesale fish markets.

Commercial pressure is now focused on the giant members of the bluefin, placing the very existance of the bluefin in extreme jeopardy. It is literally fighting for its life. Yet despite the dramatic decrease in numbers of the bluefin tuna, recreational angling possibilities still exist although today's catches are a shadow of what they were 30 years ago. Recreational fishermen have the advantage of being able to tag and release, thus protecting the future of the species.

It seems fitting to place the Atlantic bluefin tuna in a separate chapter because many of the trolling techniques, lures and strategies are unique to the bluefin, although there is some overlap with other species of tuna. I've trolled cedar plugs, an ideal school bluefin lure, successfully for yellowfin tuna, and, I have caught bluefin on daisy chains of lures usually thought of as bigeye lures.

Many offshore fishermen, hearing the sad tales of the decline of the bluefin, don't spend much effort trolling for these fish. Happily for those who still fish for bluefin, that leaves the ocean wide open to good fishing opportunities. If you are worried about keeping a fish that is so hurt by commercial fishing, then get out the tagging stick and release the catch.

ATLANTIC BLUEFIN TUNA

When bluefin were a sport fish, charter boats flourished. This catch came from Brielle, New Jersey in the late 1940s. John Geiges photo.

Giant bluefin were once valued only for their angling challenge. Several line the dock at Cat Cay in the late 1940s. John Geiges photo.

Trolling for Giant Bluefin

Trolling techniques for giant bluefin tuna began off Bimini many years ago using single, large baits, usually a Spanish mackerel. The trolling technique was improved in the Canadian Maritime Provinces when daisy chains of mackerel were employed to look like a school of fish. The daisy chain was later fine tuned off the New England bluefin grounds where a spreader bar was added to the chain and the spreader bars eventually made their way to Montauk and New Jersey waters. Each area enhanced the tactics, added its own special nuances and today the art of trolling for bluefin seems much different than it was 50 years ago.

Giant Atlantic bluefin tuna dwarf other tunas, and fishermen who specialize in catching these huge fish, believe bluefin outperform the mighty blue marlin when it comes to sheer pulling power. There is nothing quite like the feeling of being hooked to a giant bluefin as it lifts you from the fight chair, bucket harnesses snapped to a rod and reel with 45-pounds of drag, and a half ton of tuna pulling for its life.

After wintering in the Gulf of Mexico, bluefin begin a 3000 mile journey past Bimini, the Carolina and Virginia Outer Banks, New Jersey's Mud Hole, Montauk and Block Island and finally to the Canadian provinces of Nova Scotia and Newfoundland. In the fall, they return to their primal spawning grounds in the Gulf to complete the centuries old migration ritual.

Recreational anglers get their first opportunity at giant bluefin as the fish swoop out of the Gulf and head northward on the east side of the Gulf Stream past the Bahamas. For decades, many of America's top anglers have been meeting each spring to do battle with these grand fish. Tournaments held at Bimini and at nearby Cat Cay saw famous anglers like Ernest Hemingway, and innovative captains like Tommy Gifford, who added to the aura of the festivities.

The bluefin were sight-fished as mates perched precariously in the tall tuna towers of the nimble Merritt and Rybovich sportfishermen built specifically for giant tuna action. Many of today's modern fishing boat innovations were developed, or improved upon, on the Bahama giant tuna grounds. Fight chairs, tuna towers, lever drag reels, rod and reel tactics, and boat designs were fine tuned with the help of the bluefin boats, captains and anglers.

Once the fish were spotted, the captain quickly maneuvered the boat ahead of the tuna so a single, rigged mackerel or squid could be presented to the lead fish. Luck, skill, teamwork and nerve all played a part in the strike, hook-up and eventual boating of the fish.

Gifford developed a technique to beat these enormous fish on relatively light tackle and he changed the way bluefin were fought for the next 40 years. His radical, at the time, boat handling allowed many

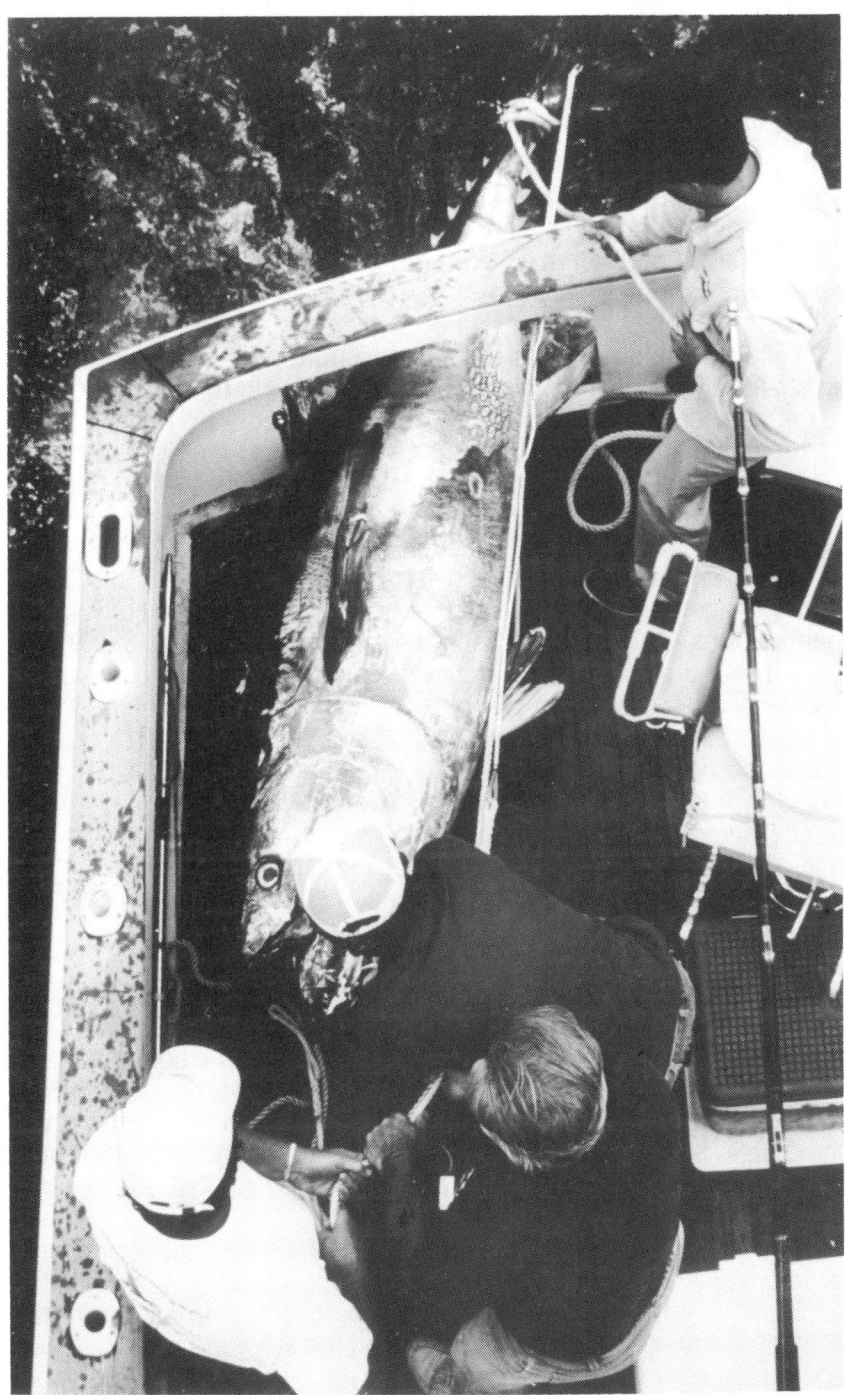

A June giant bluefin tuna caught on a spreader bar rigged with whole, fresh mackerel. Rich Barrett Photo.

more giants to be successfully brought to the boat. The fish usually moved along the Bahamas Coast on the shallow edge of the drop off to deep water. Once solidly hooked, Gifford maneuvered his boat to corral the bluefin forcing the fish to remain in the relatively shallow water, never allowing the fish to submarine into the depths where sharks or an exhausted angler meant a lost trophy.

Cat Cay still hosts its annual tuna tournament and although the giant bluefin tuna are not so abundant, the stakes are still high as the mates who spot the fish, the competition is terrific and many of the world's top anglers strive for a win.

In May, the bluefin continue to move northward, switching to the west side of the Gulf Stream, probably off the North Carolina Coast. Tarheel fishermen report huge bluefin not far from The Point, a crack in the Continental Shelf offshore of Oregon Inlet where three ocean currents brew a delightful mix of tuna and billfish. Once off the Virginia Coast, giants are not so easy to find, although fish of just under 300 pounds do show up in local catches.

Bluefin appear in June around the Bacardi Wreck and the Texas Tower off the New Jersey Coast, and in the famed Butterfish Hole just below Montauk. Seasoned bluefin veterans troll spreader bar rigs armed with a string of mackerel on a center leader and four or more mackerel draped on each arm of the bar. The strike is an eye-popping experience as a 400 to 1000-pound bluefin attacks the rig. Water bulges below the rig seconds before the bluefin engulfs one of the mackerel, hopefully the hooked bait, and takes off like a rocket.

The summer fishery, depending on weather, ocean currents and availability of bait, will position the bluefin from Block Island north into Canada. Spreader bars or daisy chains rigged with mackerel, natural squid or artificial rubber squids are trolled in many areas, such as Cape Cod, Gloucester and Nova Scotia.

I owe a special "Thank you" to to Captains Bob Pisano and Gary Kannel of the Tuna Hunter for their help in the fine points of the techniques when fishing spreader bars rigged with whole mackerel. They are professional bluefin tuna fishermen and were regulars at the Rhode Island docks at the start of each bluefin season, but they knew the bluefin had to pass the Jersey Coast to reach the Rhode Island waters. The thought of catching these fish in waters closer to home was appealing.

Back in 1987, Bob and Gary decided to put some serious effort into developing what was at that time, an untapped bluefin fishery located each June in the area near the Bacardi Wreck just inshore of the Hudson Canyon. Initial attempts at finding the fish were rewarded with hook-ups on two of the prized giant bluefin. Unfortunately both were lost but with renewed efforts in 1988, the Tuna Hunter team landed three large bluefin.

Nothing turns heads, or makes believers out of skeptics, more than seeing the real thing on the dock for weigh-in. Other boats began searching for bluefin before that summer was finished. By the 1989 June season, it was a wide open new bluefin tuna fishery and it was repeated in most seasons that followed.

The methods used near the Bacardi are basically the same methods used by New England charters skippers but refined one more step up the evolutionary ladder. The new rigs, devised off the New Jersey Coast soon appeared in tackle shops in New England, too, further enhancing the original spreader bar rigs. No doubt the evolution will continue in coming seasons.

Not all the fish are giants of better than 310 pounds. Over 1000 mediums were reported boated or released by New Jersey boats from these same ports and an equal number were probably caught from New York ports. It was bluefin tuna action like few had ever seen before.

Biologists, like Bruce Freeman of New Jersey's Marine Fisheries Division, was not surprised. Before hitching up with New Jersey's Fish and Game Department, Freeman spent several years studying the bluefin and had seen the herds of bluefin in the areas from the Virginia and Bacardi Wrecks to the Texas Tower, the Chicken Canyon and even closer to the coast in the Glory Hole and Mud Hole areas.

Early attempts at light weight spreader bars rigged with artificial squids had worked with some success, especially in New England waters, but you can't beat the real thing and many captains realized that whole, rigged mackerel made a better presentation. The theory says that a giant bluefin tuna needs a mouthful of real bait to keep its interest peaked as the huge fish attacked the spreader rigs. With natural baits, even if the bluefin hit the rig and peeled off one of the baits, the quick meal would only make the fish more aggressive.

The bluefin often came back again and again to strike at the rig until finally eating the one bait with the 12/0 hook. Witnessing the repeated strikes of a 500-pound tuna beating up on a spreader bar rig is awesome to say the least. Even hardened pros who have been at the game for many years get audibly excited as they relay radio messages of their good luck to nearby boats.

The beauty of the spreader bar rigged with mackerel is visual appearance it gives as it is trolled in the wake. The bluefin expects a school of baitfish to panic as the giant approaches the school. The spreader rigs give the very real appearance of a school of frantic bait trying to escape certain death as an afternoon snack for a bluefin.

To keep up the appearance of the frenzied baitfish, it is critical to quickly reel the spreader bar back to surface whenever a rig is blasted but no hook-up occurs. The rig must be on the surface, baits splashing like real live fish, to be effective.

Initial attempts at using standard spreader bar rigs was less than satisfactory because of the increased weight of the natural mackerel. Rigs that worked fine with artificials ended as a twisted mess after each strike and run of a bluefin. Working with Dave Arbeitman and Grant Toman of the Reel Seat in Point Pleasant, New Jersey, Pisano helped develop a beefier spreader bar constructed of 3/16" stainless steel with arms of three feet in length. A cable runs through the center of the rig where the stainless is bent into a 15 to 20 degree angle. Two mackerel are added to each side of the bar and another four or five mackerel are rigged on the center leader. Only the last mackerel is a hooked bait.

Waxed rigging twine is favored by many captains as the best way to attach the mackerel to the bar, mounted with the nose tight to the bar or center cable so the baits lay on their sides as the rig is trolled, flapping with plenty of commotion. Mackerel are prepared ahead of time with rigging twine tied in place on the nose to keep the mouth shut with the tag ends ready for attaching to the leader. The gills are also sewn shut so the gill plates don't flare and look unnatural.

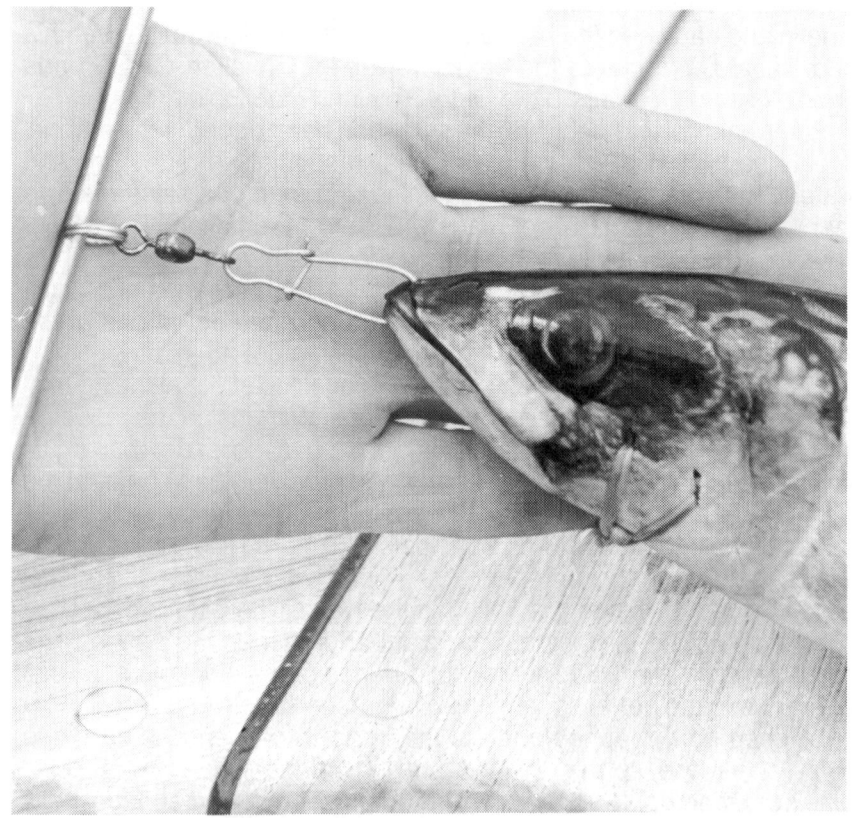

Close up of a mackerel rigged for use on a spreader bar.

The rigged baits are placed on ice in a cooler to be ready for instant rigging. Depending on the number of strikes from bluefin, or from devastating attacks by marauding bluefin, it pays to have a minimum of 45 mackerel rigged; enough for three rigs to be fished and back up baits for two more rigs.

A variation of the rig was successfully tried by Captain Bill Horvath of the Variety. Bill also worked with the Reel Seat to develop a way to mount large Duo-Lock snaps onto the bar and central cable by utilizing the same crimps and eyes used by longliners to rig their deadly lines. The snaps are pushed through the nose of a fresh mackerel and are thereby quickly attached to the rig without the hassle of rigging twine. The last update to the rig now uses very large stainless steel snaps in place of the Duo-Lock snaps.

When trolling the rigs, the boat needs to move ahead only fast enough to get the rigs on top of the water, splashing seductively without spinning or cartwheeling. If the rigs dive below the surface too frequently the boat speed should be picked up another 25 or 50 rpms. Cartwheeling rigs call for a slight slow down in speed. The actual speed is usually somewhere in the range of two to five knots depending on water conditions. Calmer days require a bit more speed than rough water days.

Three rigs are trolled. One is placed in the center of the pattern about 30 to 50 feet back in the wake. Two more rigs are dropped back at varying distances of up 50 to 100 or more feet in the wake. Closer is usually better than a far drop back but on any given day the giants, or mediums, may show a marked preference for one particular distance back in the wake over another.

The bluefin can be found over a wide area and the hot spot of the previous week may be a desert the next week. Trolling mackerel spreader bars allows the captains to cover a wide area of water but before the trolling even begins, the boats are looking for the presence of bait and especially whales. If the big humpbacks, blue or fin whales can be located, the bluefin are usually right nearby. A careful eye on the color scope may show locations of bait that can be trolled over repeatedly. Water temperature, currents and time of day don't seem to have as much affect as a ready supply of bait. Giants eat up to 10% of their body weight each day; 80 pounds of bait for an 800-pound bluefin. Without a ready and abundant source of food, the giants will travel to better feeding grounds.

Baitfishing for Giant Bluefin

Rhode Island and New York giant tuna specialists tend to fish bait from an anchored boat, rather than troll during the warmer months.

One theory why these fish don't respond well on the troll in this area is that the fish are deeper because the thermocline is deeper. In these waters, captains anchor and chum with ground mossbunker and chunked butterfish, ling, whiting and bunker. Baits will be whole mackerel, whole squid, butters, bunker or a live whiting. Three lines are fished, possibly a fourth, with one or more baits positioned away from the boat suspended off floats and another bait actively worked.

The active bait usually gets the most strikes. Line is pulled from the reel a foot or two at a time until the bait is about 100 to 150-feet from the boat. As the line is retrieved, it is coiled into a 5-gallon bucket filled with water, then the bait is let out again. At the strike of a fish, the line streams from the bucket protected from a tangle by the cushioning effect of the water.

The last hurrah of each giant tuna season takes place off the traditional grounds in the New York Bight near Sea Bright where so many early world records were caught. Giants can be taken here from early September to late October, perhaps later, depending on the mix of bait, water temperatures and the urge of the fish to head south.

Tackle Choices for Giants

Tackle for giants is always on the beefy side. I've used the Beastmaster 80/130 lever drag reels loaded with a 100-foot length of 130-pound test monofilament spliced to 800-yards of braided Dacron. Trolled fish rarely get spooked by a leader, but when bait fishing, the bluefin can be notoriously leader shy. Many anglers, therefore, tie their hooks directly to the 130-pound line. Others, fearing a break off from line chafing during a long fight, still use 200 or 300-pound test leaders.

Fighting a giant bluefin is unlike any other angling experience. Reels are fished with the drags set 45 pounds of pull, 33% of the line's breaking strength, allowing the angler to apply awesome pressure against these powerful fish. With legs locked, fanny firmly seated in a bucket harness connected to the reel, the angler rises from the seat of the fight chair, rocking back and forth gaining line a foot at a time.

A few anglers still prefer to fish with an eye towards International Game Fish Association (IGFA) standards and use a hefty fly gaff secured to the base of the fight chair stanchion to gaff a trophy bluefin. Anglers with an eye to the dollar value of the fish, use harpoon darts on 12 to 16-foot long poles to assure their catch will be boated, but not IGFA legal for world record consideration.

Many giant tuna fishermen are looking for "Him," that fish over 1000 pounds that dreams are made of and therefore they fish very heavy tackle with bent butt rods and 130-class reels. Unfortunately, most of the boats throw IGFA regulations right out the window when rigging for giant tuna. A typical rig would be a Penn 130 with 500 to 700 yards of 200-pound test Dacron backing, then spliced with 100 feet of Momoi 200-pound test flourocarbon monofilament at the business end of the tackle. A large snap with a 500-pound test ball bearing swivel is added to the end of the mono. A Hi-Seas crimp is used to crimp the mono to the snap.

Drags are usually set at 30% of the breaking strength of the line when the lever is at Strike position, up to 60% of the line strength at Full drag. While trolling, the lever is brought back to apply about 20 pounds of drag. The strike of giant bluefin on a spreader rig is jaw dropping and the sheer power and speed of these fish can cause tackle problems and failure if the drag is set too tight while trolling and waiting for the strike.

Captains who fish primarily for giants prefer to mount Lee clutch-style, 90 degree, vertical flush mount rod holders in the transom covering boards to better work the bent butt rods. A rod holder is mounted at each transom corner and a third at the center of the covering board. The clutch style rod holders are necessary in case a giant takes off at an angle after striking the rig and getting itself firmly hooked. The first run of a big fish, if it is hard away from the angle of

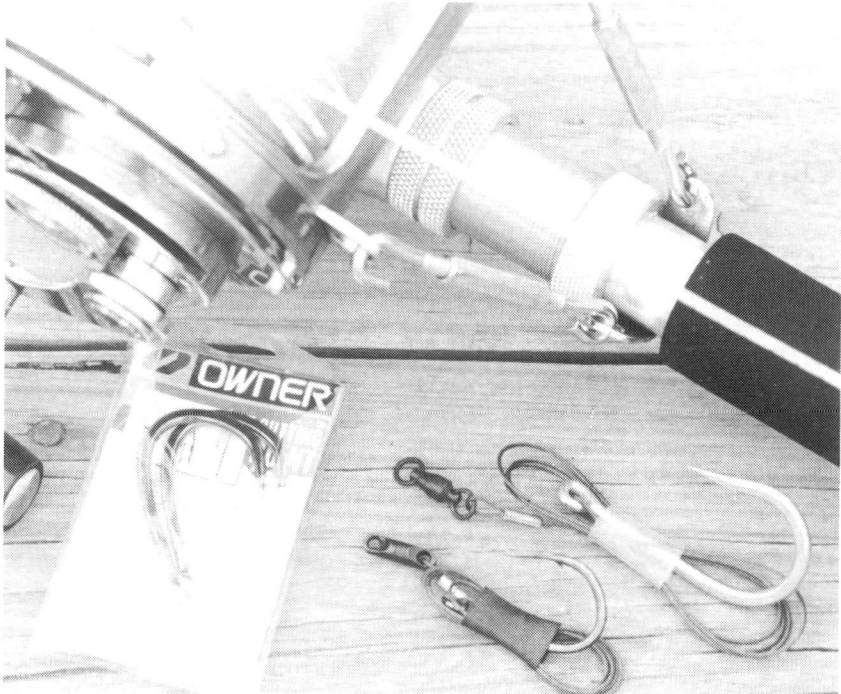

Lever drag 80TW or 130 reels are favored by most giant tuna anglers. Mouse trap rig allows heavy cable to be hidden inside bait so tuna cannot detect terminal gear.

the rod holder gimbal pin, will result in a sheared pin and ruined rod holder.

It is also much easier to remove a bent butt rod from a vertical flush mount rod holder as compared to the more usual 60 degree rod holders employed for smaller tuna, marlin and sailfish. A quick and efficient conversion to save standard rod holders is made by dropping a golf ball into the rod holder. The free spinning ball prevents the gimbal on the rod butt from grabbing the gimbal pin and the rod tip can swing in whatever direction the fish heads off to.

A smaller number of fishermen do fish by IGFA regulations and use 130-pound test tackle and line. The sport value goes way up, although it may take longer to boat the fish. This point is argued by some who believe the angler is better able to apply maximum pressure to the fish with 45 pounds of drag on the reel with 130-pound line, than when trying to apply 65 pounds of drag with 200-pound test line. Many anglers just can't handle the intense drag settings and once tired, the 200-pound tackle is not doing its job.

Steve Sloan, IGFA representative from New York, commented at a meeting of the Manasquan River Marlin and Tuna Club that prior to the bluefin becoming so valuable to the Japanese, thousands of big bluefin, and some up to the 1200-pound mark, had been landed for nearly a half century on IGFA 130-pound line. No doubt they can still be landed on 130-pound gear; it's the dollar signs in the eyes of some sportsmen that calls for excessively heavy tackle. But, this is a judgment call each of us must make on a personal basis.

School Bluefin

As the bluefin season progresses, giants and mediums continue to move up the coast, usually to Montauk, Massachusetts and the Canadian Maritime Provinces. In their wake come the schoolies which provide some excellent action for the Outer Banks of North Carolina, then Virginia and Maryland, Delaware and finally New Jersey and New York as the migration moves up the coast.

In 1992, faced with still declining stocks, the National Marine Fisheries Service further refined the size categories of bluefin tuna as follows:

Young school	less than 26"	less than 14 pounds
School	26 to 44"	15 to 65 pounds
Large school	45 to 56"	66 to 134 pounds
Small medium	57 to 69"	135 to 234 pounds
Large medium	70 to 76"	235 to 309 pounds
Giant	77" or larger	310 pounds or larger

East Coast inshore trollers are most likely to encounter greater numbers of young school fish in the spring than the slightly larger school fish. The large school bluefin are not as common as their smaller brothers. Be aware that young school fish must be released unharmed.

Tackle can be on the light side and I've enjoyed using the Penn 113H and 114H reels, the 12T and 20 Internationals, Daiwa 50H and 400H Sealine and similar light tackle offshore reels. Rods suited for 20 to 30-pound line are ideal, especially the lighter stand-up rods of 6-feet in length. My ideal inshore school bluefin outfits are based on the 113H matched to a Calstar 660L blank made into a 6-foot rod with roller guides and an aluminum butt. The reel is fished with 30-pound mono and we've taken fish up to 120 pounds with this gear with no problems, and quite a lot of fun.

Favorite lures include cedar plugs in natural wood or red and white paint, and spoons like the Huntington Drone in sizes 2½ and 3½, Hopkins 550, Clark squid spoon and the Crippled Alewife in silver or red/white. Small skirted lures like the Sevenstrand Tuna Clones, Zuckers, Mold Craft, C & H Stubbies, Ilander and chrome-headed Hex Heads are also good catchers. Many old-timers still use feathers in red/white, red/black and green/yellow. Dark purple lures have been favorites of mine for the last few years and I often add a strip bait to the lure for extra flash and perhaps some scent. Certainly the wiggling belly strip adds an extra dose of motion.

Nine rods can be effectively fished; two as flat lines with the lures right on the face of the first wake behind the boat, two more flat lines on the fourth wake, two off the riggers on the fifth and sixth wakes and another run down the middle back on the seventh or eighth wake. A pair of spoons fished in place of the two close-in flat lines is a proven variation of this pattern.

Skirted lures and feathers work better on the riggers, while spoons and cedars work best when fished tight in to the transom. Wachapreague boats use daisy chains of cedar plugs fished far back in the pattern, or in close but not usually from the riggers. A variation of the spoon is to slide an egg sinker down the leader so it rests just ahead of the nose of the spoon. The added weight gets the nose down and keeps the spoon under water most all the time.

Trolling speeds will vary from 6½ to 8 knots depending on which captain you talk to. I generally troll slower in rough water, slightly faster in calm water, watching the lures to see that they are working well at whatever speed I've selected. If they are jumping out of the water too much, I drop a few rpms, kick up a few rpms if the lures are never skipping the surface. Typically we'll catch a mix bag of skippies, little tunny, bonito and dolphin while trolling for the school bluefin.

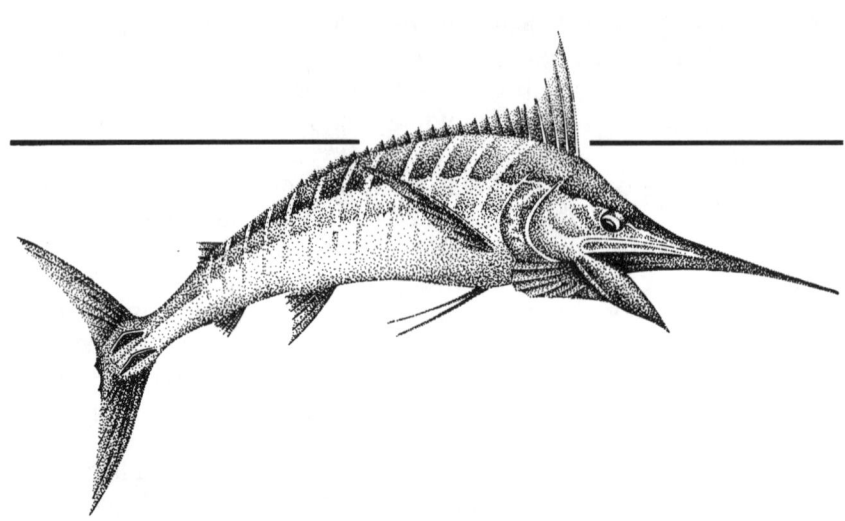

Chapter Eleven

FISH ON!

Hooking, playing and landing an offshore fish takes planning and team work. A good game plan develops a strategy that clearly assigns each crew member, and the angler, specific jobs so everyone knows exactly what is expected of them, and they know what is expected of companion team members. No single member of the team is better, or more important, than the other members, because without any one of them, the team falls apart and a trophy fish could be lost. While some captains and mates may look down their noses at the angler, the best captains know that the angler, especially a good one, is much more than just a "winder" who cranks in the slack line.

Watching the well-drilled moves of an experienced crew is poetry in motion. The hook-up, ensuing battle and final boating of the fish will look relatively easy to the untrained eye. On the other hand, watching an inexperienced crew can be a barrel of laughs and the catching of an offshore fish may seem impossible.

Most of us never get as much experience as the truly top-notch captains of the world who fish full time and travel the world's oceans in quest of mammoth fish. We settle for a pleasant lifetime of 50 to 250-pound fish, but just like the pros, the average Joe offshore fisherman can carefully fine tune his plan of attack, the set of the lures or baits, the actions of his crew and his boat handling to become a better fisherman with a slick, smooth fishing team and greatly improved chances of fishing success.

Hey, this is the fun of fishing. This is why we go offshore. The chance to catch a big one is appealing and challenging, but the day to day catches of smaller fish are the real crowd pleasers. The enjoyment of offshore fishing comes not so much from the actual catch of a giant fish, but from the cumulative memories and experiences of handling the boat, choosing the lures, seeing the strike, working the tackle, leadering and gaffing the fish and sharing the victories, and defeats, with friends on the run back home to the marina. The expectation we feel as the boat leaves the inlet to begin a new day is as much a part of fishing as the backslaps after decking a good fish.

The most high brow of anglers shun the use of the boat to help land the fish. The Masters Tournament of Palm Beach requires anglers to play their sailfish from a dead boat and the fish must be boated within an allotted time or points are lost! This adds an extra measure of challenge for light tackle fishing but some anglers may wonder how this could be done with a 500-pound blue marlin, or a 300-pound bigeye. We each have different levels of angling skills and therefore different ideas on what makes the finest sport. For some, the thrill lies in getting into the fight chair, to others it's getting strapped into the gimbal and harness to fight the fish stand-up style. Others enjoy working the cockpit, others want to handle the wheel and hunt the fish.

Ready for Action

Before the first fish hits, it pays to have everything ready for action with the decks clear so coolers, tackle, towels, boat shoes and soda cans are not in the way. Gaffs are stowed so they are easily accessible without having to dig into the engine room, tackle locker, the cabin or under a bench seat to find them. Gloves for leadering, pliers or knife for cutting the leader when releasing the catch, the tag stick with tag mounted in the pin are handy, not stowed in a hidden drawer somewhere. The fight chair is adjusted for the physical size of the angler who is designated as "first up."

On a slow day it's easy to daydream and lose focus of the game plan. Sometimes a ten minute nap, or few stretches in the cockpit are valuable to perk up the captain, mate or angler dulled under a melting hot sun. The captain and mate are always looking and analyzing. The captain scans around and in front of the boat for fish sign, birds, nervous water, color change, weed line and keeps an eye on the color scope for signs of bait, thermocline changes and schools of game fish. The mate watches the lure or bait pattern keeping an eye on the motion of the lures, expecting that dark shadow of a blue one, or a bigeye, to smash one of the offerings.

The rods and reels are positioned in the cockpit with a pre-planned pattern so the same rod and reel always goes into the same rod holder. Each reel is marked with a small stick-on number. The rods are positioned in numerical order from the left forward rod holder in the coverboards, through the flat lines, the rods in the strike arms of the fight chair, and forward to rod holders in the right coverboards, when viewing the cockpit looking aft from the helm. After the strike of the first fish, the rods that were not hit, are stowed in the rocket launcher, tower leg rod holders or as close to their fishing position as possible. On my boat, the short 12-foot leaders allow the lures to be stowed easily by just reeling the lure to the rod tip, placing the rod in the rocket launcher holder and letting the lure lay on the deck with the leader hanging loose. You can neaten this up if you have longer leaders by coiling the excessive leader around the reel.

Once the first fish is boated, we want to get the lures back in the water quickly. The neatly stored rods make this a snap and we can have our pattern loaded and ready to go in less than a minute or two with no wasted effort untangling lures or twisted leaders.

While trolling, the numbered rods allow the captain and mate to communicate without shouting. If I'm in the tower and see that the bait on the #3 rod and reel has a weed on it, or that the lure's position needs to be changed slightly, I can get the mates attention, hold up three fingers and make motions to check the bait or to let it out or pull it in to adjust the pattern.

Don't Stop the Boat!

The strike is exciting and it's easy to lose your cool. Some captains are not always calm people. At the dock, they can be laid back and tell funny stories that make your cheeks hurt from laughing so much but on the boat they can be much more intense. Do something to cause a missed fish, especially a tuna or billfish, and it's mayhem.

"You idiot!" a friend of mine yelled at a mate who took the boat out of gear just after a fish hit one of the lures, "Don't stop the boat. Keep going!"

We had just made a set across the edge of a 30-fathom lump and a yellowfin had crashed a ballyhoo bait trolled off one of the riggers. The clicker on the reel literally screamed as 100 pounds of power yanked line from the reel. One of the crew grabbed the rod and got ready to do battle. I waited next to another rod, ready to grab it should a second tuna eat another lure. That's when the mate pulled back on the throttle and dumped the boat out of gear.

The captain blew off a long stream of colorful expletives, some of them clearly describing what he thought of the mate's parentage. All of them turned the sky a few shades bluer than it had been a few moments earlier. Not a petite guy, the captain literally flew to the helm and shoved the shift levers back into gear and the boat surged forward again. Moments later, the second rod, then a third, bent hard over and two more tuna were solidly hooked.

Later at the dock we all laughed at the experience. The captain apologized for getting so excited, the mate apologized for being so foolish. He had learned a good lesson, and quickly too, as he had two more occasions that morning to handle the boat and get us some double headers by taking the advice of "don't stop the boat."

Many more fish can be caught if the boat is kept in gear after the initial strike. It doesn't matter whether you are trolling for school bluefin in New England, trolling yellowfin off the Outer Banks, trolling longfin albacore at the Hudson Canyon or blackfin tuna at the Hump off Islamorada, the advice works everywhere along the coast.

At the strike, it may seem like line is literally pouring from the reel. Outdoor writers exaggerate with prose describing "line melting from the reel," and back at the dock, nearly every fisherman will embellish their stories of a good fishing day with "the fish nearly spooled me."

In reality, though, most tuna or white marlin would find it impossible to empty a typical offshore reel with 500 to 700 yards of line on the spool. A tuna will only run so far before he has to catch his breath and stop. The exception to this, of course, is a truly huge fish, a blue marlin or giant bluefin of better than 800 pounds or so, that could spool a reel if the crew were poorly organized or the tackle too light for the job.

With tackle matched to the quarry, the only way a fish can spool a reel is if the drag has not been properly set. The largest bigeye ever caught on my boat barely had a Penn 50 to the half-spool mark. A 250-pound class blue marlin took awhile to get to the boat, but we caught it on a Daiwa 300H with 450 yards of 30-pound line. A 122-pound yellowfin that ate a school bluefin lure, was beaten handily by an Ambassaduer 9000 with 20-pound test. Many, many fishermen have similar stories of respectable fish taken on reasonabe tackle.

With the drag set at 33% of the breaking strength of the line and with the tackle reasonably matched to the fish, there should be no problem handling the fish. The biggest enemy is time, not the tackle.

Keeping the boat in gear often results in multiple hook-ups because many offshore fish travel in schools, loosely or in tight packs. As the trolled lures cross over the edge of some structure or big pod of bait, there may be several fish that give the lures the look-see. The most aggressive fish will strike and get himself hooked. His buddies, seeing the commotion, get their competitive juices flowing and get ready to strike also. They'll be hooked in a moment if the boat is kept in gear, they won't be hooked if the throttle is dumped and the engine(s) taken out of gear so the boat slows to a stop.

Out of gear, the lures that didn't get bit by the first fish, will slow down and stop, losing their life-like action. Keeping the boat in gear maintains the lure speed for a few seconds, which is just enough time for one, two or a bunch of other fish to grab the lures.

With tuna, waiting for the extra fish can be mind boggling. It takes steady nerves to wait a few seconds for the next strike. Admittedly the line does look like it's never going to stop. My son, Rich, was at the helm on a trip to the canyons one June and played the waiting game to the limit. He kept the boat in gear at the first strike and we shouted out loud "two, three, four" fish as one by one the other rods bent over in succession. We didn't stop counting until all nine rods were fast to a fish. This time, the cry "Fish on!" really meant something. These were all small bigeye of 125 to 150 pounds and none, not one, came close to spooling our 50TW reels, even with Rich keeping the boat in gear for about 10 extra seconds.

No matter how often any of us gets to fish, it's never enough. Time on the water is precious and we have to make the most of it. Keeping a steady hand on the throttles while trolling and waiting that extra few moments can pay off big.

With billfish it's a different matter, especially if the fish that crashed a lure is a big fish. Most marlin captains will jump the boat speed up a few knots to help set the hook and to maintain a tight line. Marlin have an uncanny knack for running a large loop in the line, then doubling back to cause an excessive amount of slack line, thereby assuring their escape. So, it's best to keep the boat in gear. At least for a few moments until the fish, crew and boat are settled down.

Six fish on; only 4 anglers! This is the wild action of tuna fishing at the Continental Shelf.

Setting the Hook

When trolling with lures, a fish will usually hook itself, but the angler can still give the rod tip two or three smart lifts to be sure the hook has been driven home. The lever on the reel would have been set below the Strike position while trolling. For tuna, the angler would move the lever to Strike as the captain slows the boat after the initial delay in hopes of hooking a second or third fish. For marlin, the angler would move the lever to Strike as the boat is slowed after the initial speed up to help set the hook and maintain line control.

When fishing with baits for billfish, especially live baits, a brief slack line drop back is needed after the line has been released from the rigger clip. Most captains will speed up the boat to maintain line control while the angler transfers the free spooling tackle from the rod holder to the fight chair gimbal and gets seated in the chair. Once in the chair, the reel lever is shoved forward to Strike and the rod is lifted several times to get the hook buried in flesh. At the same moment, the boat is slowed to a crawl to avoid excessive line drag from the boat's speed.

Now What?

What the captain does after the strike and hook-up can be just as important as finding the fish and getting the right lure to them. On a slow day, it's especially tough to lose what might be the only trophy catch (maybe the only catch) of the day. The best trolling fishermen, whether they are looking for tuna or billfish, will use the boat, the wind and current to their advantage. Once the fish are hooked-up, team work from the crew and angler, careful boat handling by the captain and quick use of a pencil are essential to play the fish quickly and to get back to the school of fish quickly.

Several things happen all at once after the fish are hooked. Let's say we had the strike, kept the boat in gear for a few seconds and two other fish jumped on the lures. Now what? As the captain throttles back to idle speed, he leaves one engine in gear to maintain a slight forward motion to the boat. A pencil is used to scribble down the loran numbers on a pad at the helm. Most every loran unit has a memory button, but in the excitement and commotion of the strike, it's too easy to "think" the memory button was pressed. Later when the numbers are called up, it is discovered, too late, that they aren't saved. It's impossible to miss with a pencil and a scratch pad, and the numbers can be saved forever.

As the boat slows to a crawl, the anglers take the "fish on" rods out

TURN WITH THE WIND

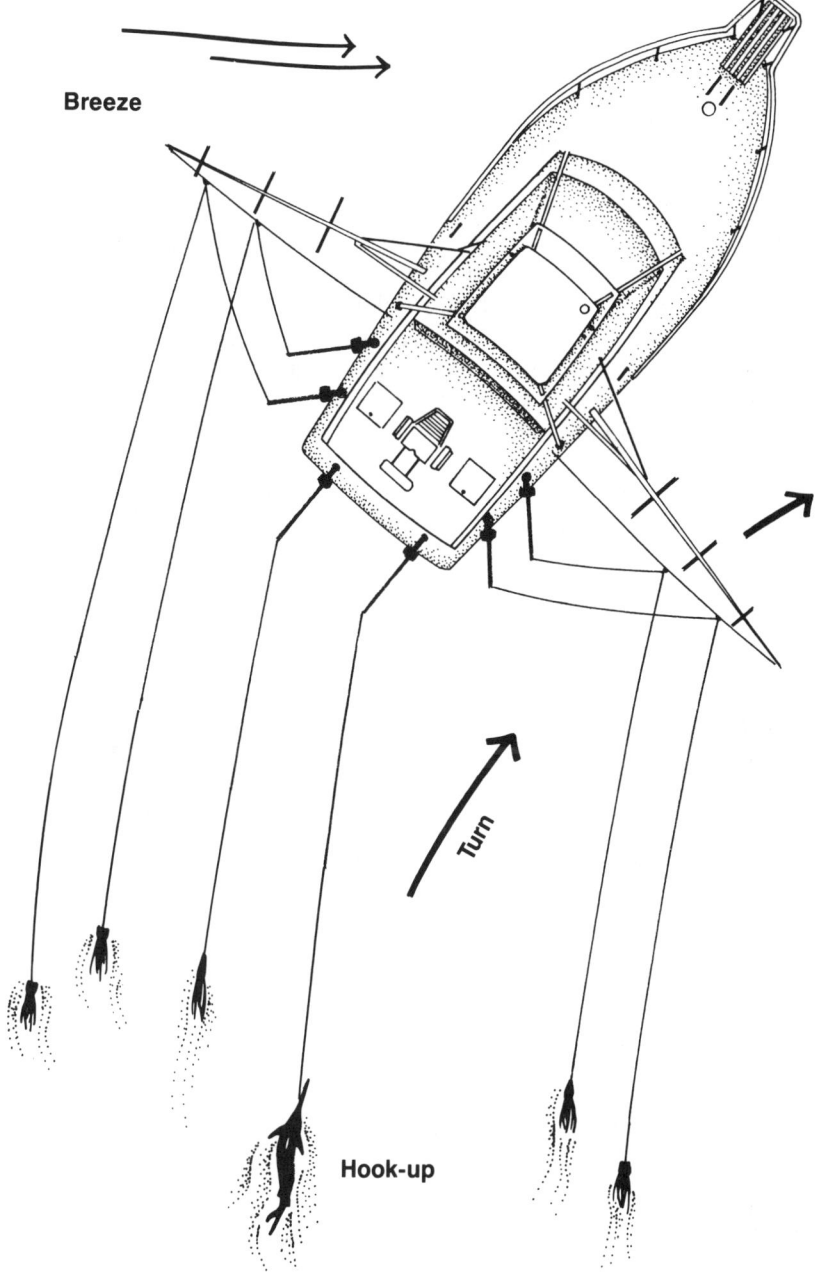

At the strike of a fish, make a slow turn to get the wind off the stern of the boat to help keep a tight line to the fish.

of the gunnel rod holders and get in the chair or get the rod butt firmly into a gimbal belt. On offshore fish, like tuna or billfish, the lever is moved from trolling setting to the Strike position, pre-set to 1/3 the breaking strength of the line.

Other crew members not working fish would clear the decks and reel in any rods not hit. Gimbal belts are slipped around the waists of anglers with fish on and anything lying on the deck is cleared away.

You usually know right away what size fish have been hooked. If the fish are less than 75 pounds, it can save time and effort if the outrigger lures that weren't bit are reeled only close enough so they dangle off the outriggers, the lures just splashing the water. It takes only seconds to get these lures back into the pattern after the fish is boated. Other rods are cleared and put into rod holders at the forward bulkhead of the cockpit, in a hard top rod holder, rocket launcher or tower rod holders so this tackle is completely out of the way.

Gaffs are readied but not left lying on the deck ready to poke a foot or leg. On small boats, place the gaffs so the hook end is nestled into a bow rail. On tower boats, the gaff can hand from a tower leg. I lay my gaffs over the stern cleat just below the cover boards so the hook is out of harms way but the gaff is ready for instant use.

Depending on the direction of the wind and the location of nearby boats, the captain may have to veer the boat to the right or left. It's moved from trolling settling to the Strike position, pre-set to 1/3 the breaking strength of the line.

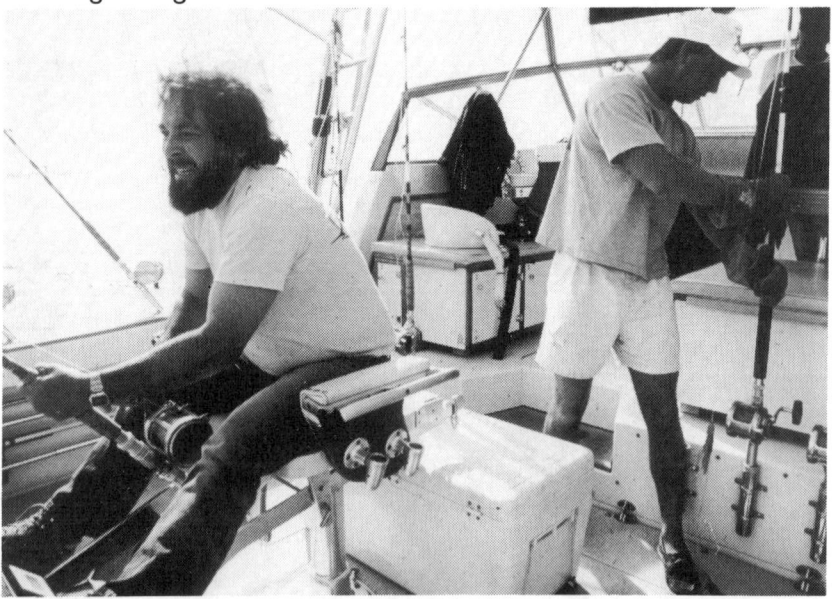

Everyone has a job to do. Angler gets set in the chair while mate stows rods and reels not whacked by a fish. Captain writes LORAN TDs, wind, temperature and other useful information on note pad.

It's tough to fight a fish with the boat heading directly or quartering into the seas and wind. A slow turn to the lee will get the wind off the beam, then off the stern where there's less chance of tangled lines. The wind helps keep the lines tight and the fish directly off the stern. The veering turn should be very shallow, not sharp to cause lines to cross or excess line to be lost from the reel.

On calm days, small center console boats offer 360 degree fishing room and it's a lot of fun to walk the boat as the fish is fought. On rough days when just standing is a victory, trying to stand with a big tuna at the end of the line, pulling for all it's worth can be nearly impossible. It's helpful in these rough seas to again keep the stern to the fish so the angler can get support by leaning against a rocket launcher, cooler, or gunnels, or get seated in the fight chair.

Maintaining some slight forward motion after the hook-up saves many fish. Alternately bump the boat in and out of gear for two or three seconds to keep some forward motion to the hull. It keeps the line tight and prevents the loss of many fish. This is especially true as the fish gets nearer to the boat. The shorter the amount of mono between the boat and the fish, the less of a safety factor from line stretch is available.

Come On Aboard!

Slight forward motion is also a big help in the last few seconds just before sinking the gaff or tagging the fish. The slow forward motion keeps the line and leader tight and keeps oxygenated water flowing over the gills of fish about to be released. Many fish, from blue marlin to bluefin, will swim towards the boat as a mate places firm pressure on the leader while maneuvering the fish within gaffing or tagging range. With no forward motion to the boat, the leader man can run out of options real quick, before the mate is ready to gaff the fish. The result is a lost fish as it spits the hook from slack line or as it rolls under the boat. Let me relate a story that happened to a friend of mine who lost a big fish at the stern.

"It's over 200 pounds for sure!" Jimmy shouted. The bigeye lay only a few feet away, inches under the water, dorsal fin just barely creasing the surface. I had a good hold of the leader and the lure was solidly hooked in the tuna's jaw. The fish should have been ours.

Jim took the boat out of gear to grab the gaff. This trophy, he believed, was going home with us. As the boat's momentum slowed, then stopped, I had to keep pulling in more leader to keep a tight line to the fish. I ran out of leader as my hand came within inches of the lure. There was no more room to maneuver or keep a tight line.

"Get the boat in gear," I shouted, but Jim was already walking to the

FISHING FOR TUNA AND MARLIN

WIRE A FISH - SMALL BOAT TACTICS

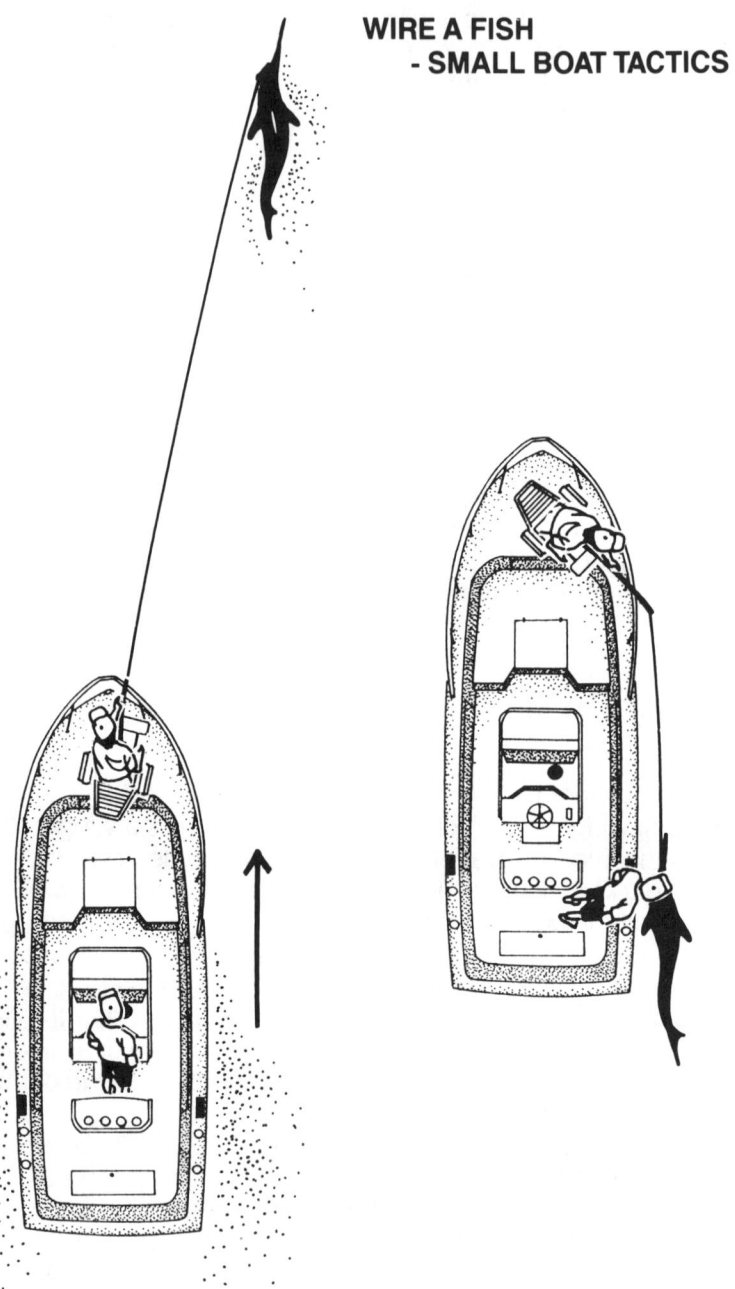

In a center console, fight the fish from the bow. As the leader gets near the rod tip, angler turns so his buddy at the helm can grab the leader.

FISH ON!

WIRE A FISH
- BIG BOAT TACTICS

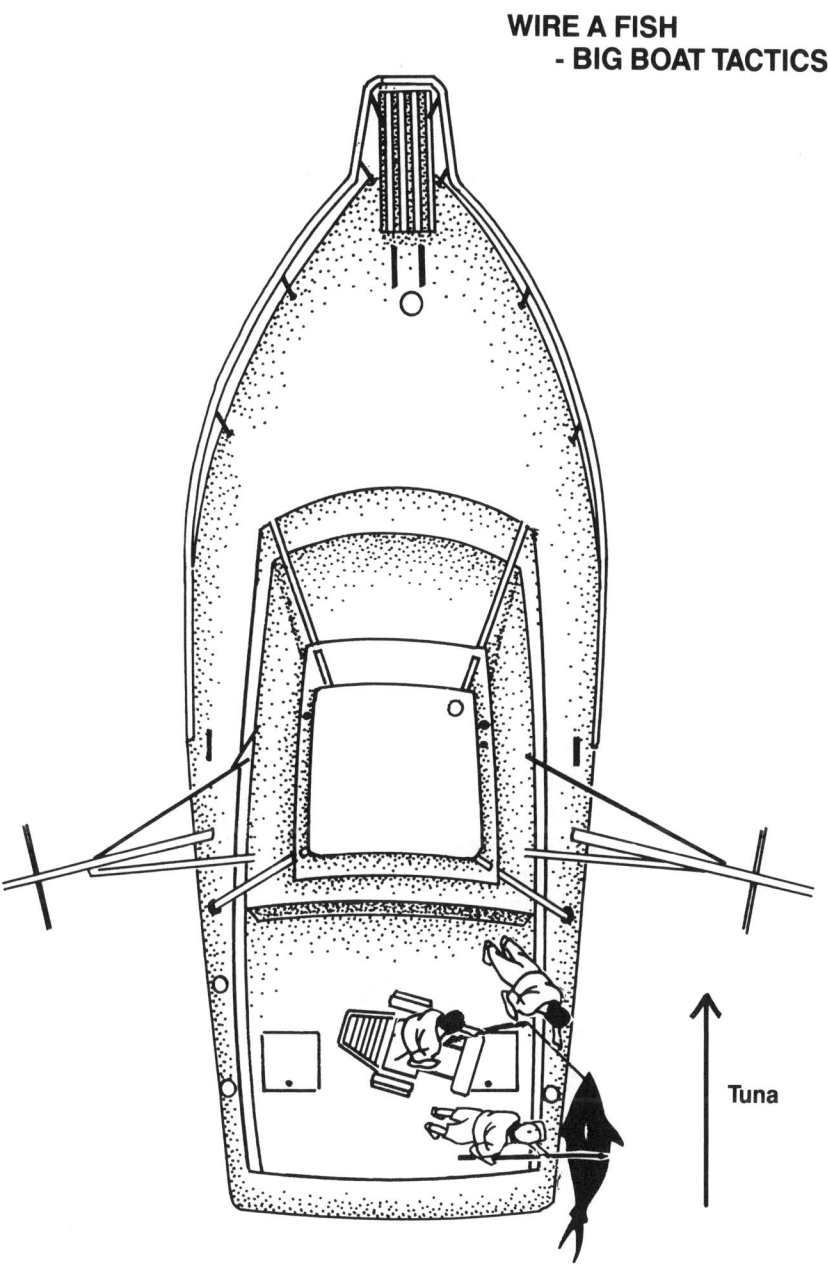

Angler turns in chair as leader touches the rod tip. Leader man brings fish alongside boat for clear shot at gaffing or tagging.

transom corner, gaff in hand, where I was leaning over the gunnel looking eyeball to eyeball at the bigeye. Do fish sense moments of weakness in anglers? This one must have. It rolled slowly on its side, angled its head and before Jim could reach the fish with the business end of the gaff, the tuna dodged under the boat. I pulled back on the leader trying to turn its head away from the rudders but a leader can only deliver so much pressure before it pops.

The leader rubbed against the rudder and I felt it vibrate in my hands for a brief instant before it snapped. The tuna, the lure, the trophy and the dozens of stories that could have been told back at the dock disappeared in a heart beat. The great fish was gone. All I had left was frayed mono, rubbed blue with bottom paint. Jim moaned, his arms ached and his back hurt.

Later that night while re-living the tale with a few friends over a late dinner, Jim admitted, "I should have kept the boat moving. The wind blew us right back over the fish. It was a goner the moment I left the throttle to get the gaff. You can bet I'll never do that again."

The safest procedure is to put the boat into gear, at idle rpms, just as the leader man grabs the leader. This forward motion usually causes the fish to rise to the surface and lay on its side or belly, parallel to the direction of the boat. Ideally the leader man should move to the closest transom corner. Which corner is usually the decision of the fish as it favors one direction as it swims in protest near the transom. School tuna are less of a problem than a marlin or large tuna. A few wraps of the leader with gloved hands and the fish should be laying in perfect position for the gaff man to lean over the corner and do his job, neatly and cleanly.

The captain only applies enough motion to keep the line tight. Too much speed can cause the fish to be pulled from the leader man's grasp. I shift the engine in and out of gear several times, applying only enough power to keep slight headway. If the fish makes a hard turn away from the boat, the leader man releases the leader and the angler again plays the fish. Since the boat is moving away from the fish there is less chance of a cut off on props or underwater gear like rudders or struts. As the fish turns, the boat moves away and the fish dodges into the wake, not under the boat.

Assuming all went well and the gaff man has a clear shot, the gaff hook should be placed into the head area so no meat is destroyed and to get a firm bite into muscle and bone, not soft flesh that may tear and cause a lost fish.

The instant the gaff is struck home, the angler should back off the drag to Strike position. The leader man would prepare a second gaff if the catch is a very big fish. Only after the fish is securely gaffed should the angler leave the chair and place the rod and reel in a nearby rod holder. He can assist the mates lifting the fish aboard.

The best place to lift the fish is at the transom corner, at the side of the hull, not over the transom. This is the only clear spot for outboards, stern drives and bracket drives. Even inboards with their clean transoms usually have the lowest gunnels at the transom corners so the lifting distance from water to cover board is minimized. Fish of 10 to 30 pounds, like dolphin or school tuna, can often be managed by the gaff man all alone, but bigger fish need a second man, perhaps a third man on the gaff as the fish is hauled aboard. To avoid the destruction of valuable meat on a hefty bigeye or medium bluefin, we prefer to use a tail rope to help lift the fish from the water to the deck. The process of hauling the fish aboard is, of course, made much easier with a transom door or a block and tackle secured to a tower leg.

Working the Tackle

Watching a real fine fisherman work the rod and reel is a pleasure. It's what separates the winders and grinders from the superior angler. As the spool diameter changes so does the effective drag setting so the angler has to use the lever drag to adjust the drag at various stages of the fight. With a full spool, 25 pounds of drag for 80-pound line is about right. After a good run where a fish pulls enough line to reduce the spool diameter by half, the drag setting is effectively doubled to 50 pounds. More drag is added from the resistance of the line in the water and the line could pop.

If you have set the drag at 33% of the breaking strength of the line with the lever at the Strike position, the lever would be backed off slightly on every run of the fish, returned to Strike at the end of the run to gain line. At boat side, when the fish may be holding just below the boat and a few extra pounds of drag are needed to lift the fish, the lever is moved forward to the Full setting. On most reels this setting is about 40 to 50% of the breaking strength of the line.

The angler must have fast reflexes to back off the drag lever if the fish suddenly makes a dash from the boat. The hefty drag setting could result in a pulled hook or a broken line unless the drag is returned to the Strike position the instant the fish makes the lunge away. With heavy tackle, and with the angler in a gimbal belt and kidney harness, or seated in the fight chair with a bucket harness, the left hand is placed over the back of the reel so the thumb and forefinger are in the ideal position to move the lever while the right hand cranks the handle. With lighter tackle, standing up or in the chair, but with no kidney or bucket harness, use the left hand to support the rod, the right hand to work the drag lever and the reel handle. Always stop the reel handle on the down stroke so you have clear access to the lever.

Short Stroke

We've all seen movies where the fisherman lifts the rod tip so the blank arcs in a high, graceful bend. The angler is usually sweating, but grinning as if he's having the time of his life. Later in the battle, he may shows signs of agony as each mighty bend of the rod causes arm muscles to shudder and ache with each pull against the fish. This may look great for a movie or video but it shows how NOT to fight the fish.

The long, slow lift of the rod works against the angler and most of the line gained on the lift is lost as the rod tip is lowered and the reel cranked. The fish senses the momentary reduced pressure as the rod tip is lowered and swims a few feet back down into the depths so the angler has to lift the fish that same distance again before getting the fish any closer to the boat.

Aggravating this is the stretch factor inherent in monofilament line. For every 6-foot lift of the rod tip, 2 feet of the lift are lost as the fish swims back down, 2 feet are lost to line stretch resulting in the gain of only perhaps 2 feet of line. To accomplish the 6-foot lift, the angler had to bend his arms, using relative weak muscles to work the rod. His high lift line retrieve is very tiring and a very slow process to get the fish to the boat.

Short, but quick, lifts of the rod tip will work far better and get the fish to the boat in less time, with less effort and fewer lost fish. With the left arm held nearly straight to the rod, the angler makes a short lift of the rod tip by leaning back with his legs, thereby reducing the fatigue of arm muscles and using the much stronger leg muscles to work the rod. The tip is lifted only 2 to 3 feet, then quickly lowered while the right hand makes one turn of the reel handle. Only 2 feet of line was gained but when this motion is repeated, rapidly, the angler can gain much more line with far less fatigue than with the high rod lift. The fish is kept off balance and does not have the chance to regain line after each pull.

The short stroke technique works equally well with the angler fighting the fish standing up and wearing a gimbal belt, or seated in the fight chair. Big fish may require the addition of the kidney harness or the bucket harness but the technique of leaning back and using leg muscles instead of arm muscles is still the same.

Fight Chair

In its simplest form, the fight chair provides a place for the angler to sit. Rough sea conditions may prevent a stand-up battle with small fish so the fight chair comes to the rescue. Much bigger fish are most effectively fought from the chair. As we discussed in Chapter Two, the fight chair actually does allow the fisherman to put more pressure to bear against a big fish.

A fight chair allows the angler to use powerful leg muscles to slide his body back and forward on the fight chair seat to work the tackle. On the back slide, the rod is lifted; on the forward slide the reel is cranked to gain line as the rod tip is lowered. On very big fish, this action is modified slightly so the angler rocks back and forth, braced against his legs, his fanny not resting on the fight chair but lifted by a bucket harness against the pull of the fish. This rocking action is a truly awesome feeling and works best with bent butt rods for maximum pulling power for the ultimate short stroke technique.

During the fight the captain will use engines and rudders to help keep the angler facing directly towards the fish. The mate, however, must assist by turning the chair at those times when a particularly fast moving fish makes dashes to the right or left of the transom, or when the chair must face off to the side of the cockpit and slightly forward when the boat is maneuvered to run forward against a fast running marlin. It is helpful to have the back of the fight chair removed so the angler has the greatest area of movement if he needs it. I like to leave the fight chair back in place, but lower it to the dropped down position.

A bucket harness and fight chair brings maximum pressure to bear against big fish. Angler uses legs to slide himself back and forth in chair, thereby raising and lowering rod tip to gain and retrieve line.

It serves as a convenient handle to swing the chair right or left to keep the fisherman facing the fish.

The usual position for a fight chair is in the cockpit of a fly bridge boat, facing aft towards the transom. In a center console, however, the best position for the fight chair is in the bow. The boat can be quickly turned to follow a big fish and to keep the angler in excellent control of the tackle. Outboard boats with chairs in the stern are often unwieldy to handle backing down, and excessive water may flush onto the deck through the splash well. Lee Wulff was one of the pioneers in developing this technique about 30 years ago to catch giant bluefin tuna of nearly 1000 pounds off Newfoundland in a 17-foot Whaler on 80-pound tackle.

Fish-Fighting Antics

The fish you have hooked is concerned with only one thing, trying to escape, and it will do everything it possibly can to accomplish this. As the fish moves in the fight against the angler, the boat will have to be maneuvered to keep the angler working the fish properly. However, the maneuvering of the boat may cause other problems. Let's take a look at some typical fish-fighting situations that are encountered while trolling.

The End Run: Many billfish will hit the lure, run away from the boat, then angle towards the right or left and eventually try to move ahead of the boat. The fish can move much faster than most boats can go in reverse, so the best tactic here is to swing the bow towards the fish, get the angler facing forward and race after the fish. Once the fish is close to the boat, the more traditional tactics of placing the angler and boat so they are stern to the fish can be used.

Whether to run forward or back down is dependent upon how much line has been dumped from the reel in the initial run. If the fish is relatively close to the boat, the forward run works beautifully, but if too much line has been lost from the spool, the water drag against the line may cause the line to break. It's a judgment call only experience can help you make.

Running With The Current: Many fish will conserve their own energy by swimming away from the boat with the help of the prevailing water current. The typical maneuver would be to back down to follow the fish, but when the fish slows or stops the run, the current, or wind, will now continue to move the boat towards the fish with the possibility that the boat may overrun the fish causing a snapped line.

The captain who is trying to keep the angler in the stern facing the fish will have to move off to the side of the fish to avoid the cut off, but now the angler is no longer facing the fish off the stern. If the boat is

FISH ON!

END RUN

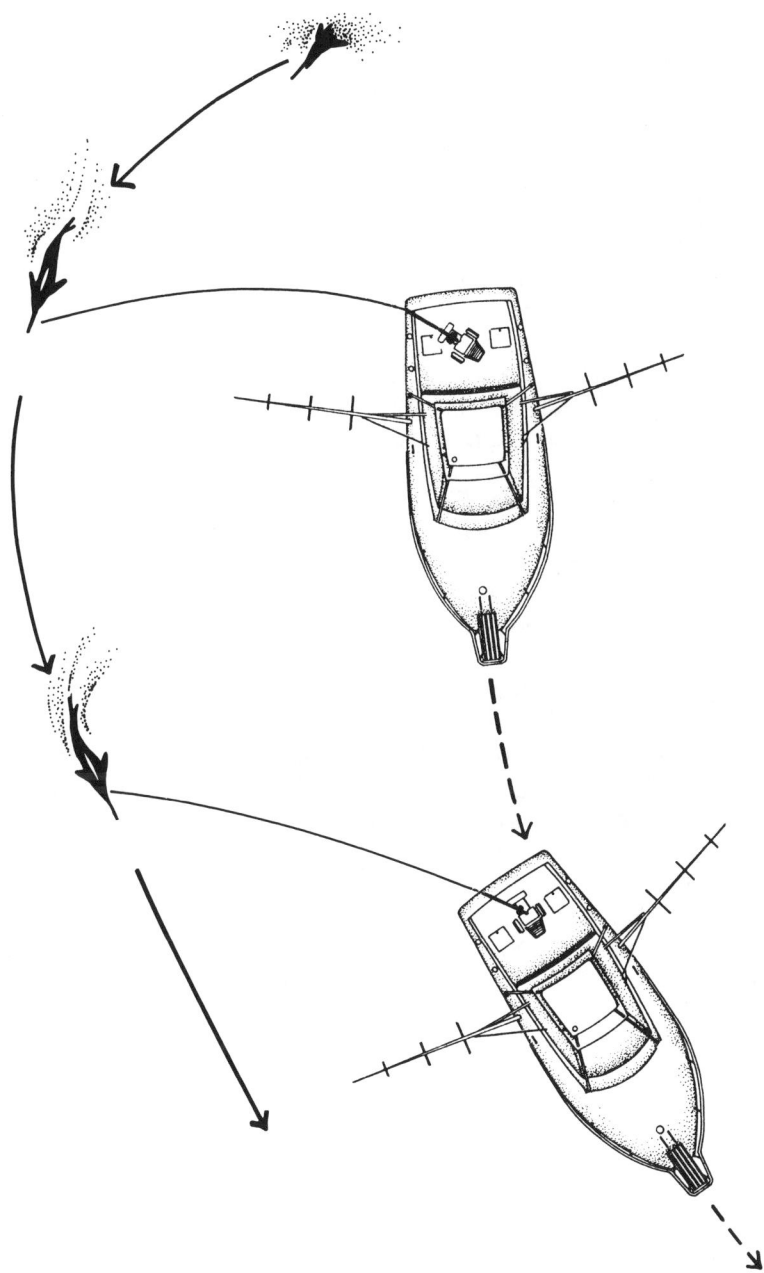

As a fish tries to make an end run around the bow, captain moves boat forward to prevent a cut off while angler fights fish off transom corner.

maneuvered to get the angler facing the fish, the wind and current again move the boat towards the fish causing a repeat possibility of over-running the fish.

The solution here is to have the stand-up angler or the fight chair face to the side of the cockpit so the boat can be maneuvered alongside the fish. When the fish is close to the boat, on a short line, the captain must be especially careful to be ready to pull away from the fish if it moves to dart under the boat. The stand-up angler would be ready to move to a new position in the cockpit to thwart the fish's efforts, or the fight chair angler would be assisted by the mate as the chair is swiveled to turn towards the new position of the fish as the captain moves the boat.

A variation of this technique uses the boat to cork screw a fish towards the surface. The angler always faces the side of the cockpit, the captain continually moving the boat in a controlled circle around the fish to gain the best line angle to constantly apply lifting pressure to bring the fish towards the surface.

Pull Away From Deep Fish: A big fish may hold several fathoms below the boat and pull with tremendous power against the angler. This vertical, straight up and down line angle is to the fish's advantage, not the angler's and can prolong the struggle. With pectorals flared out like wings, the fish requires little effort to stay down deep below the boat, yet the angler cannot exert any dramatic pressure to lift the fish. In essence all the angler can do is hang on.

An effective solution to throw deep holding fish off balance utilizes the boat to pull away from the fish thereby gaining a better line angle that places more pulling power at the angler's end. While some line is lost as the boat pulls away from the fish, the improved line angle usually allows the fisherman to not only recapture the line lost as the boat moved away from the fish, but also additional line because of the advantageous line angle. After several maneuvers like this, the fish will be within gaffing range.

Wild Fish: Marlin are famous for boat side antics that try the skills of the captain, mate and angler. A quick hand on the throttle and shift controls can save the loss of a wild fish that makes a dash under or along side the boat. The captain will rely on hand signals from the mate to indicate the position of the fish as it nears the transom, or if the fish suddenly changes direction.

Tuna can also do some unpredictable things at boat side. A 200-pound class Allison tuna gave me a few good fits as it neared the boat. Rather than fight deep, this fish aggressively turned first to the left then the right as it darted from side to side only 30 or 40 feet from the transom. Here's where a nimble boat and skillful handling make or break a trophy catch. The angler in the chair, I'm sure remembers the hard pulling power of his big fish, but I remember the challenge of

FISH ON!

PULL AWAY

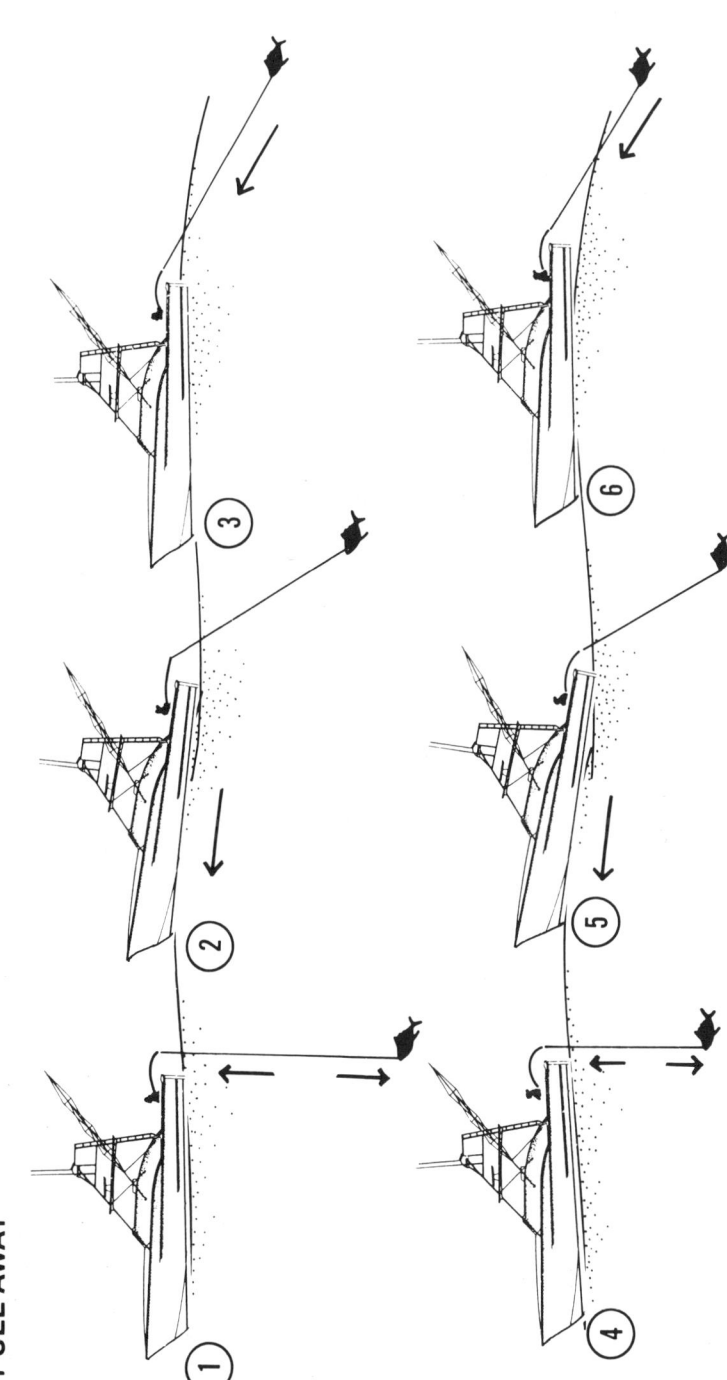

When a stubborn fish is below the boat (1), line can be hard to gain. By moving the boat away from the fish (2), the angler gets a better line angle to lift fish and gain line (3). Repeat (4, 5 and 6), until fish is ready for gaff or tag.

working the boat, shifting, turning and accelerating to keep the fish from cutting off and escaping. Watching the dances of a sharp looking sportfishing boat as a blue marlin or gutsy tuna goes ape is the stuff that fishing memories are made of.

Catching Number Two

The time to start catching the second fish is the moment you hook-up with the first fish. Trollers who follow a pre-planned drill for the captain and crew will add many extra fish to the day's catch with a few simple procedures that can be adapted to fit any boat or species of fish. We use the same basic plan on the Linda B for inshore bluefish, kingfish and striped bass, as we do for tuna and billfish. After you do it for a while, it becomes second nature. We don't consciously think about the plan any more, we just do it.

At the first strike, the captain should write down some vital information to get prepared for catching the second fish. A small spiral notebook stashed at the helm is handy for this. If it's inconvenient to use a pad that might get soaked with spray or rain, a grease pencil can be used to jot down this information directly on the console or any flat area at the steering station. The waxy pencil marks can be easily cleaned with Spray Nine or acetone.

Jot down the loran TDs first. To save time, only use the last three numbers, plus the number after the decimal. 26410.8 over 42238.9 becomes 410.8/238.9 for simplicity.

It can be helpful to jot down which rod, or rods, got hit and the direction of the troll. A tuna crashing the right rigger preferred the color, shape and action of the lure that was trolled off that rigger. That's vital information. After boating the first fish, we may want to change one or two other rods to add more of the fish-catching lure to the pattern to increase our chances for catching the next fish. If several tuna hit kept hitting the starboard rigger line that has a red and black lure fished on the fourth wake, we change several rods so they place the lures on the fourth wake. On many days it gets us shots at multiple hook-ups on yellowfin, bigeye or albacore.

Knowing the compass heading is helpful because there will be times when fish will hit the lures only when trolled in a certain direction. Because of currents, the angle of the sun or wind which causes surface water movement, tuna, or billfish, may only attack lures trolled, let's say, north to south, not south to north. They can be, and often are, that particular at times.

My scribbled note would look something like this: 410.8/238.9 - right rig - 140. It gives the abbreviated loran TDs, identifies the rod that was hit and the direction of the troll.

CATCHING NUMBER TWO

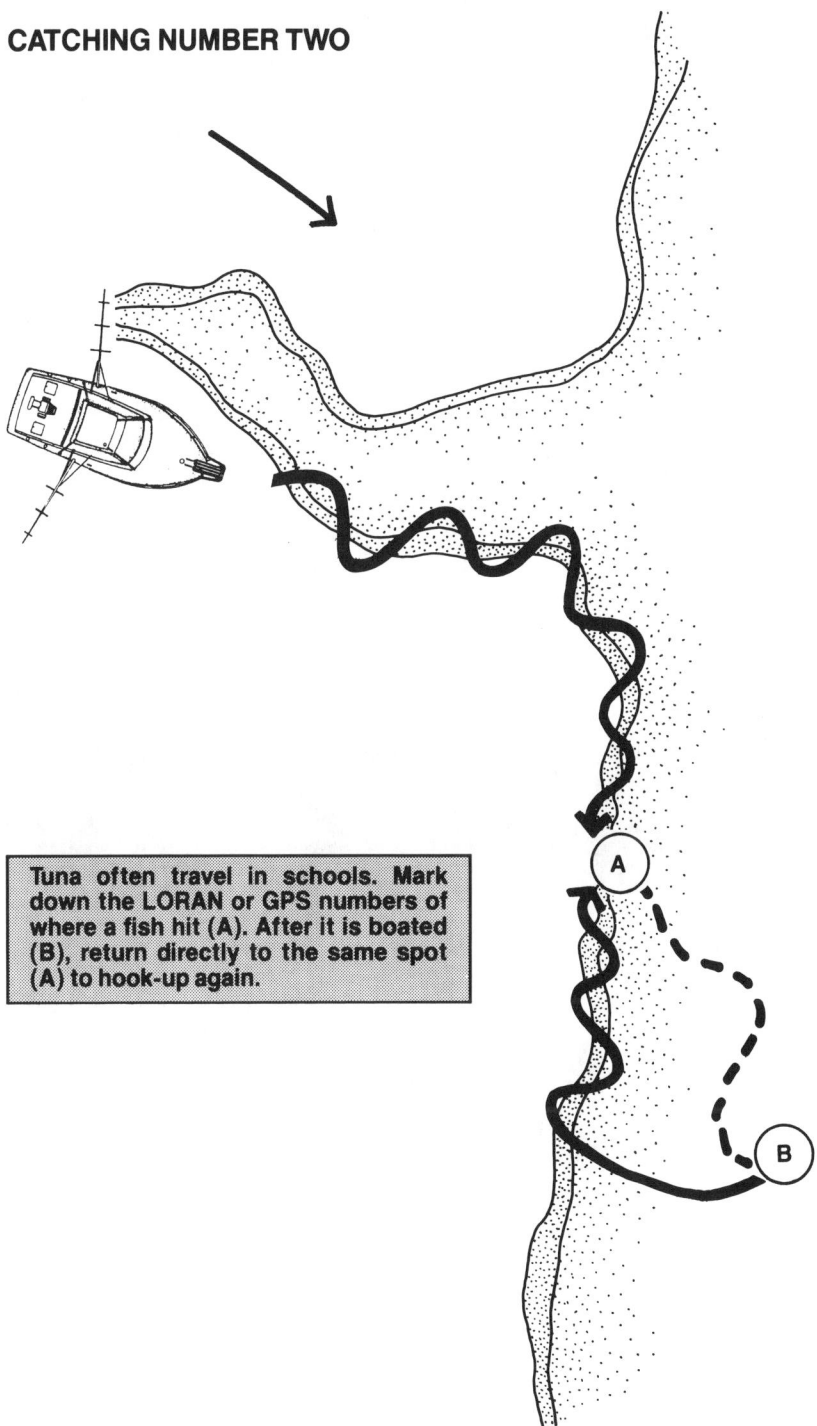

Tuna often travel in schools. Mark down the LORAN or GPS numbers of where a fish hit (A). After it is boated (B), return directly to the same spot (A) to hook-up again.

FISH ON!

As the first fish hits the deck, one of the crew works that fish to unhook it, gut it, clean the deck and slip the fish into the fish box, cooler or tuna bag. The other crew are getting the rods back in position and the lines back in the water. A small point, but five guys oohing and aahing over a fish flopping on the deck doesn't get number two in the boat. Sometimes the bite lasts for only a short time so it can be critical to quickly get back in action. Take pictures later.

While the cockpit crew is working the fish, stowing the rods, clearing the decks and getting prepared to boat the fish, the captain has a few moments to get answers to some important questions. He should think about the color of the lure that was hit, the lure size and style, how much line was out, the position of the lure in the pattern, the lure depth and trolling speed.

If necessary, a few more scribbled bits of info jotted down in the notebook can be helpful. It's easy to lose valuable information in only a few seconds because of the excitement of boating a fish. The extra note for a trolled bluefin, written below the TD info, might look like this: green/yellow - left flat - 2nd wake. I'd know the bluefin hit a green and yellow feather on the left flat line in close to the boat.

While the angler fights the fish, the captain should coach one or two of the crew to change one, two or several of the lures on the rods.

With each reel marked with a stick-on number, once baits are positioned in the trolling pattern on the first day of a new season, the line is marked so the baits can be quickly placed in the same location next time the line is let out.

Adding more of the same lure that got bit by the first fish, can only add more fish to the day's catch. We change the lures now so we don't waste time while getting back into trolling position.

When the fish is swung aboard, I immediately start moving the boat back into position. Usually we have to make a 180 degree swing to get the bow pointed towards the place we got the strike. I do this quickly with no wasted time making a long leisurely turn. It's a tight turn to get the boat aimed in the right direction. As the crew gets the rods back into the gun'l rod holders, I check the notes and make some suggestions on how far back and how deep to run the lures.

A small, but valuable tip I learned years ago from a bluefin charter captain, uses a marking pen to color the line on the first trip of each season. The mark is then an easy reference point to set the lures out to the best position on every other fishing trip. I like a black pen to make a dark gray mark on the line, just above the reel, but before the lower guide, and it lasts for quite a long time. The reel is free-spooled until the mark shows, then the reel is re-engaged into gear or the lever moved towards Strike. A few minor adjustments to the lure positions can be made by letting out a little more line, or taking some line in, so the lures work properly in the pattern.

The line marks are a great advantage when putting the lines out after a fish is boated and they make re-setting the lures a quick job. As the original hook-up location is approached, I check the color scope for fish marks and the changing bottom structure. If we fail to get a hook-up right away, running a figure eight trolling pattern will take us over a wide, but predictable, area around the spot where we caught the first fish. If we've been doing it right, fish number two should be on the line in no time.

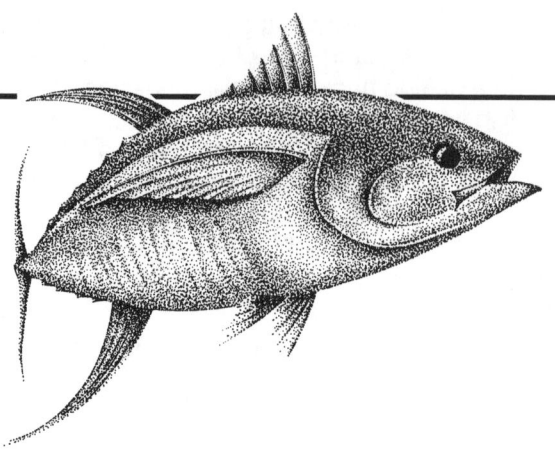

Chapter Twelve

CARING FOR THE CATCH

The big yellowfin had blasted a black and red lure about 20 minutes ago and Jeff was the first to grab the rod. He made fast work of the fish, fighting the yellowfin without aid of the fight chair. His finesse with the 50-pound tackle was about to pay off as the fish neared the transom. We could see color coming from the depths and Jeff kept the pressure on until the snap swivel touched the rod tip. "There he is!"

As Rich grabbed the leader, I bumped the port engine into gear to move the boat slowly ahead. Water pressure laid the tuna out on its side, yellow finlets glistening in the sun and the vibrant gold splash down its side glowing like a bright light. With a good wrap on the leader, Rich lead the fish forward two steps so Jeff could move to the transom corner to do the gaffing honors. The tuna lay within easy reach and he deftly gaffed the yellowfin with a perfect head shot. I pulled the boat out of gear.

The tuna was held in the water along side the boat until a tail rope was slipped down the gaff handle, then over the fish and finally cinched tightly at the tail. With a mighty heave, the 130-pound fish came over the cover boards and the 6-foot yellowfin flopped onto the deck. An ice pick to the brain dispatched the fish quickly to avoid prolonged pounding and flopping on the deck that could damage valuable meat.

Since this fish was not taken in a tournament there was no need to weigh in a whole fish. We had already tagged several smaller fish earlier in the day and had agreed that we'd keep one "big boy" for the table. To be sure the meat was kept in first class condition, the entire crew pitched in to prepare the fish for the great dining we'd have for the next few weeks.

Jeff Merrill is the swordsman on the Linda B and he makes fast work of the yellowfin, bigeye or longfin that we take home for dinner. We've enjoyed many a fine meal with barbecued or marinated tuna steaks because Jeff takes the time to "do it right" when preparing the fish.

While others readied the cooler bag, cleared the decks and started a new trolling pattern, Jeff lifted the pectoral fin and slid the knife into the lateral line about an inch deep, being careful not to go too deep to penetrate the heart. The tuna pumped blood onto the deck which Jeff quickly hosed down. He then slit the base of the tail and the gill latch under the chin.

When the bleeding stopped, the fish was collared, or cut around the gills, so the head could be pulled free. A small circular cut around the vent allowed the entire body cavity to be emptied with one hard pull on the head. The head and guts were tossed over the side providing a feast for huge oceanic deep water crabs.

The body cavity was washed and the blood veins slit at the top center of the belly cavity, rubbing the cavity clean with deft fingertips. A 6-foot length of 400-pound test stiff mono leader was uncoiled and pushed through the center of the spine, feeding it through the backbone until it came out at the tail end. Working the mono back and forth, the nervous system of the tuna was destroyed to prevent the spoilage of any meat.

The soft-sided, insulated tuna bag already had two packs of ice slid into the bottom. Tuna are warm blooded and the battle with rod and reel can heat up the body muscles causing deterioration of the meat. A bag of ice was stuffed into the body cavity of the tuna to chill the fish from the inside out, preventing the fish from cooking itself.

As the carcass was slipped into the bag, more ice was added on top of the fish and the zipper closed. Shoved under the foot rest of the fight chair, the bag now lay out of the way giving us a clear deck to fish from. The tuna was encased in a frigid chamber of ice, the meat preserved perfectly for some exquisite dining in the weeks to come.

While Jeff had done his sword trick, Rich and Matt had put out the lure pattern, hosed down the deck and everything was again ready for the next tuna attack. The entire fish cleaning and set up of the trolling pattern had taken less than 5 minutes. Not much time at all to assure some fine eating.

The two most important parts of tuna preparation are the crew and the tuna bag. Neither works well without the other. Mishandled tuna cannot be saved even with a bag; properly prepped tuna won't last

CARING FOR THE CATCH

BLEEDING THE CATCH

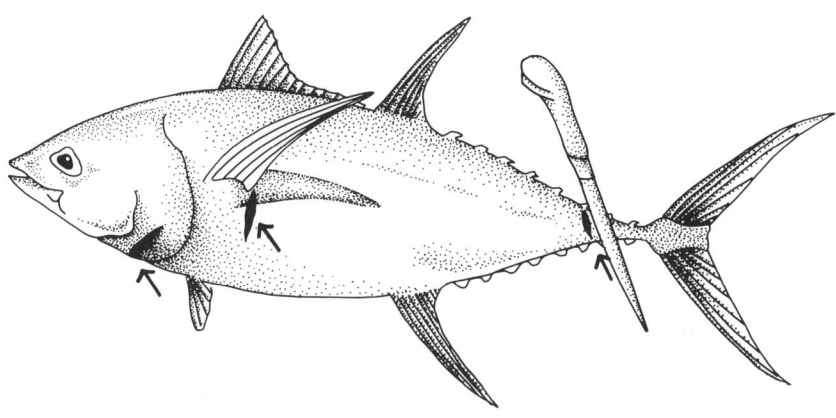

Drain the blood by making three small cuts at throat latch, at base of pectoral fin and at tail.

GUTTING THE CATCH

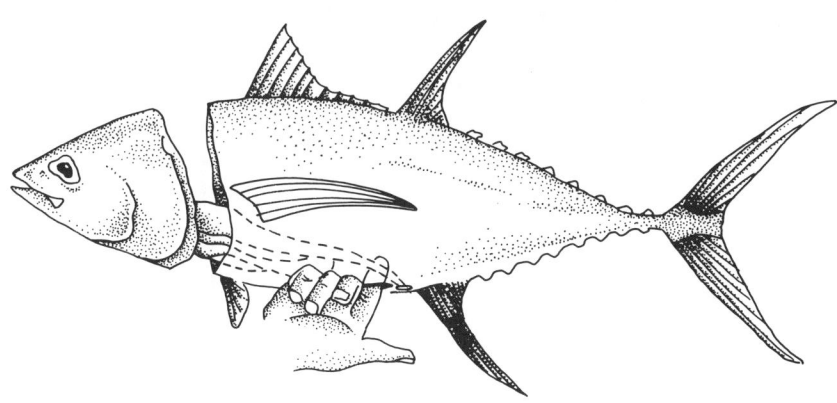

Make a 1-inch cut just forward of the vent. Reach in with finger and pull intestine free of vent. Cut around head of fish behind the gills. Remove head and entrails by twisting backbone to break free from body.

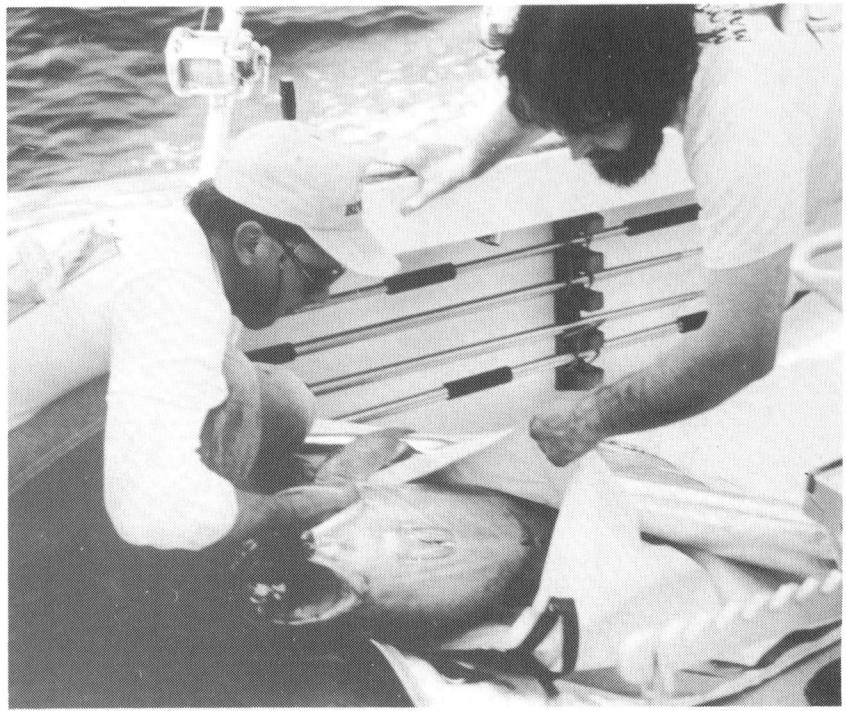
Collared, gutted and washed, a yellowfin is slid into an ice-filled, insulated Canyon Products fish bag.

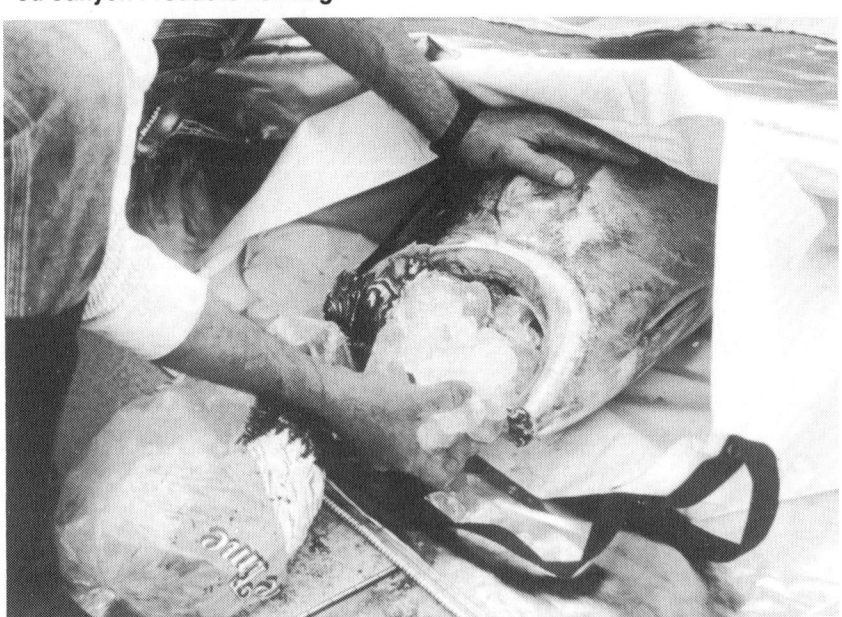
Tuna heat up internally during the fight. A bag of ice stuffed into the body cavity helps cool down the fish and assure prime meat.

without lots of ice to chill the carcass. Small tuna can be headed and iced in a large cooler, in-deck fish boxes or make-shift systems to keep tuna in good shape but for most small boats (up to 30 feet) the insulated tuna bags, like those made by Canyon Products are the only way to keep tuna fresh. The larger the boat, the larger the chance that an in-deck fish box capable of handling many fish will be available.

My own experiences fishing for tuna have been in boats that ranged in size from 23 feet to 38 feet and with no huge, below decks refrigeration system, the tuna bags are the only way to go. They assure proper care of the fish.

It's a shame to see spoiled marlin, or tuna, at the docks, or fish being dumped after weigh-in because the meat is no good. There is no excuse for this waste. An insulated fish bag solves all the problems for small boaters. They stow easily and last a long time. I have a pair of tuna bags now in their fifth season and they are still in perfect shape.

While most marlin are released today, thanks in large part to the efforts of The Billfish Foundation, the reality of big game fishing is that a few marlin are killed each year. Some expire after a long battle, simply too exhausted to live, while others get killed by shark attacks while still on the line, or from strange accidents. I watched one marlin get slashed by boat props as it dashed under the boat before the leader could be cut to release it. Some marlin are still kept for a trophy mount or in tournaments where the winning fish can only be verified by weigh-in at the dock.

Thankfully, most folks don't know that marlin are delicious eating so marlin are rarely served at the dinner table and are avoided by Americans. However, should you catch a marlin and not be able to release it, there's no need to be shy about steaking your catch and getting the barbecue grill ready. A few fishermen might look at you a little weird, but it would be a greater waste to kill such a magnificient fish and to then dispose of it.

Back at the Dock

A jumbo cooler, in-deck fish box or a large insulated tuna bag will do a good job of keeping the tuna chilled all through the trip back to the dock. Finishing up the preparation chores is not time consuming, but attention to a few small details helps assure the best meal possible.

The tuna should not be bounced against the dock, the side of the boat or dropped heavily on the dock since this bruises the meat. Small fish, those school-sized yellowfins and longfins should be iced, but not allowed to crush one another, which also spoils the eating quality of the meat.

I prefer to do the final steaking of the fish on the dock behind the boat. Wet the dock thoroughly so tuna slime and chunks of meat don't stick to the boards to cause a fishy odor the day after, and so you don't slip or get full of fish slime while you are working.

Shallow cuts along the back and belly, and on either side of the lateral line, allow the skin to be pulled off the carcass with a hefty tug, exposing the meat. Make these cuts with a sharp, but short knife, like the kind used for rigging baits.

An 18-inch slicing knife will quickly fillet the meat. With this large knife, make one deep cut down to the backbone along the top side of the fish from just behind the gills along the dorsal fins and on down to the tail. The second cut is also down to the backbone, with the slice running just above the lateral line. Both cuts should cut cleanly to the backbone. A quarter fillet can now be lifted off the skeleton.

Make similar cuts along the belly and just below the lateral line to slice a second quarter fillet from the fish. Roll the fish over and cut two more quarters from the other side of the fish. You now have four big fillets.

A large cutting board is handy to trim the quarter fillets so they are neat with no ragged or torn edges and no remnants of skin. Trim off any dark red meat that remains from the lateral line. This dark meat is very strong in flavor and can spoil what should be a fine meal.

Depending on the size of the fish being butchered, the fillets will measure from 2 to 4 feet in length. Lay them on the board, one at a time, and with a 12 inch slicing knife, cut the fillets into 3/4 or 1-inch thick steaks. A gentle rinse with fresh water will wash off any scales or fish slime on the board. Place the steaks into sealed plastic bags and put the steaks on ice.

School-sized tuna would not be filleted before steaking but I still like to remove the skin and I take extra care to be sure that the body cavity is clean before the steaking. Some fishermen use a stainless saw to cut through the backbone so the knife isn't dulled too quickly during the steaking procedure.

Freezing Tips

To be sure I get the very best possible steaks, I finish the final packing of the tuna in the kitchen, not on the dock. On a clean cutting board, I trim any discolored meat, ragged edges, or dark meat. Each steak is gently rinsed, then patted dry on a clean towel and packed in groups of 2 to 6 steaks per bag for freezing.

Freezer burn used to be a problem for me until I purchased a vacuum bagger to seal the steaks in an air-tight environment. Tuna now keep up to 6 months in our freezer with no trace of discoloring or spoiling. At about $200, the vacuum bagger has been worth the added expense. There are lesser priced vaccuum naggers available at many kitchen supply stores and department stores and they should work just as well.

At the Dinner Table

There are many excellent cook books readily available at book and gourmet food stores that do a better job than I can when it comes to cooking fish. My favorite way to prepare tuna, wahoo and marlin is on the barbecue grill because it is simple, quick and it fits our casual life style. Best of all, the fish is absolutely delicious when served for dinner.

I prefer the meat in steak form, cut about 3/4-inch thick, and marinated with special sauces. Among our favorites are salad dressings such as honey-mustard and Italian vinigrette, store-bought sauces such as ginger-terryaki and dijonaise, or any of the various barbecue sauces like Texas Best. We often try sauces found in local markets near fishing areas we visit. They usually have unusual names like Cajun Jack's or Bahama Mama's and they can be fun to try.

I start with one or two steaks per person. The marinade sauce is poured into a large zip lock bag and the steaks placed in the sauce. After sealing the zip strip, the bag can be hand massaged to work the marinade so it thoroughly cover the fish. Strong flavored marinades require a much shorter marinating time than mild flavored sauces. When I'm in a hurry, I use a stainless mixing bowl and simply stir the steaks and marinade until the fish is well covered, then let stand for 15 minutes before placing on the grill.

Tuna and wahoo steaks hold together very well on a grill and can be tuned with a grill spatula several times if necessary. I use a brush to continue to apply any of the sauce that was left over from the bag or bowl until the fish is cooked.

Fish fanciers know the best way to ruin a good tuna steak is to over cook it. The 3/4-inch steaks cook on a medium-high grill setting in no more than 10 to 12 minutes. This short time allows for thorough cooking with no undue drying out of the natural fish juices. They are superb, piping hot off the grill. In the summer, the tuna is served with a mixed salad of fresh garden vegetables and corn on the cob. Winter meals seem more appropriate with hot rice and vegetables. Either way, in either season, the dining is very fine.

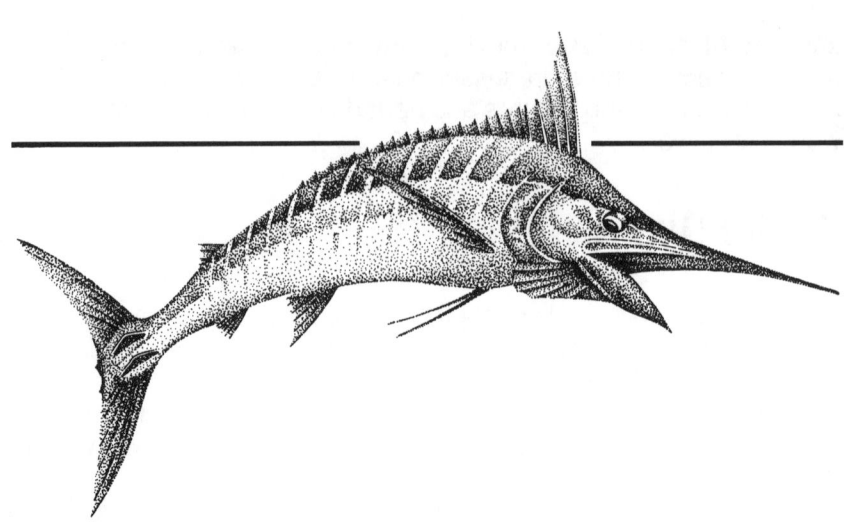

Chapter Thirteen

TAGGING FOR THE FUTURE

The barrel-sized yellowfin turned away from the boat in the dawn light, the inky black water contrasting sharply against the bright, silver-white belly and sides of the 100-pound fish. Yellow tipped finlets along the tail caught the faint glow of the morning sun and shimmered like Aztec gold - an absolutely incredible sight.

Suddenly, the dorsal fin raised rigidly from its streamlined groove along the fish's back; both pectorals flared away from their recessed body pockets and the streamlined power house was ready again for its perpetual ocean flight. Pulsing once more with vibrant life, a powerful swipe of its tail sent the big fish downward into the darkness, only the yellow tag glinting like a badge of freedom for a magnificent fish.

"Let's get another one," someone said and we quickly resumed the business and rhythm of chunking the next yellowfin into our slick. Sagging bodies, sore eyes and tired muscles had taken just about all they could but the thrill of battling just one more canyon tuna could not yet be beaten by sleep. That would come in another hour, but for now we still had a few more fish to catch.

An increased awareness for tuna tagging got its start when many tuna hunters experienced the oftentimes incredible action while chunking at the Continental Shelf. The action was red hot on many a summer night and many fishermen caught amazing numbers of fish. This new blitz of action was like a dream come true. Unfortunately for the tuna, the fast action became a nightmare as slob fishermen, with no regard for their catch, but with a greedy eye towards selling their catch, quickly tried to capitalize on the situation by bringing home dozens of fish for the market.

The worst insult to the tuna came when the markets became glutted and fish spoiled on the long ride home. So-called sportsmen in many coastal ports were seen throwing tuna carcasses over the side because the fish could not be sold. So much for sportsmanship, so much for pointing guilty fingers at the longliners.

Luckily for the tuna many canyon fishermen have begun to swing away from the "load the boat" attitude and are stressing a more conservation minded approach by simply releasing their excess catch or by going the extra measure and tagging the fish before releasing them. Several fishing clubs, like the Thousand Fathom Club have voluntarily begun to promote a two fish per man limit for their members. With a six-man crew that's still 1000 pounds of tuna on a good night's fishing so there's not much hardship, but lots of opportunities to release plenty of fish. Charter boat captains fishing out of North Carolina's Oregon Inlet have a voluntary three fish per man limit and many other ports are beginning to follow in their footsteps.

The voluntary limit works well and from my own experience not one of my charter fares ever voiced any opposition to it. In fact, they enthusiastically participated in the program and helped fill out tags and record cards. There have been nights when we saw between 20 and 30 fish brought to the boat with most of them tagged and released, after the anglers kept a few for themselves.

Some fishermen say the fish won't live after they've been played out, but this is pure baloney. Sure there must be a few fish that die

Tagging and releasing fish adds an extra measure of sport and challenge to the offshore game. This yellowfin will yield valuable data when it is recaptured in the future.

after being tagged, but they have absolutely no chance at all of survival once laid on the deck, calmed down with an aluminum baseball bat!

Many tagged tuna have lived for a long time before being recaptured again. Scott Matthews, a member of the Manasquan River Marlin & Tuna Club, released a bluefin he estimated at ten pounds in July of 1974. Twelve years later the same fish was re-caught in Cape Cod Bay and weighed 605 pounds!

So much for the "They all die theory." I've had tag returns from fish that traveled across the Atlantic Ocean to be recaptured off the west coast of Africa two years later. There are approximately 14 yellowfins that have been recaptured after making the transAtlantic crossing and this information has been eye opening to fisheries biologists who previously believed there was perhaps minimal migrations of this type.

Release With Care

So, they don't all die from exhaustion, but care must be taken to release the fish with as little harm as possible. Fish taken while chunking are the easiest to release. Just get them up to the boat and cut the leader as close as possible to the mouth. The hook, unless stainless steel, will rust out in a matter of days leaving the fish none the worse for wear. In fact, two tuna have been taken on my boat with someone else's hook still in their mouth. The annoying bit of rusting metal didn't seem to hurt their appetites one bit!

Fish caught on lures offer problems. No one is going to cut off a $30 lure, especially a lure that is a proven fish catcher. My son, Rich, has been my mate the last few years and at 190 pounds and 6 feet tall he has the power to speak with the fish on a personal level. He just leans over the covering boards and grabs the fish by the jaw, twisting the hooks free. It's awesome to feel their life so close when you are staring eye to eye with a 100 to 200-pound tuna, or a billfish, before releasing him. We got all our lures back and the fish only had jaw aches.

The only fish that can be a problem are those that may be bleeding profusely through the gills. These are best kept for the table. Minor bleeding, according to biologists at the National Marine Fisheries Service is probably not harmful. One yellowfin of about 50 pounds that we tagged a few years ago was bleeding slightly from the gills as we tagged it. Before we could change our minds and boat the fish, the tuna turned hard against the 80-pound chunking leader and released itself. Two years later it was alive and well before being caught by another fisherman and the tag returned to NMFS.

The Tagging Program

The tagging program got started back in 1954 with Dr. Frank Mather, who probably knows more about tuna, especially bluefin tuna than any other man alive. Carrying on the tradition and research are a new group of people at the National Marine Fisheries office in Miami, Florida headed by Dr. Eric Prince.

Eric's team makes tags available at no cost to individual anglers; just write a note requesting tags to:

Game Fish Tagging Program
Southeast Fisheries Center
National Marine Fisheries Service
75 Virginia Beach Drive
Miami, FL 33149-9986

A supply of tags and supporting information will be sent to you in short order. No bulk orders of tags can be shipped for tournaments, however. Eric's records show that the rate of use of the tags is highest among those anglers who request them, not those who get them as part of tournament package.

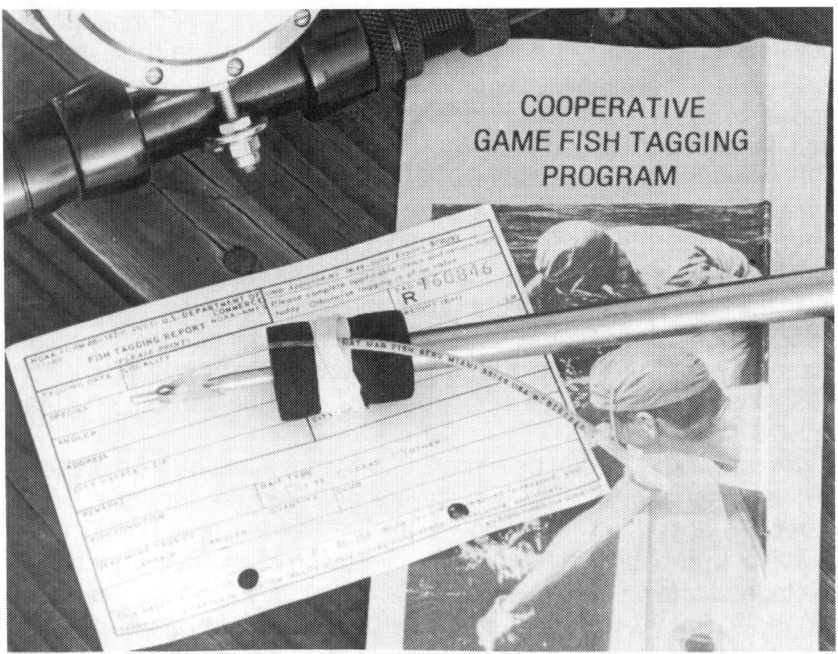

Originally developed by Frank Mather, the Cooperative Game Fish Tagging Program has provided essential management data for the past 40 years.

The tags are made up of several parts; the tag itself, the record card and tagging stick. The tags are numbered and attached to a record card with the same number. After the fish is tagged, the important information such as length, weight, location and fish condition are written on the card which is then returned postage free to NMFS. Should your fish be recaptured at a later date, that angler will read the address on the tag and return it to NMFS where the record will be pulled from the files and the information about size, weight and location gets updated.

A tagging pin is supplied with the tag kit so you can easily make your own tagging stick from a broom handle. Or, you can spring for $25 and buy one of the beautiful gold anodized aluminum AFTCO tagging sticks.

The Billfish Foundation (TBF) has been instrumental in advocating the catch, tag and release of billfish since its inception. Led by an aggressive board of directors, TBF has done extensive studies on white marlin, blue marlin and sailfish with special sonar tags, tetracycline dyes and has even developed a new tag made of surgical quality plastic that shows great promise since the dart tag will not be rejected by the body of the fish being tagged. Once implanted in a billfish, there seems to be little chance of infection or rejection as the

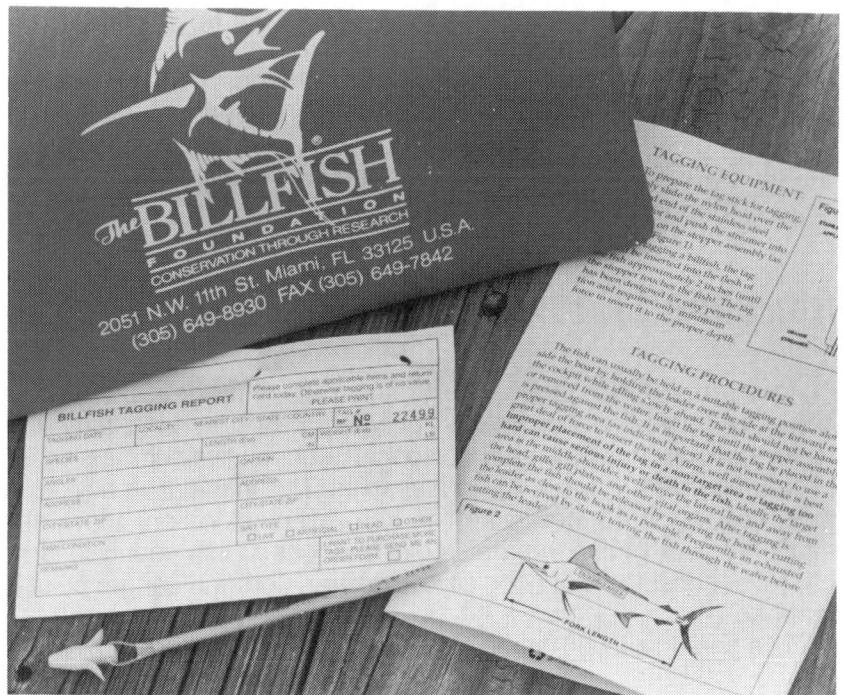

The Billfish Foundation introduced a new tag and has helped expand the tagging ethic, especially among billfish anglers the world over.

fish continues on its watery lifetime journey.

AFTCO's Bill Shedd helped organize a new wrinkle in the tagging program that should help expand the tagging effort on the East Coast. The annual AFTCO Tag Flag Program awards commemorative flags to those anglers who tag a minimum number of offshore species.

Sailfish	10
Longfin albacore, bluefin, yellowfin and bigeye	5
White marlin	5
Blue marlin	3

Points are awarded for first through tenth place in each species category and the angler who receives the most number of points wins the honor of the Atlantic Angler of the Year Award and a special trophy bearing their name resides in the IGFA office.

Detailed Records

When filling out the tagging data cards, specific information about location should be given, preferably in latitude/longitude or Loran TDs, not as general descriptions like SE of Mud Hole (which Mud Hole, how far south, how far east, etc?).

For accurate records, Dr. Prince recommends that recreational anglers keep a log book that tracks the most important information from the tag card. Several times, tag cards have been lost in the mail on the way to the NMFS offices and the invaluable information became lost forever.

Increased Knowledge

Among the things tagging helps scientists find about our favorite game fish are migration routes, growth rates, how long they live, relative population of the specific species and relative numbers of fish in spawning year classes within a species. This information helps plot facts needed to protect game fish from overexploitation, shows the effects of over fishing and helps plot changes in fish populations so effective measures can hopefully be taken before the danger point is reached.

On a personal level, the actual release of a tagged tuna provides a feeling that's hard to put into words. You've met one of nature's ultimate creatures on equal terms and you let it live another day. For some anglers who have built a habit of hanging fish for photos back at the dock to impress friends, it takes a lot of effort to release a fish. Once you do it, however, it becomes addictive and you can't stop.

Tagging is a lot of fun with great rewards in sportsmanship. Why not help the fish who make our fishing such great sport? They deserve it.

Tagging for Tomorrow

As fish populations fluctuate, usually downward, with the increased pressure from growing commercial effort, more recreational effort and from the spoiling of the world's oceans, the tag and release ethic becomes even more important. The simple release of a fish is a good idea, but tagging that fish to aid science in gathering more information is an even better idea.

The tag and release of marlin is just about unanimous by American boats, no matter what country they fish in. Tuna, however, are a different story, and a sad one at that. Giant bluefin tuna are worth such an incredible amount of money and it is a rare angler who will release giant bluefin. Tuna have sold for over $90.00 per pound and one fish in particular that weighed in excess of 900 pounds sold for more than $90,000! No wonder few giant tuna are released unharmed. Yellowfin and bigeye are gaining in importance to the commercial fishing fleets and these tunas are now on the verge of overfishing.

It is discouraging to hear of so-called sport fishermen, who would not think of killing a marlin, selling their catch of tuna. Perhaps more than the marlin, the tunas of the world may be in greater danger of overfishing because they command so little conservation attention from fishermen, scientists and the public. Commercial fishermen "care" more for the tuna than sports anglers seem to, but only because they want to assure their livelihood.

Science aside, the act of catching a fish, then releasing it to fight again, to spawn and to stabilize the population of its species is a special part of fishing. My son observed, "It's like adopting a fish as your own."

Save it for Science

To assess the well-being of an entire population of fish, it is imperative that scientists have accurate data of growth rates, reproduction and even death rates of tagged fish. Tagging can supply this data, but only tagged fish that are later recaptured and examined more closely. This means that a previously tagged fish, when recaptured, should be killed and samples of the fish shipped to NMFS.

During the past 40 years, over 65,000 billfish have been tagged and

FISHING FOR TUNA AND MARLIN

SAVE IT FOR SCIENCE - BILLFISH

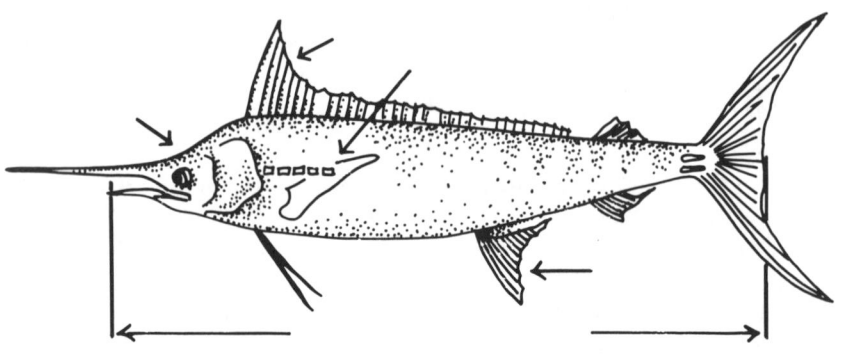

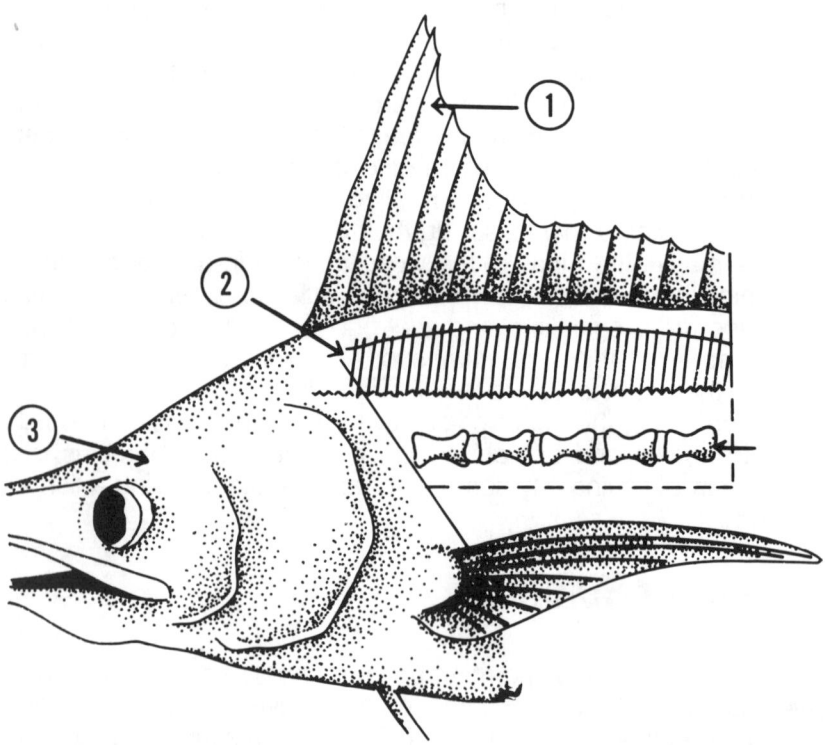

Dorsal spines (1), backbone (2) and otoliths (3) hold valuable information about age and growth rates. Measure the fish from tip of jaw to fork of tail.

TAGGING FOR THE FUTURE

SAVE IT FOR SCIENCE - TUNA

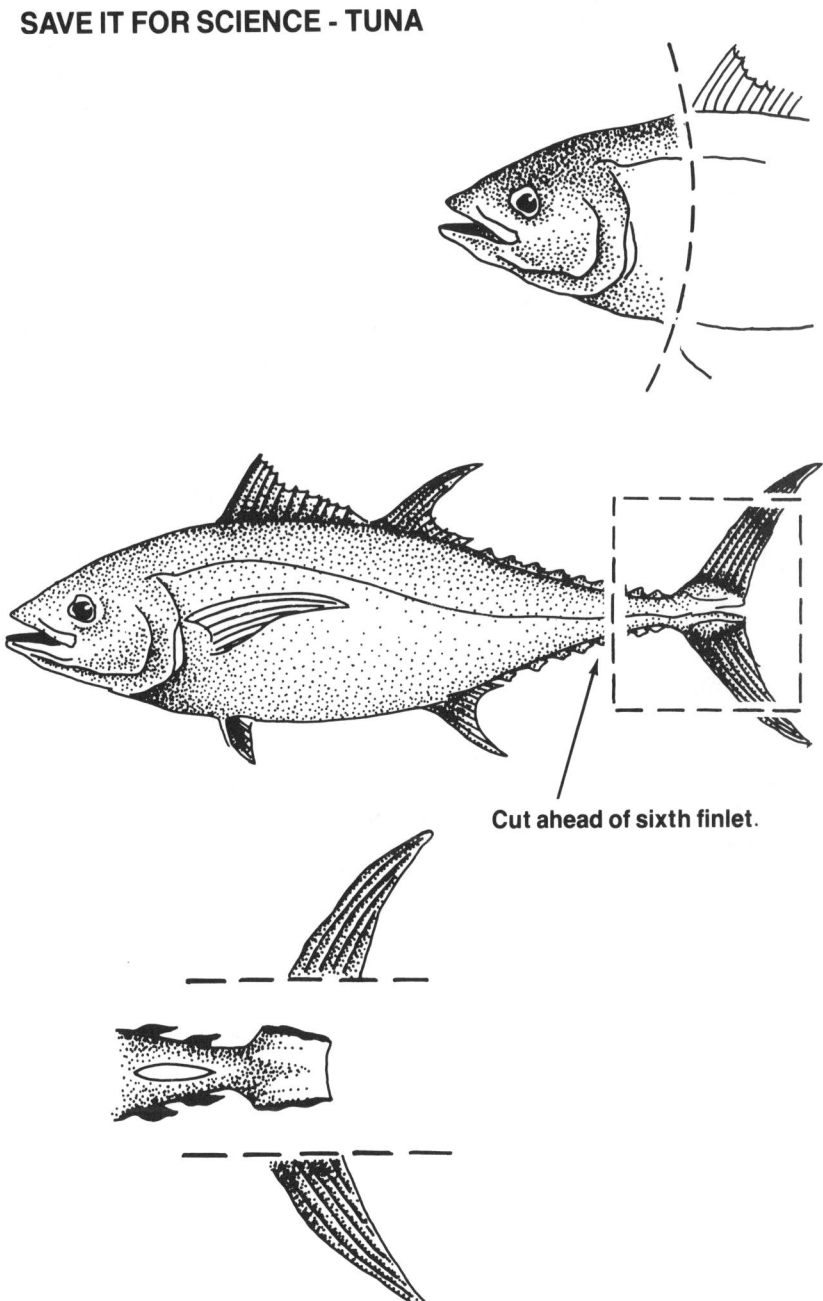

Cut ahead of sixth finlet.

Save the head which contains the otoliths and the tail for the skeletal structure. Refrigerate both parts and call NMFS at (305) 361-4248 or 4225 for information about shipping.

released but less than 2% of these fish have ever been recaptured and an even smaller percentage have been available for scientific examination. "People talk about our tag and release program," says Dr. Prince, "but it is really a tag, release and recapture program. A tagged fish is worth a gold mine of biological information."

Most fishermen who participate in tagging are probably not aware of the importance and potential contribution to science of saving the skeletal structures of the fish for growth and age research analysis. Unlike humans, the older fish are larger fish, and all billfish and tuna continually grow during their lives. The rate of growth is dependent on several factors such as food availability, water quality, water temperature, genetics and the overall health of that particular fish.

Fisheries biologists can use several methods to figure age and growth rates but the most widely used is a microscopic examination of the "hard parts" to count the growth rings, much like a tree trunk shows annual growth rings in its trunk. The hard parts of a billfish or tuna are the scales, first six dorsal spines, the otoliths or earstones and the backbone. For billfish, the prime hard parts are the dorsal spines, otoliths and backbone. For tuna, the best parts are the otoliths, backbone and dorsal fins. These parts can be saved for examination by cutting off the head of the marlin, and head and tail of a tuna, then freezing these parts for shipment to NMFS.

Each time a major change of growth occurs, a growth ring appears in these hard structures. The skeletal parts are thinly sliced and examined under a scanning electrograph microscope. The growth rings are compared to the known date of original tagging and the final recapture date. This direct comparison allows biologists to more accurately calculate real aging data, fish life spans and growth rates.

Dr. Eric Prince who heads up the Cooperative Game Fish Tagging Program is delighted with the increased tagging effort of the last few years, but is hoping to see a corresponding increase in the number of recaptured tagged fish kept for biological examination. "Many fishermen think they are helping the program when they re-release a fish that was previously tagged. The best thing they could do would be to kill the fish, ice it down and call our office when they get back to the dock so we can make arrangements to have the fish delivered to us for study and in-depth examination.

According to Prince, the data that can be obtained from microscopic study of bone growth rings, aging data and detailed dissection of the fish can be of far greater value than its re-release. If you catch a previously tagged marlin or tuna call 1-800-437-3936 for information on how to preserve and ship the catch to NMFS. Remember that billfish must be larger than the minimum federal size limit and school bluefin must be 15 pounds or more.

Recapturing a tagged fish is a rare event, especially for blue marlin and white marlin, so every recaptured fish has the potential to serve up a generous menu of scientific knowledge. The store of data is relatively small for many offshore species and even small discoveries can seem like breakthroughs of extreme value to biologists; and ultimately to support fisherman who depend on stable fishing population to assure expectations of good fishing opportunities

Be sure to call the folks at the National Marine Fisheries Service whenever you catch a previously tagged fish. They'll give you all the details on how to ship the important parts of the fish to them, or make arrangements for an agent to pick up the fish from you.

The assurance of good fishing in the years to come depends on your help.

ABOUT THE AUTHOR

Pete Barrett has been writing about his fishing experiences along the East Coast for the past 30 years and his travels have taken him from New England to the Outer Banks of North Carolina and to Florida and the Bahamas. His favorite fish are found beyond the green slope waters, where the Gulf Stream meets the deep abyss of the Continental Shelf.

Since 1973, Pete has worked for The Fisherman, a weekly magazine with editions in New England, Long Island, New Jersey, Mid Atlantic and Florida. He is now the Associate Publisher of the magazine and of The Fisherman Library book series. A licensed charter captain, his Linda B frequently fishes the canyons.

An advocate of tagging and releasing game fish, especially tuna and marlin, he has won several awards for his tagging efforts, including the 1990 AFTCO Atlantic Angler of the Year Award, and awards for tagging yellowfin tuna in 1989 and 1991, and longfin albacore in 1992.

His wife, Linda, is a full-time partner in their writing and publishing activities. Their son, Rich, is also a licensed charter captain and devoted fisherman.